International Series in Operations Research & Management Science

Volume 311

More information about this series at http://www.springer.com/series/6161

Fausto Pedro García Márquez • Benjamin Lev
Editors

Introduction to Internet of Things in Management Science and Operations Research

Implemented Studies

Springer

Editors
Fausto Pedro García Márquez
Ingenium Research Group
University of Castile-La Mancha
Ciudad Real, Spain

Benjamin Lev
LeBow College of Business
Drexel University, Decision Sciences and MIS
Philadelphia, PA, USA

ISSN 0884-8289 ISSN 2214-7934 (electronic)
International Series in Operations Research & Management Science
ISBN 978-3-030-74643-8 ISBN 978-3-030-74644-5 (eBook)
https://doi.org/10.1007/978-3-030-74644-5

This Springer imprint is published by the registered company Springer Nature Switzerland AG
The registered company address is: Gewerbestrasse 11, 6330 Cham, Switzerland

Preface

This edited volume uses Operations Research and Management Science (OR/MS) disciplines together with the new advances in information systems and technologies to follow the recent market needs. Most of the services in OR/MS will be done employing Internet of Things (IoT). The main functionality of IoT is to connect devices in large networks, favoring information transfer, e.g., images, data, videos, and files. It is applied to all disciplines such as business, energy, transport, financial, and health. Advanced analytics is needed to cover the treatment of this information, for example, deep learning, machine learning, and data mining.

This volume provides an overview of thematic analysis, an exhaustive state-of-the-art analysis, and the main different novel techniques applied to many case studies, where the results are discussed and validated. We present 12 chapters where different authors demonstrate their models, cases, implemented studies, or theory of Internet of Things using Management Science and Operations Research tools and techniques.

Ciudad Real, Spain — Fausto Pedro García Márquez
Philadelphia, PA, USA — Benjamin Lev

Introduction

The emerging field of Internet of Things (IoT) will utilize Operations Research and Management Science (OR/MS) disciplines together with recent advances in information systems and technologies to follow the recent market needs. Most projects in OR/MS will be done employing IoT. The main functionality of IoT is to connect devices in large networks, favoring information transfer, e.g., images, data, videos, and files. It is applied to disciplines such as business, energy, transport, financial, and health. Advanced analytics is needed to cover the treatment of this information, for example, deep learning, machine learning, and data mining.

This volume provides an overview of thematic analysis, an exhaustive state-of-the-art analysis, and the main different novel techniques applied to many case studies, where the results are discussed and validated.

This book is intended for professionals in the field of engineering, information science, mathematics, economists, and researchers who wish to develop new skills in IoT or who employ the IoT discipline as part of their work. The authors who contributed to this book describe their original work in the area or provide material for cases and studies successfully applying the IoT discipline in real life cases and theoretical approaches.

Internet and Internet of Things (IoT)-based applications have brought a global change in bridging the virtual world with the real world. Chapter "Internet of Things: Technologies and Applications" aims at providing an overview of IoT, its contribution in improving the quality of life, the technologies involved in its implementation, and IoT applications that brought comfort in the lives of many. An overview of the technologies included in the implementation of IoT, such as Radio frequency Identification (RFID), Near Field Communication (NFC), and Machine-to-Machine Communication (M2M), has been provided. The emergence of IoT and its incorporation in various applications of healthcare, education, and rehabilitation has made IoT an important part of Assistive Technology (AT). Assistive technologies have greatly impacted the lives of disabled people in performing their daily activities. While IoT is still in the development stage, its integration into AT services is challenging while the benefits are unlimited. Chapter "Internet of Things:

Technologies and Applications" includes the introduction, state-of-the-art technologies and applications of IoT, case studies, followed by conclusion and future recommendations.

Broad utilization of IoT in different industries and manufacturing segments, from healthcare to transportation and supply chain, smart house, smart city, and smart medicine, generated a huge amount of data through such smart devices. Prescriptive analytical power of firms enables them to gain a competitive advantage from generated data. Prescriptive analytics can be enabled by deep learning to overcome the complexity of pattern recognition and data analysis of censored data. Deep learning with learning (un)structured data has great capability in identifying hidden knowledge. Therefore, deep learning plays an enabler role for prescriptive analytics. The goal of prescriptive analytics is to create business value by enhancing firms' performance by offering optimal solutions. In chapter "Prescriptive Analytics in Internet of Things with Concentration on Deep Learning," absorptive capacity theory is deployed and explains that to the extent that firms can empower prescriptive analytics with deep learning technology and optimization algorithms to identify and leverage external knowledge, firms can gain advantage of exploitative innovation capability and enhance their performance significantly.

Chapter "IoT Security and New Trends of Solutions" focuses on the security issues of the IoT. It explores the development direction of IoT security through discussion of technology. The IoT can make individuals more closely connected, but it may spread individual or local insecurity factors further apart. Specifically, the chapter addresses IoT security in detail in the following six sections. The first section discusses the foundation of IoT security. Then, it presents the security issues in perception layer. This layer is the core of IoT, and its security is a prerequisite for information security and privacy protection of IoT. The third section is IoT security in the network layer and then it analyses the security in IoT applications. In terms of security in application layer, it considers security technologies and security strategies for IoT applications. As more and more applications are running with cloud service, this chapter focuses on the security issues of cloud computing applications. Section 5 discusses some case studies of IoT security, and the last section discusses possible future research directions for IoT security.

In recent years, there has been an intense debate surrounding two modalities of learning in higher education, the traditional and the innovative. The model presented in chapter "A Hybrid Model of Learning Methodology Analyzed Through the Use of Machine Learning Techniques" aims to combine the best of both methodologies, thereby creating and developing a hybrid learning model. The model includes multimedia tools, traditional tools, and techniques derived from the field of neuroscience. Using IoT through the Canvas digital learning platform, which monitors the student during the course, a large amount of data can be obtained. These data are analyzed and employed to evaluate the hybrid model using machine learning techniques to support the decision-making in the learning methodology. The obtained results show: (1) a change in the traditional structure of a class; (2) a positive effect on performance, especially through video lessons; (3) both the hybrid model and the Canvas digital learning platform generated positive effects within the learning environment.

When Industrial Internet of Things (IIoT) appears in our enterprise network, a new security breach arises, with new possibilities, and at least with a request of one special layer of cybersecurity (CS) which should be applied to it. One of the methods which is growing in popularity due to its simplicity and inner strength is the use of Blockchain (BC) as a first layer to secure the sensors, the data, the actuators, and the actors, persons who access and monitor IIoT information from smart devices, existing in this special part of our enterprise network. The aim of chapter "Internet of Things Cybersecurity: Blockchain as First Securitisation Layer of an IoT Network" is to set some of the bases of this mix of IIoT and Blockchain for enterprise cybersecurity.

For a smart city with stochastic demand, a data-driven signal control is considered for traffic responsive and time-varying road traffic networks. For period-dependent stochastic demand, a flow-based scenario design for traffic assignment can be formulated as a complementarity. A new solution using stochastic gradients is proposed in chapter "A Data-Driven Traffic-Responsive Signal Control for a Smart City Road Network Under Uncertainty." To demonstrate feasibility of the proposed approach, numerical experiments using real-world example road networks are performed. To investigate computational tractability of the proposed approach, numerical comparisons are made with the state-of-the-art existing traffic signal control strategies. These results reported indicate that the proposed data-driven traffic responsive signal control can achieve reliably better results for a smart city road network than did those recently proposed against a high consequence of stochastic demands.

Chapter "Utilization of Consumer Appliances in Smart Grid Services for Coordination with Renewable Energy Sources" presents an innovative model for increasing consumer participation in smart grid electricity markets. The goal of the research is twofold. Firstly, we aim to develop business models that offer a potential solution to the unpredictable output of solar and wind power plants. The model assumes consumers' positive attitudes toward green energy and allows them to take an active role in lessening the unpredictability of renewables by offering their household devices in smart grid services. Secondly, we aim to design an IoT infrastructure for the realization of the proposed model based on smart plugs working within a Blockchain environment. The software component is extended with a collaborative Blockchain-based loyalty scheme with the goal of allowing further consumer incentives. The proposed model has been evaluated through a pilot study of consumer' attitudes and the model is expected to be accepted and implemented in the smart grid in Serbia.

A smart grid is a new concept that provides two-way information and electricity connection that has prepared an opportunity to involve customers for awareness of load profile, the participation of distributed generation, demand management, cost optimization, and variety in customer services. With the emergence of newer technologies in the fifth generation (5G) and beyond, like the IoT, devices tend to be always online. IoT provides the necessary platform for the exchange of information. Running demand-side management (DSM) needs technologies such as advanced metering infrastructure (AMI) on the consumption side. On the other hand, new devices can connect to the Internet. By sending a signal from the utility and receiving it by the AMI, a shiftable home appliance can work to low price without human activity. Chapter "Application of Internet of Things (IoT) to Demand-Side Management in Smart Grids" focuses on providing an overview of the smart grid and the application of IoT in smart grids by focusing on DSM. Accordingly, well-known IoT algorithms based on DSM used in smart homes are reviewed and investigated in this chapter. Accordingly, the basics of IoT and DSM and their application to the smart grids are investigated and reported in this study.

In chapter "A Hybrid Model of Learning Methodology Analyzed Through the Use of Machine Learning Techniques," the key determinants or factors influencing consumers' behavioral intention to accept autonomous vehicles (AVs) are explored and tested. Although there is a plethora of studies in the literature evaluating various technologies, most of the models of technology acceptance and theories selected are applied on barriers to successful IT implementation in organizations or generally on technologies that have long been deployed. There are very few studies conducted on disruptive technologies such as AV. In chapter "Understanding the Factors Influencing Consumers' Behaviour Towards Autonomous Vehicles Adoption," this issue is addressed with the identification of context-related constructs partly retrieved from existing literature that describe a modeling process for a technology acceptance attempting to explain the main factors influencing people behavioral intention to adopt autonomous vehicle technology. Constructs such as trust, self-efficacy, anxiety, perceived safety, and legal regulation are considered. The main contribution of the study is the detailed exploration on the users' acceptance of AV. It proposes a theoretical model called Autonomous Vehicle Technology Acceptance Model (AVTAM) that gives us a better understanding of what will eventually influence future AV customers. The main findings of this work suggest that users' safety on the road, the cost associated with the technology, and the trust on car manufacturers will play a very important role for large-scale AV adoption.

IoT in Wuxi city has grown energetically and boomingly with a series of remarkable development achievements. In chapter "Development Path, Experience and Implications of the Internet of Things Industry in Wuxi, Jiangsu Province, China," development path of the IoT industry in Wuxi is analyzed. Then, the development experience and implications of the IoT industry are summarized. At the same time, existing problems in the development process of the IoT industry are also discussed. At last, countermeasures are proposed to promote the sustainable development of the IoT industry in Wuxi city. The special Wuxi intelligence and Wuxi experience in the IoT industry could provide reference for developing the IoT industry in the other cities.

The automotive industry is composed of multiple manufacturing processes of primary parts for assembly of assemblies. These parts are generally built on massive manufacturing processes, based on stamping and simple assemblies, through nailing, welding, grinding, adding components, etc. Defects in elements that affect the process can lead to the generation of whole batches of defective parts. The inspections are carried out by artificial vision cameras based on pattern recognition algorithms. The efficiency to recognize patterns depends on many variables such as the position of the pieces, changes in the brightness, appearance of dust, and sensor deterioration. The use of convolutional neural networks has proven to be an effective method to perform this type of recognition in images. Furthermore, automotive industry requires more information and data on what is happening at each stage of the process. This means that it is no longer useful to send a few digital signals to make the process work. The massive sending of data that has been processed apart from the process is required to be adjusted constantly and in real time, before, during, and after the stage it is, based on the information received. This is achievable using the IoT. A new approach based on algorithm (You Only Look Once) YOLO v3 and IoT is presented in chapter "Use of Convolutional Neural Networks for Quality Control in Automotive Industry." A comparison of the performance with other neural networks architectures is performed. The accuracy is studied with different conditions to check the performance of the classification for real-time applications.

Finally, chapter "Using Other Multi-Attribute Decision-Making Techniques to Measure Efficiency When Data Envelopment Analysis Fails" shows an example of data envelopment analysis that does not provide us with efficiencies based on the same selection of inputs and outputs that were provided by the decision maker. Therefore, it selects another multi-attribute decision-making tool such as TOPSIS (Technique for Order of Preference by Similarity to Ideal Solution). TOPSIS is modified to calculate "efficiency" and uses entropy weighting method to use all the inputs and outputs in our efficiency decision process. A case study is applied to an example of sensor procurement within the IoT.

Ingenium Research Group, University of Castilla-La Mancha, Ciudad Real, Spain
Fausto Pedro García Márquez
FaustoPedro.Garcia@uclm.es

LeBow College of Business, Drexel University, Decision Sciences and MIS, Philadelphia, PA, USA
Benjamin Lev
bl355@drexel.edu

Contents

About the Editors

Fausto Pedro García Márquez works at the University of Castilla-La Mancha as Full Professor (Accredited as Full Professor since 2013), Spain, Honorary Senior Research Fellow at Birmingham University, UK, Lecturer at the Postgraduate European Institute, and he has been Senior Manager in Accenture (2013–2014). He obtained his European PhD with the highest distinction. He has been awarded these prizes: Runner Prize for Management Science and Engineering Management Nominated Prize (2020), Advancement Prize (2018), First International Business Ideas Competition 2017 Award (2017); Runner (2015), Advancement (2013) and Silver (2012) by the International Society of Management Science and Engineering Management (ICMSEM); and Best Paper Award in the international journal of *Renewable Energy* (Impact Factor 3.5) (2015). He has published more than 150 papers (65% International Scientific Indexing, 30% Journal Citation Reports, and 92% internationals), some recognized as: "Applied Energy" (Q1, as "Best Paper 2020"), "Renewable Energy" (Q1, as "Best Paper 2014"), "ICMSEM" (as "excellent"), "Int. J. of Automation and Computing" and "IMechE Part F: J. of Rail and Rapid Transit" (most downloaded), etc. He is the author and editor of 25 books (Elsevier, Springer, Pearson, Mc-Graw Hill, Intech, IGI, Marcombo, AlfaOmega. . .) and holds 5 patents. He is the editor of 5 international journals and committee member of more than 40 international conferences. He has been Principal Investigator in 4 European Projects, 6 National Projects, and more than 150 projects for universities, companies, etc. His main interests are Artificial Intelligence, Maintenance, Management, Renewable Energy, Transport, Advanced Analytics, and Data Science. He is an expert of the European Union in AI4People (EISMD), and ESF. He is the Director of www.ingeniumgroup.eu. More information in https://blog.uclm.es/faustopedrogarcia.

Benjamin Lev is the University Trustee Professor at LeBow College of Business, Drexel University, Philadelphia, Pennsylvania, USA. He holds a PhD in Operations Research from Case Western Reserve University. Prior to joining Drexel University, Dr. Lev held academic and administrative positions at Temple University, University of Michigan-Dearborn, and Worcester Polytechnic Institute. He is the Editor-in-Chief of *OMEGA-The International Journal of Management Science* www.OmegaJournal.org; Co-Editor-in-Chief of *International Journal of Management Science and Engineering Management*; and serves on several other journal editorial boards (*INFORMS JAA* (formerly Interfaces), *IAOR*, *ORPJ*, *Financial Innovation*, *OPSEARCH*, *IDIM*, *IIE-Transactions*, *ERRJ*, *INFORMS JOR*). He currently holds faculty appointments at seven Chinese Universities (Beijing Jiaotong University, Chengdu University, Nanjing University of Aeronautics and Astronautics, Nanjing University of Information Science and Technology, Nanjing Audit University, Xidian University, Tianjin University). Professor Lev is the former TIMS VP-Meetings and INFORMS VP-Meetings. He is INFORMS Fellow since 2003. He has published sixteen books, numerous articles, and organized many national and international conferences including ORSA/TIMS Philadelphia; INFORMS Israel; IFORS Scotland; ALIO-INFORMS Buenos Aires; and ICMSEM Philadelphia (https://en.wikipedia.org/wiki/Benjamin_Lev).

Internet of Things: Technologies and Applications

Seema Ansari, Tahniyat Aslam, Adeel Ansari, Pablo Otero, Irfan Ahmed, and Fatima Maqbool

1 Introduction

The main objective of the Internet of things (IoT) is to link present and future electronic devices to the Internet. The IoT connects a huge number of electronic devices or objects to the Internet in order to facilitate high-level interaction and

S. Ansari (✉)
College of Engineering and Sciences, Institute of Business Management, Karachi, Pakistan

Telecommunication Engineering department, University of Malaga, Spain, Malaga, Spain
e-mail: seema.ansari@iobm.edu.pk

T. Aslam
College of Engineering and Sciences, Institute of Business Management, Karachi, Pakistan

Department of Electronic Engineering, NED University of Engineering and Technology, University Road Karachi, Karachi, Pakistan
e-mail: tahniyat.aslam@iobm.edu.pk

A. Ansari
Computer Science Department, Shaheed Zulfiqar Ali Bhutto Institute of Science & Technology, Karachi, Pakistan
e-mail: adeel.ansari@szabist.edu.pk

P. Otero
Telecommunication Engineering department, University of Malaga, Spain, Malaga, Spain
e-mail: por@uma.es

I. Ahmed
Department of Electronic Engineering, NED University of Engineering and Technology, University Road Karachi, Karachi, Pakistan
e-mail: irfans@neduet.edu.pk

F. Maqbool
College of Engineering and Sciences, Institute of Business Management, Karachi, Pakistan
e-mail: fatima.maqbool@iobm.edu.pk

F. P. García Márquez, B. Lev (eds.), *Introduction to Internet of Things in Management Science and Operations Research*, International Series in Operations Research & Management Science 311,
https://doi.org/10.1007/978-3-030-74644-5_1

communications between virtual and real world [1]. Physical devices or objects of the real world can be embedded with sensing, identifying, communicating, and networking facilities, which will allow them to interact with other devices via Internet to accomplish the dedicated tasks [2].

Transforming daily objects into smart devices supports vast promises and advantages like improving the condition of human and enhancing business procedures. Eventually, the aim of IoT is to allow "things" to be linked every time, everywhere, with everyone, via every network and service [3]. The concept of this visualization will need major research development in technologies. Technologies including Radio Frequency Identification (RFID), Machine-to-Machine (M2M) communication, wireless actuator and sensor networks and ubiquitous computing have been employed to a number of applications, varying from manufacturing and industrial environment to end user for observing and automation. Vermesan and Friess [3] broadly categorized IoT technologies into three groups. (1) To facilitate devices in IoT systems for allocating and obtaining related data, (2) To allow devices in IoT systems for processing the contextual data, and (3) To enhance the quality of IoT systems. The initial groups are mutually recognized as the functional units of IoT. The other group is not a functional although it helps in the penetration of the IoT.

Currently the Internet has become universal, linking nearly each corner of the world, and is affecting individual life in incredible ways. We have entered into an era of wide-ranging connectivity, where a wide range of devices are connected to the Internet [4]. The major initiative behind the IoT model is to deploy billions or even trillions of smart devices, that are capable to detect the environment, communicate and transmit required information, and then receive response from the environment. It is predictable that in 2021, there will be nearby 28 billion connected equipment and devices. The huge IoT market division comprises of numerous applications which are extensively used in manufacturing and societies [5]. loT will create the impression of the Internet even more ubiquitous, personal, and familiar in everyday life [6]. The Internet of Things is bridging the virtual world with the real world and finds several applications in entertainment, social life, health care, environment observing, smart home, fitness, education, transport systems, and energy conservation as shown in Fig. 1.

2 State-of-the-Art Technologies and Applications of IoT

2.1 Technologies

IoT has turned out to be the innovative model of Information and Communication Technology (ICT) [7]. IoT-based architecture requires devices to be connected together in a network, to provide specific facilities and services. They are beneficial for various everyday applications like smart residences where some appliances linked with the sensors collect the information, while other actuators use it for counteraction initiating. IoT solutions can be comprised of different equipment

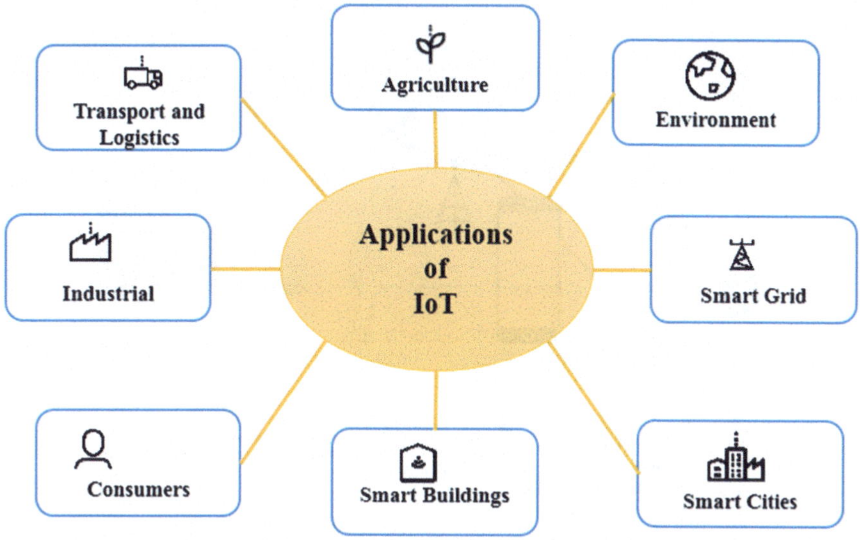

Fig. 1 Application of IoT. (Source: [5])

and devices that would be offered with effective methods of exchanging the information. Increasing the transmission distance between the inter-devices and reducing the consumption of power are main challenges in the field of IoT [8]. There are many enabling technologies used in IoT networks, for example Radio Frequency Identification (RFID), ZIGBEE, Bluetooth, 6LoWPAN, Wireless Sensor Network (WSN), Wi-Fi, Cellular networks as illustrated in Fig. 2. Some of these technologies are discussed below:

Radio Frequency Identification (RFID) RFID uses RFID tags embedded in objects which can be wirelessly identified and tracked. It uses electromagnetic energy that transmits data wirelessly from the RFID tag to the RFID receiver [10]. RFID tag comprises a small radio transponder, a radio receiver and transmitter. The tag is triggered by the electromagnetic wave from an RFID reader and transmits digital data that contain identification and other information required. RFID, shown in Fig. 3, is a method of identifying objects automatically and capturing data [11].

Wireless Sensor Network (WSN) It is the technology that is acquiring momentum in the IoT business. It is based on an architectural paradigm comprising of a number of central nodes also known as hub and sensor nodes. In WSN, the gathered information from the actuators nodes is transmitted to the hub for further processing. Bluetooth Low Energy (BLE) is a wireless communication protocol that can be employed for node communication.

Other possibility for using less energy and comparatively wide range in communication is the Zigbee wireless communication standard. Zigbee sustains the foundation of IoT networks with around 64,000 devices [12]. The dissimilarity among

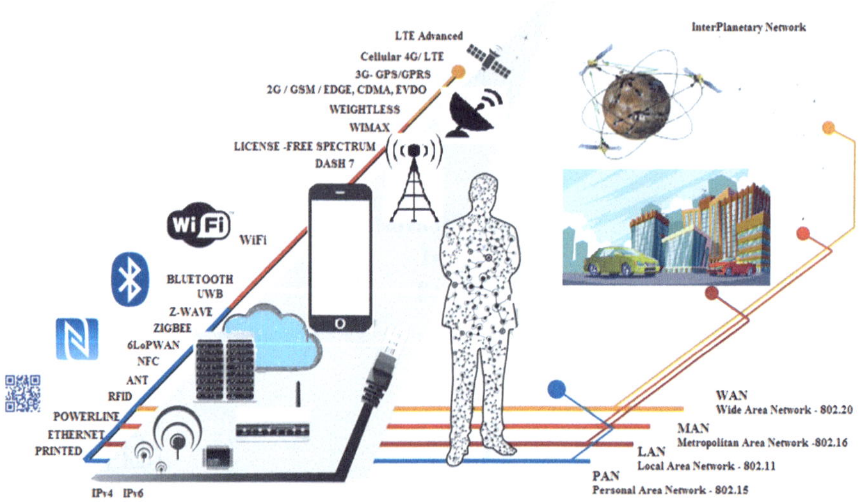

Fig. 2 An overview of IoT systems and devices [9]

Fig. 3 FasTrak, an RFID chip used for automatic toll collection in California. (Source: [11])

BLE and Zigbee depends on the bandwidth of channel, amount of cell nodes, frequency and supported range. BLE, Wi-Fi, and RFID are usually operated in the communication technologies. Actuators and sensors like light, temperature, and power are mounted and linked to a WSN architecture mode wirelessly [13].

Currently, due to the heterogeneous nature of linked devices, several communicating technologies are emergent in the period of IoT. The promising ones are cellular networks 4G and 5G, Wireless Sensor Networks (WSNs), Wireless Local Area Networks (WLANs), Vehicular Ad hoc Networks (VANETs), etc. Through proposing wireless connectivity with various data rates and network coverage, they normally support heterogeneous IoT and machine-to-machine (M2M) applications. For improving the IoT services, facilities, and applications, many researchers and industries are currently showing their concern to improve the proficiency and efficiencies of these communication systems [14].

Bluetooth It is a wireless technology, used for wireless data transmission over a short range [15]. It can be used for short wavelength radio transmission in the ISM band ranging from 2.4 to 2.48 GHz from stationary and mobile devices, thus forming a Wireless Personal Area Network (WPAN) [9].

Wi-Fi It is a Wireless Local Area Network (WLAN) technology that is created by Institute of Electrical and Electronics Engineers (IEEE) 802.11 standards [16]. It allows exchange of information with all electronic devices like computers, mobile phones, tablets, and laptops connected through high-speed Internet connections. The range of communication is up to 100 meter but it can be extended [9].

2.2 *Internet of Things in Smart Cities*

Today, human beings are more relied on the Information and Communication Technologies (ICT) networked than before [17]. Smart city denotes to novel industries using information and communication technologies (ICT) together with the functions and environmental operations of metropolitan areas [18]. The smart city term can also be defined as the merging of ICT, the natural environment, energy and power technologies, and provides services within city and in-house environments [19]. A smart city is formed by linking the physical and social infrastructure with the business and the ICT infrastructure in order to control the combined intelligence of the metropolitan city [20].

The Internet of Things (IoT) is an innovation prospect for providing novel services by connecting virtual and real worlds with the massive amounts of electronic equipment or devices distributed in homes, automobiles, roads, buildings, and many other public places [21]. Metropolitan IoTs are intended to support the vision of smart city and aim to use the innovative technologies to aid the value-added facilities for the management and citizens of the city [22].

IoT is a network of connected devices with innovative abilities to communicate with other devices on the network, humans, and their surrounding world to carry out various tasks. By integration of IoT with the smart city, flexible management of recourses can be achieved in various application domains to the urban areas [23]. A smart city is an advanced metropolitan area that excels in the field of governance, economy, and citizen's life because of very strong social and human capital, along with the ICT infrastructure. It is a novel approach to dealing with the complexity of urban life, increase efficacy, decrease expenses, and improve the condition of citizen's life [24].

2.2.1 Smart Lighting System

The major concern of IoT-based smart city is the efficient management of power and energy. As the population is growing, the need and demand of electricity is increasing. Electricity is necessary for the public places, malls, industries, residential and commercial areas. Currently, about 10% of the overall energy supply is consumed by public lighting [25]. A Smart Lighting System (SLS) integrated with various IoT technologies for managing and controlling lighting system in the smart city. It is an automatic and intelligent light controlling system that is operated in a centralized and distributed way by different protocols, devices, and sensors. Efficient lighting system can control the energy consumption in residences, offices, malls, streets, etc.

The objective of an SLS is to achieve an independent and more effective light managing system. Sikder et al. [26] analyzed different scenarios of IoT-based indoor and outdoor SLS. The results showed that SLS reduces the power consumption around 33.3% in both scenarios. Figure 4 illustrates the SLS architecture. There are three components of the SLS architecture:

Lamp Unit (LU)

LED has reduced the power consumption in the lighting systems. A Lamp Unit (LU) comprises of different sensors and controller, which collects the data and transmits it to the Control Center (CC). The data can be collected by using motion and light actuators. The motion sensor can detect the automobile and pedestrians, while light sensors can be used to check the intensity of day light. Temperature sensors are also used to detect the fault in power lines.

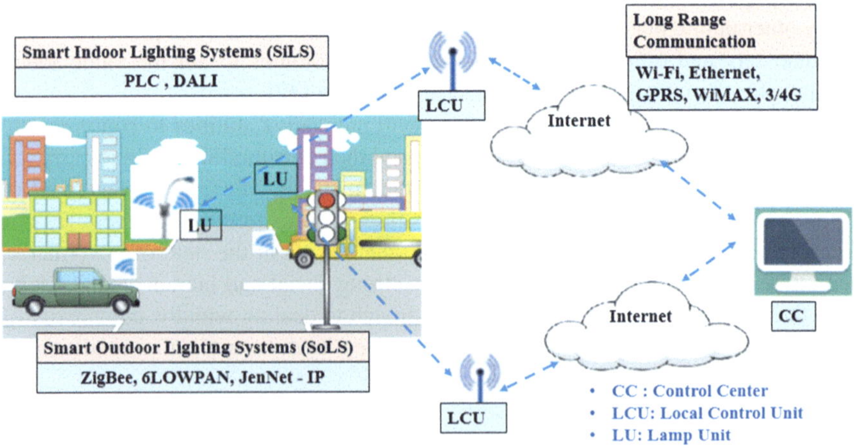

Fig. 4 Smart lighting systems architecture. (Source: [26], p. 640)

Local Control Unit (LCU)

It gathers the data from different LUs by using a short range communication protocol (IEEE 802.15.4 protocols for example ZigBee, 6LoWPAN, or Bluetooth Low Energy (BLE)) and transfers the data to the control center.

Control Center (CC)

It gathers data from LCUs and saves it on a cloud. It is the most effective way of storing large amount of data for the large urban areas. Different tool and techniques are used to analyze the data.

2.2.2 Waste and Garbage Management

Bonino et al. [27] introduced a Smart City Platform (SCP) established in the context of the ALMANAC FP7 EU research project and discussed the scenarios of the smart city waste management in a European city. The aim of this project is to incorporate the IoT, with the capillary networks and metro access networks to propose smart facilities to the citizens. The platform creates an active federation of public and private networks, sustaining end-to-end privacy and security.

It has been observed that the enormous amount of garbage including the plastic wastage causes a life threat to the human as well as the earth's environment. So, it is necessary to cope with this issue by developing a well-structured and organized mechanism. The world is moving toward the smart systems to have an efficient structure in dealing with the daily wastage and garbage. Smart cities with the smart garbage management can make the lives of citizen more secured and comfortable. One of the main applications of smart city is the effective garbage management that would guarantee the healthy environment to the citizen. Memon et al. [28] developed an IoT-based cost-effective and real-time monitoring system that can observe the garbage daily via smart technology by using WeMos and ultrasonic actuators. The study proposed an automated waste observing and collecting process which is more effective embedded system that senses the level of the waste in the bin and transmits the obtained data via Internet using Wi-Fi. So, it is convenient to access the citizen by following their particular IP address.

2.3 Internet of Things in Smart Homes Domain

A house equipped with a network of advanced domestic appliances and devices, sensors and actuators that can be able to distantly access, observe, control and deliver facilities upon residents' requests is referred to as an IoT-based smart home [29]. Though the extensive analysis of high-speed Internet in the later 1990s delivered the chance for the business of home-based network to develop, it was not up to the end of 2000s that smart home environment started to be established, which is when smart cell phones were promoted. Originally, a smart home was described using numerous names, like a digital house, a home-based network, home automation, and an intelligent residence. Around the mid-2010s, it has been tending to an amalgamation of Internet of Things (IoT) and a condition-aware smart house.

The innovative form of conventional home automation is a smart home. In initial home automation, the communication devices are installed, for providing multiple services at home [30]. Therefore, smart home facility was utilized to control environmental usages like lighting and heating system [31]. Nowadays due to advancement in technologies, a smart home system observes residence activities and the in-house surroundings shown in Fig. 5. Furthermore, a smart home delivers facilities that achieve the demands and requirements of a user. Now, the smart home amenities are developing as they move toward AI.

"Alexa" the smart personal assistant is invented by Amazon Lab126. It has been set up in a broad variety of devices and equipment. Alexa has been installed in many smart homes product by LG Electronics. China smart home maker Xiaomi is preparing to target the market of smart home systems. Xiaomi introduced an air purifier that is able to distantly control through a cell phone and invented a module that can be introduced into all household appliances like refrigerators, air conditioners, and laundry machines. Apple is emerging an AI speaker that sustains "Apple Home Kit," predictable to deliver voice support as a core to control home-based

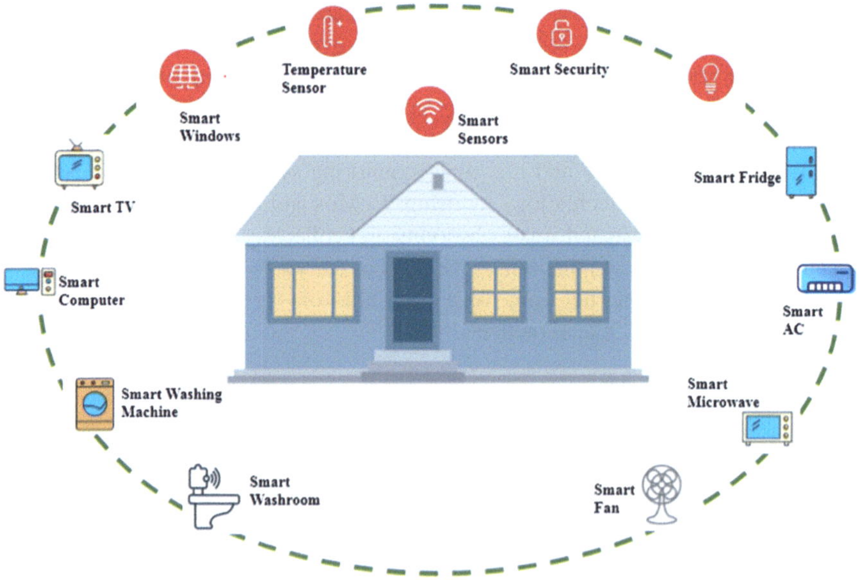

Fig. 5 Smart home ([31], p. 3)

products. Therefore, smart home services are emerging and flourishing by implementing IoT and AI.

2.4 *Internet of Things in Agriculture Domain*

Agriculture has an important role in serving the world. In recent years, the food and agriculture sector has already achieved in meeting the challenges regarding the foodstuff safety and security. These developments have been achieved in farming field methods and breeding of plants and animals. The agriculture and farming is a challenging field for IoT from a technical and organizational perception [32]. Because the "things" are natural and living, like animals, plants, crops, soils, and fresh foodstuffs, so it's difficult to embed IoT devices (for example microprocessors, actuators, antennas) into the foodstuffs and products. In addition, agriculture and farming depends on environmental conditions such as weather, temperature, soil, diseases, and pests. Therefore there is a wide range of unpredictability and irregularities in agricultural things. The integration of wireless sensor networks (WSN) and IoT in agricultural sector can raise the level of agriculture [33].

IoT-based smart agricultural systems are constructed for observing the crop field with the help of actuators and sensors such as light, humidity, temperature, soil moistness, and automating the irrigation system. The agriculturalists can observe the condition of fields from everywhere. The goal of IoT-based smart farming is not limited to traditional farming operations, but it could also be used in regular trends in farming like organic agriculture, household farming and it also improves the quality of agriculture [34]. IoT-based smart agriculture can provide great benefit, including effective usage of water, or optimization of treatments [35]. IoT current developments in agriculture are depending on the technologies in order to make better decisions, reduction in costs, and enhancement in production.

2.4.1 Sampling and Mapping of Soil

The soil sampling is used to determine the status of nutrient in a field in order to measure the nutrient deficiencies. This can be done normally in fall or winter depending upon the soil conditions of soil and climate [36]. Soil mapping helps in seeding different varieties of crops in a specific area to improve and enhance the properties of soil accordingly, such as suitability, sowing time, and planting depth of the seeds. Moreover, raising various crops collectively leads to the smart agriculture, by making the best usage of resources. There is a wide variety of tool kits and sensors are used for tracking the quality of soil. They are used for observing the properties of soil, such as texture and surface, rate of absorption, and capacity of water holding in order to reduce the effects of salinization, erosion, acidification, densification, and pollution. Agro Cares developed a soil testing kit named Lab-in-a-Box [37].

This kit helps the farmer to examine up to 100 samples a day, without any lab experience. Another major issue that limits the productivity of the crops is drought. In 2009, Soil Moisture and Ocean Salinity (SMOS) satellite was launched, which offers soil mapping globally. Martínez-Fernández et al. [38] used SMOS L2 in Spain, to analyze the Soil Water Deficit Index (SWDI). Vagen et al. [39] used moderate resolution imaging spectro-radiometer (MODIS) sensor for mapping the degradation risk in lab of sub-Saharan Africa.

2.4.2 Irrigation

Earth covers 97% with the salty water by seas and oceans, and only the 3% covers fresh water, in which two-third are stored in the form of polar ice caps and glaciers. Barely 0.5% of the fresh unfrozen water is present in the air, ground or lies in the underground [40]. Several irrigation methods like sprinkler irrigation and drip irrigation are used for tackling the usage of water. The quality and amount of crops are severely affected by shortage and excess amount of water and irregular irrigation that reduces the nutrients of soils and causes various microbial infections. In recent years, the irrigation methods are adopting the IoT technologies. Crop Water Stress Index (CWSI)-based irrigation methods are used to increase the efficiency of crops by using IoT technologies [41].

In a wireless sensor based soil observing system, field sensors are used to gather the soil data and transfer it to the processing center for further analysis of the soil. Other parameters like climate change data and satellite images of soil are applied to CWSI model for measuring the absolute irrigation index value for each field. Another method like Variable Rate Irrigation (VRI) which works according to variability of soils, helps in improving the efficiency of water usage [42].

2.4.3 Fertilizer

It is a chemical or natural element that can deliver essential nutrients for the fertility and growth of the crops. Plants require three basic macronutrients, nitrogen N for the growth of the leaf; phosphorus P for the roots, fruits, and flowers growth; potassium K for the water movement and growth of stems. The deficiency or improper nutrients and fertilizer can harm the health of plants and crops. IoT-based fertilizing methods are used to estimate the requirement of nutrients efficiently. Benincasa et al. [43] proposed the Normalized Difference Vegetation Index (NDVI) that uses satellite pictures to observe the status of crop nutrients. Different IoT-based enabling technologies are used for smart fertilization such as geo mapping [44], autonomous vehicles [45], and Variable Rate Technology (VRT) [46].

2.4.4 Crop Disease and Pest Management

IoT-based wireless robot and drones are used to slash insecticide by identifying the pest and crop disease in real time [47]. Normally, for observing the pest management and plant disease three phases are required such as identifying, estimating, and treatment. The advanced approaches depend on image processing, in which various raw images are taken from the crops via sensors, UAVs, and remote sensing satellites. The field sensors are capable to gather the data related to crop health. The IoT-based automated traps can take images and identifies the insect types through remote sensing and transfer the data to the cloud for further processing [48].

2.4.5 Crop Monitoring, Forecasting, and Harvesting

It is used to examine different features of agricultural crop, for example plant moisture, harvested grain quality and quantity. Crop estimating is an art of predicting the production before the harvest. It helps the farmer in decision-making related to farming. Moreover, examining the crop quality determines the correct phase for harvesting. Forecasting the correct harvesting time helps in maximizing the quality of crop and production. Figure 6 illustrates a Farm Area Network (FAN) that can represent the entire farm in real time to the agriculturalist. A Farm RTX mobile app invented that can deliver the harvest data in real time and automatically upload the data on user web based platform [49]. Satellite images can be used to monitor the crops. Torbick et al. [50] used Sentinel-1A Interferometry pictures to analyze the rice crop in Myanmar. Wang et al. [51] stated the fruits size and color are important during harvesting period. They analyzed and tracked the different conditions of mangos in a farm.

2.5 *Industrial Internet of Things (IIOT)*

The industrial internet of things (IIoT) signifies to the additional usage of internet of things (IoT) in the field of industries and applications [52]. Due to an influential emphasis on big data, machine learning, and machine-to-machine communication, the IIoT allows industries and enterprises to have improved efficacy and integrity in their operations. IIoT supports industries and companies to have better operational efficacy and reliability because of big data, machine learning, and machine-to-machine devices communication. Figure 7 illustrated that IIoT is made up of variety of connected devices by communication software. Every single device or combined systems can monitor, gather, transmit, or receive information intelligently without any human intervention. The IIoT can be differentiated as a large number of

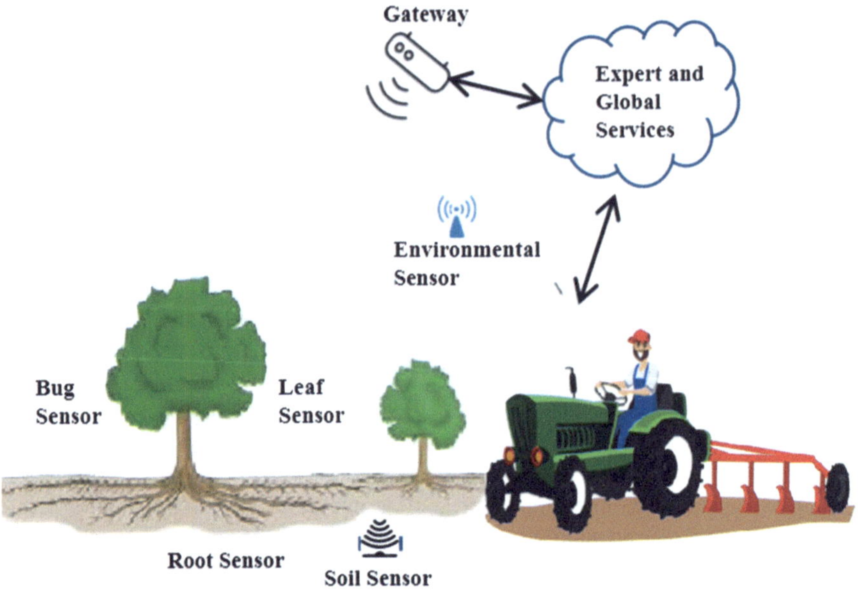

Fig. 6 An IoT-based farm area network (Source: [33])

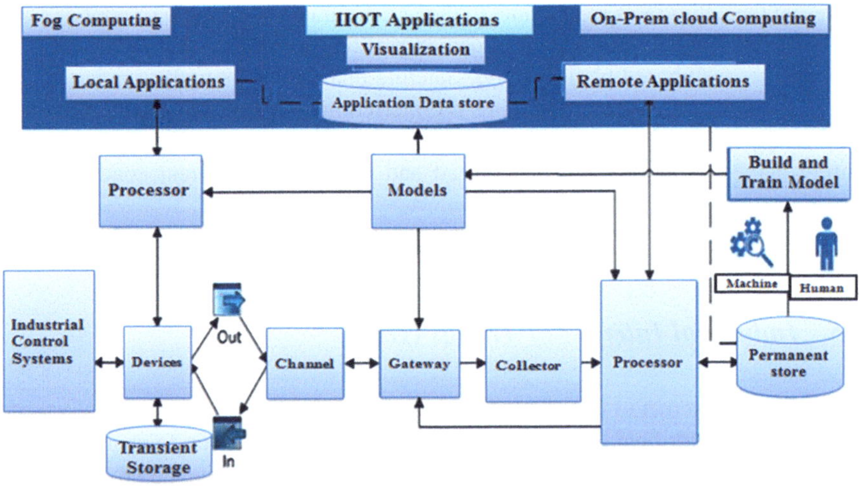

Fig. 7 The industrial internet of things (IIoT) architecture (Source: [53–55], p. 37)

interlinked [56] industrial organizations that are communicating and managing their data analytics and proceedings to improve industrial operation. Cyber-physical system refers to as an industrial system that links the real world with digital world through actuators and sensors that can solve many control issues.

There are two different perceptions on how the IoT varies from industrial IoT. The first observation is that there are two different areas. The IIoT links various critical machines and actuators in high risk industries such as healthcare sector, energy, transportation and industries control. IoT manages to be customer-level devices like home-based thermometers, wearable fitness gadgets, and programmed pet feeders [53–55]. They are vital and applicable, but failures do not directly form emergency situations. Another view is to realize the IIoT as the structure that must be created earlier than IoT.

The IIoT emphasizes on smart cyber-physical structures. They comprise of machines linked with computers that analyze and create decisions promptly, based on actuator information received from numerous broadly divided sources. The IIoT allows the smart system in your vehicle that automatically brakes when it senses an obstruction in the street. It facilitates the patients observing system in clinics to follow every detail from their heart rate to their medicine. It allows a mining instrument or a robot to protect and proficiently function where humans can't [53–55]. The large number of information are created and communicated among systems, devices, actuators, and sensors. The connectivity software works promptly, despite of how many devices and systems are participated and collaborated, confidentially and privately.

2.6 *Internet of Things in Energy Conservation*

At present, IoT has begun to create an influence in the sector of energy. Starting from monitoring the temperature in a room through sensors, to state-of-the-art applications that regulate the usage of energy of an entire building. IoT technology is reducing the costs and producing more products in the energy sectors [57]. The energy sector and industry explores for a new paradigm for distributing and managing facilities to incorporate the renewables into the grid, the IoT technology provides the solution to this demand. The Energy Internet of Things (EIoT) can reduce the challenges by managing the demand of electricity with the supply. This technique can help to adopt renewable and sustainable technologies [58]. IoT plays an important role in managing energy regulation. But there is a limitation in renewable energy, because it relies directly on the environmental natural inputs. This is because of inconsistence in the distribution of energy generated from windmill or by solar. Energy Internet of Things (EIoT) has developed smart home appliance with programmable thermostats that manage the power and energy consumption, in the absence of the people from home or offices. IoT delivers prominent ways for managing and monitoring problems in energy sector and provides best solutions [59].

In conventional power grids, the quality and consistency are the main challenges for both consumers and service providers. Because of increasing the power requirement, delay in the response time of automated switches, insufficiency in automated analytics gradually causes more and more shutdowns and power failures. The era of IoT provides an optimal solution by introducing a Smart Grid (SG) system.

Smart grid is based on the concept related to digital technology and electrically powered network. It comprises of electrical network, smart monitoring systems and automatically control devices and appliances. Smart grid supplies electricity from producers to customers, regulates the flow of energy, decreases the energy loses, and makes the electrical network performance more consistent and reliable. Smart grid technologies included sensing and integrating communication technologies, advanced machineries, improved controlling and interfacing methods. Smart grid depends on quality of power, self-restoring, participation of consumer, enables electrical energy market, improves the assets and enables the generations and high penetration of erratic generation sources. Based on the benefit and cost analysis, smart grid can deliver a better and improved quality of life to the customers. In contrast to the current existing power system, many questions arise about its capability to continue delivering the residents and businesses with comparatively reliable and affordable power facility.

Smart grid can propose many prospective economic and environmental aids and implication, mainly in energy conservation:

1. Enhance the reliability of power transmission.
2. Improve the distribution of power conservation and efficiency.
3. Reduction in the costs for electrical utilities.
4. Decreases the electricity expenses by households and industries.
5. Reduce the emission of greenhouse gas (GHG).

As the technology evolves, customer can use power more effectively and manageably. As per research analysis, energy will be saved as around 53 million vehicles GHG emission, if the power grid can work efficiently by 5%. If each American family uses compact fluorescent bulb instead of incandescent bulb, the entire country will save enough amount of electrical energy, which provides power to the other three million residents and saves as a minimum $600 million yearly [60].

Technologies like Smart Metering (SM) and Advanced Metering Infrastructure (AMI) are invented, to introduce the bidirectional communication between service providers and customers during the process of power transactions [61]. Smart meter allows the consumer to monitor, manage, and control power usage and optimizing the performance and reducing the power losses. Smart metering can also improve the outage detection, power restoration and verification. Both utilities and consumers can have benefits from smart grid based net meter, service providers could be able to handle the peak demand, while the customer can observe, optimize their power consumption based on real-time price of electricity and offset their increasing power bills [62]. By implementation of smart meter, utilities will be able to provide best targeted tariffs and initiate a new model based on real-time controlling, which can aid to decrease the high consumption cost [63].

2.7 Internet of Things in Healthcare

Internet of things (IoT) is one of the main advancement in the field of healthcare sector. It connects all medical equipment embedded with sensors and working devices of all-IP based architecture, hence linking the real-world objects with the virtual world objects. Smart IoT-based healthcare system has capability to monitor patients distantly with the help of wireless sensors, and helps in the improvement of healthcare, possibly saving the life of patients. It helps in reducing the cost of healthcare which is the main concern of the world, by the effective utilization of the resources [64]. Healthcare and medical care are the vital application areas of IoT. The IoT has the potential to increase various medical and healthcare applications, for example in distant health monitoring, observing of elderly and chronic disease patients, etc. Medication and compliance with treatment by doctors and healthcare providers at home are other vital applications. So, many medical equipment or devices, sensors or actuators, and diagnostic devices can be considered as smart objects or devices. IoT-based healthcare facilities improve the quality of patient's life and reduces the overall cost [65].

Figure 8 illustrates the IoT-based healthcare scenario designed by Pang [66]. In this situation, all medical gadgets and devices are embedded with actuators and sensors that collect the data related to the patients continuously and transfer it in real time [67]. These healthcare services are extended from clinics and hospitals to the home. They delivered medical and healthcare services like medicine and diet management, emergency services, telemedicine facilities, health and social

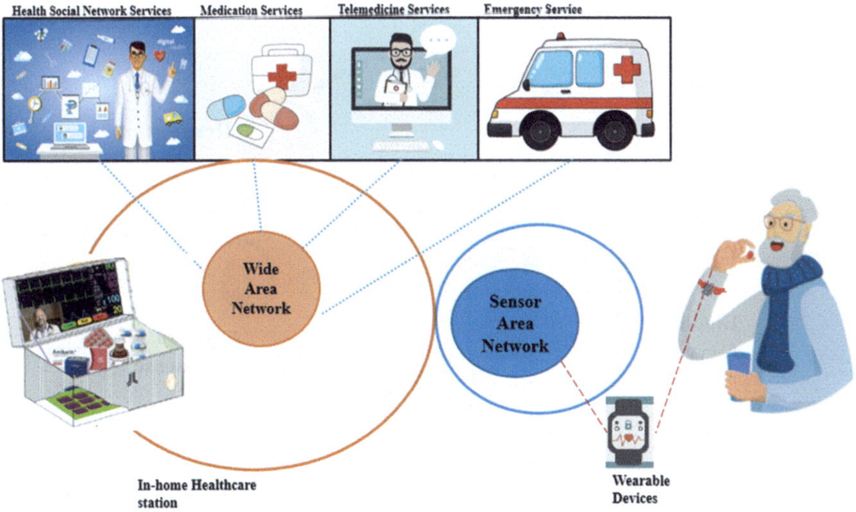

Fig. 8 Internet of things based healthcare scenario ([66], p. 8)

interaction services. The patient's health records are stored constantly [68]. The gathered medical record are collected from these medical devices and examined by physician and doctors remotely.

2.7.1 IoT Healthcare Applications

There are several applications of IoT in healthcare sectors. These applications are user-centric and can be directly accessed by the patients and users. The IoT in healthcare sector can connect any medical device or equipment embedded with sensors that enables them to transmit and receive patient's data. These devices can be linked through internet or via Bluetooth. The IoT-based healthcare devices commonly measure heart rate, blood oxygen, blood glucose, body temperature, etc., as shown in Fig. 9. The patient's record can be accessed by the doctors and physician remotely [69].

Monitoring of Blood Glucose Level

Diabetes is a disease in which patients' suffer from high blood glucose or sugar levels. Monitoring of blood glucose level indicates the changes in pattern and assists in planning of medication and meals times. An IoT-based invasive method of continuous glucose monitoring (CGM) approach is explained by Gia et al.

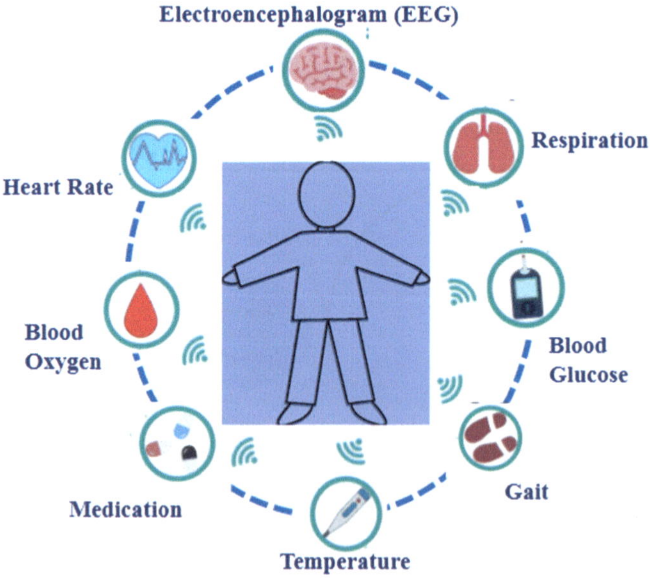

Fig. 9 IoT-based healthcare applications [69]

[70]. An RF communication protocol is adapted for glucose monitoring. This architecture provides push notification services for informing the doctors and patients in case of irregularities in blood glucose (such as in case of too high and too low blood sugar level). An IoT-based non-invasive blood glucose monitoring is explained by Alarcón-Paredes et al. [71]. This framework is based on Raspberry Pi Zero (RPi) empowered with a power bank, depending on a Raspberry Pi Camera and visible laser beam, all embedded in a glove. Data is acquired by taking a set of images of the patient's fingertip and compute its histogram for non-invasive observing. The collected data is processed through an artificial neural network (ANN). The obtained data is verified with laboratory blood glucose test.

Electrocardiogram Monitoring

The electrocardiogram (ECG) is the heart activity, noted by electrocardiography, which comprises of measuring of heart rate and the determination of the basic rhythms. Heart failure is one of the main causes of unexpected and sudden death in old and middle aged people. An IoT-based ECG examining system has been proposed [72]. This system is designed to continuously monitor the electrocardiogram (ECG) signal gathered from the patients through wearable devices embedded with sensors. The collected data is stored in the database which can be accessed by doctor and physician only. When any abnormalities are detected in the ECG signal of the patient, an automatic signal is generated to the doctors and family members about the serious conditions and provides urgent health assistance.

A Wearable Heart Monitoring Inductive Sensor (WHMIS) developed by Brezulianu et al. [73] monitors the heart activity using inductive sensor that are interleaved in the clothes fabric. In this monitoring system, only one inductive sensor is required in the front area of the patients' clothes near heart to examine the cardiorespiratory activity, while in the previous methods many sensors were placed on the different parts of the body. Both respiration and heart rate activity can be monitored continuously.

Blood Pressure Monitoring

Blood pressure can be monitored by a blood pressure monitoring device that can collect the records of patients' blood pressure and transmit it to the doctors via an IoT network. This device is comprised of blood pressure apparatus and a communication module [74]. Numerous smart wearable devices depend on various technologies that have been established and promoted for blood pressure measurement [75]. There are two methods of monitoring blood pressures. First method is based on oscillometric Method. In this method, piezoelectric sensors are embedded in cuff based device. Most popular smart devices include Qardio arm system [76] and HeartGuide device [77]. Second method depends on photopletismographic method. In this system, camera and flash LED are equipped with the mobile device, and the software are used to analyze the signal to estimate the value of blood pressure. Some of the related devices are DreamCare Blood Pressure Monitoring Smart Bracelet [78] and Asus VivoWatch BP [79].

Body Temperature Monitoring

The important part of healthcare services is monitoring of body temperature. Because it is a vital sign that indicates the maintenance of homeostasis. A temperature monitoring system is installed via IoT on the home gateway. The home gateway transfers the patient's body temperature using infrared detection [80]. A tool is invented for monitoring patient's body temperature in real time using android smart phone equipped with telemedicine which can send sms whenever patient's body temperature is not in normal limits. This tool used DS18B20 sensor for examining and gathering the body temperature data that will be processed by microcontroller, and transmit it to the smartphone via Bluetooth [81].

Monitoring of Blood Oxygen Saturation

Pulse oximetry is applicable for observing of blood oxygen saturation. The integration of pulse oximetry with IoT is useful in medical applications. Khattak et al. [82] discussed Co-AP based pulse oximetry. A wearable pulse oximeter comes with connectivity-based healthcare device, which can be used to constantly observe the patient's health via IoT network. A new method for examining blood oxygen saturation has been developed. A multispectral photodiode has been operated to examine the SpO_2 through a LED [83].

Rehabilitation System

The IoT has the potential to improve the rehabilitation methods that are linked with elderly population and lack of healthcare experts or physician. Rehabilitation and physical medications can help in restoring the quality of life for the disabled and physical impairment patients. Fan et al. [84] proposed an IoT-based smart rehabilitation system that connects all resources in real time.

Wheelchair Management

A number of people are suffering from permanent or short-term disabilities because of various disorders, diseases, weakness, or accidents. Wheelchairs are becoming important for those cases in which patients are facing difficulties in walking. Smart wheelchairs are designed for patients who can use it independently, but there are some cases in which patients or users rely on somebody and cannot handle wheelchair independently [85]. An IoT-based wheelchair is designed by Intel [86]. It is a notable invention of IoT, as this development shows the "things" can change into connected devices directed by data. This wheelchair can monitor the persons sitting in the chair and gathering the surrounding data and allowing for accessing the locations.

Tetraplegia is a pathological condition, caused by any injury, illness, or disease that effects in the partial or complete loss of the limbs and torso. IoT-based smart wheelchairs are developed for the people who are restricted completely or partly by their hand movement. There are three types of modes proposed by Garg et al. [87], which assist the wheelchair user to move freely and their information are transmitted to the nearby person and to the cloud. Accelerometer-based hand glove is designed for wheelchair movement. Wheelchair users can easily transmit their information via RF transmission through hand gesture and their information can also be accessed by their family and doctors. Joseph et al. [88] designed an Arduino microcontroller and voice recognition systems to assist in the wheelchair movements. User can control the direction through voice and gesture. Ultrasonic sensors are used for obstacles detection.

3 Case Studies

In this section, an overview of the most popular case studies is discussed.

3.1 Efficient Water Supply and Management

The IoT can change the method of how water is consumed in a town. The smart meters can detect leakage, data integrity, prevent revenue loss due to inefficiency and enhance productivity by saving time spent in data entry and its analysis. Further, these smart meters can have features such as consumer portals, providing real-time access to residents to find out about their water consumption and supply [53–55].

The usage of water was measured and analyzed for residents of Surrey, Canada. A case study of efficient water supply and management is presented [89].

3.1.1 Water Usage and Management: City of Surrey, Canada

Analysis was done on a total of 61,263 houses with complete house address and water consumption. The data analysis helps to manage the water resource for each hold data consumption. The water requirement for next year can also be predicted and controlled. The analysis of water usage of each house showed more than 6000 houses use water more than 8000–9000 m^3. This showed the normal consumption of the water at maximum houses.

The amount of water used by all cities was different, depending upon the population present in a city and the facilities such as schools, universities, industries, and hospitals present in a city. The statistics collected helped in determining the water requirement at a particular house in a city. The consumption of fresh water could also be maintained based on requirement of each house.

Furthermore, it also assists the authorities to control the water resources relying on their reservoirs. For example, if one has more water reservoir, then he can only store the required amount of water by finding the smart city parameters. Similarly, if one has a shortage of water reservoir, then one can predict the need of water beforehand and then use it accordingly.

It was noticed that in industrial areas, the consumption was high compared to residential areas. This helped in the designing of a system where flow of water can be increased or decreased based on area requirement. Likewise, an effective drainage system can also be designed keeping in mind the above statistics. Thus on the basis of water usage, a billing system can be designed for a specific city.

The analysis showed that in a total of 61,263 houses, the average consumption was 57,877.937. Yet, 50% of the citizens used less than 58,186 m^3 of water and 25% of the citizens use less than 26,893 m^3 of water while 75% of the people use less than 81,983 m^3 water. The data were positively skewed means more than 50% use more than average consumption of water. The water consumption analysis assists smart authorities to manage billing system, by deciding a limit for less fixed bill payments and for charging extra amount to those citizens whose consumption is more compared to other users. The same technique of water management can be applied to energy management such as electricity and gas.

3.2 *IoT in Traffic Control and Management*

Smart traffic management and control refers to the application of integrated technologies and management strategies in transport system. The development of IoT and implementation enable users to utilize innovative services and reach their destination safely by smarter use of transport networks. The technology uses different types of sensors that bring in GPS data from smart phones of drivers to monitor the traffic, location of vehicles and their speed. Green light timings are monitored and automatically changed to avoid traffic congestion. This is achieved through smart traffic lights connected to cloud management platform [53–55].

Let's take a look at how smart transport system is being used around the world to reduce traffic congestion and improve efficiency of the transport system.

3.2.1 Dallas' Traffic Management System, Texas

In the city of Dallas, Texas, traffic management system has been automated by the Ericsson's Connected Urban Transport suite. They provide data analysis, monitor and manage transport system by reducing congestion and improving traffic flow for car drivers. Ericsson, Head of IoT Jeff Travers believe that managing the good traffic quality attracts investors and business industry in decision-making. Dallas is considered to be the fastest growing region in the country, in terms of growing traffic management and drivers' safety at a much reduced cost. It requires an integrated dashboard available to several government sectors; KPI tracking; and computerization characteristics "in which a system will prompt or alert another system when thresholds are disobeyed—for quicker retorts and decreased load" [90].

3.2.2 Management of Railway in Germany

German company Telent had been a reliable coworker to Deutsche Bahn AG in the telecommunications sector for several years and has established its strength as part of countrywide partner. Telent will provide Deutsche Bahn the smart multi-channel systems, at around 7000 points. The IoT solution of Telent is capable of detecting defects in the railway infrastructure before they occur by centralized remote monitoring of the machines at each point. The Dutch company Strukton Systems, a project partner of Telent, measures, digitizes and processes the relevant data using its multi-channel measurement systems.

Deutsche Bahn targets to apply prognostic safeguarding tools for maintenance to monitor its points. This is enabled by measuring the current pulse from the cable connection to the point in the signal box. The status data is measured by special sensors, and then centrally analyzed at related parts of the point controller. If any deviation from the reference value is found such as occurrence before the defect appears, the smart system will detect it at an initial phase. The service teams then inspect closely on site the affected parts and if needed replace them, to avoid disruption in operations. The contract among Telent and Deutsche Bahn includes system components, planning services, installation and commissioning of the solution, which inspects almost 7000 point machines at 305 operative control points all over Germany [90].

3.3 Garbage and Waste Management

With the increase in population, keeping the city clean is very important to avoid diseases that may erupt due to unhygienic environment caused by overflowed garbage containers. IoT platform supports smart garbage collection and waste management, thus helping to maintain a clean and hygienic environment. This smart garbage system uses sensors, System on Chip, micro-controllers, and GPS module to assure dustbins cleaning as soon as it reaches the maximum level. If the garbage is not picked up on time, a report is then sent to the concerned authority, who takes action against the contractor [91].

IoT facilitates garbage collection in an efficient manner. Generally, the garbage is collected by the garbage collecting operators at fixed schedules. This is an inefficient process that leads to unneeded fuel consumption by the garbage collectors and unproductive use of wastage containers. In IoT-based smart city solutions, each garbage bag or container has a sensor that measures the level of the garbage and sends the data to the garbage management center. When the level of the garbage reaches a certain threshold, the data is sent to garbage management center, where it is processed and sends an alert to a truck driver's mobile app. The truck driver then empties a full container rather than emptying half or less than full containers [53–55].

3.3.1 A Case Study: Peninsula Sanitary Service Inc. (PSSI) Implements Container Monitoring Sensors

Picking up garbage from the waste containers in a traditional manner has been a tedious and inefficient task. The hauler was compelled to empty the container on their scheduled route, irrespective of whether the containers were empty, half-full, or spilling over. This system was uneconomical in terms of labor, fuel, and maintenance cost.

Compology a San Francisco based company developed a solution to solve the problem via data collection. They installed sensors into the waste container to collect data, which is then analyzed and displayed through web-based software. The technology measures the fullness level of the trash containers and allows haulers to empty only the containers that are full, thus saving time and labor and improving customer service.

3.3.2 How One Waste Hauler Implemented Image-Based Container Sensors to Manage Inventory and Streamline Services

The Challenge

Stanford University is a world renowned university with a huge campus, uses services of Peninsula Sanitary Service Inc. (PSSI), for waste collection. In addition to the daily waste produced by a large population of the campus, PSSI also provides services collecting debris boxes for a large number of construction projects in progress at 8000+ acre campus.

The big challenges for PSSI were:

1. Anticipating service needs
2. Managing container inventory

The Solution

In 2016 summers, the Operations Manager for PSSI, Andrew Pellegrini, referred to Compology for the solution. Compology provides a web-based container monitoring solution. Software powered by container-mounted sensors that use automatic GPS location tracking, image-based fullness monitoring, and motion-based service verification. With the combination of location and fullness data along with access to container images, PSSI hoped to address their main challenges of managing container inventory and anticipating service needs. Compology technicians quickly installed sensors on all 104 PSSI roll-off containers and worked with PSSI so they could hit the ground running [92].

The Results

With the container monitoring solution provided by Compology, PSSI managed to meet the challenges:

1. *Anticipate Service Needs*
   The Compology's services provided accurate information about fullness of containers with images for error proofing, for verifying remotely. PSSI managed to anticipate service needs, by providing quick service to each site by receiving accurate information about the fullness of containers.
2. *Manage Container Inventory*
   The Compology's software resolved the problem by showing the containers on site details, location, customer's information and date and time of last service and the containers available in inventory, this enables PSSI to manage and swap the containers immediately [92].

3.4 Smart and Efficient Parking

Smart and efficient parking refers to creating a real-time parking map to assist drivers in parking their cars in parking spaces. The GPS data from drivers' smart phones assist in finding available parking space. When the nearest parking space is free, the driver gets the alert and using the map on their phone finds the parking easily and faster. This saves the driver from driving around in search of parking. An example of smart and efficient parking in the city of Burlington, Canada is given as a case study [93, 94].

3.4.1 Smart Parking System in Burlington, Canada

The aim of this project is to provide real-time information about available car parking spaces to the drivers. To do the task, Telefonica and Urbiotica have been selected by ATM. They have equipped ten areas with the U-Flow Parking system. The system counts the number of vehicles entering and leaving the area and provides real-time information of the available parking space, with great accuracy. It also provides information about the normal and booked car parking spaces such as those for people with less mobility, electric vehicles, and employees. This is done by U-Spot single space detection sensors. U-Spot is an autonomous wireless parking sensor that detects real-time incoming and outgoing vehicles in parking lots along with their parking periods, using magnetic technology. The information from both systems are combined by U-Admin platform, which generates and transmits the information about the normal parking space availability to FIWARE Telefonica platform which is integrated with Mou-te.

With more than 180,000 population, and direct access to the Lake Ontario, the City of Burlington (Ontario, Canada) is a perfect site for visitors with short- and midterm vacations and leisure. The City thus faces issues of managing daily and summer car parking for locals and visitors.

3.4.2 Solution for Guided Parking

Services End-to-End

In order to improve the vehicles movement condition in Burlington, the metropolis chose to invest in a smart parking system. The system is now being used by Burlington, for monitoring the drivers within a city during peak hours, average hours, use of parking off-street, etc. The parking manager accesses the key information provided by the system in a quick and effective way. He can analyze the parking situation, on-street rotations, off-street arrivals and departures. Thanks to Urbiotica's Parking U-Admin Control Center.

Following are the details of the installed system:

- On-street parking is monitored by **U-Spot** sensors, used for the main streets of the city center.
- **Flow parking** sensors monitor off-street parking. They are configured for two-way count.
- Free spots in the main street are indicated by Variable Message Sign in the city center.
- Real-time management and data analysis is controlled by the **Parking U-Admin Control Center.**

Advantages of the Result

- Lessens stress and anxiety for users.
- Reduction in vehicle congestion in the street.
- Improved standard of living for inhabitants [92].

4 Conclusion and Future Prospects of IoT

IoT has become a technological reality today. The use of IoT is gaining momentum. Currently, it has become a need, bringing comfort to human's life. The day when every device will be able to communicate with the other device through the internet is not far-off. The purpose of this chapter is to evaluate the effectiveness of IoT in many domains like healthcare, industry, manufacturing, agriculture, environments, smart cities, transport, etc. This chapter covers the state-of-the-art IoT applications, the technologies supporting IoT in real-world applications and case studies of smart cities. Due to large production of data, diversity, and speed by IoT devices, a quick analysis is required to ensure minimum delay, higher bandwidth, reliability, and data security. IoT can be further advanced with the implication of fog computing, to meet the evolving demands of high speed processing and lesser time delay. If security risks in WSN are resolved, the use of this mechanism will be far more.

References

1. Teixeira, T. V., Hachem, S., Issarny, V., & Georgantas, N. (2011). Service oriented middleware for the internet of things: A perspective. In *Proceedings of the 4th European conference on towards a service-based internet* (pp. 220–229).
2. Whitmore, A., Agarwal, A., & Xu, L. D. (2015). The internet of things—A survey of topics and trends. *Information Systems Frontiers, 17*, 261–274.
3. Vermesan, O., & Friess, P. (2014). *Internet of things—Converging technologies for smart environments and integrated ecosystems*. River Publishers Series in Communications.
4. Perwej, Y. (2017). An experiential study of the big data. *International Transaction of Electrical and Computer Engineers System, 4*(1), 14–25.
5. Kuhlins, C., Rathonyi, B., Zaidi, A., & Hogan, M. (2020, January). *Cellular networks for Massive IoT*.Ericsson.com. Retrieved March 30, 2020, from https://www.ericsson.com/assets/local/publications/white-papers/wp iot.pdf adresinden alındı.
6. Evans, D. (2011). *The internet of things: How the next evolution of the internet is changing everything*. Cisco Internet Business Solutions Group (IBSG), Cisco Systems, Inc., San Jose, CA, USA, White Paper. Retrieved March 30, 2020, from http://www.cisco.Com/web/about/ac79/docs/innovlIoT_IBSG 0411 FINAL.pdf adresinden alindi.
7. Atzor, L., Iera, A., & Morabito, G. (2010). The internet of things: A survey. *Computer Networks, The International Journal of Computer and Telecommunications Networking*.
8. Nair, K., Kulkarni, J., Warde, M., Dave, Z., Rawalgaonkar, V., Gore, G., et al. (2015). Optimizing power consumption in IoT based wireless sensor networks using bluetooth low energy. In *International conference on green computing and internet of things, ICGCIoT, Greater Noida, Delhi, India* (pp. 589–593). https://doi.org/10.1109/icgciot.2015.7380533.

9. Harwood, T. (2019, November 1). *IoT technology guidebook*. Postcapes. Retrieved April 7, 2020, from https://www.postscapes.com/internet-of-things-technologies/.
10. Want, R. (2006). An introduction to RFID technology, pervasive computing. *IEEE, 5*(1), 25–33. https://doi.org/10.1109/MPRV.2006.2.
11. Radio-Frequency Identification. (n.d.). *Wikipedia*. Retrieved April 20, 2020, from https://en.wikipedia.org/wiki/Radio-frequency_identification.
12. Ndih, E. D., & Cherkaoui, S. (2016). On enhancing technology coexistence in the IoT era: ZigBee and 802.11 case. *IEEE Access, 4*, 1835–1844. https://doi.org/10.1109/ACCESS.2016.2553150.
13. Piyare, R., & Lee, S. R. (2013). Smart home-control and monitoring system using smart phone. In *Conference: 1st international conference on convergence and its application (ICCA)* (Vol. 24).
14. Palattella, M. R., Dohler, M., Grieco, A., Rizzo, G., Torsner, J., Engel, T., et al. (2016). Internet of things in the 5G era: Enablers, architecture and business models. *IEEE Journal on Selected Areas in Communications, 34*.
15. Patel, M., & Wang, J. (2010). Applications, challenges, and prospective in emerging body area networking technologies. *IEEE Wireless Communications*, 80–88.
16. Mandal, S. (2016). *Internet of things (IoT)—Part 4 (network protocols and architecture)*. Retrieved from https://www.c-sharpcorner.com/UploadFile/f88748/internet-of-thingsiot-part-4-network-protocols-and-arc/.
17. Kaushal, A. (2015). *Role of information & communication technology (ICT) in smart city*. Newgen Soft. Retrieved March 29, 2020, from https://newgensoft.com/blog/role-of-information-communication-technology-ict-in-smart-city/ adresinden alındı.
18. Sterbenz, J. P. (2017). Smart city and IoT resilience, survivability, and disruption tolerance: Challenges, modelling, and a survey of research opportunities. In *Proceedings of the 2017 9th international workshop on resilient networks design and modeling (RNDM), Alghero, Italy* (pp. 1–6).
19. Collignon, C., Haberleithner, J., & Reyes, M. (2017). Creative industries in the smart city: Overview of a liability in emerging economies. In *Handbook of research on entrepreneurial development and innovation within smart cities*. IGI Global.
20. Harrison, C., Eckman, B., Hamilton, R., Hartswick, P., Kalagnanam, J., Paraszczak, J., et al. (2010). Foundations of smarter cities. *IBM Journal of Research and Development, 54*(4), 1–16.
21. Moreau, E. (2012). *Towards smarter cities*. Internal white paper v3.0, Dar Group.
22. Zanella, A., Bui, N., Castellani, A., Vangelista, L., & Zorzi, M. (2014). Internet of things for smart cities. *IEEE Internet of Things Journal, 1*(1).
23. Jin, J., Gubbi, J., Marusic, S., & Palaniswami, M. (2014). An information framework for creating a smart city through internet of things. *IEEE Internet of Things Journal, 1*(2), 112–121.
24. Dlodlo, N., Gcaba, O., & Smith, A. (2016). Internet of things technologies in smart cities. In P. Cunningham & M. Cunningham (Eds.), *IST-Africa 2016 conference proceedings*. IIMC International Information Management Corporation.
25. Lombardi, P., Giordano, S., Yousef, W., & Farouh, H. (2012). Modelling the smart city performance. *Innovation: The European Journal of Social Science Research, 25*(2), 137–149.
26. Sikder, A. K., Acar, A., Aksu, H., Uluagac, A. S., Akkaya, K., & Conti, M. (2018). IoT-enabled smart lighting systems for smart cities. In *IEEE 8th annual computing and communication workshop and conference (CCWC)*.
27. Bonino, D., Alizo, M. T., Alapetite, A., Gilbert, T., Axling, M., Udsen, H., et al. (2015). ALMANAC: Internet of things for smart cities. In *3rd International conference on future internet of things and cloud*.
28. Memon, S. K., Shaikh, F. K., Mahoto, N. A., & Memon, A. A. (2019). IoT based smart garbage monitoring & collection system using WeMos & ultrasonic sensors. In *International conference on computing, mathematics and engineering technologies—iCoMET 2019*.
29. Balta-Ozkan, N., Davidson, R., Bicket, M., & Whitmarsh, L. (2013). Social barriers to the adoption of smart homes. *Energy Policy, 63*, 363–374.

30. Lutolf, R. (1992). Smart home concept and the integration of energy meters into a home based system. In R. Lutolf (Ed.), *Smart home concept and the integration of energy. Seventh international conference on metering apparatus and tariffs for electricity supply, Glasgow, UK, IET* (pp. 277–278).
31. Ricquebourg, V., Menga, D., Durand, D., Marhic, B., Delahoche, L., & Loge, C. (2006). The smart home concept: our immediate future. In V. Ricquebourg, D. Menga, D. Durand, B. Marhic, L. Delahoche, & C. Loge (Eds.), *Th1ST IEEE international conference on e-learning in industrial electronics, Hammamet, Tunisia* (pp. 23–28). IEEE.
32. Talavera, J., Tobón, L., Gómez, J., Culman, M., Aranda, J., Parra, D., et al. (2017). Review of IoT applications in agro-industrial and environmental fields. *Computers and Electronics in Agriculture, 142*(Part A), 283–297.
33. Ayaz, M., Ammad-Uddin, M., Sharif, Z., Mansour, A., & Aggoune, E.-H. M. (2019). Internet-of-things (IoT)-based smart agriculture: Toward making the fields talk. *IEEE Access, Special Section on New Technologies For Smart Farming 4.0: Research Challenges and Opportunities*.
34. Lee, M., Nat, S., & Hwang, J. (2013). Agricultural production system based on IoT. In *Computational science and engineering (CSE) IEEE 16th international conference* (pp. 833–836).
35. Ma, J., Zhou, X., & Li, Z. (2011). Connecting agriculture to the internet of things through sensor networks. In *Internet of things (iThings/CPSCom) 2011 international conference on and 4th international conference on cyber physical and social computing* (pp. 184–187).
36. Dinkins, C. P., & Jones, C. (2013). *Interpretation of soil test reports for agriculture*. Tech. Report. Montana State University.
37. AgroCares Lab-in-a-Box. (n.d.). *Agrocares nutrient intelligence*. Retrieved April 2, 2020, from https://www.agrocares.com/en/products/lab-in-the-box/.
38. Martínez-Fernández, J., González-Zamora, A., Sánchez, N., Gumuzzio, A., & Herrero-Jiménez, C. M. (2016). Satellite soil moisture for agricultural drought monitoring: Assessment of the SMOS derived soil water deficit index. *Remote Sensing of Environment, 177*, 277–286.
39. Vagen, T.-G., Tondoh, J. E., Desta, L. T., Gumbricht, T., & Winowiecki, L. (2016). Mapping of soil properties and land degradation risk in Africa using MODIS reflectance. *Geoderma, 263*, 216–225.
40. Water Facts—Worldwide Water Supply. (2019, November 12). *Bureau of reclamation*. Retrieved April 2, 2020, from https://www.usbr.gov/mp/arwec/water-facts-ww-water-sup.html.
41. Irrigation & Water Use. (2019, September 23). *Farm practices & management*. Retrieved April 4, 2020, from https://www.ers.usda.gov/topics/farm-practices-management/irrigation-water-use/.
42. LaRue, J., & Frederick, C. (2012). *Decision process for the application of variable rate irrigation*. American Society of Agricultural and Biological Engineers.
43. Benincasa, P., Antognelli, S., Brunetti, L., & Fabbri, C. A. (2018). Reliability of NDVI derived by high resolution satellite and UAV compared to in-field methods for the evaluation of early crop N status and grain yield in wheat. *AGRIS, 54*(4), 1–19.
44. Suradhaniwar, S., Kar, S., Nandan, R., Raj, R., & Jagarlapudi, A. (2018). *Geospatial technologies in land resources mapping, monitoring and management*. Springer.
45. Khan, N., Medlock, G., Graves, S., & Anwar, S. (2018). GPS guided autonomous navigation of a small agricultural robot with automated fertilizing system. *SAE Technical Paper 2018-01-0031*.
46. Colaço, A. F., & Molin, J. P. (2017). Variable rate fertilization in citrus: A long term study. *Precision Agriculture, 18*(2), 169–191.
47. Kim, S., Lee, M., & Shin, C. (2018). IoT-based strawberry disease prediction system for smart farming. *Sensors, 18*(11), 4051.
48. Integrated Pest Management. (n.d.). *Seimos, variable rate mating disruption and automated pest camera traps*. Retrieved April 4, 2020, from https://semios.com/ipm/.
49. Farm RTX. (n.d.). *Retrofit yield monitor & automatic yield maps*. Retrieved April 5, 2020, from https://www.farmtrx.com/.

50. Torbick, N., Chowdhury, D., Salas, W., & Qi, J. (2017). Monitoring rice agriculture across Myanmar using time series Sentinel-1 assisted by Landsat-8 and PALSAR-2. *Sensors, 9*(2), 119.
51. Wang, Z., Walsh, K., & Verma, B. (2017). On-tree mango fruit size estimation using RGB-D images. *Sensors, 17*(12), 2738.
52. Xu, L. D., He, W., & Li, S. (2014). Internet of things in industries: A survey. *IEEE Transactions on Industrial Informatics, 10*(4).
53. Perwej, Y., AbouGhaly, M. A., Kerim, B., & Harb, H. A. (2019). An extended review on internet of things (IoT) and its promising applications. *Communications on Applied Electronics (CAE), 9*, 8–22. https://doi.org/10.5120/cae2019652812.
54. Perwej, Y., Haq, K., Parwej, F., & Mumdouh M. (2019, April). The internet of things (IoT) and its application domains. *International Journal of Computer Applications, 182*(49).
55. Perwej, Y., Parwej, F., Hassan, M. M., & Akhtar, N. (2019). The internet-of-things (IoT) security: A technological perspective and review. *International Journal of Scientific Research in Computer Science, Engineering and Information Technology (IJSRCSEIT), 5*(1), 462–482. https://doi.org/10.32628/CSEIT195193.
56. Wollschlaeger, M., Sauter, T., & Jasperneite, J. (2017). The future of industrial communication: Automation networks in the era of the internet of things and industry 4.0. *IEEE Industrial Electronics Magazine, 11*(1).
57. Pan, J., Paul, R. J., Vu, T., Saifullah, A. S., & Sha, M. (2015). An internet of things framework for smart energy in buildings: Designs, prototype and experiments. *IEEE Internet of Things Journal, 2*(6), 527–537.
58. Kabalcı, E., Gorgun, A., & Kabalci, Y. (2013). Design and implementation of a renewable energy monitoring system. In *Power engineering energy and electrical drives (POWERENG), fourth international conference.*
59. Spanias, A. S. (2017). Solar energy management as an internet of things (IoT) application. In *8th International conference on information, intelligence, systems & applications (IISA), IEEE, Larnaca, Cyprus.*
60. Ma, X. (n.d.). *Smart grid*. Retrieved July 30, 2020, from https://www.cse.wustl.edu/~jain/cse574-10/ftp/grid/index.html.
61. Al-Turjman, F., & Abujubbeh, M. (2019). IoT-enabled smart grid via SM: An overview. *Future Generation Computer Systems, 96*, 579–590.
62. Chen, C., Nagananda, K., Xiong, G., Kishore, S., & Snyder, L. (2013). A communication-based appliance scheduling scheme for consumerpremise energy management systems. *IEEE Transactions on Smart Grid, 4*(1), 56–65.
63. Xiong, G., Chen, C., Kishore, S., & Yener, A. (2011). Smart (in home) power scheduling for demand response on the smart grid. In *Innovative smart grid technologies (ISGT), IEEE PES* (pp. 1–7).
64. World Health Organization. (2014). *Obesity and overweight*. Retrieved April 1, 2020, from http://www.who.int/mediacentre/factsheets/fs311/en/ adresinden alındı.
65. Islam, S. M., Kwak, D., Kabir, M., Hossain, M., & Kwak, K. S. (2015). The internet of things for health care: A comprehensive survey. *IEEE Access, 3*, 678–708.
66. Pang, Z. (2013). *Technologies and architectures of the internet-of-things (IoT) for health and well-being*. Doctoral thesis, in Electronic and Computer Systems,Kista Sweden: KTH Royal Institute of Technology, 2013. p. xiv, 75.
67. Bertholdo, L., Granville, L., Tarouco, L., Arbiza, L., Carbone, F., Marotta, M., et al. (2012). Internet of things in healthcare: Interoperati-bility and security issues. In *IEEE international conference communications (ICC, IEEE)* (pp. 6121–6125).
68. Domingo, M. C. (2012). An overview of the internet of things for people with disabilities. *Journal of Network and Computer Applications, 35*(2), 584–596.
69. Linkous, L., Zohrabi, N., & Abdelwahed, S. (2019). Health monitoring in smart homes utilizing internet of things. In *MCPS workshop in CHASE 2019 conference in Washington D.C.*

70. Gia, T. N., Ali, M., Dhaou, I. B., Rahmani, A. M., Westerlund, T., Liljeberg, P., et al. (2017). IoT-based continuous glucose monitoring system: A feasibility study. In *8th International conference on ambient systems, networks and technologies (ANT-2017)*. Elsevier.
71. Alarcón-Paredes, A., Francisco-García, V., Guzmán-Guzmán, I. P., Cantillo-Negrete, J., Cuevas-Valencia, R. E., & Alonso-Silverio, G. A. (2019). An IoT-based non-invasive glucose level monitoring system using Raspberry Pi. *Applied Sciences, 9*(15), 3046.
72. Shaown, T., Hasan, I., Mim, M. R., & Hossain, M. S. (2019). IoT-based portable ECG monitoring system for smart healthcare. 2019 1st International conference on advances in science, engineering and robotics technology (ICASERT). IEEE.
73. Brezulianu, A., Geman, O., Zbancioc, M. D., Hagan, M., Aghion, C., HemanthJ, D., et al. (2019). IoT based heart activity monitoring using inductive sensors. *Sensors, 19*(15), 3284.
74. Xin, T. J., Min, B., & Jie, J. (2013). Carry-on blood pressure/pulse rate/blood oxygen monitoring location intelligent terminal based on internet of things. In *Chinese Patent 202875315 U*.
75. Lamonaca, F., Balestrieri, E., Tudosa, I., Picariello, F., Carnì, D. L., Scuro, C., et al. (2019). An overview on internet of medical things in blood pressure monitoring. In *2019 IEEE international symposium on medical measurements and applications (MeMeA)*.
76. Qardio. (2013). Retrieved April 6, 2020, from https://www.getqardio.com/.
77. OMRON. (n.d.). Retrieved April 5, 2020, from https://omronhealthcare.com/products/heartguide-wearable-blood-pressure-monitor-bp8000m/.
78. Pioneer DreamCare Blood Pressure Monitoring Smart Bracelet. (n.d.). Retrieved April 6, 2020, from http://pioneeriot.com/?product=pioneer-dreamcare-bphr-smart-monitoring-bracelet-watch.
79. Asus VivoWatch BP. (2018). Retrieved April 6, 2020, from https://www.cnet.com/pictures/asus-vivowatch-bp-is-a-wrist-sized-blood-pressure-monitor/2/.
80. Jian, Z. (2012). Temperature measurement system and method based on home gateway. In *Chinese Patent 102811185 A*.
81. Fajrin, H. R., Ilahi, M. R., Handoko, B. S., & Sari, I. P. (2019). Body temperature monitoring based on telemedicine. *Journal of Physics: Conference Series, Volume 1381. The 1st international conference on engineering and applied science, Madiun, Indonesia.*
82. Khattak, H. A., Ruta, M., & Sciascio, E. D. (2014). CoAP-based healthcare sensor networks: A survey. In *11th International Bhurban conference on applied sciences & technology (IBCAST) Islamabad, Pakistan*.
83. Chong, A., Terosiet, M., Histace, A., & Romain, O. (2019). Towards a novel single-LED pulse oximeter based on a multispectral sensor for IoT applications. *Microelectronics Journal, 88*, 128–136.
84. Fan, Y. J., Yin, Y. H., Xu, L. D., Zeng, Y., & Wu, F. (2014). IoT-based smart rehabilitation system. *IEEE Transactions on Industrial Informatics, 10*(2), 1568–1577.
85. Sibai, M. H., & Manap, S. A. (2015). A study on smart wheelchair systems. *International Journal Of Engineering Technology And Sciences (IJETS), 4*(1).
86. Mendoza, M. (2014). *Intel, Stephen Hawking showcase connected wheelchair project.* Tech Times. Retrieved April 1, 2020, from https://www.techtimes.com/articles/15367/20140911/intel-stephen-hawking-showcase-connected-wheelchair-project.htm adresinden alındı.
87. Garg, U., Ghanshala, K. K., Joshi, R., & Chauhan, R. (2018). Design and implementation of smart wheelchair for quadriplegia patients using IOT. In *2018 First international conference on secure cyber computing and communication (ICSCCC)*. IEEE.
88. Joseph, C., Aswin, S., & Prasad, J. S. (2019). Voice and gesture controlled wheelchair. In *2019 3rd International conference on computing methodologies and communication (ICCMC)*. IEEE.
89. Huang, J., & Hua, K. (2017). *Managing the internet of things: Architectures, theories and applications*. The Institution of Engineering and Technology.
90. Kinney, S. (2018, January 26). *Three smart transportation case studies.* IoT insights. Retrieved April 1, 2020, from https://enterpriseiotinsights.com/20180126/transportation/three-smart-transportation-case-studies-tag17-tag99 adresinden alındı.

91. Chavhan, R. V., & Rojatkar, D. V. (2017). IoT based garbage management system. *International Journal of Trend in Scientific Research and Development (IJTSRD), 1*(6), 815–817.
92. Pellegrini, A. (2017). *A case study: Peninsula Sanitary Service Inc. (PSSI) implements container monitoring sensors.* Complology. Retrieved April 1, 2020, from https://compology.com/blog/pssi-implements-container-monitor adresinden alındı.
93. Perez, D. (2020). *Smart parking systems in Burlington, Canada.* Urbiotica. Retrieved April 1, 2020, from https://www.urbiotica.com/en/examples-smart-cities/smart-parking-system-burlington-canada/ adresinden alindi.
94. Perez, P. D. (2020). *Smart parking.* Urbiotica. Retrieved April 1, 2020, from https://www.urbiotica.com/en/category/smart-parking/ adresinden alındı.

Prescriptive Analytics in Internet of Things with Concentration on Deep Learning

Iman Raeesi Vanani and Setareh Majidian

1 Introduction

In digital era, Internet of Things (IoT) has been introduced with the aim of empowering human in doing tasks with higher productivity concentrating on Artificial Intelligence (AI) and power of involving things connected with each other [1]. By emerging of IoT, a paradigm shift has happened in businesses to develop added value services, creating novel business model and sustainable competitive advantages through the machine and gadgets networked with each other [2]. Different industrial domains gain advantage of IoT applications such as "health," "traffic," "logistic," "retail," "agriculture," and "smart cities" [3]. IoT with its significant development in recent 20 years brings effective impact on different areas of "market channel transparency" by enabling enterprise to track items [4]. IoT offers many innovative, reliable and safe solutions for high risk environment where human safety is under risks [5]. It provides real-time information flow about indoor climate conditions which have vital impact on plant growth [6]. By improving resource and energy productivity, IoT brings huge opportunity for monitoring manufacturing environment [7]. IoT support decision making in cyber security [8], tracing system design [4] and many other fields on the base of gathered data. Despite the fact that research assign added value to IoT, in fact, data analytics brings the fundamental base for that valuable output. It analyzes huge amount of relevant data in order to bring business value [9]. As IoT technology generates big data, big data analytics deploy novel analytical tools such as python and R in order to analyze data with the

I. Raeesi Vanani
Associate Professor, Allameh Tabataba'i University, Tehran, Iran

S. Majidian (✉)
Alumni of University of Tehran, Tehran, Iran

F. P. García Márquez, B. Lev (eds.), *Introduction to Internet of Things in Management Science and Operations Research*, International Series in Operations Research & Management Science 311,
https://doi.org/10.1007/978-3-030-74644-5_2

main features of variety, volume, and velocity with the aim of extracting insight from them [10, 11]. Besides the most famous characteristics of big data veracity, validity, volatility, and value are comprised in big data characteristics, as well [12]. Data analytics has three phases, namely descriptive analytics, predictive analytics, and prescriptive analytics. As the level of analytics goes from descriptive to predictive and prescriptive, the depth level of analysis will be increased [13]. IoT as a new technology has provided businesses with accurate and meticulous prescription which generated from prescriptive analytics to improve decision making functions [14]. On the other hand, deep learning technology provides data analytics with great data processing and big data analysis power. It also helps to create highly optimized decision making [15, 16]. In fact, growth rate of IoT will be increased by application of data analytics. Furthermore, significant role of deep learning in IoT data analytics is irrefutable, as it can fulfill the rising analytical demands of IoT systems [17]. So deep learning with its potential power of improving prescriptive analytics plays an enabler role for prescriptive analytics. In this research, absorptive capacity is taken to explain how prescriptive analytics can be improved by deep learning technology which results in gaining advantage from exploitative innovation to enhance firm performance and decision making function. In this research, we aim to introduce prescriptive analytics generated from IoT data through deep learning. The rest of the chapter is constructed as follows. Firstly, a brief overview on each concept of IoT, deep learning, and prescriptive analytics is outlined. Then, previous research working on prescriptive analytics of IoT data through deep learning will be presented and it will be shown that each research has worked effectively in solving related problems. Next, comprehensive research model will be introduced. At the end, conclusion future research will be presented.

2 Literature Review

2.1 Internet of Things (IoT)

IoT has been first used by Kevin Ashton in 1999 in field of supply chain management [18]. In a simple way, IoT has been defined as the association of things over internet via "Wireless Sensor Networks (WSN)," "Radio-frequency Identification (RFID)," "Bluetooth," "Near-field communication (NFC)," "Long Term Evolution (LTE)," and other smart communication devices and technologies. Information gathered from various devices with the aim of sending to an internet-based destination [19]. Processes that are involved in gathering and distributing data are "identifying," "sensing," "networking," and "computation" which allows personalized communication with smart things [3]. Figure 1 shows application of IoT in different industries [20]. Two main IoT applications are device-to-device and human-to-device.

The IoT on device needs to ensure the transmission and reception of data and accurate and on time decision making. Device-to-human applications have higher

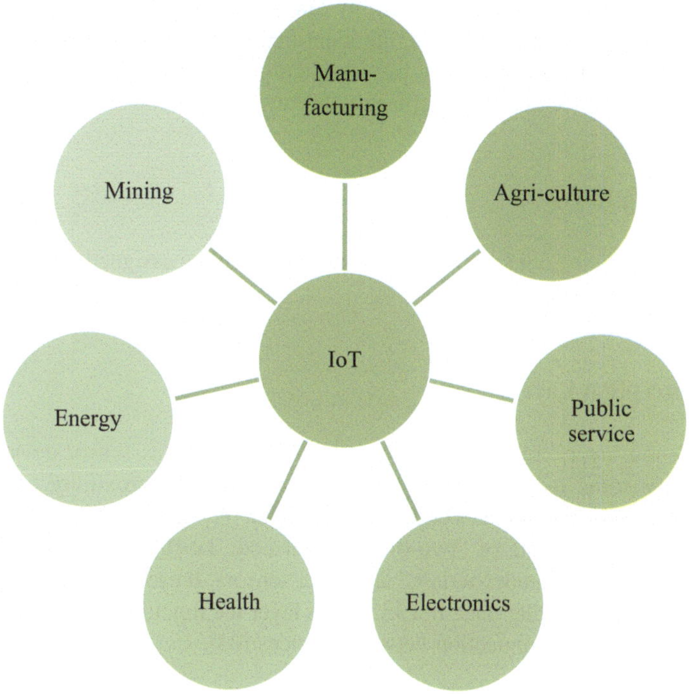

Fig. 1 Application of IoT in industries [20]

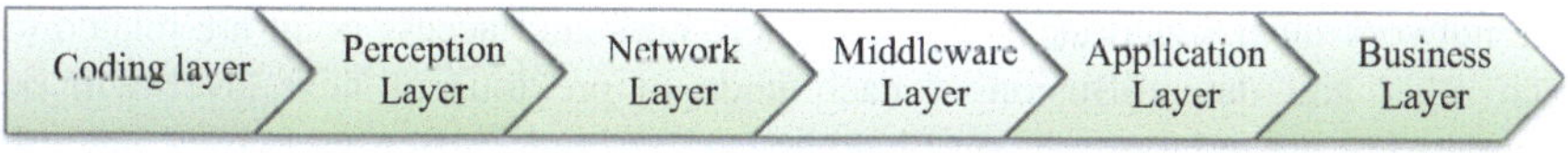

Fig. 2 Multilayered IoT architecture [21]

needs of visualization in comparison with device-to-device applications, which put intelligence on device that helps them to monitor the environment, find out problems, even solve the problem needless of human intervention and also interact with other devices.

2.2 IoT Architecture

IoT deploys a multilayered architecture which is shown in Fig. 2, which consists of "coding layer," "perception layer," "network layer," "middleware layer," "application layer," and "business layer" [21]. Data generated via sensors can be categorized into three classifications, which are data generation, the main features of this classification are "velocity," "scalability," "dynamics," and "heterogeneity"; data interoperability, this category is known by "incompleteness" and "semantics" features; and data quality classification, the identified data in this category is with low level of certainty, "redundancy," high level of ambiguity and inconsistency [22]. The layers of IoT Architecture are described as follows.

2.2.1 Coding Layer

In "coding layer," the object is identified and an ID will be assigned to the identified object [21].

2.2.2 Perception Layer

In "perception layer," other technologies like RFID work as sensor device which may identify some useful information, such as humidity, proximity, speed, and location [21]. This layer creates connection between physical world and information world. The layer consists of "two-dimensional code label," "code reader-writer," "RFID tags and RFID reader-writer," and other sensors. It uses different information sampling devices to gather data. In fact, in this layer the function of data collection is done through internet connection between devices [23].

2.2.3 Network Layer

The network layer functions as a point where node and access point are related to each other and data diffusion of each node in previous or next layer will be completed or moved forward. Wi-Fi, ad hoc, Mesh, and ZigBee are known network layer [23].

2.2.4 Middleware Layer

After transforming the information to digital signals, in "network layer" those signals will be passed to the "middleware layer" through Wi-Fi and WiMAX with identified protocols. In "middleware layer," the gathered data will be processed and the automated actions will be taken [21]. In this layer data exchange is monitored and data transmission is done through different networks like satellite, mobile, or any private networks [23].

2.2.5 Application Layer

In "application layer," the usability area of IoT will be determined which can be smart houses, smart cities, smart manufacturing and the list goes on [21]. In this layer, sharing information through any intelligent applications happens which consists of any device and expert systems [23]. This layer is responsible for translation of request to an identified language for the platform [24].

2.2.6 Business Layer

In "business layer," the strategic approach will be taken in order to form appropriate business model to create value from identified applications [21]. Human computer interface, virtual reality, and other applications of intelligent information are involved in this layer [23].

Other IoT applications that bring value for customers, namely automated controlling, data analytics, and information sharing [25] are discussed in the following sections.

2.3 Automated Controlling

By flourishing applications of automation industry and wireless connections, automated controlling creates an avenue for new usage of IoT. For example, "Smart Automated House Application" which is deployed on the basis of IoT systems provides people to control household devices remotely. The remote control consists of turning on and off light, fan, water pump, gardening of water or other electronic devices with feature of connecting to the internet [26]. Automated controlling is deployed by application of mobile phones, tablets, and computers that connect things to internet and can bring intelligence and safety to the environment. Many places like banks, hospitals, and public environment that become hazardous in disaster can be controlled through IoT [27]. In addition to the cited areas of automated controlling based on IoT, firms in area of crops growing gain advantage of the technology. It helps company to have meticulous monitoring and analyzing over crops growth process which brings cost saving advantage and high quality production [28]. IoT also helps immediate assistance to the cardiac arrest. They can be assessed by IoT automated controlling and GPS system which shows the exact location of patient [29].

2.4 Data Analytics

On the rise of IoT data which has five features of variety, volume, velocity, veracity, validity, and volatility is generated enormously. Firms are faced with challenges of storing and analyzing a huge amount of data that are extracted from small constructions [30]. However, the data cannot be useful without any analytical power [31]. Big data analytics can help the IoT output by providing data collection efficiency, or other fields like processing, analytics, and security [30]. Data analytics in area of IoT is identified as process of clarifying trend, hidden patterns and extracting insight from the structured, semi-structured, and unstructured data. It helps firms to take advantage from the information covered in data by making insightful decisions. Data mining techniques, statistic methods, and machine learning algorithms are widely used in IoT data analytics [31]. By leveraging data analytics, data from different applications like e-healthcare to GPS sensors are gathered in order to analyze and deploy in generating strategies for transportation system, emergency and developing quick response to criminal warning. It even helps in understanding customer interest and behavioral pattern [32].

2.5 Information Sharing

Information sharing in context of IoT has been generated by development in IoT technology and it refers to exchanging information with other partners in order to improve strategic decisions. It can be done by developing supporting capabilities related to IoT. It is divided into two types: internally and externally. The former indicates the relation of focal firm with other partners inside the focal firm's industry and the latter refers to information exchanging between focal firms and firms outside the industry of focal firm [33]. The mechanism of IoT information sharing is improved through block chain which covers shortcomings like processing huge amount of data with lots of expenses and energy and inefficiency in guaranteeing the validity, authentication, and security issues of data [34].

3 Deep Learning

From 2006 deep learning as a subset of machine learning has been faced with augmented area of applications. Wide applications of deep learning can be found in image recognition, "machine translation," IoT, and other data-driven technologies [35]. Deep learning has changed analyzing human data generated such as video, image, and audio. It also significantly impacts the next generation applications of IoT in tasks of sensing and recognition [36]. Conventional machine learning techniques suffer from processing natural data with the raw form; however, deep learning methods take multilayer representation which is generated through nonlinear modules with working on raw data and transforming the representation in one level and create a higher level of representation. This composition method helps to learn even most complex functions [37]. Artificial algorithms motivate deep learning as simulator of human brain in deep layered structure in order to extract features and create an abstract picture of data. The output of deep learning is deployed in big data analytics. The way that deep learning algorithms process raw data to extract complex and nonlinear pattern results in using a simpler linear model for big data analytics process [38]. Deep learning with its multiple hidden layers "(deep networks)" face with high level of difficulty with learning various features. In fact, deep learning learns the process in multiple levels of concepts. There is hierarchy architecture in building the concept with each concept built on the top of others. As the level of learning goes up, the complex concept has been represented. So, in lower level simple representation is outlined [39]. Deep learning deploys a massive amount of nonlinear filter in advance of offering solution which is generated through automatic hierarchical feature extraction which makes deep learning needless of extracting feature with some traditional way such as trial and error or manual processes. The model built through deep learning algorithms comprises of multilayer neural networks. In this architecture, neurons link two subsequent features layers with initially having nonlinear transformation parameters. The input will be transformed passing layer to layer till reaching the target layer where decision is made [40]. Deep learning architecture flexibility can be customized with various types of raw data. Training on deep learning is based on back propagation process that results in efficient data representation [41]. Three main features of deep learning play critical role in outstanding performance of it, which are "unsupervised feature learning," "strong generalization capability," and "big-data training." On the base of these characteristics, the method face with overwhelming success in various fields such as pattern recognition, forecasting, classification, and image processing [42]. Deep learning automatically learns structured/unstructured data in order to extract feature. The process is done efficiently which covers the lack of conventional machine learning techniques. Considering the application of deep learning in big data analytics, two famous architectures are Deep Belief Network (DBN), working with labeled/unlabeled data with three layers of input, hidden, and output, and Convolutional Neural Network (CNN), working with hierarchical layers, namely, feature maps and classification layers [38]. Deep learning methods are discussed as follows.

3.1 Deep Belief Network (DBN)

DBN consists of a "multilayer restricted Boltzmann machine (RBM) as a stochastic neural network." The process is done through three layers of visible and hidden and output layer. It trains the data via two processes of pre-training and fine-tuning phase where pre-training phase tries to predict parameters and the trained data is fine-tuned through back propagation [43]. DBN performs like DNN that uses restricted Boltzmann machines (RBMs) [44].

3.2 *Convolutional Neural Network (CNN)*

CNN has significant ability in feature extraction on the way of reducing the complexity of model and parameter number [45]. It is known through three features of "local field," "subsampling," and "weight sharing" where acting in three layers. The first layer is input layer, the second layer is the hidden layer which consists of "convolutional layer" and "subsampling layer" and the last layer is the output layer [46]. CNN technique can be used for processing big data, especially image data, gathered from IoT devices [47]. It is cited that CNN is powerful technique in classification of IoT data with high level of accuracy [48].

3.3 *Artificial Neural Network (ANN)*

Another deep learning method is Artificial Neural Network (ANN), which is one of the most widely used techniques [49] and it is inspired from human brain. The method is used a specific processing model which is known as artificial neurons, that the neurons are interconnected to each other. Each layer takes the output of previous layer as input. The main issue in ANN is learning ability of the model which tries to balance the weights and biases to reach the desired output [50].

3.4 *Deep Neural Network (DNN)*

DNN is an imitation of human brain in data processing and has several diverse supervised and unsupervised architectures. "Restricted Boltzmann machine," "deep belief networks," "convolutional neural networks," "recurrent neural network," "long short term memory," "auto-encoders," and "generative adversarial networks" represent DNN architectures [17]. DNN has a layered architecture which consists of "stacked denoising auto-encoder (SDAE)," cascade auto-encoder layer, and softmax classifier. The structure extracts features from raw data and then uses them in classification process [46]. By deploying DNN methods, IoT problems are solved effectively as the intelligence level of problem solving is dramatically increased [51].

4 Prescriptive Analytics

Big data analytics are massively used to create value for the businesses. It deploys advanced technologies to uncover hidden pattern and information [52]. Advanced analytics with focus on business takes different techniques aim to build scenarios and help in simulating the outcome and improving insight related to realities and hypothesizing future events [53].

Advanced analytics comprises of five types of analytics, namely, descriptive, predictive, prescriptive, detective, and cognitive analytics.

4.1 Descriptive Analytics

Descriptive analytics put focus on required data and decision model for company activities in three levels of short term, medium term, and long term. It also helps organization with improved performance of integrated functions, resulting in intelligent decision making [54]. Real-time information that can specify delivery planning, point of material order or answering to emergency orders can be analyzed through descriptive analytics [55].

4.2 Predictive Analytics

Predictive analytics is deployed to answer questions of "what will be happening," like demand forecasting, using past data. Time series, data mining techniques and linear, nonlinear regression are the methods used in predictive analytics [55].

4.3 Prescriptive Analytics

The aim of prescriptive analytics is to suggest alternatives with optimal value [52]. It also enables decision makers to have a simulation on the proposed decision options and the outcome of undertaking course of actions [56]. Prescriptive analytics is the most complex kind of business analytics. It takes predictive analytics output and artificial intelligence, "optimization algorithms," "probabilistic models of expert system" to generate results which is optimal, compatible to situations, "automated" and "constrained" with dependency to time solutions [14]. Prescriptive analytics goes beyond the predictive analytics by answering the questions such as "why it would happen." It is deployed to give recommendation to decision makers [55].

It also works with IoT principals, big data and business rules to fine the optimal solution [57]. Some different features of prescriptive analytics are shown in Table 1.

Table 1 Features of prescriptive analytics

Studies	Definition
Harikumar et al. [58]	Method of extracting corrective action which leads toward desired and optimum decision making
Wang et al. [15, 16]	Propose responsive action plans through deploying quantitative optimization model and stochastic simulation which leads toward data-driven decision making model
Appelbaum et al. [59]	It hinders uncertainties through using mathematical simulation and optimization algorithms which are based in "business rules" "constrained" and "thresholds"
Stefani and Zschech [60]	It enables decision makers to be aware of the output of each action plan and recommend the one with optimized result

4.4 Detective Analytics

In detective analytics, data is gathered to diagnosis biased values which are extracted in predictive analytics. It helps to have an effective and accurate results in prescriptive analytics [54].

4.5 Cognitive Analytics

Cognitive analytics deploys machine learning and artificial intelligence in order to process data with high level of complexity. The method is powerful in recognizing heterogeneous and qualitative data in both types of structured and unstructured. Another important feature of cognitive analytics is that it not only extracts hidden knowledge but also it finds out underlying ideas and concepts which is a simulation of human cognitive ability and brain performance [61]. There are two streams that make the cognitive analytics improved. Advances in big data, cloud computing, and other computer science issues helps to create business value from hidden knowledge. Growth in area of cognitive and neuroscience research like brain function, cognitive processes, and models also helps cognitive analytics improved [62].

5 Methodology

The methodology used in this chapter has been widely used previously in different fields of science [63–65]. The searching strategy in this methodology is initiated by general phrases of "deep learning in prescriptive analytics," "deep learning in data analytics," "IoT and deep learning," "IoT and data analytics," smart city/house/farm/agriculture/medicine/manufacturing/factories/shop floor, and "deep learning." There are many works which have been done in the fields of data analytics, especially in predictive analytics and deep learning. For example, deep learning can improve

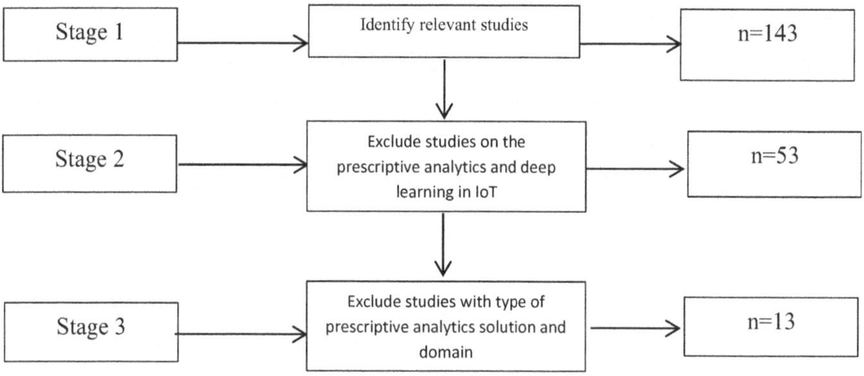

Fig. 3 Stage of the study selection process

education quality through processing educational data which is used to predict learning outcomes [66]. The aggregation of deep learning and predictive analytics also deploys to predict congestion states, traffic loads, and alternative routes especially when an incident happens [67, 68]. Deep learning also creates a ground for predicting security and cyber-attack based on data gathered from IoT devices [69]. Deep learning helps in other industry like farming to have unbiased and effective decision, especially when real-time data is gathered from IoT devices. For example, data gathered from sensors about soil and temperature are entered as an input of deep learning methods in order to predict irrigating the soil with water [70].

Various databases have been searched which are Science Direct, Springer, Emerald, IEEE with emphasizing on journals, conference papers and books and filtering blog in our search. The stage of the search is as below and in Fig. 3:

1. The chapter found on the basis of defined criteria is in the area of big data analytics, particularly in predictive analytics or prescriptive analytics. The former covers three main aspects of big data analytics so the part that have focus on prescriptive analytics is our aim to understand on the basis of prescriptive analytics and deep learning in IoT environment which problem has been solved. The papers which are working on predictive analytics are excluded, otherwise the output is deployed in solving a problem intelligently and the latter is our main aim of search to find the particular problem and decision making is done through futuristic analytics in IoT environment through deep learning.
2. When the particular article has been gathered, they have been reviewed to find the domain, type of problem, and the outcome of solving the problem in smart environment with prescriptive analytics and deep learning.
3. Based on the review, the area that prescriptive analytics work better and more and the type of decision that has been made in addition to the outcome of it on firms' performance has been identified.

Table 2 Research phase

Sources	First level	Second level	Third level
ScienceDirect	94	40	7
Springer	8	4	4
Emerald	21	8	1
IEEE	20	1	0
Total	143	53	12

The three phase of search is shown in Table 2. In the first phase, 143 papers related to the issue have been found but in further steps when the content of them is reviewed based on the problem that is solved with prescriptive analytics approach and deep learning with IoT device, the number of papers has been diminished to 12 in addition to a book chapter.

6 Prescriptive Analytics in IoT Through Deep Learning

It is forecasted that till 2020 IoT will reach to 26 billion units with high impact on firms' performance, supply chain, work flow, material tracing, etc. [25]. IoT processes comprise of "sensing," "actuation," "control," and "monitoring activities" when exchanging data. The data is processed in ways of locally or in server or even cloud environment [71]. Many industries like manufacturing put focus on analyzing IoT data as it brings significant performance in designing product, cost reduction and sustainability [72]. With wide growth of devices connected to IoT and the huge amount of data generated with these tools, big data analytics can cover perfectly data "processing," "analytics," and "security." In brief, big data analytics can manage IoT data [30]. Big data analytics and machine learning match well with predictive and prescriptive analytics [73]. Analyzing IoT data brings knowledge and insight from generated data to have a clear picture of future. It is crucial as it will lead to create value for business and society. So deep learning as advanced machine learning technique creates a ground for having a strong data training and prediction [74]. Prescriptive analytics has been introduced by IBM in 2010 with the aim of improving capabilities of descriptive and predictive analytics through creating optimal decision making and performance and also a strong data-driven optimization which makes decision support and planning much more effective [75].

Table 3 outlines the recent researches that use deep learning algorithms in IoT data to generate prescriptive analytics. On the basis of Table 1, it can be concluded that prescriptive analytics as a result of deep learning algorithm in IoT data creates productivity, intelligent and agile control, improved performance, accurate determination, high quality recommendation, accurate treatment, and smart decision making. It is also viable in smart manufacturing, smart medicine, smart car, and smart city industries.

Table 3 Deep learning in IoT with prescriptive analytics perspective

Study	Research outcome
de Aguiar et al. [76]	The authors presented a generic model through predictive and prescriptive analytics which is ideal for IoT. This will lead toward productive of businesses
Vater et al. [77]	Prescriptive analytics on shop floor has been introduced to control the shop floor intelligently
Wang et al. [15, 16]	Deep learning algorithms have been deployed on sensory data in order to improve performance through strong data analytics
Liu et al. [78, 79]	The authors prescribe recommendation by using medical IoT data in medicine which leads toward successful clinical performance. It helps inexperienced and traditional medicine to make accurate differentiation between serious fever and complex symptoms
Ullah et al. [80]	The authors pointed out the improved performance in disease detection and prescribing appropriate drugs and also they also identified "security of health-oriented IoT devices" and the role of it in proposing proper drugs
Liu et al. [78, 79]	In this research, deep learning algorithms deployed on medical IoT data detect lung tumor which impacts the effectiveness of lung survival and treatment
Yao et al. [81]	The authors used smart medical data generated through IoT technology to determine the composition of gallstone which has significant impact on treatment recommendation for gallbladder stones
Chen et al. [82]	In this paper, the authors deploy a smart in-car camera system which uses cloud computing and deep learning in order to decide which part of the videos of detected objects should be stored. The result is significant decrease in storage size
Bu and Wang [83]	In this paper, IoT data is analyzed through deep learning algorithm in order to make emergency decision on the water intake which has impact on crop growth conditions
Mohammadi et al. [84]	In this paper, the indoor localization system problem as a matter of smart house issues has been solved via deep learning and prescriptive analytics which results in improved 23% localization accuracy
Park et al. [85]	In this paper, crop disease has been detected and through deep learning the healthy and ill strawberry leaves are differentiated. The accuracy level of disease detection in smart farming has been increased specially in detection of leaves healthiness
Othman and Aydin [86]	In this paper, deep learning solves the problem of detecting fake anonymous student entering the exam hall through with face detection technology and smart alert which is powered by IoT
Dash et al. [87]	In this research, health record in different data sources has been analyzed through deep learning which leads toward prescribing affordable and pertinent treatment. IoT plays a mediated role in relating biomolecular and clinical datasets. The quality of decision making has been smarter and cost effective

7 Research Model and Discussion

Sensor data gathered from different firms and industries and with 7Vs characteristics enter into deep learning algorithms as inputs. In this model, sensory data are gathered from Internet or various protocols such as WSN, RFID, Bluetooth, NFC, LTE, or other protocols. Then, the data will be processed locally, on central server or cloud space. Deep learning algorithms can be used in data processing to uncover hidden pattern and insight. On the base of results generated through deep learning algorithms, the problem will be solved with optimum value. This will bring improved firm performance which can be represented in accurate decision making, high level performance, agile control, and productivity. IoT technology generates big data through smart devices that integrated with each other and enables sensing by RFID. The combination of "sensors," "TFID tags," and "communicating technologies" comprises the IoT fundamental elements [88]. Smart data generated through IoT has the potential to bring both chance and challenge of mining to extract value because of size and complexity [89]. In IoT sensory data, the volume, variety, and velocity are significantly growing [90–92]. It also needs a proper analytical framework for knowledge discovery [93].

As IoT big data needs models and analytical technologies to meet analytical need of complex and various data, deep learning with its applications in structured and unstructured method can uncover hidden pattern and classify data through hierarchical learning [94]. Data analytics which is defined as three major phases of descriptive analytics, predictive analytics, and prescriptive analytics are well supported by deep learning algorithms which brings efficient, effective, and proper data analytics [95, 96]. The fundamental elements of prescriptive analytics are "optimization," "simulation," and "evaluation methods" [97]. When prescriptive analytics deploys in organization as a "recommender or guidance," it has the potential to improve firm performance, empower firm's competition power, make optimal decision, and increase business value through prescribing course of action with the result of each action [98, 99]. It is cited that three main elements of prescriptive analytics are optimization, simulation, and evaluation methods [97]. So, in order to gain optimum results, it is proposed to accompany deep learning with optimization algorithms that listed in Sec. 3.

Figure 4 shows research model. This model creates a relation between IoT data (big data with characteristics of Variety, Volume, Velocity, Veracity, Validity, Volatility, Value), prescriptive analytics (futuristic approach), deep learning (with algorithms of CNN, RNN, RBM, DBN, LSTM, auto-encoders, and generative adversarial networks), optimization algorithms (ACB, BCO, FFA, PSO, and Genetic Algorithm), dynamic capabilities (Exploration and Exploitation), and firms' performances (productivity, intelligent and agile control, improved performance, accurate determination, high quality recommendation, accurate treatment, and smart decision making).

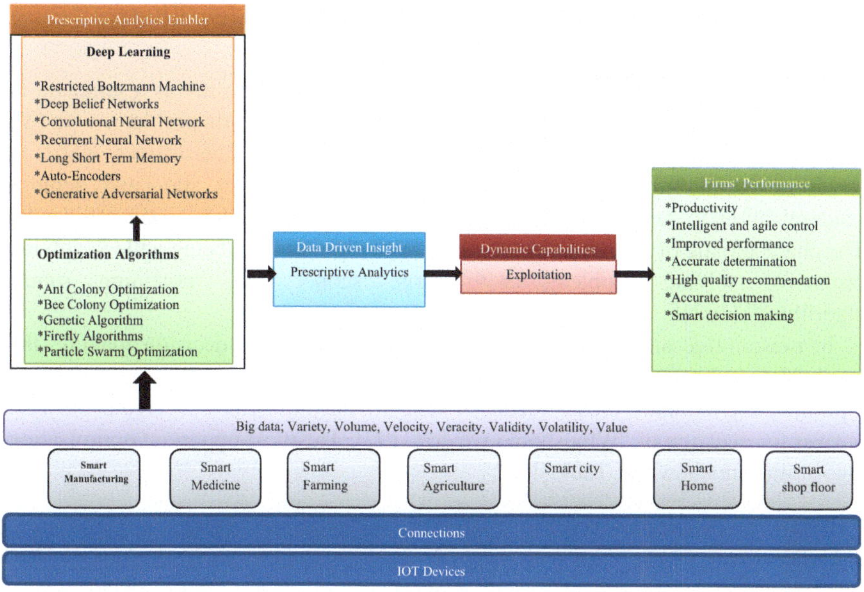

Fig. 4 Research model

7.1 Deep Learning and Prescriptive Analytics

Deep learning with its powerful computational strength and mining algorithms to extract hidden knowledge play a critical role in decision making. It also makes data analytics strong by bringing intelligent facilities for businesses in addition to overhead cost cut, being updated with demand and keeping up with taste change of customers [15, 16]. Prescriptive analytics as the most difficult data analytics phase needs powerful tools to create accurate data processing with high potential of learning. Deep learning capabilities in processing IoT big data are not ignorable [17]. Deep learning has the ability to overcome traditional machine learning problems and gain high level of accuracy [100]. Deep learning is powerful, efficient, and effective for all phases of big data analytics especially for predictive and prescriptive analytics. Deep learning with its potential of overcoming inefficiency of neural network empowers data analytics [101]. Therefore, as prescriptive analytics is the most complex data analytics and deep learning offers strong and accurate data processing, in this model deep learning has been introduced as an enabler that has empowered prescriptive analytics.

7.2 Optimization Algorithms and Prescriptive Algorithms

Optimization algorithms which are meta-heuristic algorithms act as a template to design underlying heuristics with the aim of solving optimization problems with two main features of "intensification" and "diversification." The former refers to searching locally to find the best current answer. However, the latter deploys randomization to assure that the algorithm explore the search space efficiently. The characteristic of meta-heuristic optimization algorithms is being agile in solving problems, solving problems with large scope, and "obtaining robust algorithms" [102].

In prescriptive analytics which is an optimization-based decision making, the feedback loop brings validation on the result of provided prescription and solutions. Optimization methods create feedback data to business rules to create the best answer for question of "Why should we do?" [97]. The most important optimization algorithms are shown in Table 4.

7.3 Prescriptive Analytics and Exploitation Capability

According to "Absorptive Capacity" theory which is defined as "the ability of a firm to recognize the value of new, external information, assimilate it, and apply it to commercial ends," absorptive capacity is crucial for organizations to bring innovative capabilities. The level of knowledge that organizations absorb can have impact on innovative capabilities which are "exploitative learning" and "exploratory learning" [107]. It is proved that prescriptive analytics can impact on exploitative innovation significantly. In other words, optimal solutions made and course of actions proposed by prescriptive analytics improve exploitation aspects of innovation [108]. It is defined that exploitation innovation is related to developing current

Table 4 Optimization algorithms

Meta-heuristic optimization algorithms	Definition
Particle swarm optimization (PSO)	It was developed in 1995 by Kennedy and Eberhart. It is based on natural behavior of fish and bird's schooling [103]
Firefly algorithm (FFA)	It was introduced by Yang. It is inspired from fireflies' behavior and flashing patterns [103]
Ant colony optimization (ACO)	It was developed in the 1990s to overcome optimization problems with the feature of hard combinatorial [104]
Tabu search algorithm (TS)	It was introduced by Glover and Laguna in 1997 in order to solve optimization problems with "adaptive memory" and "responsive exploration" [105]
Genetic algorithm	Nature-inspired algorithm, useful in finding optimization solution [106]

product and services to meet the existing customer needs in an effective way which can be attained through current firms' capabilities [109].

7.4 *Exploitation Capability and Firms' Performance*

Exploitative innovation is one of main parts of firms' dynamic capability which refers to leveraging current facilities and logic to create incremental but not radical improvements in products and services [110] and is widely used in prescriptive analytics [108]. In IoT environment, the problems which are solved and pointed out in Sect. 4 create exploitative innovation to increase firms' performance in various ways which are listed below:

1. Productivity.
2. Intelligent and agile control.
3. Improved performance.
4. Accurate determination.
5. High quality recommendation.
6. Accurate treatment.
7. Smart decision making.

8 Conclusion

The main objective of this study was to address an important area of research that besides its capability in creating business value is novel and sophisticated to deploy. However, by ever increasing role of IoT in daily life, manufacturing, health, medicine, etc. and improved analytical needs for analyzing generated data via smart devices, there is a need to understand the role of the most powerful analytical phase of big data analytics which is named as prescriptive analytics. Data generated through IoT devices has different characteristics of big data which are variety, volume, velocity, veracity, validity, volatility, and value and comprised of 7Vs in addition to complexity, which needs to be strongly analyzed in order to extract knowledge, pattern, and hidden information. This will be overcome by deep learning algorithms with the feature of learning structured and unstructured raw data that take nonlinear models in order to understand the most complex functions. Optimization problems can have better solution with nature-inspired algorithms, so they can be accompanied with deep learning to empower prescriptive analytics in order to show different alternatives and their results and the most optimal solutions. In fact, in this chapter the combination of optimization algorithms and deep learning has been introduced as enabler of prescriptive analytics. Through this enabler, prescriptive analytics can exert more powerful futuristic predictions and offer course of actions which leads toward exploitative capability. Exploitative capability deploys current resources for creating improved decision making which can be enhanced with prescriptive analytics. The result of deploying exploitative innovation business value is represented in productivity, smart decision making, agile decision making, and accurate treatment. According to investigation on previous research, a full list of business value as a result of prescriptive analytics in IoT field that is generated through application of deep learning algorithms has been generated. The outcomes of such application are productivity, intelligent and agile control, improved performance, accurate determination, high quality recommendation, accurate treatment, and smart decision making. In this chapter, the combination of meta-heuristic optimization algorithms (ACO, BCO, FFA, GA, and PSO) and deep learning algorithms have been introduced as the enabler for prescriptive analytics by deploying various algorithms, namely, RBM, DBN, CNN, RNN, LSTM, autoencoder, and generative adversarial networks.

9 Future Research

This study has several potential limitations. First, prescriptive analytics is investigated which takes into account in different industries. Therefore, future research can be concentrated on the impact of prescriptive analytics on different categories of industries, like the impact of prescriptive analytics on smart manufacturing or smart medicine, etc. Second, prescriptive analytics is in the center of concentration in this chapter. However, business analytics are comprised of various analytical phases such as descriptive, predictive, prescriptive, detective, and cognitive in which the input of each phase is the results of previous phase. Hence, researchers can work on business analytics as a whole and shows how outputs of each phase bring business value for firms.

References

1. Ly, P. M., Lai, W. H., Hsu, C. W., & Shih, F. Y. (2018). Fuzzy AHP analysis of internet of things (IoT) in enterprises. *Technological Forecasting & Social Change, 136*, 1–13. https://doi.org/10.1016/j.techfore.2018.08.016.
2. Lee, I. (2019). The internet of things for enterprises: An ecosystem, architecture, and IoT service business model. *Internet of Things, 7*, 100078. https://doi.org/10.1016/j.iot.2019.100078.
3. Čolaković, A., & Hadžialić, M. (2018). Internet of things (IoT): A review of enabling technologies, challenges, and open research issues. *Computer Networks, 144*, 17–39. https://doi.org/10.1016/j.comnet.2018.07.017.
4. Ding, L., Hu, B., Ke, C., Wang, T., & Chang, S. (2019). Effects of IoT technology on gray market: An analysis based on traceability system design. *Computers & Industrial Engineering, 136*, 80–94. https://doi.org/10.1016/j.cie.2019.06.038.

5. Thibaud, M., Chi, H., Zhou, W., & Piramuthu, S. (2018). Internet of things (IoT) in high-risk environment, health and safety (EHS) industries: A comprehensive review. *Decision Support Systems, 108*, 79–95. https://doi.org/10.1016/j.dss.2018.02.005.
6. Haruna, A. N., Mohamed, N., Ahmad, R., Abdul Rahim, A. R., & Najwa Ani, N. (2019). Improved internet of things (IoT) monitoring system for growth optimization of Brassica chinensis. *Computers and Electronics in Agriculture, 164*, 104836. https://doi.org/10.1016/j.compag.2019.05.045.
7. Li, W., & Kara, S. (2017). Methodology for monitoring manufacturing environment by using wireless sensor networks (WSN) and the internet of things (IoT). *Procedia CIRP, 61*, 323–328. https://doi.org/10.1016/j.procir.2016.11.182.
8. Thramboulidis, K., & Christoulakis, F. (2016). UML4IoT—A UML-based approach to exploit IoT in cyber-physical manufacturing systems. *Computers in Industry, 82*, 259–272. https://doi.org/10.1016/j.compind.2016.05.010.
9. Nie, X. T., Fan, T., Wang, B., Li, Z., Shankare, A., & Manickam, A. (2020). Big data analytics and IoT in operation safety management in under water management. *Computer Communications, 154*, 188–196. https://doi.org/10.1016/j.comcom.2020.02.052.
10. Ghasemaghaei, M. (2020). The role of positive and negative valence factors on the impact of bigness of data on big data analytics usage. *International Journal of Information Management, 50*, 395–404. https://doi.org/10.1016/j.ijinfomgt.2018.12.011.
11. Amanullah, M. A., Ariyaluran Habeeb, R. A., Nasaruddin, F. H., Ganide, A., Ahmed, E., Salam Mohamed Nainar, A., Md Akim, N., & Imran, M. (2020). Deep learning and big data technologies for IoT security. *Computer Communications, 151*, 495–517. https://doi.org/10.1016/j.comcom.2020.01.016.
12. Khan, M. A., Uddin, M. F., & Gupta, N. (2014). Seven V's of big data understanding big data to extract value. In *Conference of the American Society for engineering education* (pp. 1–5). IEEE.
13. Ghasemaghaei, M. (2018). Improving organizational performance through the use of big data. *Journal of Computer Information Systems, 60*(5), 395–408. https://doi.org/10.1080/08874417.2018.1496805.
14. Lepenioti, K., Bousdekis, A., Apostolou, D., & Mentzas, G. (2020). Prescriptive analytics: Literature review and research challenges. *International Journal of Information Management, 50*, 57–70. https://doi.org/10.1016/j.ijinfomgt.2019.04.003.
15. Wang, J., Ma, Y., Zhang, L., Gao, R. X., & Wu, D. (2018). Deep learning for smart manufacturing: Methods and applications. *Journal of Manufacturing Systems, 48*(Part C), 144–156. https://doi.org/10.1016/j.jmsy.2018.01.003.
16. Wang, C., Cheng, H., & Deng, Y. (2018). Using Bayesian belief network and time-series model to conduct prescriptive and predictive analytics for computer industries. *Computers & Industrial Engineering*, 486–494. https://doi.org/10.1016/j.cie.2017.12.003.
17. Saleem, T. J., & Chishti, M. A. (2019). Deep learning for internet of things data analytics. *Procedia Computer Science, 163*, 381–390. https://doi.org/10.1016/j.procs.2019.12.120.
18. Kim, H., & Kim, J. (2017). A load balancing scheme based on deep-learning in IoT. *Cluster Computing, 20*, 873–878. https://doi.org/10.1007/s10586-016-0667-5.
19. Khanna, A., & Kaur, S. (2019). Evolution of internet of things (IoT) and its significant impact in the field of precision agriculture. *Computers and Electronics in Agriculture, 157*, 218–231. https://doi.org/10.1016/j.compag.2018.12.039.
20. Dachyar, M., Zagloe, T., & Saragih, L. R. (2019). Knowledge growth and development: Internet of things (IoT) research, 2006–2018. *Heliyon, 5*(8), e02264. https://doi.org/10.1016/j.heliyon.2019.e02264.
21. Farooq, U., Muhammad, W., Sadia, M., Anjum, K., & Talha, K. (2015). A review on internet of things (IoT). *International Journal of Computer Applications, 113*(1), 1–7.
22. Qina, Y., Sheng, Q. Z., Falkner, N. J. G., Dustdar, S., Wang, H., & Vasilakos, A. V. (2016). When things matter: A survey on data-centric internet of things. *Journal of Network and Computer Applications, 64*, 137–153. https://doi.org/10.1016/j.jnca.2015.12.016.

23. Zhong, C., Zhu, Z., & Huang, R. (2015). Study on the IOT architecture and gateway technology. In *14th International symposium on distributed computing and applications for business engineering and science (DCABES)* (pp. 196–199). https://doi.org/10.1109/DCABES.2015.56.
24. Nitti, M., Pilloni, V., Giusto, D., & Popescu, V. (2017). IoT architecture for a sustainable tourism application in a smart city environment. *Mobile Information Systems, 2017*, Article ID 9201640, 9 pages. https://doi.org/10.1155/2017/9201640.
25. Lee, I., & Lee, K. (2015). The internet of things (IoT): Applications, investments, and challenges for enterprises. *Business Horizons, 58*(4), 431–440. https://doi.org/10.1016/j.bushor.2015.03.008.
26. Durani, H., Sheth, M., Vaghasia, M., & Kotech, S. (2018). Smart automated home application using IoT with Blynk App. In *Proceedings of the 2nd international conference on inventive communication and computational technologies*. IEEE Xplore Compliant—Part Number: CFP18BAC-ART; ISBN: 978-1-5386-1974-2.
27. Pavithra, D., & Balakrishnan, R. (2015). IoT based monitoring and control system for home automation. In *Proceedings of 2015 global conference on communication technologies (GCCT 2015)*.
28. Mentsiev, A. U., Gerikhanov, Z. A., & Isaev, A. R. (2019). Automation and IoT for controlling and analysing the growth of crops in agriculture. *Journal of Physics: Conference Series, 1399*, 044022.
29. Namee, K., Panong, N., & Polpinij, J. (2019). Integration of IoT, edge computing and cloud computing for monitoring and controlling automated external defibrillator cabinets in emergency medical service. In *5th International conference on information management (ICIM), Cambridge, United Kingdom* (pp. 237–241). https://doi.org/10.1109/INFOMAN.2019.8714717.
30. Ahmed, E., Yaqoob, I., Hashem, I., Khan, I., Ahmed, A. I. A., Athanasios, M. I., & Vasilakos, V. (2017). The role of big data analytics in internet of things. *Computer Networks, 129*(Part 2), 459–471. https://doi.org/10.1016/j.comnet.2017.06.013.
31. Marjani, M., Nasaruddin, F., Gani, A., Karim, A., Hashem, I., Siddiqa, A., & Yaqoob, I. (2017). Big IoT data analytics: Architecture, opportunities, and open research challenges. *IEEE, 5*, 5247–5261. https://doi.org/10.1109/ACCESS.2017.2689040.
32. Sharma, S. K., & Wang, X. (2017). Live data analytics with collaborative edge and cloud processing in wireless IoT networks. *Special Section on Future Networks: Architectures, Protocols, and Applications*. https://doi.org/10.1109/ACCESS.2017.2682640.
33. Li, Y., Hou, M., Liu, H., & Liu, Y. (2012). Towards a theoretical framework of strategic decision, supporting capability and information sharing under the context of internet of things. *Information Technology and Management, 13*, 205–216. https://doi.org/10.1007/s10799-012-0121-1.
34. Si, H., Sun, C., Li, Y., Qiao, H., & Shi, L. (2019). IoT information sharing security mechanism based on blockchain. *Future Generation Computer Systems, 101*, 1028–1040. https://doi.org/10.1016/j.future.2019.07.036.
35. Zhao, R., Yan, R., Chen, Z., Mao, K., Wang, P., & Ga, R. X. (2019). Deep learning and its applications to machine health monitoring. *Mechanical Systems and Signal Processing, 115* (15), 213–237. https://doi.org/10.1016/j.ymssp.2018.05.050.
36. Niu, W., Zhang, X., Du, X., Zhao, L., Cao, R., & Guizani, M. (2020). A deep learning based static taint analysis approach for IoT software vulnerability location. *Measurement, 152*, 107139. https://doi.org/10.1016/j.measurement.2019.107139.
37. LeCun, Y., Bengio, Y., & Hinton, G. (2015). Deep learning. *Nature, 521*, 436–444. https://doi.org/10.1038/nature14539.
38. Najafabadi, M., Villanustre, F., Khoshgoftaar, T., Seliya, N., Wald, R., & Muharemagic, E. (2015). Deep learning applications and challenges in big data analytics. *Journal of Big Data, 2*, 1. https://doi.org/10.1186/s40537-014-0007-7.
39. Wani, M., Bhat, F., Afzal, S., & Khan, A. I. (2020). *Advances in deep learning*. Springer.

40. Singh, A. K., Ganapathysubramanian, B., Sarkar, S., & Singh, A. (2018). Deep learning for plant stress phenotyping: Trends and future perspectives. *Trends in Plant Science, 23*(10), 883–898. https://doi.org/10.1016/j.tplants.2018.07.004.
41. Torrisi, M., Pollastri, G., & Le, Q. (2020). Deep learning methods in protein structure prediction. *Computational and Structural Biotechnology Journal*. https://doi.org/10.1016/j.csbj.2019.12.011.
42. Wang, H., Lei, Z., Zhang, X., Zhou, B., & Peng, J. (2019). A review of deep learning for renewable energy forecasting. *Energy Conversion and Management, 198*, 111799. https://doi.org/10.1016/j.enconman.2019.111799.
43. Song, W., Feng, N., Tian, Y., Fong, S., & Kyungeun, C. (2018). A deep belief network for electricity utilisation feature analysis of air conditioners using a smart IoT platform. *Journal of Information Processing Systems, 14*(1), 162–175. https://doi.org/10.3745/JIPS.04.0056.
44. Sohn, I. (2020). Deep belief network based intrusion detection techniques: A survey. *Expert Systems with Applications*. https://doi.org/10.1016/j.eswa.2020.114170.
45. Rui, H., Yunhao, Z., Shiming, T., Yang, Y., & Wenhai, Y. (2019). Fault point detection of IOT using multi-spectral image fusion based on deep learning. *Journal of Visual Communication and Image Representation, 64*, 102600. https://doi.org/10.1016/j.jvcir.2019.102600.
46. Vanani, I., & Majidian, R. S. (2019). Literature review on big data analytics methods. In *Social media and machine learning*.
47. Shin, M., Paik, W., Kim, B., & Hwang, S. (2019). An IoT platform with monitoring robot applying CNN-based context-aware learning. *Sensors, 19*, 2525. https://doi.org/10.3390/s19112525.
48. Motamedi, M., Portillo, F., Saffarpour, M., Fong, D., & Ghiasi, S. (2018). *Resource-scalable CNN synthesis for IoT applications*. arXiv:1901.00738.
49. Sengupta, S., Basak, S., Saikia, P., Paul, S., Tsalavoutis, V., Atiah, F., Ravi, V., & Peters, A. (2020). A review of deep learning with special emphasis on architectures, applications and recent trends. *Knowledge-Based Systems, 194*, 105596. https://doi.org/10.1016/j.knosys.2020.105596.
50. Razafimandimby, C., Loscri, V., & Vegni, A. M. (2016). A neural network and IoT-based scheme for performance assessment in internet of robotic things. In *2016 IEEE first international conference on internet-of-things design and implementation (IoTDI)* (pp. 241–246). https://doi.org/10.1109/IoTDI.2015.10.
51. Mehra, M., Saxena, S., Sankaranarayanan, S., Tom, R., & Veeramanikandan, M. (2018). IoT based hydroponics system using deep neural networks. *Computers and Electronics in Agriculture, 155*, 473–486.
52. Ghasemaghaei, M. (2019). Are firms ready to use big data analytics to create value? The role of structural and psychological readiness. *Journal of Enterprise Information Systems, 13*(5), 650–674. https://doi.org/10.1080/17517575.2019.1576228.
53. Saheb, T., & Izadi, L. (2019). Paradigm of IoT big data analytics in the healthcare industry: A review of scientific literature and mapping of research trends. *Telematics and Informatics, 41*, 70–85. https://doi.org/10.1016/j.tele.2019.03.005.
54. Menezes, B. C., Kelly, J. D., Leal, A. G., & Le Roux, G. C. (2019). Predictive, prescriptive and detective analytics for smart manufacturing in the information age. *IFAC-PapersOnLine, 52*(1), 568–573. https://doi.org/10.1016/j.ifacol.2019.06.123.
55. Souza, G. C. (2017). Supply chain analytics. *Business Horizons, 57*(5), 595–605. https://doi.org/10.1016/j.bushor.2014.06.004.
56. Ghasemaghaei, M., Hassanein, K., & Turel, O. (2017). Increasing firm agility through the use of data analytics: The role of fit. *Decision Support Systems, 101*, 95–105. https://doi.org/10.1016/j.dss.2017.06.004.
57. Balali, F., Nouri, J., Nasiri, A., & Zhao, T. (2020). Data analytics. In *Data intensive industrial asset management*. Springer. https://doi.org/10.1007/978-3-030-35930-0_7.

58. Harikumar, H., Rana, S., Gupta, S., Nguyen, T., Kaimal, R., & Venkatesh, S. (2018). Differentially private prescriptive analytics. In *2018 IEEE international conference on data mining (ICDM)* (pp. 995–1000). IEEE. https://doi.org/10.1109/ICDM.2018.00124.
59. Appelbaum, D., Kogan, A., Vasarhelyi, M., & Yan, Z. (2017). Impact of business analytics and enterprise systems on managerial accounting. *International Journal of Accounting Information Systems, 25*, 29–44. https://doi.org/10.1016/j.accinf.2017.03.003.
60. Stefani, K., & Zschech, P. (2018). Constituent elements for prescriptive analytics systems. *Association for Information Systems.*
61. Handfield, R., Jeong, S., & Choi, T. (2019). Emerging procurement technology: Data analytics and cognitive analytics. *International Journal of Physical Distribution & Logistics, 49*(10), 972–1002. https://doi.org/10.1108/IJPDLM-11-2017-0348.
62. Gudivada, V. N., Irfan, M. T., Fathi, E., & Rao, D. L. (2016). Chapter 5—Cognitive analytics: Going beyond big data analytics and machine learning. *Handbook of Statistics, 35*, 169–120. https://doi.org/10.1016/bs.host.2016.07.010.
63. Barbosa, M. W., Vicente, A. C., Ladeira, M. B., & Valadares de Oliveira, M. P. (2018). Managing supply chain resources with big data analytics: A systematic review. *International Journal of Logistics Research and Applications, 21*(3), 177–200.
64. Duan, Y., Edwards, J. S., & Dwivedi, Y. K. (2019). Artificial intelligence for decision making in the era of big data—Evolution, challenges and research agenda. *International Journal of Information Management, 48*, 63–71.
65. Tranfield, D., Denyer, D., & Smart, P. (2003). Towards a methodology for developing evidence-informed management knowledge by means of systematic review. *British Journal of Management, 14*(3), 207–222.
66. Doleck, T., Lemay, D. J., Basnet, R. B., & Bazelais, P. (2020). Predictive analytics in education: A comparison of deep learning frameworks. *Education and Information Technologies, 25*, 1951–1963. https://doi.org/10.1007/s10639-019-10068-4.
67. Kumar, V., & Garg, M. L. (2017). Deep learning in predictive analytics: A survey. In *International conference on emerging trends in computing and communication technologies (ICETCCT), Dehradun* (pp. 1–6). https://doi.org/10.1109/ICETCCT.2017.8280331.
68. Saha, R., Tariq, M. T., & Hadi, M. (2020). Deep learning approach for predictive analytics to support diversion during freeway incidents. *Transportation Research Record: Journal of the Transportation Research Board, 2674*(6), 480–492. https://doi.org/10.1177/0361198120917673.
69. Al-Garadi, M. A., Mohamed, A., Al-Ali, A. K., Du, X., Ali, I., & Guizani, M. (2020). A survey of machine and deep learning methods for internet of things (IoT) security. *IEEE Communications Surveys & Tutorials, 22*(3), 1646–1685. https://doi.org/10.1109/COMST.2020.2988293.
70. Garg, D., Khan, S., & Alam, M. (2019). Integrative use of IoT and deep learning for agricultural applications. In *Proceedings of ICETIT. Lecture notes in electrical engineering* (Vol. 605). Springer. https://doi.org/10.1007/978-3-030-30577-2_46.
71. Ray, P. P. (2018). A survey on internet of things architectures. *Journal of King Saud University - Computer and Information Sciences, 30*(3), 291–319. https://doi.org/10.1016/j.jksuci.2016.10.003.
72. Bradley, R., Jawahir, I. S., Murrell, N., & Whitney, J. (2017). Parallel design of a product and internet of things (IoT) architecture to minimize the cost of utilizing big data (BD) for sustainable value creation. *Procedia CIRP, 61*, 58–62. https://doi.org/10.1016/j.procir.2016.11.213.
73. Armoogum, S., & Li, X. M. (2019). Chapter 2—Big data analytics and deep learning in bioinformatics with hadoop. In *Deep learning and parallel computing environment for bioengineering systems* (pp. 17–36). https://doi.org/10.1016/B978-0-12-816718-2.00009-9.
74. Mohammadi, M., Al-Fuqaha, A., Sorour, S., & Guizani, M. (2018). Deep learning for IoT big data and streaming analytics: A survey. *IEEE Communications Surveys & Tutorials, 20*(4), 2923–2960. https://doi.org/10.1109/COMST.2018.2844341.

75. Frazzetto, D., Nielsen, T. D., Pedersen, T. B., & Šikšnys, L. (2019). Prescriptive analytics: A survey of emerging trends and technologies. *The VLDB Journal, 28*, 575–595. https://doi.org/10.1007/s00778-019-00539-y.
76. de Aguiar, M., Greve, F., & Costa, G. (2017). PrescStream: A framework for streaming soft real-time predictive and prescriptive analytics. In *Computational science and its applications*. Springer. https://doi.org/10.1007/978-3-319-62392-4_24.
77. Vater, J., Harscheidt, L., & Knoll, A. (2019). Smart manufacturing with prescriptive analytics. In *2019 8th International conference on industrial technology and management (ICITM), Cambridge, United Kingdom* (pp. 224–228). https://doi.org/10.1109/ICITM.2019.8710673.
78. Liu, Z., Bai, C., Yu, H., Zhu, Y., Wu, T., Bu, F., & Zhang, Q. (2019). An adaptive deep learning model to differentiate syndromes of infectious fever in smart medicine. *Future Generation Computer Systems, 111*, 853–858. https://doi.org/10.1016/j.future.2019.09.055.
79. Liu, Z., Yao, C., Yu, H., & Wu, T. (2019). Deep reinforcement learning with its application for lung cancer detection in medical internet of things. *Future Generation Computer Systems, 97*, 1–9. https://doi.org/10.1016/j.future.2019.02.068.
80. Ullah, Z., Al-Turjman, F., Mostarda, L., & Gagliardi, R. (2020). Applications of artificial intelligence and machine learning in smart cities. *Computer Communications, 154*, 313–323. https://doi.org/10.1016/j.comcom.2020.02.069.
81. Yao, C., Wu, S., Liu, Z., & Li, P. (2019). A deep learning model for predicting chemical composition of gallstones with big data in medical internet of things. *Future Generation Computer Systems, 94*, 140–147. https://doi.org/10.1016/j.future.2018.11.011.
82. Chen, C. H., Lee, C. R., & Lu, W. C. H. (2017). Smart in-car camera system using mobile cloud computing framework for deep learning. *Vehicular Communications, 10*, 84–90. https://doi.org/10.1016/j.vehcom.2017.10.001.
83. Bu, F., & Wang, X. (2019). A smart agriculture IoT system based on deep reinforcement learning. *Future Generation Computer Systems, 99*, 500–507. https://doi.org/10.1016/j.future.2019.04.041.
84. Mohammadi, M., Al-Fuqaha, A., Guizani, M., & Oh, J. (2017). Semisupervised deep reinforcement learning in support of IoT and smart city services. *IEEE Internet of Things Journal, 5*(2), 624–635. https://doi.org/10.1109/JIOT.2017.2712560.
85. Park, H., JeeSook, E., & Kim, S. H. (2018). Crops disease diagnosing using image-based deep learning mechanism. In *2018 International conference on computing and network communications (CoCoNet), Astana* (pp. 23–26). https://doi.org/10.1109/CoCoNet.2018.8476914.
86. Othman, N. A., & Aydin, I. (2019). A smart school by using an embedded deep learning approach for preventing fake attendance. In *2019 International artificial intelligence and data processing symposium (IDAP)* (pp. 1–6). https://doi.org/10.1109/IDAP.2019.8875883.
87. Dash, S., Shakyawar, S. K., Sharma, M., & Kaushik, S. (2019). Big data in healthcare: Management, analysis and future prospects. *Journal of Big Data, 6*, 54. https://doi.org/10.1186/s40537-019-0217-0.
88. Ullah, F., Habib, M. A., Farhan, M., Khalid, S., Durrani, M., & Jabbar, S. (2017). Semantic interoperability for big-data in heterogeneous IoT infrastructure for healthcare. *Sustainable Cities and Society, 34*, 90–96. https://doi.org/10.1016/j.scs.2017.06.010.
89. Ren, L., Cheng, X., Wang, X., Cui, J., & Zhang, L. (2019). Multi-scale Dense Gate Recurrent Unit Networks for bearing remaining useful life prediction. *Future Generation Computer Systems, 94*, 601–609. https://doi.org/10.1016/j.future.2018.12.009.
90. Goswami, P., & Madan, S. (2017). A survey on big data & privacy preserving publishing techniques. *Advances in Computational Sciences and Technology, 10*(3), 395–408.
91. Leung, C. K., Zhang, H., Souza, J., & Lee, W. (2018). Scalable vertical mining for big data analytics of frequent itemsets. In *International conference on database and expert systems applications* (pp. 3–17). https://doi.org/10.1007/978-3-319-98809-2_1.
92. Yu, S. C., Shin, D. B., & Ahn, J. W. (2016). A study on concepts and utilization of geo-spatial big data in South Korea. *KSCE Journal of Civil Engineering, 20*, 2893–2901. https://doi.org/10.1007/s12205-016-0504-7.

93. Mishra, N., Lin, C. C., & Chang, H. T. (2014). A cognitive adopted framework for IoT big-data management and knowledge discovery prospective. *International Journal of Distributed Sensor Networks (IJDSN)*. https://doi.org/10.1155/2015/718390.
94. Li, P., Chen, Z., Yang, L. T., Zhang, Q., & Deen, M. J. (2018). Deep convolutional computation model for feature learning on big data in internet of things. *IEEE Transactions on Industrial Informatics, 14*(2), 790–798.
95. Fan, C., Xiao, F., & Zhao, Y. (2017). A short-term building cooling load prediction method using deep learning algorithms. *Applied Energy, 195*, 222–233. https://doi.org/10.1016/j.apenergy.2017.03.064.
96. Xiong, Y., Zuo, R., & Carranza, E. J. M. (2018). Mapping mineral prospectivity through big data analytics and a deep learning algorithm. *Ore Geology Reviews, 102*, 811–817. https://doi.org/10.1016/j.oregeorev.2018.10.006.
97. Soltanpoor, R., & Sellis, T. (2016). Prescriptive analytics for big data. *Databases Theory and Applications*, 245–256. https://doi.org/10.1007/978-3-319-46922-5_19.
98. Bertsimas, D., & Kallus, N. (2019). From predictive to prescriptive analytics. *Management Science, 66*(3). https://doi.org/10.1287/mnsc.2018.3253.
99. Kwon, O., Lee, N., & Shin, B. (2014). Data quality management, data usage experience and acquisition intention of big data analytics. *International Journal of Information Management, 34*(3), 387–394. https://doi.org/10.1016/j.ijinfomgt.2014.02.002.
100. Guo, Y., Liu, Y., Oerlemans, A., Lao, S., Wu, S., & Lew, M. S. (2016). Deep learning for visual understanding: A review. *Neurocomputing, 187*(26), 27–48. https://doi.org/10.1016/j.neucom.2015.09.116.
101. Ren, L., Cui, J., Sun, Y., & Cheng, X. (2017). Multi-bearing remaining useful life collaborative prediction: A deep learning approach. *Journal of Manufacturing Systems, 43*(Part 2), 248–256. https://doi.org/10.1016/j.jmsy.2017.02.013.
102. Gandomi, A. H., Yang, X. S., & Alavi, A. H. (2013). Cuckoo search algorithm: A metaheuristic approach to solve structural optimization problems. *Engineering with Computers, 29*, 17–35. https://doi.org/10.1007/s00366-011-0241-y.
103. Yang, X. S. (2011). Metaheuristic optimization: Algorithm analysis and open problems. *Lecture Notes in Computer Science, 6630*, 21–32. https://doi.org/10.1007/978-3-642-20662-7_2.
104. Socha, K., & Dorigo, M. (2008). Ant colony optimization for continuous domains. *European Journal of Operational Research, 185*(3), 1155–1173. https://doi.org/10.1016/j.ejor.2006.06.046.
105. Bilge, Ü., Kıraç, F., Kurtulan, M., & Pekgün, P. (2004). A tabu search algorithm for parallel machine total tardiness problem. *Computers & Operations Research, 31*(3), 397–414. https://doi.org/10.1016/S0305-0548(02)00198-3.
106. Jan, B., Farman, H., Khan, M., Imran, M., Islam, I. U., Ahmad, A., Ali, S., & Jeon, G. (2017). Deep learning in big data analytics: A comparative study. *Computers and Electrical*, 1–13.
107. Gassmann, O., & Frankenberger, K. (2016). *Exploring the field of business model innovation. New theoretical perspectives.*
108. Ghasemaghaei, M., & Calic, G., (2019). Does big data enhance firm innovation competency? The mediating role of data-driven insights. *Journal of Business Research, 104*, 69–84.
109. Ngo, L.V., Bucic, T., Sinha, A., & Lu, V. N. (2019). Effective sense-and-respond strategies: Mediating roles of exploratory and exploitative innovation. *Journal of Business Research, 94*, 154–161. https://doi.org/10.1016/j.jbusres.2017.10.050
110. Limaj, E., & Bernroider, E. W. N. (2019). The roles of absorptive capacity and cultural balance for exploratory and exploitative innovation in SMEs. *Journal of Business Research, 94*, 137–153. https://doi.org/10.1016/j.jbusres.2017.10.052.

IoT Security and New Trends of Solutions

Xiaoyu Gu and Zhe Zhang

1 IoT Security Foundation

The IoT is now widely used in various areas of society, such as agriculture, industry, urban management, intelligent transportation, and healthcare. The IoT industry has made some progress, but the IoT security and privacy issues have become one of the decisive factors for the stable and rapid development of the IoT [1, 2]. Compared to the Internet and wired and wireless communication networks that have been developing for years, research on IoT security, which has been in development for many years, is still in a rapid development phase. The characteristics of the IoT itself pose a greater challenge to the study of its security issues. At the same time, some manufacturers may not take safety into account when producing equipment in order to save costs or for other reasons [3].

As the various sensing nodes in the IoT scenario (e.g., sensors, wearable devices, surveillance cameras) have certain sensing, computing and execution capabilities, the widespread presence of these devices may pose new threats to the security of personal and public information. On the one hand, since IoT has the characteristics of network compatibility and unlimited expansion of business scope, when all kinds of information (as big as national traffic and electricity data, as small as personal travel and household data) are connected to the seemingly borderless IoT, it will likely lead to illegal access to data at any time and anywhere; on the other hand, if the operation of key areas of the country and society (such as electricity, medical care, etc.) are dependent on IoT-aware business, dynamic information in the country's basic and key service areas will likely be illegally stolen, thus affecting national

X. Gu (✉) · Z. Zhang
Nanjing University of Science and Technology, Nanjing, China
e-mail: x.gu@njust.edu.cn

F. P. García Márquez, B. Lev (eds.), *Introduction to Internet of Things in Management Science and Operations Research*, International Series in Operations Research & Management Science 311,
https://doi.org/10.1007/978-3-030-74644-5_3

development and social stability. It's not hard to imagine that if the IoT were to be attacked, its security and privacy would be at great risk, and could even trigger a series of malignant consequences, such as a grid shutdown, runaway traffic, and factory shutdowns.

IoT nodes are often deployed on the existing networks, while also enhancing the perception and application platform of existing networks. IoT security will also be challenged if traditional network security measures are not sufficient to provide reliable security. Therefore, in solving IoT security issues, it is also necessary to design relevant security mechanisms based on the characteristics of the IoT itself. At the same time, the realization of information security and network security is a necessary condition for large-scale applications of the Internet of Things, as well as an important sign of the maturity of the Internet of Things application system.

In general, IoT security refers to the combination of physical security, information gathering security, information transmission security, and information processing security of the Internet of Things. IoT security refers to the protection of IoT hardware, software, and data in its systems, which can operate continuously and reliably without any interruption of IoT services, without being tampered with, altered or leaked by chance or malicious reasons [4]. Furthermore, the data-centric factor of IoT and its close relevance to applications determine the overall security objectives of IoT need to be (1) Confidentiality to prevent illegal users from reading confidential data; (2) Data identification capabilities to prevent nodes from being maliciously injected with false information; (3) Device identification to prevent illegal devices from accessing the IoT; (4) Integrity to verify whether data has been modified; and (5) Availability to ensure that the services of the perceived network are available to legitimate users at all times.

The specific forms of IoT security are [3, 5]: (1) physical security, which mainly includes the prevention of sensor interference, shielding, signal interception, etc., which is a manifestation of the specificity of IoT security that distinguishes it from traditional networks; (2) operational security, which exists in various elements, involving the normal operation of sensors, transmission systems, and processing systems, which is basically the same as traditional information system security; (3) data security, which also exists in various elements, requiring that information in sensors, transmission systems, and processing systems will not be stolen, tampered with, forged, denied, etc.

Sensors and IoT may not operate under overly complex protection systems due to power consumption issues, and IoT faces threats and attacks that are unique to IoT, in addition to the security issues associated with general information networks. The related threats mainly include physical capture, transmission threats, selfishness threats, denial of service threats, and perceived data threats; the related attacks mainly include blocking interference, collision attacks, depletion attacks, non-fair attacks, selective forwarding attacks, vulnerability attacks, witch attacks, information tampering, etc. [6]. In general, the relevant security countermeasures mainly include cryptographic mechanisms and secret key management, aware layer identification mechanisms, secure routing mechanisms, access control mechanisms, secure data fusion mechanisms, invasion and fault tolerance mechanisms, etc.

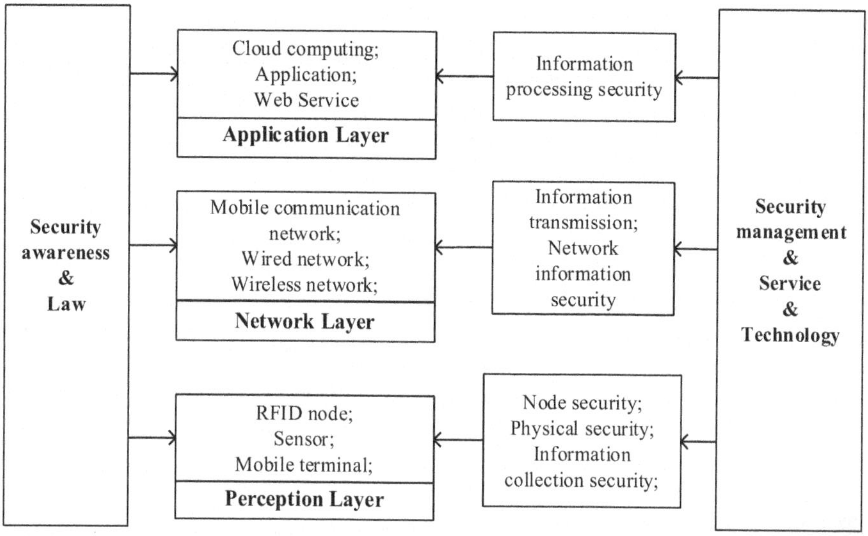

Fig. 1 Security hierarchy model

However, while some work has been done to classify the characteristics of the IoT, associated threats and attacks, there is currently no overall security architecture that supports formal authentication, which is an important foundation for security.

On the other hand, security threats to the structural aspects of IoT exist in every structure of the perception layer, network layer, and application layer [7]. In conjunction with the Distributed Connectivity Management (DCM) model for the IoT, the following figure depicts the corresponding security hierarchy model [8] (Fig. 1).

The following sections will provide a systematic description of the keys and technologies involved in conjunction with the characteristics of security of each layer.

2 IoT Security in Perception Layer

The IoT perception layer mainly consists of devices for data acquisition such as sensors and networks of sensors before accessing the network gateway. In this layer, various sensors, cameras, or other devices first collect data from the physical environment, and then work together or transmit data directly to the gateway device (i.e., the network layer) through industrial fieldbus, infrared, Wi-Fi, Bluetooth, ZigBee, and other short-range wired or wireless transmission technologies. Therefore, the main task of the perceptual layer is to interact with the real world and intelligently perceive information from the physical environment. At the same time, this information and data will be used in specific areas and industry applications. For example, cameras and various sensors installed on highways are collecting information such as images, environmental data at all times to monitor the status of the entire road and vehicles by the traffic control department. Some of this information can be shared with navigation Apps to help users make travel plans. However, it should be noted that the vehicle's license plate number information cannot be disclosed to those navigation Apps users for privacy reasons.

Typically, many devices in the IoT are deployed in unsupervised locations, where attackers have relatively easy access and then compromise these devices or sensors, or even manipulate them illegally by breaking the sensor communication protocols. It can be summarized that the security threat to the perception layer comes, on the one hand, from illegal intrusion into the perception layer nodes, stealing information, obtaining or tampering with data, resulting in information leakage and distortion, and on the other hand, it comes from the occupation of the perception channel of the perception layer, which leads to the inability of the perception layer to perceive and collect information from the outside environment, which ultimately interrupts information transmission. In this section, we will focus on two of the most important parts of the perception layer, namely RFID security issues and sensor technology and sensor network security.

2.1 RFID Security

Nowadays, RFID (Radio Frequency Identification) tags are widely used in the IoT to identify the static properties of objects. RFID is mainly through near-field communication technology and biometric identification technology for automatic identification without human intervention, which is convenient and fast [9]. As an example, there are two obvious things in an access control system of your office, a pass card and a card reader installed on the door. Just swipe the card on the reader and we are legally through the access control system and open the office. This process completes the RFID communication between the card reader and the card. In addition to this, many other systems such as campus card systems and bank card systems are using RFID for communication. There is a chip in each of these cards that can be energized and emits a radio magnetic signal to communicate with the card reader when touching with the card reader (Fig. 2).

The main security issues involved in RFID are: (1) the tag's own access defects, that is, any user (authorized and unauthorized) can read the RFID tag through a legitimate reader, while the tag's re-writability makes the tag's data security, validity, and integrity cannot be guaranteed; (2) the security of the communication link; (3) the security of mobile RFID, this type of security mainly involves counterfeit and unauthorized service access problems.

In theory, the main attacks of RFID include active and passive attacks [10]. Active attacks include (1) to obtain the RF tag entity, remove the chip package, then obtain the internal sensitive data; (2) through the software, use of hardware vulnerabilities, delete or tamper rewritable content inside the RF tag; (3) denial of service attacks through channel jamming or other means to disrupt legitimate operations. Passive

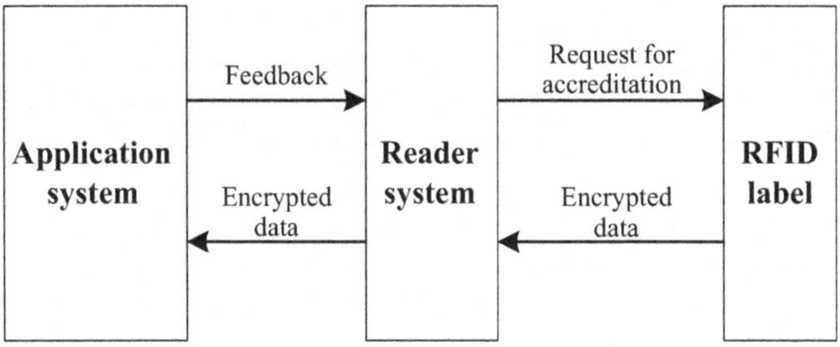

Fig. 2 Schematic diagram of RFID system

attacks include (1) through eavesdropping technology, analysis of the electromagnetic characteristics of the processor in normal operation, in order to obtain communication data; (2) through illegal reader, directly read and track the information of items.

In practice, current methods used to achieve RFID security are mainly physical methods, cryptographic methods, and a combination of the two methods:

1. *Physical methodological aspects*
   - *Kill tag*: The Kill tag mechanism uses a method of physically destroying RFID tags so that once a Kill command is applied to a tag, the tag will no longer be available.
   - *Faraday cage*: This is an electrostatic shielding mechanism which uses Faraday Cage to shield labels from receiving signals from any reader in order to protect consumer privacy.
   - *Active Interference*: The basic principle of Active Interference is to use a device to continuously send an interfering signal to interfere with the signal sent by any reader that is close to the label.
   - *Blocker Tag*: Blocker Tag is a special type of tag, unlike normal tags that are generally used to identify items; Blocker Tag is a passive jammer.
2. *Cryptographic methodological aspects*
   - *Hash-Lock Protocol*: The Hash-Lock protocol was proposed by Sarma, Weis, and Engels [11] to use a metal ID instead of a real tag ID to avoid information leakage and being tracked, with each tag having its own access key. The protocol is able to provide access control and tag data privacy protection. But since the ID does not use a dynamic refresh mechanism, the metal ID remains unchanged and the tag is easy to track and locate.
   - *Random Hash-Lock Protocol*: Since the Hash-Lock protocol uses a metal ID that can be used by privacy invaders to track location, to address the issue of tag traceability in this protocol, Weis, Sarma, Rivest, and Engels [12] proposed a random Hash-Lock protocol. In this protocol, for different queries of the label reader, the label will return the return value of the random number pattern to the reader to avoid tracking. However, since the ID is still

transmitted in plaintext, the acquisition of this information makes it possible to counterfeit the tag. In addition, each time for the label authentication, the database need to send all the label identification information, which is large, to the label reader, and it is also difficult to quickly handle the sudden response, the protocol is not quite practical.

- *Hash-Chain Protocol*: Syamsuddin, Dillon, Chang, and Han [13] has proposed a Hash-Chain protocol, which is essentially a query-response protocol based on shared secrets. In the Hash-Chain protocol, a tag is an active tag with autonomous ID update capability, avoiding the leak of tag-location privacy information. But in order to minimize the production cost of the label, this protocol is just a one-direction authentication protocol, and the label cannot confirm the legitimacy of the reader.
- *Distributed RFID Inquiry-Response Protocol*: Rhee, Kwak, Kim, and Won [14] propose an RFID authentication protocol for distributed database environments, which is a typical query-response two-way authentication protocol. However, in this scenario, performing the authentication protocol once requires the tag to perform two hash operations which is not quite suitable for low-cost RFID systems.

2.2 Sensor and Sensor Network Security

If RFID tags are considered to identify the static properties of objects, sensors and sensing technology can be considered to identify dynamic properties of different objects. Sensor technology underpins the entire IoT technology and applications. As the fundamental unit of the IoT, the ability of the sensors in the perception layer to complete their tasks as designed has become one of the keys to the success of IoT.

The sensor senses the information of the object and RFID gives it the encoding of electromagnetic information. Sensing technology uses sensors and multi-hop self-organizing networks to collaboratively sense, collect information about sensed objects in the region, and send the information to the upper levels. A sensor node mainly consists of sensor module, processor module, wireless communication module, and energy supply module. In practical applications, a wireless sensor network consisting of sensor nodes can facilitate the user to monitor and control the IoT nodes in the area through the Internet, and facilitate the user to better collect, process, and fuse data.

Due to the weakness of the wireless link of the sensing network itself, the limited computing power, storage capacity and energy of the nodes, the traditional security mechanisms cannot be directly applied to the sensing network. Moreover, there are two main types of attacks on sensor networks:

- *External attack.* An attacker is an unauthorized user of a sensor network, but because the sensor network communicates on a wireless channel, the attacker can easily eavesdrop on data transmitted on the channel and thereby gain access to private or confidential data.

- *Internal attack.* Node capture is a larger security threat to wireless sensor networks. An internal attack here refers to the capture of a node in a sensor network by an attacker, who can use this defective node to launch an internal attack on the entire network, bringing the entire network down.

Currently, sensor network security mainly considers three aspects, namely, authentication and encryption, secure routing, intrusion detection, etc.

For authentication and encryption, secret key technology is often used. The main factors considered of sensor network secret key management include [10]: (1) the mechanism can safely distribute the key to the sensor nodes; (2) the share-key process is safe and can prevent eavesdropping, counterfeiting, and other attacks; (3) nodes in the network are less exposed to security threats after the keys of small number of nodes are leaked; (4) the key update and revocation can be carried out safely and conveniently; (5) the key management mechanism has little impact on the connectivity and scalability of the network.

For secure routing, the IoT connects sensor networks of different structures, and how to securely connect these networks and the nodes in the network is necessary to think about for secure routing. A multi-path secure routing technique can be used. First establish a primary path from the data source node to the destination node, and then establish multiple alternate paths; data is transmitted through the primary path, while using the alternate path to transmit data at low speed to maintain data validity; when the primary path fails, a sub-optimal path is selected from the alternate path as the new primary path.

For intrusion detection, this technology is often used as another line of defense for information security, which consists of two main categories: passive listening and active monitoring [5]. In fact, wireless sensor network intrusion detection systems differ greatly from those of traditional networks, which is mainly manifested in: (1) No fixed network foundation. Wireless sensor networks do not have a central point of operation and intrusion detection systems do not have good statistics; (2) Type of communication. Communication links in wireless sensor networks are characterized by low rates, limited bandwidth, and high bit error rate, and broken links are very common in wireless sensor network data transmission, which often leads to false alarms in detection systems. (3) Limited resources available (e.g., energy, CPU, memory). Traditional intrusion detection systems require a large amount of computation, the available resources of wireless sensor networks are extremely limited, so it is necessary to design a lightweight intrusion detection system with less computation and communication overhead.

In addition to the above security protection techniques, due to the limited resources of IoT's own nodes and the high-density redundant distribution, it is impossible to run a full-featured intrusion detection system (IDS) on every node. Therefore, further research is necessary on how to rationally distribute IDS in the sensing network.

Generally, the main means and technologies to achieve security of sensor networks are described below:

On the physical level: (1) For wireless interference attacks, we can use spread spectrum and frequency hopping techniques, switch communication mode techniques or periodically detect the existence of attacks and return to normal working status when the attack is terminated; (2) For physical tampering attacks, we can add physical damage detection mechanisms, encrypt sensitive information, physical disguise or hiding nodes and other methods.

On the transmission link: (1) For link-layer collision attacks, we can use error correction coding and channel listening and retransmission mechanisms; (2) For resource consumption attacks, we can limit the data transmission speed, automatically discard redundant data requests, and we can also develop some policies in the implementation of the protocol to ignore the overly frequent requests, or limit the number of retransmissions of the same packet, etc.

Furthermore, there are also many types of encryption for sensor networks, the most common of which are: (1) Symmetric key encryption algorithms, such as TEA encryption algorithm, RC5, RC6 encryption algorithm; (2) Asymmetric key cryptography algorithms such as RSA, Diffe-Huffman, elliptic curve cryptography (ECC) algorithm [10].

3 IoT Security in Network Layer

The network layer of the IoT mainly includes information storage and query, network management, and other functions, and it builds on the existing mobile communication network and the Internet. It mainly implements the forwarding and transmission of data acquired by the perceptual layer to the remote server, providing strong support for the intelligent processing and analytical decision-making of data at the remote server. The amount of data being transmitted in the IoT network layer is huge and the requirements for transmission speed are high. And IoT network layer security mainly includes network security, information security, and infrastructure security [5]. The basic network of the network layer of IoT can be the public Internet in general, or a specific LAN (local area network). In general, the network layer of IoT can be broadly classified into the access layer and the core layer.

Information from the perception layer enters the network layer through the access layer. The security technologies of the access layer mainly include: sensor network security, network node and private key management; denial of service attack and denial of sleep attack of nodes in the perception layer; node identification, authentication and control; repair of nodes after damage; integrity identification, message authentication, watermarking technology, and other mechanisms to ensure confidentiality and security of mission deployment and execution; lightweight cryptographic protocol and key management [15]. It is important to note that, since the access layer is a transition sublayer for information from the perception layer upward into the network layer, some of the techniques overlap with security technologies in the perception layer.

The core layer of the IoT network layer can also be called the core switching layer. In addition to the existing SSL (Secure Sockets Layer) and TLS (Transport Layer Security) protocols, the core layer of the IoT network layer also needs to consider the hierarchical control of access rights to the databases in the perception layer, behavioral authentication and recording, information security, digital signatures (watermarks), authentication, cryptographic algorithms, etc.

In fact, the network layer security of IoT is similar to those of general Internet network security, with two main areas of focus being addressed below:

1. *Security issues from the Internet's own architecture, access methods, and various devices.*

   The access layer of the IoT will use a variety of access technologies such as mobile internet, wired networks, Wi-Fi, and WiMax. Since a large number of IoT nodes are mobile devices, the heterogeneous nature of access technology at the access layer makes it a focus of research on how to provide mobility management for these terminals to ensure handover of nodes and services between networks. The solution to this security problem will benefit from further research in switching technology and location management techniques. In addition, access to IoT relies primarily on mobile communication networks, where all communication between mobile stations and the fixed base station is conducted through wireless interfaces. Due to the openness of the wireless interface, any individual using a wireless device can obtain the information transmitted therein by eavesdropping on the wireless channel, or even modify, insert, delete, or retransmit the transmitted information in the wireless interface, so the mobile communication network has wireless eavesdropping, identity impersonation and data tampering and other insecurity challenges.

2. *Security issues from data transmission networks.*

   The implementation of IoT network core layer functionality relies heavily on traditional network technologies, the biggest problem currently facing is the shortage of existing network address pool, and the main solution is pinned on the advancing IPv6 technology [16]. IPv6 technology uses IPsec protocol, which provides high strength security processing of data packets at the IP layer, providing secure services such as data source address verification, data confidentiality, and limited business flow encryption. But no technology is perfect, and many of the security risks in the current IPv4 network environment will still exist in an IPv6 network environment, and some security risks will become more serious with the introduction of new IPv6 features. First, anomalous traffic attacks such as distributed denial of service (DDoS) attacks are still rampant; second, attacks against domain name servers (DNS) will continue to exist. Again, IPv6, as a network layer protocol, only affects network layer security, and the security risks of the other layers (including the physical layer, data link layer, transport layer, and application layer) will remain the same in IPv6. Finally, it will take some time to replace the IPv4 protocol with IPv6, and the transition to IPv6 can only take an evolutionary approach, with the measures taken to address the current interoperability between the two potentially creating new security risks [17].

In addition, in the network layer, the QoS (quality of service) security of the IoT network layer is still to be discussed. QoS security is a quality-of-service constraint framework of security technologies for the IoT network layer. A QoS security strategy for IoT networks should first and foremost reflect a commitment to meeting security needs. For example, in IoT systems for automobiles, various sensors and cameras in vehicles may need to read and analyze data every 5 ms, otherwise they may not be able to perceive the surrounding environmental information in a timely manner, which may lead to safety accidents. For another example, when a building has a minor fire incident, the building's IoT system needs to immediately send abnormal environmental information to the property or fire department for a quick response and to avoid a disaster.

The peculiarities of IoT network QoS that differ from traditional network QoS can be summarized as follows: (1) IoT devices are usually resource-constrained devices, and there are processing limitations. When a large number of devices are connected to the network layer, various types of data competing for system resources are likely to occur; (2) For different applications and service scenarios and different customers, QoS services should be different, which leads to different requirements for confidentiality, delay, and packet loss rate of the collected data, and security services should be differentiated [5, 17].

4 IoT Security in Application Layer

The main role of the IoT application layer is to provide users with various services such as information collaboration, sharing and interoperability using analyzed data [18]. The various applications of IoT are the product of close integration of information technology and industry expertise, which fully reflects the characteristics of intelligent processing of IoT, which involves technologies such as business management, middleware, and data mining. In addition, the mission of application layer also includes the collection, storage, and management of the data passed on from the previous layer. In general, security threat attacks against the application layer of IoT spread quickly and have far-reaching effects.

The data in the application layer may carry private data of the user of the item. Malicious attacks on the application layer, resulting in malicious tracking of data in the system to locate and steal, can lead to the leakage of people's informational data, which is not conducive to the protection of people's privacy. Since the IoT involves multiple industries, the processing of massive data information and business control strategies will pose huge challenges in terms of security and reliability, especially in terms of business control, management and authentication mechanisms, privacy protection, and mobile end devices.

Attacks against the application layer usually come from: viruses, worms, Trojan, unwanted applications, remote attacks, personnel threats, etc. [10, 15, 19].

1. *Viruses, worms, and Trojan*
   - *Viruses*. A computer virus is a program that disrupts the normal operation of a computer and makes it unusable.
   - *Worms*. A worm is defined as "a malicious program that replicates itself through a computer network and, when proliferated, can cause network congestion and paralysis."
   - *Trojan*. The term Trojan is used to describe all penetrations that do not fall into any particular category.
2. *Undesired apps*
   - *Rootkit*. Rootkit is a malicious program that gives attackers unrestricted access to their systems while concealing its existence.
   - *Adware*. Adware is an abbreviation for software that can support advertising.
   - *Spyware*. Spyware includes all applications that can send private messages without the user's consent/knowledge.
3. *Remote attacks*
   - *DoS attacks*. DoS, or denial of service, is an attack that makes computer resources unavailable to their target users. Computers that are subject to DoS attacks usually need to be rebooted, otherwise they will not work properly.
   - *DNS poisoning*. By poisoning the DNS (Domain Name Server), hackers can trick any computer's DNS server into believing that the false data they provide is legitimate and trustworthy.
   - *SMB Relay*. SMB Relay are special programs that can perform attacks on remote computers.
   - *ICMP attacks*. ICMP (Internet Control Message Protocol) is a popular and widely used Internet protocol that enables networked computers to send various error messages.
4. *Threats from personnel*
   - *Hackers*. Hacker means "cracker" who mainly engaged in malicious cracking of business software, malicious hacking of other people's websites, etc.
   - *Internal staff*. The threat of insiders is often the primary enemy of cybersecurity. Malicious system administrators may cause unanticipated disruptive effects.

4.1 General Application Layer Security

Therefore, we can try to think about application layer security from the following three perspectives:

1. *Security of operational control, management, and certification mechanisms*

   Since IoT devices may be deployed before connecting to the network, and IoT nodes are unattended, how to remotely contract for IoT devices and configure business information becomes a problem. In addition, the vast and diverse IoT requires a strong and unified security management platform, otherwise a single security management platform will be overwhelmed by the variety of IoT applications.
2. *Privacy protection security*

   In the development of the IoT, a large amount of data concerns the privacy of individuals (e.g., personal travel routes, consumption habits, individual location information, health status, corporate product information), so privacy protection is an issue that must be considered. How to design different scenarios and different levels of privacy protection technology is a hot topic in IoT security technology research.

   Privacy protection includes identity privacy and location privacy [12]. Identity privacy refers to not revealing the identity of the sending device when passing data; location privacy refers to telling a data center that a device is operating properly, but not revealing the specific location of the device. In fact, privacy protections are all relative. Non-disclosure of privacy does not mean that no information about privacy is disclosed. For example, for location privacy, information about an area (sometimes public or easily guessed information) is often leaked, but the precise location within the area needs to be protected; for identity privacy, information about a group is also often leaked, but the identity of individuals within this group needs to be protected as well.

   In IoT industry applications, if the information targeted by the privacy protection is not compromised, it means that the privacy protection is successful. In academic research, however, a quantitative description of privacy leakage is needed, i.e., a system may not have fully compromised the privacy of the protected object, but the information that has been leaked makes the privacy information very vulnerable, at which point it can be said that the privacy information can be guessed successfully with a high probability.
3. *Mobile terminal device security*

   The popularity of smartphones and other mobile communication devices, while bringing great convenience to life, also brings many security issues. So how to protect this data from loss and theft is one of the important challenges of mobile device security. When a mobile device is stolen and the mobile device becomes the control terminal of an IoT system, the loss from theft can be far greater than the value of the data in the device. Due to the incalculable damage caused by malicious control of terminals, security protection of mobile devices as IoT terminals is an important technical challenge.

4.2 Cloud Computing Security

Also, a very important part of the application layer is cloud computing, where cloud computing and cloud services can serve as a managed services platform to support IoT applications [20]. Specifically, the IoT requires three main supports: sensor devices for perception; transmission devices for IoT devices that need to transmit large amounts of information to each other; and dynamic, highly efficient, massively scalable intelligent processing centers, or computing resource processing centers, that control and dominate objects. This resource processing center, which is now commonly used, is the cloud computing platform. Using the cloud computing model, it is possible to process huge amounts of data, dynamic management, and intelligent analysis in real time, and send dynamic information to the computing resource processing center via wireless or wired transmission for data aggregation, analysis, management, and processing.

Due to the virtualized factor of cloud computing resources, cloud computing security has some new features compared to traditional security [21]: (1) Traditional security boundaries have disappeared, but as a result of the adoption of virtualization technologies in cloud computing, traditional physical boundaries have been broken and protection mechanisms based on physical security boundaries are difficult to apply effectively in a cloud computing environment; (2) Dynamism, where the number and classification of users in a cloud computing environment are different, frequent and mobile, and the security needs to be dynamically adjusted accordingly; (3) Data security protection, since data in cloud computing is not stored locally, data encryption, data integrity protection, data recovery, and other means of data security protection are more important for the privacy and security of data; (4) Third-party regulation and auditing, because of the cloud computing model, which makes the rights of service providers huge, the rights of users can be difficult to guarantee, and therefore requires third-party regulation and auditing.

In order to achieve cloud computing security and combine the characteristics of cloud computing technology and services, on the basis of clear security protection needs, it is necessary to adopt a comprehensive variety of security technology means, from physical security, network security, system security, application security, management security, virtualization security, data security, to build a hierarchical and in-depth security defined system to safeguard cloud computing applications [5, 15, 20, 21]:

1. *Physical security*

   Physical security is a prerequisite for the security of the entire cloud computing system, which mainly includes the security of physical devices, the security of the network environment, etc. to protect the cloud computing system from various natural and man-made damages.
2. *Network security*

   Network layer security mainly refers to the security of network architecture, network equipment, security equipment, mainly reflected in network topology security, security domain delineation and boundary protection, network resources access control, remote access security, routing system security, intrusion detection means, network facilities antivirus, and other aspects. The main security measures and technologies adopted include delineation of security domains, implementation of secure border protection, deployment of firewalls, IPS/IDS, deployment of Dos/DDoS attack prevention system, network security audit system, antivirus gateway, strong authentication, etc.

3. *System security*

   System security mainly refers to the security at the operating system and database level of all computer devices, including host servers and maintenance terminals in the cloud computing system. The security of the operating system is mainly reflected in the insecurity caused by defects in the operating system itself, such as access control, authentication, system vulnerabilities, security configuration problems of the operating system, virus threats to the operating system, etc. The security of the database is mainly reflected in security patches, account passwords, role permissions, logging and auditing, parameter settings, etc.

4. *Application security*

   Application security mainly refers to the security of applications running on cloud computing host systems with different functions. Since cloud computing is a new web service model, application security is mainly reflected in web security.

   Web security includes two aspects: first, the security of the web application itself, that is, the use of web application vulnerabilities (such as SQL injection, cross-site scripting vulnerabilities, directory traversal vulnerabilities, sensitive information leakage vulnerabilities) to obtain user information, damage the application, and obtain control rights of the web server, etc.; second, content security, that is, the use of vulnerabilities to tamper with web page content, implant malicious code, spread improper content and a series of other problems.

   For web application vulnerabilities, we should focus on the full lifecycle security management of web application systems and adopt different methods to improve the security of application systems according to the characteristics of different stages of the system life cycle. We can take protection measures such as web filtering, anti-spyware, email filtering, web page tampering, and web application firewall. While at the same time, strengthen the security configuration, such as regular check account and password policy settings, regular check system logs and abnormal security events, etc.

5. *Management security*

   The most secure network equipment cannot be managed without people, and the best security policy is ultimately implemented by administrators. With regard to the characteristics of cloud computing systems, emphasis should be placed on strengthening the management of user management, access authentication, security auditing, etc.; and establishing a security audit system to improve the ability to review violations after they have occurred.

   It is also necessary to strengthen the management of cloud computing security incidents, establish a sound emergency response mechanism, improve the emergency response capability for abnormalities and emergencies, and ensure that cloud services can be quickly restored in the event of a security incident.

6. *Virtualization security*

   In response to the threats posed by virtualization, security isolation and access control of virtual machines, virtual switches, virtual firewalls, encrypted storing of virtual image files, load balancing of storage space, redundancy protection and backup recovery of virtual machines can be used to ensure high availability of cloud computing services.
7. *Data security*

   Confidentiality, integrity, availability, authenticity, authorization, and non-repudiation of data are all key issues in a cloud environment. In cloud computing, we need to design for redundancy in modules (e.g., power modules, control modules). There is also a need to digitally sign data to ensure that it is not modified or changed during transmission and to have multiple backups. In addition, the security and importance of the data to the user varies, due to the importance of the information involved in the data. The level of privacy of data in the cloud needs to be linked to the level of privacy of the user. This means that the above data is graded according to its importance, which can be based on the importance of the data and the sensitivity of the data.

5 Case Studies About Future IoT Attacks

Currently, the world is becoming more dependent on IoT devices and it is needed to think about the possible current and future threats to the IoT and security solutions. This section will present some case studies and discuss the future development direction of IoT security.

5.1 Automotive IoT Security

With the rapid development of the mobile Internet and the IoT, the automotive industry is also constantly changing towards intelligence and connectivity. With advanced IoT sensors and intelligent control systems, information exchange and sharing between vehicles and people, vehicles and vehicles, vehicles and roads, and vehicles and cloud service platforms could be realized. This brings great convenience to people's transportation and helps to establish an intelligent transportation system [22]. With the rapid development of the automotive Internet of Things (IoT), its security issues are likely to become increasingly prominent in the future. For example, Yan et al. have been able to successfully hack into Tesla by using RF technology to forge the original RF signal from the key to control the engine ECU unit [23]. Security experts also tamper with the protocol transmission data in various other ways in order to modify the user's commands or send forged commands to the vehicle CAN bus [24].

In brief, the main security threats to the automotive IoT arise from three areas:

1. *Network-based communication attacks*: Automotive IoT systems include a variety of wireless communication technologies. If the wireless communication itself has cyber security issues, then the automotive IoT will naturally inherit these security issues. Due to the security issues, an attacker could tamper with or forge attack signals, or attack the car's remote service app and inject attack commands into the car in order to affect the normal state of the vehicle or take direct control of it [25]. The mobile terminal in the IoT network can complete the control of the vehicle through the App, such as door lock, remote start the vehicle and other functions. For example, the attacker can obtain the communication key and analyze the communication protocol through decompiling technology, and further control the vehicle with the remote-control system. On the other hand, Android or IOS system App have the risk of malicious code implanted by attackers, when the mobile terminal communicates with the vehicle, the App can be used as a springboard to further penetrate into the intelligent car, thus stealing user privacy information or threatening the car driving safety.
2. *Attacks against automotive platforms*: In automotive platforms, various electronic control systems have been developed for safety, comfort, convenience, low power consumption, and low cost. The CAN (stands for Controller Area Network which is an internationally standardized serial communication protocol) bus communication protocol for automobiles was developed by the German electrical supplier Bosch in 1986 in order to adapt to the need to reduce the number of wiring harness connections in multiple systems and to the need for high-speed communication of large amounts of data on automotive platforms [26]. Due to the high-speed, unencrypted and unauthenticated nature of the automotive CAN bus, it is relatively easy for an attacker to forge CAN bus messages to affect the vehicle status or to illegally collect data from sensors in the vehicle, leading to a privacy breach for the user. For example, Koscher et al. have successfully implemented an interruption attack by eavesdropping and analyzing bus messages through the OBD interface, deciphering the CAN bus communication matrix, sending forged messages to the bus, and controlling the body module, engine, etc. [27]. Nie et al. has been able to crack and attack Tesla's CAN bus from wireless (Wi-Fi/Cellular) [28].
3. *Attacks against connected vehicle components and sensors*: With the development of vehicle intelligence, autonomous driving technology will gradually replace manual driving. Self-driving cars mainly use environmental awareness systems to identify their surroundings and make appropriate decisions, but environmental awareness adds a large number of intelligent devices, such as radar, cameras, and sensors, which increases the number of network nodes in the vehicle network and also increases the entry point for attackers, so that attackers can use the security loopholes of such devices or interfere with the sensing results of physical devices to cause in-vehicle. The number of nodes in the network, such as radar, cameras, and sensors, increases the number of entry points for attackers. Currently, there is not much research in this area. Zhou et al. have discussed attacks against speech sensors and speech recognition in

autonomous driving systems [29]. And Sun et al. have performed a study to explore the general vulnerability of current LiDAR-based perception architectures and discover that the ignored occlusion patterns in LiDAR point clouds make self-driving cars vulnerable to spoofing attacks [30].

5.2 Healthcare IoT Security

As the IoT becomes more prevalent in healthcare, more and more hospitals are using smart IoT devices. These devices enable doctors to quickly and accurately monitor patients as well as medical conditions. Research by Deloitte shows that the average hospital in the USA has 15 smart medical devices per bed [31]. In addition, personal consumer electronic devices have gained the attention of the medical community, such as the Apple Watch. These devices facilitate access to patient-related information, such as heart rate, blood pressure, oxygen saturation, and daily exercise.

However, an over-reliance on IoT devices in healthcare may lead to an increase in security threats. Attacks on healthcare organizations can lead to disruptions in services, financial losses, reduced patient confidence in the healthcare system, and risks to patients' health. On the one hand, there is the risk to patients' privacy and security. Meanwhile, nearly lots of medical devices run on unsupported operating systems (OS) (or older OS versions) that have also often stopped being updated for security and vulnerabilities have stopped being patched. With the proliferation of IoT devices, patient information will become vulnerable to compromise, and patients' medical records within the system could be targets for identity theft or healthcare fraud. On the other hand, damage to medical IoT devices has the potential to cause serious health problems and may even lead to death. From the hospital's perspective, the most critical, nodes that need to be secured are patient monitoring and life support systems, oxygen systems, anesthesia system, infusion pumps, and other devices. In addition, smart diagnostic equipment in hospital laboratories and radiology equipment could also have serious implications in the event of an IoT attack. Moreover, even access control systems or wireless tags that play a minor supporting role can affect the response time of medical staff. For example, during the COVID-19 pandemic, criminals are using ransomware to hack into hospital IoT systems at an increasing rate. The adverse consequences of such intrusions are not limited to damage to data or monetary loss, but also hinder the proper functioning of healthcare systems and potentially affect the health of patients, which is a matter of life and death [32].

5.3 Drone IoT Security

Currently and in the future, drones are becoming more and more technically mature and their applications in life are becoming more and more widespread. With their low cost, small size, light weight, ease of handling, high flexibility and high adaptability, safety stability and ease of concealment, drones are playing important roles in agricultural inspection, filming, natural disasters, and social security. The main attacks against the IoT system for drones are sensors attacking, GPS spoofing, communication software threats, privacy security, etc.

Specifically, a drone system consists of drone, remote-control terminals, and communication links. Attacks against the drone IoT network are mainly focused on the three systems mentioned above, which mainly undermines the confidentiality, integrity, and availability of the system. For confidentiality, the system's data needs to be protected from illegal access. Threats against this category mainly include illegal access to systems and data with software vulnerabilities, viruses, malware, Trojan horses, etc. Integrity refers to the integrity of the transmitted data and the integrity of the system. If there is no integrity constraint, an attacker can break the integrity of the data by inserting, deleting, or modifying it, making the system error. Current attacks against integrity include interference with data links or sensors, stealing data and modifying existing transmissions or generating new information. Availability means that the system should respond to legitimate access in a timely manner. Attacks against availability are primarily designed to make it impossible for drones to access appropriate data or to react accordingly to instructions. For instance, mainstream IoT security attacks such as denial of service can be used to attack the availability of drone networks and this will increase the power consumption of the drone and reduce the uptime of the drone.

6 Solutions for the Future of IoT Security

This section focuses on thinking about future solutions regarding IoT security, as well as some of the current hotspots for current research. We focus on two solutions for securing the IoT, one is the blockchain-based IoT security solution and the other is the AI (artificial intelligence)-based IoT security solution.

6.1 Blockchain-Based Security Solution

Currently, the traditional IoT security authentication technology is mainly based on a centralized system and is also limited by the topology of the IoT itself. Blockchain technology can break this limitation. Blockchain is originated from Satoshi Nakamoto's Bitcoin as the underlying technology of Bitcoin [33], which is essentially a decentralized database. It is a technical solution that collectively maintains a reliable database through decentralization and de-trusting [34, 35]. It will help establish a foundation of trust and ensure the privacy and security of the data shared through the network. It also has the following advantages: (1) Decentralization: When any two nodes in the blockchain transmit information, they need to broadcast it to all nodes in the network, which means that each node will store the information as it is broadcast. At the same time, each node will also verify the accuracy of the information, and only the successfully authenticated data will be transmitted, which can guarantee the security of data transmission in the network to the maximum extent; (2) Once the information in the blockchain is transmitted, the nodes will immediately broadcast it, which creates convenient conditions for subsequent information enquiries and also makes the transmission and recording of information more accurate and less prone to tampering, as well as reducing the cost of data maintenance; (3) Blockchain can also further improve the security of information transfer in the IoT, minimizing the risk of data loss and tampering. Blockchain can timestamp each transmission, while all nodes on the blockchain need to use a hash algorithm to determine the uniqueness of their identity and avoid data tampering.

With the use of blockchain technology in the IoT, security will be significantly improved. Currently, there are many third-party organizations involved in the IoT network as a regulatory intervention, which may listen to the transmission of information. This not only violates the privacy, but also may give the wrongdoers an opportunity to take advantage of the situation and cause greater losses. With the private chain technology of blockchain, it can allow IoT nodes to share information only to the nodes in the private network to avoid misuse of the content by others and nodes without permission.

Therefore, to conclude, blockchain technology can be one of the ways to secure the IoT in the future [36]. This has four main advantages: (1) Improve the security of data transmission. In response to the problem of forgery attacks in the traditional IoT authentication process, the blockchain authentication method ensures the integrity and non-repudiation of the device when interacting with the network information; (2) Reducing the cost of data transmission and operation management. The distributed connection method adopted by blockchain technology forms a P2P transmission network. By reasonably using this transmission network to optimize the current IoT network architecture, the operation and maintenance cost of the central server of IoT can be saved, and the low-cost connection and data transmission among IoT terminals can be realized; (3) Privacy protection: The application of blockchain technology enables the IoT network to achieve decentralized operation. The central server does not store all the interaction data to reduce the risk of information leakage to a certain extent, solving the problem of information security and user privacy protection, while also resisting Distributed Denial of Service (DDOS) attacks, etc.

6.2 AI-Based Security Solution

As the modern threat landscape continues to expand, the addition of AI to IoT security strategies is becoming critical to establishing and maintaining an effective security posture.

Currently, the most common application of AI is predictive analytics, which means that machine learning is used to analyze large amounts of data and identify anomalies from it [37]. For example, using AI to monitor network traffic or user's behavior and identify what is unusual. Or observing how humans interact with devices to identify whether this is a real human or malware pretending to be human. It can also identify false threat alerts and reduce the rate of false alarms.

Another application is intelligence consolidations, which means handing over IoT cybersecurity research to AI. Right now, IBM is teaching its AI platform Watson to read news, research reports, and Twitter feeds on cybersecurity to build a knowledge graph and find correlations between each piece of knowledge [38, 39]. Once trained, Watson can then instantly give relevant security information, thus easing the work of analysts and saving them from having to look up large amount of information.

The third application could be intelligent response, which aims to increase the efficiency of analysis over a period of time. Martin points out that in a IoT network security operation center [40], for example, 58% of an analyst's time is spent on repetitive tasks. For example, when a security monitoring system issues an alert, the analyst must compare different applications, databases, and systems to confirm whether the alert is true. As these steps are fixed, they are well suited to be assisted by artificial intelligence.

At the same time, in the face of the new field of AI where technical specifications, industry standards, laws and regulations are not yet sound, the development of a unified IoT security monitoring standard, security prevention architecture, and security assessment system are also pivotal in making IoT security an important application area for AI. It can be said that, with the increasing maturity of artificial intelligence technology, artificial intelligence in the field of "AI + security" can not only comprehensively improve the response and reaction speed of various threats in IoT security, but also comprehensively improve the foresight and accuracy of risk prevention.

7 Conclusion

In this chapter, we discuss some topics on IoT security. First, we explore the foundations of IoT security, and security issues for the perception layer, network layer, and application layer of the IoT. We then conducted some case studies to discuss possible security threats in future scenarios of automotive IoT, healthcare IoT, and drone IoT systems. Finally, we discuss possible security solutions, i.e., how blockchain technology and AI can be used to enhance the security of the future IoT. We believe that the future of IoT security for emerging industries is an issue that needs to be explored deeply. Meanwhile, how to improve the security of already deployed IoT devices and ensure system compatibility is an issue that also needs to be explored. We also believe that IoT security solutions based on blockchain and AI techniques will certainly become a wide and popular topic for research and industry application.

Acknowledgments Support by National Natural Science Foundation of China (Grant No. 71901121, 71931006, 71972101); and Support by Fundamental Research Funds for the Central Universities (Grant No. 30919013202, 30920010021).

References

1. Hassija, V., Chamola, V., Saxena, V., Jain, D., Goyal, P., & Sikdar, B. (2019). A survey on IoT security: Application areas, security threats, and solution architectures. *IEEE Access, 7*, 82721–82743.
2. McNab, C. (2007). *Network security assessment: Know your network*. O'Reilly Media, Inc..
3. Hassan, W. H. (2019). Current research on internet of things (IoT) security: A survey. *Computer Networks, 148*, 283–294.
4. Weber, R. H., & Weber, R. (2010). *Internet of things* (Vol. 12). Springer.
5. Stallings, W. (1995). *Network and internetwork security: Principles and practice* (Vol. 1). Prentice Hall.
6. Knapp, E. D., & Langill, J. T. (2014). *Industrial network security: Securing critical infrastructure networks for smart grid, SCADA, and other industrial control systems*. Syngress.
7. Weber, R. H. (2010). Internet of things—New security and privacy challenges. *Computer Law & Security Review, 26*(1), 23–30.
8. Song, H. (2019). *Internet of everything: Core technology & security of IoT*. Tsinghua University Press.
9. Kopetz, H. (2011). Internet of things. In *Real-time systems* (pp. 307–323). Springer.
10. Forouzan, B. A. (2007). *Cryptography & network security*. McGraw-Hill, Inc..
11. Sarma, S. E., Weis, S. A., & Engels, D. W. (2002). *RFID systems and security and privacy implications*. Paper presented at the international workshop on cryptographic hardware and embedded systems.
12. Weis, S. A., Sarma, S. E., Rivest, R. L., & Engels, D. W. (2004). Security and privacy aspects of low-cost radio frequency identification systems. In *Security in pervasive computing* (pp. 201–212). Springer.
13. Syamsuddin, I., Dillon, T., Chang, E., & Han, S. (2008). *A survey of RFID authentication protocols based on hash-chain method*. Paper presented at the 2008 third international conference on convergence and hybrid information technology.
14. Rhee, K., Kwak, J., Kim, S., & Won, D. (2005). *Challenge-response based RFID authentication protocol for distributed database environment*. Paper presented at the international conference on security in pervasive computing.
15. Forshaw, J. (2018). *Attacking network protocols: A hacker's guide to capture, analysis, and exploitation*. No Starch Press.
16. Tanenbaum, A., & Wetherall, D. (2013). *Computer networks* (4th ed.). Pearson New International Edition/University of Hertfordshire.
17. Khan, R., Khan, S. U., Zaheer, R., & Khan, S. (2012). *Future internet: The internet of things architecture, possible applications and key challenges*. Paper presented at the 2012 10th international conference on frontiers of information technology.
18. Atzori, L., Iera, A., & Morabito, G. (2010). The internet of things: A survey. *Computer Networks, 54*(15), 2787–2805.
19. Roman, R., Najera, P., & Lopez, J. (2011). Securing the internet of things. *Computer, 44*(9), 51–58.
20. Ruparelia, N. B., & Ruparelia, N. (2016). *Cloud computing*. MIT Press.
21. Erl, T., Puttini, R., & Mahmood, Z. (2013). *Cloud computing: Concepts, technology & architecture*. Pearson Education.

22. Saarika, P., Sandhya, K., & Sudha, T. (2017). *Smart transportation system using IoT.* Paper presented at the 2017 international conference on smart technologies for smart nation (SmartTechCon).
23. Yan, C., Xu, W., & Liu, J. (2016). Can you trust autonomous vehicles: Contactless attacks against sensors of self-driving vehicle. *DEF CON, 24*(8), 109.
24. Woo, S., Jo, H. J., & Lee, D. H. (2014). A practical wireless attack on the connected car and security protocol for in-vehicle CAN. *IEEE Transactions on Intelligent Transportation Systems, 16*(2), 993–1006.
25. Kavianpour, A., & Anderson, M. C. (2017). *An overview of wireless network security.* Paper presented at the 2017 IEEE 4th international conference on cyber security and cloud computing (CSCloud).
26. Ran, L., Junfeng, W., Haiying, W., & Gechen, L. (2010). *Design method of CAN BUS network communication structure for electric vehicle.* Paper presented at the international forum on strategic technology 2010.
27. Koscher, K., Czeskis, A., Roesner, F., Patel, S., Kohno, T., Checkoway, S., McCoy, D., Kantor, B., Anderson, D., & Shacham, H. (2010). *Experimental security analysis of a modern automobile.* Paper presented at the 2010 IEEE symposium on security and privacy.
28. Nie, S., Liu, L., & Du, Y. (2017). Free-fall: Hacking tesla from wireless to can bus. *Briefing, Black Hat USA, 25*, 1–16.
29. Zhou, M., Qin, Z., Lin, X., Hu, S., Wang, Q., & Ren, K. (2019). Hidden voice commands: Attacks and defenses on the VCS of autonomous driving cars. *IEEE Wireless Communications, 26*(5), 128–133.
30. Sun, J., Cao, Y., Chen, Q. A., & Mao, Z. M. (2020). *Towards robust lidar-based perception in autonomous driving: General black-box adversarial sensor attack and countermeasures.* Paper presented at the 29th {USENIX} security symposium ({USENIX} security 20).
31. Carroll, W., & Fingar, S. (2018). *Smart medicaid Leveraging cognitive technologies to improve health and program efficiencies.* Retrieved from https://www2.deloitte.com/us/en/insights/industry/health-care/smart-technology-in-health-care-medicaid-programs.html.
32. Burgess, M. (2020). *Hackers are targeting hospitals crippled by coronavirus.* Retrieved from https://www.wired.co.uk/article/coronavirus-hackers-cybercrime-phishing.
33. Nakamoto, S., & Bitcoin, A. (2008). A peer-to-peer electronic cash system. *Bitcoin.* Retrieved from https://bitcoin.org/bitcoin.pdf, 4.
34. Nofer, M., Gomber, P., Hinz, O., & Schiereck, D. (2017). Blockchain. *Business & Information Systems Engineering, 59*(3), 183–187.
35. Zheng, Z., Xie, S., Dai, H.-N., Chen, X., & Wang, H. (2018). Blockchain challenges and opportunities: A survey. *International Journal of Web and Grid Services, 14*(4), 352–375.
36. Khan, M. A., & Salah, K. (2018). IoT security: Review, blockchain solutions, and open challenges. *Future Generation Computer Systems, 82*, 395–411.
37. Xiao, L., Wan, X., Lu, X., Zhang, Y., & Wu, D. (2018). IoT security techniques based on machine learning: How do IoT devices use AI to enhance security? *IEEE Signal Processing Magazine, 35*(5), 41–49.
38. Marshall, T. E., & Lambert, S. L. (2018). Cloud-based intelligent accounting applications: Accounting task automation using IBM watson cognitive computing. *Journal of Emerging Technologies in Accounting, 15*(1), 199–215.
39. Strickland, E. (2019). IBM Watson, heal thyself: How IBM overpromised and underdelivered on AI health care. *IEEE Spectrum, 56*(4), 24–31.
40. Martin, J., & Lodewijkx, K. (2014). *Securing cloud environments for enterprise computing.* Paper presented at the proceedings of the 6th edition of the ACM workshop on cloud computing security.

A Hybrid Model of Learning Methodology Analyzed Through the Use of Machine Learning Techniques

Roberto Morales Arsenal and Jesús María Pinar-Pérez

1 Introduction

In recent years, the availability of data has greatly increased thanks to the internet and the abundance of sensory devices found in almost every aspect of our lives. From our watches and smartphones, to our cars, factories and businesses, schools, and universities. It is predicted that in the near future the number of devices that gather data from human beings will reach 25–50 billion [1], representing an average of 6.58 devices per person (worldwide) in 2020 [2]. As the number of devices increases and technologies become more advanced, the volume of data published will also grow exponentially. The Internet of Things (IoT) establishes a smart network of communication between people and the devices surrounding them, using the internet as a communication system [3]. The great importance of IoT stems from its ability to capture, analyze, and manage data that can be transformed into usable information. This information is used to obtain knowledge, and, finally, this knowledge is employed to generate wisdom [2]. These data provide actionable information in order to improve the decision-making of systems and processes, save time for people and businesses, and improve quality of life [4]. There are a lot of examples of IoT such as the condition monitoring of machines to improve maintenance processes [5–8], information from wearable devices to capture health data of humans [9] and data from the learning process of students [10].

In the academic education area, traditional approaches involved a limited quantity of data such as student grades, attrition rates, and instructor perceptions gathered at the end of a course [11]. In the twenty-first century, new digital technologies and

R. M. Arsenal · J. M. Pinar-Pérez (✉)
Quantitative Methods Department, University College for Financial Studies (CUNEF), Madrid, Spain
e-mail: rmorales@cunef.edu; jesusmaria.pinar@cunef.edu

F. P. García Márquez, B. Lev (eds.), *Introduction to Internet of Things in Management Science and Operations Research*, International Series in Operations Research & Management Science 311,
https://doi.org/10.1007/978-3-030-74644-5_4

resources are implemented online in the academic education process. These technologies are able to generate a large amount of data of students [11] from different devices such as computers, smartphones, tablets, and class assistance control devices. But these data must be analyzed providing important information and knowledge for the decision-making of instructors and student to improve the learning process [12]. In the last decade, Learning Analytic (LA) has increasingly been implemented in the education sector. Literature collects a lot of research works about LA, some reviews are [12–18]. Reference [13] found that the use of LA in higher education allows institutions to develop student-focused strategies, identifying the most adequate tools to improve the learning process. Reference [19] presents evidence on the use of LA in educational action list to the stakeholders. Reference [20] collects some different types of data from IoT used in LA techniques or methods in the literature. References [21, 22] employed ML techniques for LA to predict and to explain the reasons behind the failure of the students.

Reference [23] presents a flipped classroom model where a great amount of traditional lecture content is removed. This reference found that students' anxiety and tension were replaced by confidence and skill reaching general improvements in evaluations of the course. But, "some students perceive the lack of lecture and the increased expectation for personal responsibility for one's own learning outside of class time as unfair or unreasonable." Reference [24] found that the flipped model had a positive impact on students' attitudes and performances. However, the effects did not persist. Another example of an active and collaborative learning tool is mind maps. This is a powerful tool that stimulates the entire brain [25]. Other references show improvements in student's performance using video-lectures or screencasts. For example, reference [26] indicates that a very large percentage of students who watch the video-lessons improve the topic understanding and have better grades. But not all the students visualize videos. The techniques, implemented in the previous references, were analyzed without considering other alternative techniques. A combination of these techniques could improve the learning process. In a previous work developed by the authors [27, 28], a hybrid learning model was developed combining the best of both methodologies (traditional and innovative). But it was evaluated using only "traditional" data (mainly exam grades) finding better marks with lower variability.

The model developed in this manuscript improves the hybrid model presented in reference [27] considering new learning resources and neuroeducation techniques. The main objective of this chapter is to provide a deeper analysis of the hybrid model employing both traditional data and innovative data. The IoT data incorporated to the data set will allow instructors both to know the behavior of the student through his online activity and to delve into the structure and dynamics of the class. A set of a well-known ML techniques are used in order to: (1) identify the most relevant explanatory variables of the performance of students (classification techniques); (2) analyze the class structure (clustering techniques); (3) predict the performance of the students (prediction techniques); and finally (4) identify groups of variables with the same information (dimensionality reduction technique).

This chapter is structured as follows. The next section presents the hybrid learning methodology carried out. Section 3 describes the Canvas learning platform and the available data used, showing a previous statistical analysis. The ML techniques employed in this work are presented in Sect. 4. Section 5 contains the results obtained by the ML techniques applied. The last section is devoted to the final conclusions.

2 The Learning Hybrid Model Methodology

A hybrid academic methodology model has been implemented in recent years for undergraduate students in the subject of business statistics. This model improves the hybrid model presented in reference [22] considering new educational resources and neuroeducation techniques. The academic methodology used combines the best of traditional teaching such as masterclass and problem set resolution on blackboard, as well as new technologies (video-lectures, screencasts, forums, etc.) and techniques derived from the advances of neuroeducation such as gamification and flipped classrooms. The final objective is to create a more effective learning that allows the student to obtain a deep learning of the subject (more information in reference [27]).

The innovative learning methods try to bridge the gap between digital students from Generation Z and traditional teaching. Additionally, these innovative techniques, such as video-lectures and screencasts, better suit the learning rhythms of each student. The hybrid model is more adaptable and flexible to the needs of the student. Therefore, video-lectures for theory and screencasts for practice work must be complementary to traditional materials (not a substitute). These videos must satisfy the following technical characteristics: shorts (10–15 min), easy to understand and applied. The main objective of the video-lessons is to engage students (short term), motivate and maintain interest of students (medium term), and consolidate knowledge (long term).

Table 1 shows the class structure carried out during the course. The methodology is implemented in three sessions per week where only one session is related to traditional class. Session 1 includes a master class and exercises on whiteboard. Session 2 and 3 are innovative classes including practical exercises solved with a computer, online tests, and mind maps. Each session requires the reading and visualization of videos or screencasts before the session.

Neither the traditional methodology nor the most innovative methodology can substitute the effort and the work that students must carry out by themselves, but they can increase the motivation (key variable in the optimal learning process). In this sense, the Canvas learning platform offers an excellent tool to monitor the activity and results of students.

Table 1 Class structure

	Number of sessions per week		
	Session 1	Session 2	Session 3
Duration	1 h 30′	1 h	1 h 30′
Type	Traditional	Flipped	Flipped
Method	Theoretical classes + resolution of numerical exercises on whiteboard	Practical classes with computer (with R and excel)	Gamification of tests with Socrative or Kahoot, real-world exercises. Elaboration of mind maps
Requirements	Visualization of video-lectures and readings	Visualization of screencast, video-lectures, and readings	Study of the material of Session1 and Session2
Work type	Individual	In group	In group

3 Canvas Learning Platform and Data Description

Canvas is the fastest growing and the second largest learning management system (LMS) employed by higher education institutions in the United States [29]. It is used by four of the top 5 higher educational institutions according with the annual ranking of top 25 online degree programs [30], other LMS used in higher education are Angel, Blackboard, or Moodle [31]. The Canvas platform is used in this work to collect the necessary data.

Data from 80 students of an introductory course of Business Statistic at University in Spain are used in this work. Canvas is able to collect large amounts of data from different devices such as computers, smartphones or tablets, and class assistance control devices. Canvas provides continuous monitoring of student activity such as responses, accesses of reading material, visualization of video-lectures, marks from quizzes and tasks, postings on a forum, class attendance, or some other assessment. This learning management system offers a Dashboard that allows instructors to measure different indicators that can help to improve the learning process. Table 2 shows the variables directly obtained through the normal development of the course (variables 1–9) and obtained from the innovative methodology (variable 10–16). Additionally, a target variable *Outcome* was created being a binary variable where 1 represents that the student has a high performance (HP), i.e., when the student reaches a final score of more than 6.5 (out of 10); and 0 represents non-high performance (NHP), i.e., a final score lower than 6.5.

In this work, the set of information has been increased through the Canvas online learning platform (IoT information). Therefore, a set of variables and data have been incorporated into the model that the traditional one does not include. The output of the hybrid model is a function of the explanatory variables based on the information set Ω.

Table 2 Variables available from the learning system

No.	Variable	Data type	Values	Type of input
1	*Identification*	Numeric	Number case	Traditional
2	*Gender*	Factor	Female = 1, male = 0	Traditional
3	*Speciality studied in the high school*	Factor	Social = 1, technological =1, science = 1	Traditional
4	*Quizzes*	Numeric (continuous)	Between 0 and 10	Traditional
5	*Final score*	Numeric (continuous)	Between 0 and 10	Traditional
6	*Midterm*	Numeric (continuous)	Between 0 and 10	Traditional
7	*Repeating*	Factor	Yes = 1, no = 0	Traditional
8	*Attention*	Factor	Null =0, low 1, moderate = 2, high = 3	Traditional
9	*Motivation*	Factor	Low = 1, moderate = 2, high = 3	Traditional
10	*Videos (video-lectures)*	Factor	Watch = 1, Nowatch = 0	Innovative
11	*Total activity*	Numeric	Units = hours	Innovative
12	*Page views*	Factor	Low = 1, moderate = 2, high = 3	Innovative
13	*Participation*	Factor	Low = 1, moderate = 2, high = 3	Innovative
14	*Missing*	Numeric	Number of undelivered workers	Innovative
15	*Late*	Numeric	Number of workers delivered after the deadline (with penalization)	Innovative
16	*Attendance*	Numeric	Percentage of attendance during the course	Innovative
17	*Outcome*	Factor	High performance (HP) = 1, non-high performance (NHP) = 0	

Note: in some models, categorical variables were reduced to binary variables

$$Y_{\mathrm{HM}} = f\left(X_i, I_j \middle| \Omega = \{\mathrm{Traditional} + \mathrm{Innovative}_{\mathrm{IoT}}\}\right); \quad \forall\ i = 1, \ldots, t\ ;\ \forall\ j = 1, \ldots, k \tag{1}$$

where Y is the output, dependent or target variable, X_i represents the set of traditional variables (*traditional inputs*), and I_j denotes the set of innovative variables (*innovative inputs*). The inclusion of this new data set allows instructors to have a deeper understanding of the behavior, habits, and learning methods of the current generation of students.

Previous statistical analysis of the data A simple statistical analysis of the effectiveness of the online resources available to students has been carried out previously. Figure 1a shows a box plot representing the visualization of *Videos* against *Final score*. The complete visualization of the video-lectures is a good predictor of the final score obtained by the student. In this analysis, it has been considered that the student watches the video when he has visualized at least 95% of

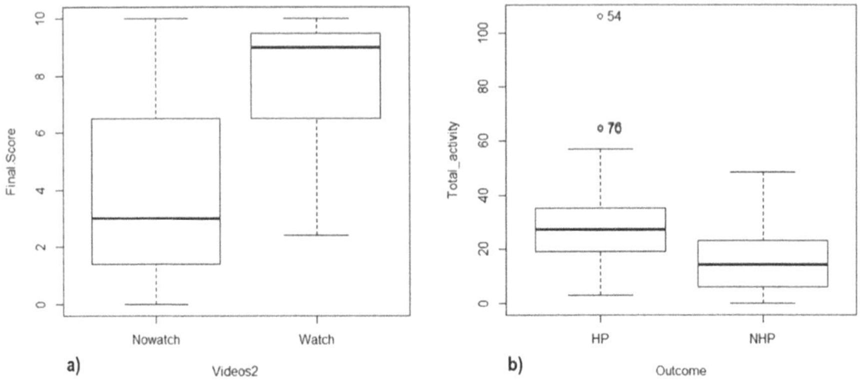

Fig. 1 Previous analysis of data. Boxplot (**a**) *Videos* vs *Final score*; (**b**) *Outcome* vs *Total activity*

Table 3 Absolute frequencies of students between videos and level of performance

		Videos	
		No watch	Watch
Outcome	NHP	43	8
	HP	8	21

the video content and Nowatch otherwise. In general, the students reach higher final scores after watching the corresponding video-lectures. Figure 1b presents a boxplot for the variable *Outcome* (HP or NHP students) versus the *Total activity* registered in Canvas. The total activity determines, by a smaller degree than the visualization of videos, the final performance of the student. In other words, the student could be connected to the Canvas platform but without interaction. The average number of hours of the total activity on the Canvas platform is 16.5 for NHP students and 31.1 for HP students. A Pearson's chi-squared test (p-value<0.05) has been carried out showing that the performance of the student (variable *Outcome*) is not independent if the student visualizes the video-lectures or not.

The IoT information gathered on video-views indicates that 72.4% of high-performing students viewed the full video-lectures. On the other hand, 84.3% of students with a lower performance did not complete the full video-lecture, possibly viewing the beginning and the end of the video (2 or 3 min only). In total, 36.25% of students completed viewing the full video-lecture. This corresponds with aspects of Generation Z: A lack of concentration and a desire for immediacy and typically losing interest after 5–10 min (Table 3).

In Fig. 2a, b, the relationship between some innovative variables and the academic performance of the student is observed. Figure 2b indicates a positive relationship between the visualization of the video-lectures and the academic performance of the student. A small proportion of HP students do not need to visualize the video-lectures to understand the subject. In general, the behavior of the student by level of performance is totally different. Figure 2c, d show the relationships between student performance and some of the traditional variables such as *Midterms*

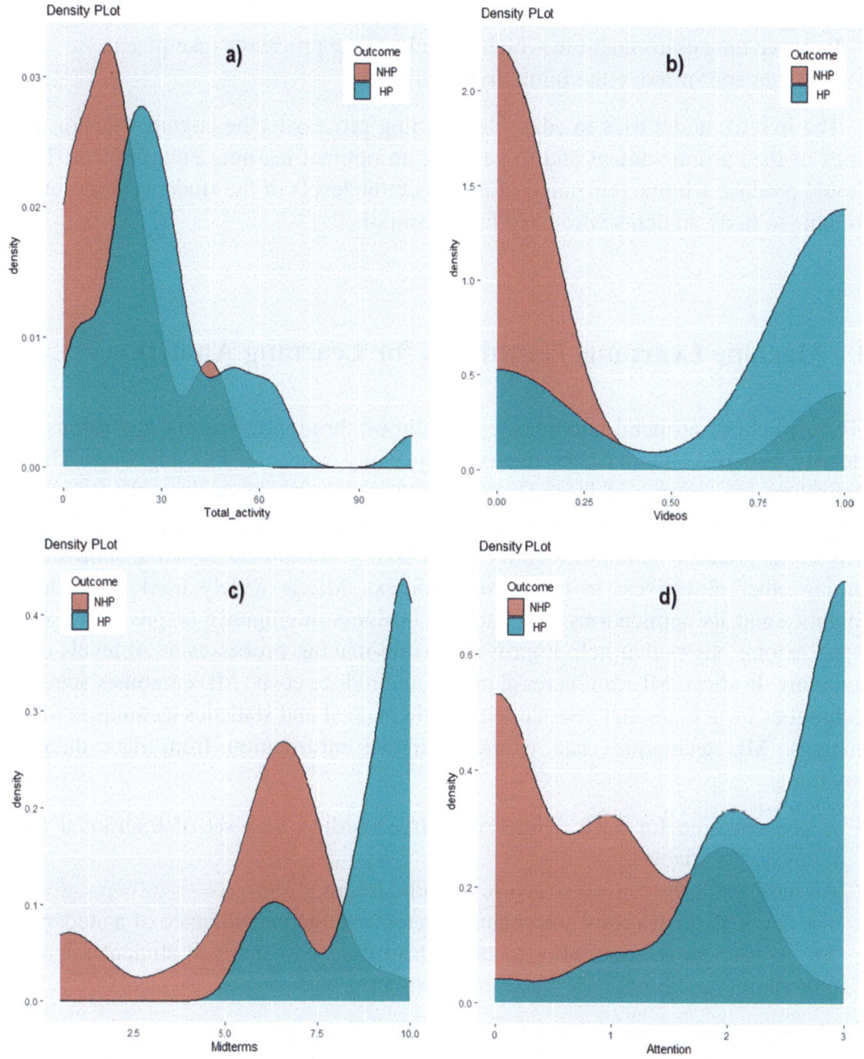

Fig. 2 Density functions for variable outcome versus (**a**)Total activity; (**b**) Videos; (**c**) Midterm scores; and (**d**) Attention

and the capacity of concentration of the student in the classroom measured by the variable *Attention*. In both cases, a direct relationship can be observed being stronger between *Attention* and *Outcome*. Density functions observed in Fig. 2c show that there are NHP students with good midterm scores and a small proportion of HP students with below average midterm scores.

Previous descriptive analysis is a good starting point to obtain information on the effectiveness of the hybrid model. In order to improve knowledge and understanding, a set of ML techniques was applied with a triple purpose:

- Design more effective and efficient learning processes.
- Improve the environment in which these learning processes take place.
- Evaluate and improve the initial hybrid model.

The hybrid model tries to adapt the learning process to the cognitive characteristics of the current student and to generate an optimal learning environment. This should produce a homogenization of the academic levels of the students (instructors are able to hook students who have fallen behind).

4 Machine Learning Techniques for Learning Analytics

ML is a field of artificial intelligence that allows, through the use of algorithms, to identify patterns and make predictions especially working with big data. These algorithms are capable of learning from experience autonomously without human intervention. ML is widely used in business decisions to determine which products will be in greatest demand, identify and classify consumers or drive innovation among other objectives. In this former context, ML is widely used in business analytics and its applications for example: business intelligence or predictive analytics among others that help improve decision-making processes at all levels of a company. In short, ML can increase profits and reduce costs. ML combines specific techniques from computer science with mathematical and statistics techniques (data mining). ML techniques can extract valuable information from data thereby obtaining:

- A classification for each of the students according to a set of traditional and innovative variables.
- An idea about the typical structure of a classroom.
- The set of variables most important to determine the performance of a student.
- An assessment of the ability of the hybrid model to increase student interest, motivation, and ultimately student performance.

ML techniques can be classified by type as follows [32]:

- *Supervised learning (SL)*: It is based on a system of labels associated with data. The model has a set of input variables (predictors or independent) that have some influence on an output variable (dependent variable). There is clear and explicit supervision.
- *Unsupervised learning (UL)*: All data is unlabeled, and the algorithms learn to inherently structure and organize from the input data. There is no explicit supervision.
- *Reinforcement learning (RL)*: Reinforcement learning is placed between supervised learning and unsupervised learning. Its objective is to obtain information about the relation between input-output variables from experience. In other words, being able to make the best decision in different situations according to

Table 4 Classification of machine learning techniques applied

	Type of technique	Objective in this study	Algorithms	Prior knowledge of classes
Classification	SL	Suggest groups of students based on patterns in data	• Naive Bayes classifier • Binary logistic regression • Neural networks	Yes
Clustering	UL	Group new student and class' structure analysis	Hierarchical models	No
Prediction	SL	Predict student performance	Binary logistic regression models	Yes
Reduction dimensionality	UL	Reduce the number of inputs. Identify types or groups of variables	Factor analysis (with principal components)	No

a trial-and-error process in which the correct decisions are rewarded. There is implicit supervision through rewards.

Table 4 presents a summary of the ML techniques applied in this study for different purposes. Supervised learning is typically done in the context of classification, (an input is mapped to an output label), or regression, (an input is mapped to a continuous output). Common algorithms in supervised learning include logistic regression, naive Bayes, support vector machines, artificial neural networks, and random forests. In both regression and classification, the goal is to find specific relationships or structure in the input data that allow to effectively produce correct output data.

With these goals, the ML methods used in this work have been briefly described below.

4.1 *Naïve Bayes Classifier*

One of the simplest classification models is the so-called Naive Bayes Classifier (NBC). It is a supervised classification algorithm, i.e., the output labels are known. The principle behind Naive Bayes is the Bayes theorem also known as the Bayes Rule. The Bayes theorem is used to calculate the conditional probability, which is nothing but the probability of an event occurring based on information about the events in the past. The main restriction of the model is that it considers all the input variables (predictor variables) independent of each other, that is, there is no relationship between them. However, in the real world, the predictor variables are not always independent of each other, hence the adjective "naive." The Naive Bayes model is easy to build and particularly useful for very large data sets. Along with simplicity, Naive Bayes is known to outperform even highly sophisticated classification methods.

The Naïve Bayes model is a binary model where the students are classified according to two categories: HP and NHP. The conditional probabilities were calculated using the following expressions:

$$P(\mathrm{HP}|\mathrm{videos},\ \mathrm{pageviews},\ \ldots) = \frac{P(\mathrm{videos},\ \mathrm{pageviews},\ \ldots|\mathrm{HP}) \cdot P(\mathrm{HP})}{P(\mathrm{videos},\ \mathrm{pageviews},\ \ldots)} \quad (2)$$

$$P(\mathrm{NHP}|\mathrm{videos},\ \mathrm{pageviews},\ \ldots) = \frac{P(\mathrm{videos},\ \mathrm{pageviews},\ \ldots|\mathrm{NHP}) \cdot P(\mathrm{NHP})}{P(\mathrm{videos},\ \mathrm{pageviews},\ \ldots)} \quad (3)$$

Since the denominators are common, the previous equation can be rewritten as follows:

$$P\left(\mathrm{HP}_i|\underbrace{\mathrm{videos}_i,\ \ldots, \mathrm{page\_views}_i}_{X_i}\right) \propto \prod_{i=1}^{n} P(X_i|\mathrm{HP}_i) \cdot P(\mathrm{HP}_i) \quad (4)$$

$$P\left(\mathrm{NHP}_i|\underbrace{\mathrm{videos}_i,\ \ldots, \mathrm{page\_views}_i}_{X_i}\right) \propto \prod_{i=1}^{n} P(X_i|\mathrm{NHP}_i) \cdot P(\mathrm{NHP}_i) \quad (5)$$

As noted above, the most restrictive assumption of the model is that the inputs are independent. In fact, it is difficult for this assumption to be fulfilled. Especially in the academic context where (to a greater or lesser extent) there is a dependency relationship between the selected variables. Therefore, the first step has been to carry out a simple analysis of the correlations between the different explanatory variables. In this context (with a large number of inputs variables), the well-known problem of multiple comparisons arises. To solve this problem, the correlation matrix was calculated, obtaining the corresponding corrected p-values using the Holm procedure or Bonferroni–Holm correction.

The corrected p-values indicate that the correlation coefficient was high for the most commonly input variables (4% of them show a correlation statistically equal to zero while 96% present a statistically significant correlation). Therefore, the variables that present a lower degree of correlation between them have been selected considering the Bayesian model as a good starting point for further analysis. In any case, the model results indicate that, although the restrictions imposed by the model are not exactly met, the predictive capacity of the model is very good and similar to more complex models.

4.2 Binary Logistic Regression

The binary logistic regression (BLR) technique is used in this work as a classification model. The BLR method tries to find the relationships between the output variable and the input variables. In other words, it uses a supervised learning method where the input variable is a binary or dichotomous variable (HP and NHP), unlike the traditional regression model where the output variable is continuous. This difference gives rise to different parametric models and different hypotheses for these models, but, once this difference is saved, the methods used in the logistic regression follow the same principles as the linear regression model.

Using the logistics distribution, the mean of *Y*, given a value of *X*, is represented by:

$$\pi(x) = E(Y|X = x) \tag{6}$$

$$\pi(x) = \frac{e^{\beta_0 + \beta_1 \text{Videos} + \cdots + \beta_k \text{Total\_activity}}}{1 + e^{\beta_0 + \beta_1 \text{Videos} + \cdots + \beta_k \text{Total\_activity}}} \tag{7}$$

Using the logit transformation, the model is as follows:

$$Y = \ln \underbrace{\left[\frac{\pi(x)}{1 - \pi(x)}\right]}_{\text{odss}} = \beta_0 + \beta_1 \text{Videos} + \beta_2 \text{Midterms} + \ldots + \beta_n \text{Total\_activity} \tag{8}$$

The model is estimated by maximum likelihood using for the Newton-Raphson method in which a backward elimination variable selection method has been used.

Odds is the quotient between the probability that the student has a good performance divided by the probability that the student has a poor performance of the course. Associated with the concept of odds, the odds ratio is defined as the quotient between the odds of an event under a certain condition, and the odds of that same event under another condition.

The odds ratio is a measure of association that approximates how much more likely, or unlikely, it is that the student performs or does not perform well among other students depending on the independent variables. For example, in the case of gender, this qualitative variable indicates if it is more, less, or equally likely to have a good performance if $Gender = 0$ (male) or $Gender = 1$ (female).

4.3 Artificial Neural Networks

One of the most used methods in ML are the so-called Artificial Neural Networks (ANN). These try to mimic the learning method of the human brain. Neural networks use nonlinear algorithms to both predict and classify. Although they have been criticized on many occasions as black box methods, ANNs have obtained excellent results in many fields of application.

The main objective of the ANN is to discover a series of characteristics from linear combinations of the model inputs that will later be used to model the output using a nonlinear function [33]. They are regression or classification models in two stages. A neural network can be mathematically expressed by Eq. (9) [18, 34]:

$$y_k = f_0\left(\sum_h \omega_{hk} f_h\left(\sum_h \omega_{ih} x_i\right)\right) \tag{9}$$

where the estimated value of the response variable y_k is a sum of products between the respective ω for i input variables x and h hidden nodes, mediated by the activation functions f_h and f_0 for each hidden and output node.

In this study, a multilayer perceptron neural network has been used as a classification method where the input variable is binary ($Y = 1$ or HP; $Y = 0$ or NHP), and the explanatory variables are both categorical variables (*Gender*, *Videos*, etc.) and quantitative variables (*Midterm*, *Total activity*, etc.).

Table 5 summarizes the main characteristics of the architecture of the network used. The network applies a type of supervised learning using a resilient backpropagation algorithm that searches for the configuration of weights that minimizes the error, reflected through a function that penalizes the failure to estimate the actual data. It is a feedforward algorithm, i.e., the network connections follow a single direction. The backpropagation algorithm is the most widely used training method. Cross entropy is employed as a loss or error function. This function measures the distance between the true probability distribution function and the estimated probability distribution function. A hidden layer has been included to increase the flexibility in the types of input-output relationships that can be handled by allowing more complex (nonlinear) relationships between variables. A sigmoid function is used as activation function in the hidden layer. The Softmax function is employed as output function. This function is a generalization of the logistic function where each output will be in the interval (0,1).

Table 5 Architecture of the network used in this work

Architecture of the network	
Covariate scaling method	Normalization
Algorithm	Resilient backpropagation with weight backtracking
Hidden layers activation function	Hyperbolic tangent
Output layers activation function	Softmax
Error function	Cross entropy
Number of hidden layers	1

4.4 Hierarchical Agglomerative Clustering (HAC)

The cluster analysis tries to classify the students without having the help of the input variable as in the case of the previously mentioned classification methods. In this case, the algorithm detects groups or clusters of students that have characteristics or similarities between them. The algorithm only takes into account the model inputs, X_i, that is, it uses an unsupervised learning method, since it does not know a priori the value or the label of the variable Y_i.The basic idea is to classify objects forming groups or clusters that are as homogeneous as possible within themselves and heterogeneous among themselves.

For unsupervised clustering analysis, the hierarchical clustering method has been selected, which has the advantage that it is not necessary to specify the number of clusters beforehand. For the study, a bottom-up approach (agglomerative clustering) has been used where the grouping begins at the base of the tree, where each observation forms an individual cluster. The clusters combine as the structure grows to converge in a single central cluster that contains all the elements. In the agglomerative approach, the type of distance and the method of grouping or linkage must be specified. The Jaccard distance (binary option in R) has been used to calculate the distance between pairs of observations and to quantify the similarity between two clusters. The Ward method of minimum variance has been used as a grouping or linkage method, which minimizes the total sum of variance intra-cluster. Additionally, this method allows to obtain the so-called dendrograms that are visualizations of a hierarchical binary grouping.

4.5 Multiple Linear Regression Model

The multiple linear regression model (MLR) is a technique that uses a set of explanatory variables X_i to predict a continuous outcome of a dependent variable Y. The model is linear or linearized. The objective is to obtain information about the quantitative linear relationship between the explanatory variables and output variable.

$$Y = \beta_0 + \beta_1 \text{Videos} + \beta_2 \text{Midterms} + \ldots + \beta_n \text{Total\_activity} + e \qquad (10)$$

where $e \sim \text{NID}\left(0, \sigma_n^2 I\right)$

The variance-covariance matrix of e is a scalar matrix (a square diagonal matrix with all its main diagonal entries equal), $\text{Var}(e) = \sigma_n^2 I$, where I is the identity matrix. (There are no correlation and heteroscedasticity.) As it has previously commented, the variables used are highly correlated, which could originate in this context an exact or approximate multicollinearity problem that could hinder the estimates or raise many doubts about the validity of the estimated parameters of the model. In this case, the selected output variable has been *Final score* being closely related to the

Outcome variable. In other words, it allows to define the variable of interest as a continuous quantitative variable necessary for this type of model. Again, the model selection technique used is the backward selection procedure by MCO.

4.6 Factor Analysis Using Principal Components

The data matrix consists of a number of rows or cases of 80 (students) and a number of columns (variables) of 15, which present statistically significant correlations in many cases due to the context in which they take place. Thus, the following question naturally arises: could these 15 input variables be grouped into a smaller set of variables? Being this smaller group of *new variables* independent of each other. To investigate, the so-called dimension reduction techniques are used, in particular, factor analysis using Principal Component Analysis (PCA) as an estimation method.

The objective is to group the set of explanatory variables (traditional and innovative) by means of their correlations, so that all the variables within a group are highly correlated with each other, but have relatively low correlations with other variables that are found in different groups. In this analysis, each group of variables represents an unobservable variable or factor, which is responsible for the observed correlations. The factorial model postulates that $X = (X_{1,} =$ Videos, $X_{2,} =$ Gender, . . ., $X_n =$ Attendance) is linearly dependent on a few unobservable random variables, F_1, F_2, . . ., F_m, called common factors and additional p sources of variation ε_1, ε_2, . . ., ε_n called specific, unique factors, or errors.

PCA has been used to estimate the model. PCA describes the variation of a multivariate data set in terms of an uncorrelated set of variables, each of which is a particular linear combination of the original variables. The new variables, called principal components, are obtained in decreasing order of importance, i.e., the first main component collects the maximum information (variation) from the original data. The second component collects the greatest amount of information, which has not been collected by the first component, i.e., the information of the initial variables that are incorrect with the first main component, and so on. Components are used to summarize data with minimal loss of information. The new axes represent the directions with maximum variability and produce a simpler and more orderly description of the structure of the variances-covariances matrix.

5 Empirical Results

The empirical results obtained by the different ML models estimated with the R statistical package and applied to the learning data are shown in this section. Table 6 collects the R libraries and functions used in this work. To allow the reproducibility of the algorithms, a seed with a value (1234) was selected.

Table 6 R libraries and functions used

ML algorithm	R libraries and functions
NBC	Naivebayes, dplyr, ggplot2, caret, pscych
BLR	glm
ANN	neuralnet, NeuralNeTools, RSNNS, and Rcpp
HC	Agnes, dendextend, dplyr, and ggplot2
MLR	R Commander
FA-PCA	psych and function prcomp

In order to evaluate the model, the cross-validation method has been implemented, i.e., the sample has been separated into two sub-samples. One called training set to adjust the model (70%) and the remainder of the dataset (30%) is used as a validation test to assess the accuracy of the model.

5.1 Naïve Bayes Classifier

As we comment is previous sections, the independence assumption is important in the Naïve Bayes Model. For this reason, and as a starting point, a simple analysis of the correlations between the different explanatory variables has been carried out (see Fig. 3). For model estimation, the following categorical variables, that showed correlations below 0.45, have been selected: *Videos, Motivation, Specialty, Attention, Page_views,* and *Gender*. This set of variables capture both characteristics the traditional model and the innovative model. The main diagonal in Fig. 3 presents thc frequency distributions for the selected variables. The values above the main diagonal are the correlation coefficients. Just below the main diagonal there are the graphical representations determining the sign of the correlation (positive slope = positive correlation, negative slope = negative correlation, and zero slope = non-correlated).

Positive or negative correlation indicates that the independence assumption is not fulfilled. For this reason, the variables with lowest correlations have been selected.

Table 7 shows the conditional probabilities for the first four students The Bayesian model correctly classifies the four students (highest conditional probability).

In order to evaluate the model, the confusion matrix presented in Table 8 is employed.

The following information about the accuracy performance of the NBC (positive class: *HP*) is observed from the confusion matrix.

- Accuracy: Total proportion of student correctly classified, 0.8261.
- Sensitivity: Proportion of "HP" students correctly classified, 0.83.
- Specificity: Proportion of "NHP" students correctly classified, 0.82.
- Kappa statistic: It is used to measure the quality of the model. For Kappa between 0.6 and 0.8, the model is considered as good.

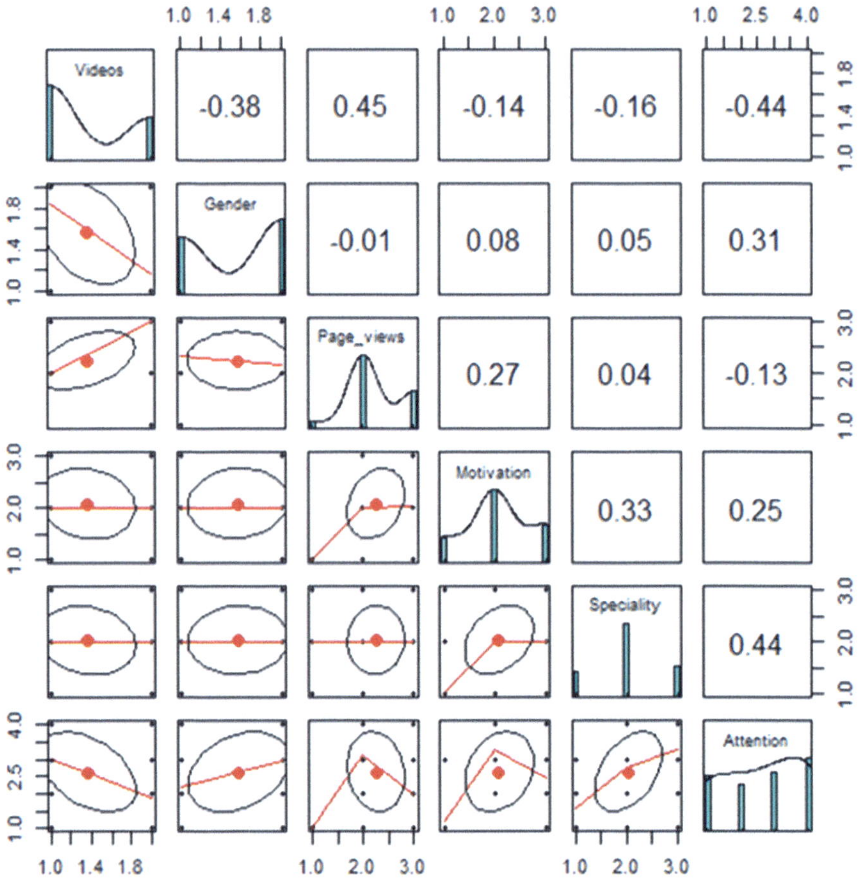

Fig. 3 Correlation map for categorical variables

Figure 4 shows the importance that the NBC model gives to each of the inputs. The NBC model attaches great importance to the visualization of the video-lectures, followed by more traditional variables such as *Attention*, *Speciality,* or *Motivation*. It also shows the gender of the student as significant.

5.2 *Binary Logistic Regression*

The adjusted BLR model including only variables *Midterm* and *Videos* is the following:

Table 7 Conditional probabilities for the first four student using NBC

P(HP)	*P*(NHP)	Videos	Gender	Page_views	Motivation	Speciality	Attention	Outcome
0.99201	0.00798	Nowatch	Male	Low	Low	Social	Moderate	NHP
0.99352	0.00647	Nowatch	Female	Low	Low	Social	Low	NHP
0.99845	0.00154	Nowatch	Male	Low	Low	Tech	Low	NHP
0.04229	0.95770	Watch	Female	Moderate	Moderate	Social	Moderate	HP

Table 8 Naïve Bayes confusion matrix

		Prediction	
		NHP	HP
Actual	NHP	14	1
	HP	3	5

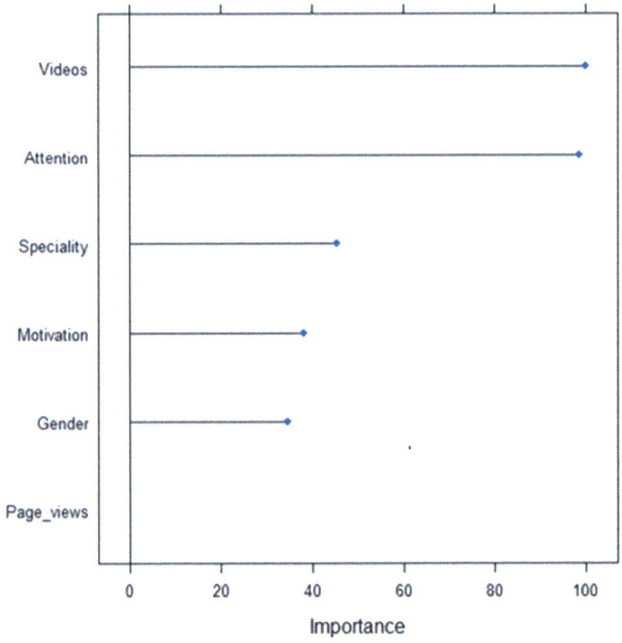

Fig. 4 Importance variables obtained by NBC

$$\ln\left(\frac{\pi(x)}{1-\pi(x)}\right) = y = \underset{(2.713)}{-9.0892} + \underset{(0.338)}{0.9933}\,\text{Midterm} + \underset{(0.970)}{3.1309}\,\text{Videos} \tag{11}$$

Or alternatively:

$$\pi(x) = \frac{e^{-9.0892+0.9933\,\text{Midterm}+3.1309\,\text{Videos}}}{1+e^{-9.0892+0.9933\,\text{Midterm}+3.1309\,\text{Videos}}} = \widehat{P}(Y=1|x_i) \tag{12}$$

being the dependent variable: $Y = 1$ (HP) and $Y = 0$ (NHP).

As a measure of the quality of the fitted model, the goodness of fit test of Hosmer–Lemeshow is used. This test gets a p-value of 0.688 (>0.05) suggesting that the model is a good fit to the data. Additionally, the value of the R^2 of Nagelkerke indicates that the model explains roughly 78% of the variation in the outcome. The confusion matrix obtained by BLR model in the train test is presented in Table 9.

Table 9 Binary logistic regression confusion matrix

		Prediction	
		NHP	HP
Actual	NHP	12	2
	HP	0	8

The computation of odds-ratios could be interpreted as follows:

- *Midterms*: $\widehat{\mathrm{OR}} = e^{0.9933} = 2.7001$. It is 2.70 times more likely that a student who has obtained a good score in the midterms will have a higher performance.
- *Videos*: $\widehat{\mathrm{OR}} = e^{3.1309} = 22.89$. It is 22.89 times more likely that a student who has viewed the full videos will reach a higher score.

5.3 *Artificial Neural Networks*

Different ANN with different groups of variables were estimated. Figure 5 shows the network and inputs selected.

The confusion matrix of the ANN to evaluate the predictive performance of the model is presented in Table 10.

Finally, the ANN model estimates the relative importance of each of the input variables (see Table 11). According to the ANN model, the three most important predictors to classify the student performance are *Midterms*, *Videos,* and *Motivation*.

5.4 *Hierarchical Agglomerative Clustering*

To build the hierarchical classification model, the following categorical variables have been selected, which have been previously transformed into binary variables: *Videos, Gender, Page_views, Participation, Motivation, Speciality, Attention, Repeating,* and *Outcome*.

Figure 6 depicts the obtained dendrogram using the R agglomerative option "ward.D" distance with an agglomerative coefficient equal to 0.9317. The horizontal axis contains all the students, the height of the dendrogram gives an idea about dissimilarities between students. The clustering algorithm clearly identifies two main groups of students: Cluster 1 (the red branch) and Cluster 2 (the green branch).

Table 12 shows the two clusters formed, one mainly by poorly performing students (43) and the other with students with good academic performance (28).

5.5 *Multiple Linear Regression Model*

In order to estimate the quantitative relationships between the output and the explanatory variables, the following multiple regression model is adjusted:

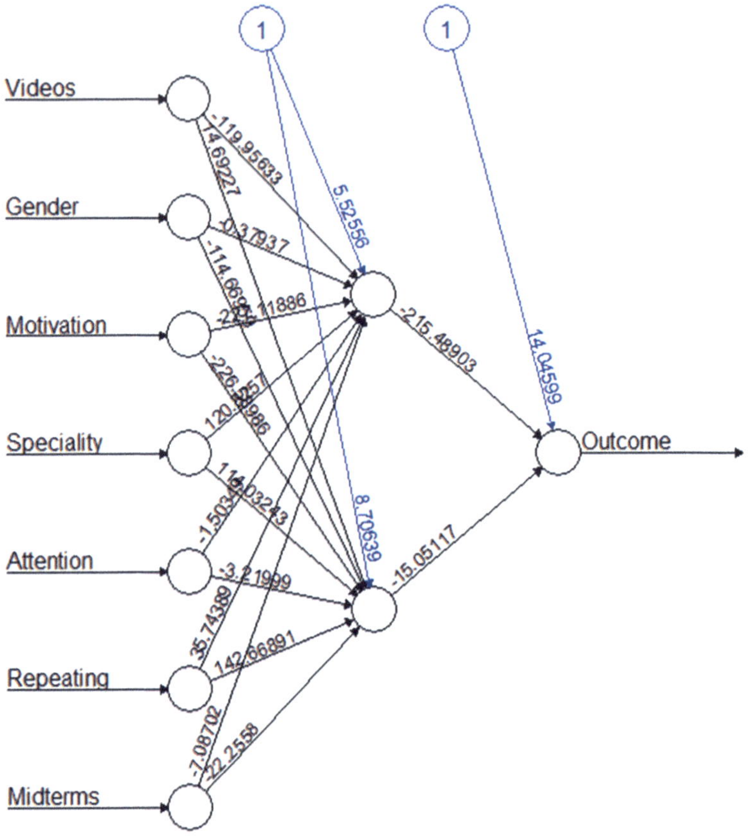

Fig. 5 Neural network graph. Error: 3.066728. Steps: 2254

Table 10 Neural network confusion matrix

		Prediction	
		NHP	HP
Actual	NHP	16	1
	HP	3	5

$$\widehat{\text{FinalScore}} = \underset{(0.6791)}{0.5771} + \underset{(0.1080)}{0.5284}\,\text{Midterms} + \underset{(0.3142)}{0.7247}\,\text{Speciality} + \underset{(0.5651)}{2.1015}\,\text{Videos} \quad (13)$$

The problem to estimate this model is the multicollinearity because there are significant correlations between the predictor variables. The adjusted coefficient of determination (measure of the accuracy of the model) is 0.533, i.e., the model is able to explain 53.3% of the total variability of the explained variable *Final score*.

Table 11 Neural network relative importance

	Importance	Normalized importance (%)
Gender	0.068	17.6
Videos	0.070	34.1
Page_views	0.037	9.6
Attention	0.076	19.7
Repeating	0.022	5.6
Participation	0.080	20.6
Motivation	0.103	26.7
Speciality	0.027	7
Midterms	0.386	100
Total_Activity	0.132	18.1

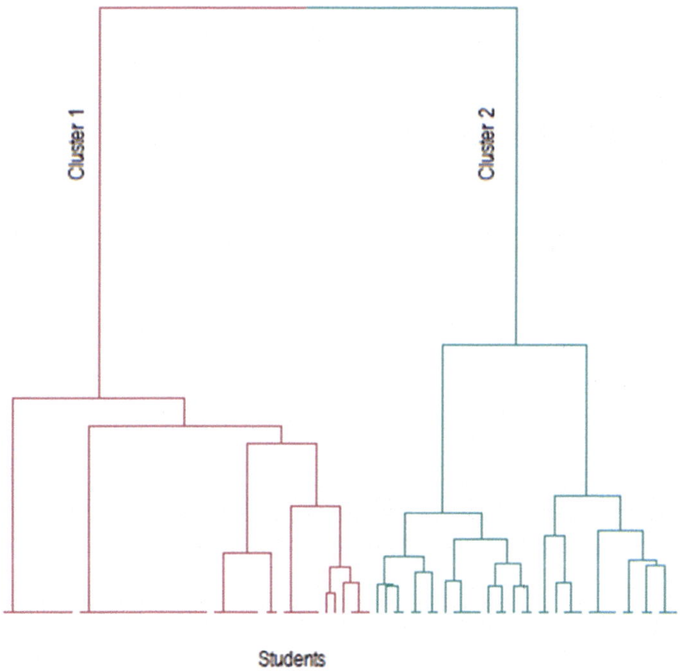

Fig. 6 Cluster dendrogram

Table 12 Cluster outcome

	Outcome	
	0 = NHP	1 = HP
Cluster 1	43	1
Cluster 2	8	28

To verify that the hypotheses of the linear regression model are met, a residual analysis of the model was carried out.

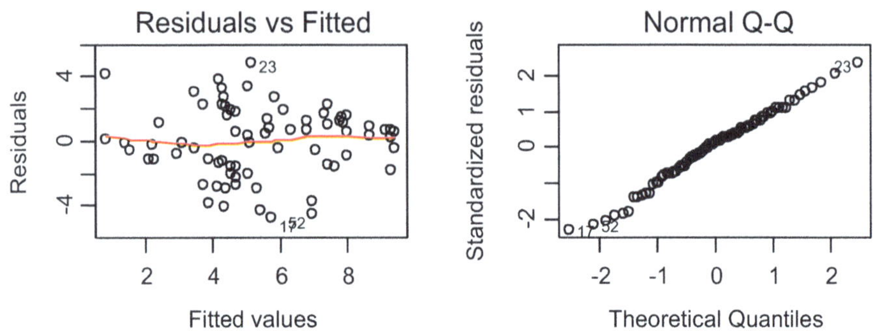

Fig. 7 Residual analysis of the MLR model

- Normality: The points reasonably follow the diagonal indicating that they follow a normal distribution (Fig. 7).
- Homoscedasticity: A changing dispersion is not observed (see Fig. 7, left graph), so the assumption of homogeneity is also fulfilled.

Therefore, the considered model is suitable, i.e., the estimated parameters are valid.

- *Midterm* coefficient interpretation: ceteris paribus, if the midterm exam score increases 1 unit, on average, *Final score* increases 0.52 points in the final grade.
- *Speciality* coefficient interpretation: If the student has taken the specialty of science in high school it increases the *Final score*, on average, by 0.72 points.
- *Videos* coefficient interpretation: The full visualization of the video-lectures increases, on average, the *Final score* by 2.1 extra points.

5.6 Factor Analysis Using Principal Components

The aim of the PCA is to reduce the number of explanatory variables to a smaller set of variables or components that are independent of each other. The first step done was to eliminate variables that are considered not very informative. Finally, the variables selected to perform the factor analysis were: *Videos, Gender, Page_views, Participation, Motivation, Speciality, Attention, Repeating,* and *Outcome*.

The first three components have been selected reaching 66.4% of the total information provided by the original variables (see Table 13). The components are displayed in order of importance. The first principal component collects the maximum information (variation) from the original data. The second component collects the greatest amount of information, which has not been collected by the first component, i.e., the information of the initial variables that are uncorrelated with the first component, and so on. Each component is a particular linear combination of the original variables. The Kaiser-Meyer-Olkin adequacy test shows a value of

Table 13 PCA total explained variance

	Initial eigenvalues		
Components	Total	% variance	% accumulated
1	4.261	42.608	42.608
2	1.291	12.914	55.522
3	1.088	10.878	66.400
4	0.889	8.886	75.286
5	0.730	7.300	82.586
6	0.576	5.757	88.343
7	0.440	4.397	92.740
8	0.369	3.686	96.426
9	0.275	2.753	99.178
10	0.082	0.822	100.000

Table 14 PCA eigenvectors

	Component		
	1	2	3
Videos	**0.730**	0.010	0.311
Total_activity	**0.485**	−0.311	−0.014
Gender	0.396	0.242	**0.709**
Page_views	**0.581**	0.433	0.035
Participation	**0.839**	0.372	−0.166
Motivation	**0.840**	0.279	−0.153
Speciality	**0.511**	0.075	−0.639
Attention	**0.750**	−0.192	0.130
Repeating	−0.452	**0.709**	−0.069
Midterms	**0.749**	−0.432	−0.074

Bold values are the highest values for each variable. Highest values identifies the associated component

0.767, therefore, the factor model is adequate. The test of Bartlett for Sphericity was also used. This test determines if the correlation matrix fits the identity matrix (absence of significant correlation between variables) and indicates that the scatterplot will fit a perfect sphere. According to this test, the null hypothesis is rejected.

The next step is to interpret the components and associate each component to the original variables. Table 14 shows the matrix of eigenvectors associated to each component. These values are useful to identify the characteristics of the components. The interpretation of the coefficients of this matrix corresponds to the correlation between the axes (component 1, component 2, and component 3) and the variables. The largest value for each variable identifies the associated component. The PCA technique selects three components: Component 1 is related to motivation and personal characteristics of the student (intrinsic motivation), Component 2 is associated with being a repeating student or not; and finally, Component 3 is related to being male or female.

5.7 Summary Results

An initial descriptive analysis shows a clear disaggregation of the polarized class structure into two large groups: students with high performance levels and students with low performance levels.

Table 15 shows a model evaluation summary and the different inputs selected for each ML technique. Regarding the classification algorithms, the best model was the binary logistics regression in terms of model accuracy. In terms of sensitivity, the best performance was achieved by NBC and ANN. Finally, according to the specificity, the best model is the BLR algorithm. With respect to the model specification (determination of which independent variables should be included in or excluded), the following variables were selected by order of importance: (1) *Videos* (selected by five algorithms). The variable *Videos* is related to the part of the hybrid model more focused on the use of multimedia tools, (2) *Midterm* (selected by four algorithms). *Midterms* are more related to the traditional evaluation system, (3) *Speciality* and *Motivation* (selected by two algorithms). *Motivation* is more associated to the implementation of the neuroeducation methods, and (4) *Gender* and *Attention* (selected by one algorithm) related to traditional evaluation system.

Table 15 shows a model evaluation summary and the different inputs selected for each machine learning (ML) technique. Regarding the classification algorithms, the best model, in terms of accuracy, was the binary logistics regression model. In terms of sensitivity, the best performance was achieved by NBC and ANN. Finally, according to the specificity, the best model is the BLR algorithm. With respect to the model specification (determination of which independent variables should be included (in) or excluded), the following variables were selected in order of importance: (1) *Videos* (selected by five algorithms). The variable *Videos* is related to the part of the hybrid model more focused on the use of multimedia tools, (2) *Midterm* (selected by four algorithms). *Midterms* are more related to the traditional evaluation system, (3) *Speciality* and *Motivation* (selected by two algorithms). *Motivation* is more associated with the implementation of the neuroeducation methods and (4) *Gender* and *Attention* (selected by one algorithm) related to traditional evaluation systems.

Table 15 ML techniques evaluation and inputs

	NBC	BLR	ANN	MLR	FACP
Accuracy	0.8261	0.9091	0.8440		
Sensitivity	0.8333	0.8000	0.8333		
Specificity	0.8235	1.0000	0.8421		
Inputs	Video	Videos	Midterms	Videos	Videos
	Attention	Midterms	Videos	Speciality	Motivation
	Speciality	Gender	Motivation	Midterms	Midterms

Note: NBC is Naïve Bayes classifier; BLR is Binary Logistic Regression; ANN is Artificial neural network; MLR is Multiple linear regression; FACP is Factor analysis using principal components

The innovative variables provide a vision of virtual student behavior through the Canvas platform: *Videos, Total activity, Page_views, Late*, discussion *forums*, etc. The variable *Videos* clearly offers the most reliable and useful information for the analysis. The reason for this could be that the visualization of videos requires greater motivation and attention from the student, unlike the *Total activity* variable, which requires less active student participation.

The HAC algorithm mainly identified two groups of students. The largest group is related to students with low performance and the smaller one is related to students with performance much higher than the rest. This breaks with the class structure of a higher education class using "traditional data" where three large groups could be identified: A small group (roughly 20%, the most applied); a second group made up of the average student (the largest), and finally another small group made up of the worst performing students (which, for the most part, was filtered by the education system).

Factor analysis identified that the main three components were related to: (1) The personal characteristics of the student. Including variables more related to the levels of intrinsic motivation of the students such as *Motivation, Attention, Videos*, etc., (2) The condition of the repeating student, and (3) The gender of the student.

There exists a clear and positive relationship between *Videos* and *Motivation* variables, indicating a positive effect of the video-lectures of the hybrid model on student motivation. Although, the direction of causality is difficult to determine.

In view of data, and through the analysis of the variable *Videos*, the hybrid model seems to have obtained partial success insofar as it has managed to increase the performance of students who are already good, but has failed to capture the attention of some of the rest.

6 Conclusions

This chapter presents a hybrid learning methodology for students of an introductory course of Business Statistics at University carrying out a deep analysis of data collected from the instructor and the learning platform.

The hybrid model combines traditional techniques with multimedia tools and neuroeducation concepts. This model has been able to bridge the gap between the digital world in which the student moves and the more traditional academic world.

Information collected by instructors in traditional form about the learning process of each student is complemented with the information provided by IoT. The Canvas platform was used to manage IoT data and to monitor the student during the course. Useful information is drawn from this data set by applying various ML techniques. This information can be used in the decision-making to improve the methodological strategy in the learning process.

The empirical results show that the hybrid model is more flexible and adaptable (self-paced learning), but it has only been able to partially improve the class level. The incorporation of multimedia tools into the learning process has had a positive impact on student motivation and therefore, on academic performance. While these multimedia tools have been taken advantage by well-performing students, they have also been able to attract a small percentage of less-motivated students. Additionally, female students performed better than male students, achieving higher scores.

More frequent application and utilization of neuroeducation techniques are required to increase student engagement (curiosity, interest, degree of attention, passion, etc.). Finally, the satisfaction survey carried out at the end of the course shows that 83% of students gave a positive response to the hybrid model.

References

1. Mahdavinejad, M. S., Rezvan, M., Barekatain, M., Adibi, P., Barnaghi, P., & Sheth, A. P. (2018). Machine learning for internet of things data analysis: A survey. *Digital Communications and Networks, 4*(3), 161–175.
2. Evans, D. (2011). The internet of things how the next evolution of the internet is changing everything. *Cisco White Paper, 1*(2011), 1–11. Retrieved November 12, 2019, from https://www.cisco.com/c/dam/en_us/about/ac79/docs/innov/IoT_IBSG_0411FINAL.pdf.
3. Ray, P. P. (2016). A survey of IoT cloud platforms. *Future Computing and Informatics Journal, 1*(1–2), 35–46.
4. James, M., Chui, M., Bisson, P., Woetzel, J., Dobbs, R., Bughin, J., & Aharon, D. (2015). The internet of things: Mapping the value beyond the hype. *McKinsey Global Institute, 3*.
5. Pérez, J. M. P., & Márquez, F. P. G. (2015). Condition monitoring and fault diagnosis in wind energy systems. In J. L. Bessède (Ed.), *Eco-friendly innovation in electricity transmission and distribution networks* (pp. 221–241). Woodhead Publishing/Elsevier.
6. Pérez, J. M. P., Márquez, F. P. G., & Papaelias, M. (2017). Techno-economical advances for maintenance management of concentrated solar power plants. In *Proceedings of the tenth international conference on management science and engineering management* (pp. 967–979). Springer.
7. Pliego Marugán, A., García Márquez, F. P., & Pinar-Pérez, J. M. (2016). Optimal maintenance management of offshore wind farms. *Energies, 9*(1), 46.
8. Ruiz-Hernández, D., Pinar-Pérez, J. M., & Delgado-Gómez, D. (2020). Multi-machine preventive maintenance scheduling with imperfect interventions: A restless bandit approach. *Computers & Operations Research, 119*, 104927.
9. Ravi, D., Wong, C., Lo, B., & Yang, G. Z. (2016). A deep learning approach to on-node sensor data analytics for mobile or wearable devices. *IEEE Journal of Biomedical and Health Informatics, 21*(1), 56–64.
10. Koren, I., & Klamma, R. (2018). Enabling visual community learning analytics with internet of things devices. *Computers in Human Behavior, 89*, 385–394.
11. Elias, T. (2011). Learning analytics. *Learning*, 1–22. Retrieved March 15, 2020, from http://citeseerx.ist.psu.edu/viewdoc/download?doi=10.1.1.456.7092&rep=rep1&type=pdf.
12. Chiappe, A., & Rodríguez, L. P. (2017). Learning analytics in 21st century education: A review. *Ensaio: Avaliação e Políticas Públicas em Educação, 25*(97), 971–991.
13. Aldowah, H., Al-Samarraie, H., & Fauzy, W. M. (2019). Educational data mining and learning analytics for 21st century higher education: A review and synthesis. *Telematics and Informatics, 37*, 13–49.
14. Avella, J. T., Kebritchi, M., Nunn, S. G., & Kanai, T. (2016). Learning analytics methods, benefits, and challenges in higher education: A systematic literature review. *Online Learning, 20*(2).

15. Gedrimiene, E., Silvola, A., Pursiainen, J., Rusanen, J., & Muukkonen, H. (2019). Learning analytics in education: Literature review and case examples from vocational education. *Scandinavian Journal of Educational Research, 64*(7), 1105–1119.
16. Leitner, P., Khalil, M., & Ebner, M. (2017). Learning analytics in higher education—A literature review. In A. Peña-Ayala (Ed.), *Learning analytics: Fundaments, applications, and trends. Studies in systems, decision and control* (Vol. 94, pp. 1–23). Springer.
17. Peña-Ayala, A. (2018). Learning analytics: A glance of evolution, status, and trends according to a proposed taxonomy. *Wiley Interdisciplinary Reviews: Data Mining and Knowledge Discovery, 8*(3), e1243. https://doi.org/10.1002/widm.1243.
18. Venables, W. N., & Ripley, B. D. (2013). *Modern applied statistics with S-PLUS*. Springer.
19. Ferguson, R., Brasher, A., Clow, D., Cooper, A., Hillaire, G., Mittelmeier, J., & Vuorikari, R. (2016). Research evidence on the use of learning analytics: Implications for education policy. In R. Vuorikari & J. Castano-Munoz (Eds.), *A European framework for action on learning analytics* (pp. 1–152). Joint Research Centre Science for Policy Report.
20. Nistor, N., & Hernández-García, Á. (2018). What types of data are used in learning analytics? An overview of six cases. *Computers in Human Behavior, 89*, 335–338.
21. Delen, D. (2010). A comparative analysis of machine learning techniques for student retention management. *Decision Support Systems, 49*(4), 498–506.
22. Lykourentzou, I., Giannoukos, I., Nikolopoulos, V., Mpardis, G., & Loumos, V. (2009). Dropout prediction in e-learning courses through the combination of machine learning techniques. *Computers & Education, 53*(3), 950–965.
23. Wilson, S. G. (2013). The flipped class: A method to address the challenges of an undergraduate statistics course. *Teaching of Psychology, 40*(3), 193–199.
24. Van Vliet, E. A., Winnips, J. C., & Brouwer, N. (2015). Flipped-class pedagogy enhances student metacognition and collaborative-learning strategies in higher education, but effect does not persist. *CBE—Life Sciences Education, 14*(3), ar26.
25. Budd, J. W. (2004). Mind maps as classroom exercises. *The Journal of Economic Education, 35* (1), 35–46.
26. Brecht, H. D. (2012). Learning from online video lectures. *Journal of Information Technology Education, 11*(1), 227–250.
27. Morales, R. (2019). *A hybrid approach in a first course of statistics, Pi-InnoMath*. Uned, 2.
28. Morales Arsenal, R., & Pinar-Pérez, J. M. (2020). The impact of new technologies in an introductory course in business statistics. In *INTED2020 proceedings* (pp. 6459–6466).
29. Baldwin, S., & Ching, Y.-H. (2019). Online course design: A review of the canvas course evaluation checklist. *The International Review of Research in Open and Distance Learning, 20* (3). https://doi.org/10.19173/irrodl.v20i3.4283.
30. U.S. News & World Report. (2018). *Best online bachelor's programs*. Retrieved March 1, 2019, from https://www.usnews.com/education/online-education/bachelors/rankings.
31. Edutechnica. (2019). *LMS data-Spring 2019 updates*. Retrieved March 17, 2019, from https://edutechnica.com/2019/03/17/lms-data-spring-2019-updates/.
32. Kotsiantis, S. B., Zaharakis, I., & Pintelas, P. (2007). Supervised machine learning: A review of classification techniques. *Emerging Artificial Intelligence Applications in Computer Engineering, 160*, 3–24.
33. Hastie, T., Tibshirani, R., & Friedman, J. (2009). *The elements of statistical learning: Data mining, inference, and prediction*. Springer.
34. Bishop, C. M. (1995). *Neural networks for pattern recognition*. Oxford University Press.

Internet of Things Cybersecurity: Blockchain as First Securitisation Layer of an IoT Network

Arturo Benayas-Ayuso, Rodrigo Perez Fernandez, and Francisco Perez-Arribas

1 Introduction

Industry 4.0 comprises a wide range of technologies, which are integrated into a single solution, merging to a point where it is difficult to distinguish between one or another technology, generating a full technological ecosystem. Based on that paradigm established by Industry 4.0, the relationship between the three technologies to be discussed is evident. Some of these technologies applied to the naval sector can be seen in Fig. 1 [1].

One of the most important technologies in industry 4.0 is cybersecurity. This step should not be overcome or either take as a simple step. Cybersecurity requires a set of layers which complicates enough the process getting away junior hackers and which doesn't't suppose a personal challenge for expert hackers, enough to bore both kind of hackers, and, at the same time, keep inner and outer communications available and well performing for all enterprise agents, virtual or real, which works in the inner network.

Security requirements, based on the definition of N. Komminos et al., need to be addressed by three main concepts: Confidentiality, Integrity and Availability, known as CIA [2]. Confidentiality is based on assure that only authorised users can read the message or access to the service. Integrity for all content of the message or service, which should be unaltered in the transmission. And Availability of the message or service at any time the agent requests it [3].

Cybersecurity in enterprise distributed networks is always a challenge, but, if we add IoT to an enterprise network, the challenge of securitisation becomes a nightmare. But, if we divide the work into smaller parts that are easier to manage, the first

A. Benayas-Ayuso (✉) · R. Perez Fernandez · F. Perez-Arribas
Marine Engineering School of the Universidad Politécnica de Madrid, Madrid, Spain

F. P. García Márquez, B. Lev (eds.), *Introduction to Internet of Things in Management Science and Operations Research*, International Series in Operations Research & Management Science 311,
https://doi.org/10.1007/978-3-030-74644-5_5

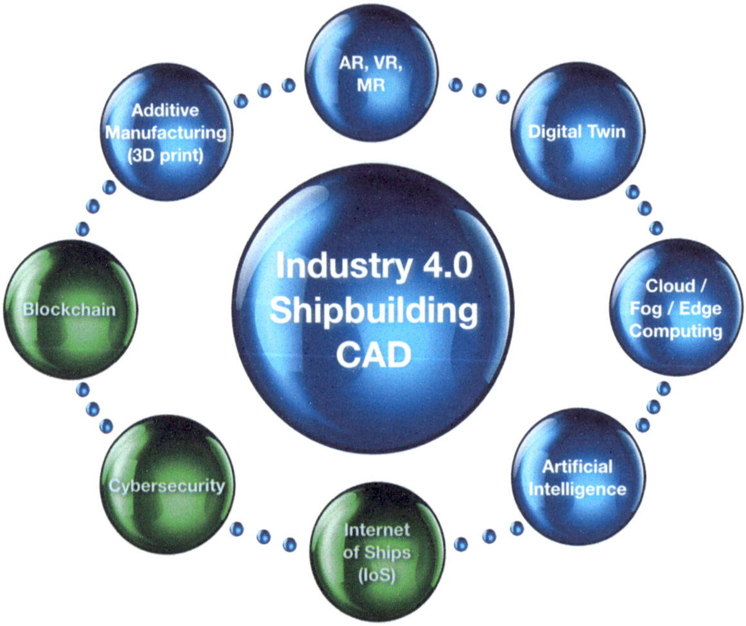

Fig. 1 Industry 4.0 paradigm: in paper technologies have been marked with a green ball

analysis should be done differentiating each small challenge. Based on the analysis of possible security failures, first division level can be: enterprise network security and IoT inner security. Other approach sets all elements inside the business network (intranet) as an IoT device with its special characteristics.

Attacks to an enterprise network can be classified in:

1. DDoS (Distributed Denial of Service), enterprise network becomes overloaded producing a slowdown or even blocking some common enterprise process or controls.
2. MitM (Man-in-the-Middle), communications can be modified by an external attacker.
3. Phishing.
4. Drive-by and, its sibling, XXS (cross-site scripting).
5. Password-steal.
6. SQL-injection.
7. Eavesdropping (passive or active).
8. Birthday attack (break the hash control generation to replace a valid message for an invalid one).
9. Malware.
10. Others.

Based on this list, not all the attacks are valid for all kinds of devices which can be connected to our network. Depending on the type of device, there are more suitable attacks which are inherent to its building technology, its fabrication process, its inner components or even, the communication protocols and ports/ways used in.

In the next sections, we are going to review which of this security breach concepts can be applied to the three technologies mentioned in this paper, IoT, Blockchain and Cybersecurity. First, we are going to describe IoT inner problems, without focusing on any type of special device, based only in common features shared by all of them. Second, we are going to study the Blockchain technology and its weakness in some scenarios. And finally, we are going to propose a set of solutions which can be applied to increase our security in the IIoT enterprise ecosystem avoiding the most common Cybersecurity problems.

2 IoT Cybersecurity Problems

The use of things which can connect to the network offering data from different parts, at first sight, do not offer a security problem meanwhile this data do not compromise any action in the enterprise ecosystem, but when things can take actions in an autonomous way based on this data, risk is increased over expectations, and the word cybersecurity gets a special meaning.

M. A. Khan et al. shows of a wide set of insecurities which are mixed on the term IoT device, due to their different building nature. This is expressed by next paradigm: "*...the Wireless Sensor Networks (WSNs) and Machine-to-Machine (M2M) or Cyber-Physical Systems (CPS) have now evolved as integral components for the broader term IoT. Consequently, the security problems related to WSN, M2M, or CPS continue to arise in the context of IoT with the IP protocol being the main standard for connectivity*" [4].

Some of the characteristics of IoT devices are: heterogeneous device types, heterogeneous communication technologies, heterogeneous connection technologies, with low or non-security embedded, with limited hardware and software capabilities, and with open-system design to make easier the integration in the network. Because the software/hardware limits, devices are cheap and affordable, but highly insecure [5].

There are IoT device suppliers which knowing all these limits, and they want to avoid all of them in each device, but this improvement requires an incremental of the price to afford it in new brand IoT devices. But, even with this upgrade, there are some other issues which still are in the enterprise scenario.

A. Banafa shows us a wide list of issues for IoT devices [6]. Completing this with known exposed limits, even if some of them can be now overcome for newest ones, most common IoT security problems can be summarised in:

1. No password or weak, guessable, or even hard-coded one, this allows easy access to the device, helping to control it directly, or after easy-password steal.
2. Hardware issues, which limits the capabilities to block the device from external non-authorised access.

3. Lack of a secure update mechanism, this allows a drive-by or XXS attacks, in which some part of the software to be updated in the device or the full one is substituted by malware in order to perform other type of attacks like: Denial-of-Sleep, to drain the battery of the device; Denial-of-Service (DoS), in which device gets a malfunction state o even, use the device to produce a Distributed Denial-of-Service (DDoS) in the enterprise data system, by incrementing the data requested/sent.
4. Old and unpatched embedded operating system and software, which allows multiple type of attacks, from eavesdropping, MitM, birthday attack, DDoS, phishing, drive-by, XXS, malware.
5. Insecure data transfer and storage, with no control over the data transmitted, one of the most common attack is eavesdropping.
6. Lack of user knowledge & awareness, this lead us to an insecure system. All attacks and even non listed ones can be applied.
7. Lack of physical hardening, allow an external noncontrolled attacker to perform: eavesdropping, birthday attack, MitM, DDoS, phishing, drive-by, XXS, malware.
8. Botnet attacks, based in corrupting our network with noncontrolled software can drive us too with malware and/or DDoS attacks.
9. Industrial espionage & eavesdropping.
10. Highjacking your IoT devices, attacks like eavesdropping, birthday attack, MitM, DDoS, phishing, drive-by, XXS, malware can be perform.
11. Data integrity risks of IoT Security in healthcare, can lead on eavesdropping and phishing attacks.
12. Rogue IoT devices allow attacks such as: eavesdropping, phishing, MitM, birthday attack, XXS, malware.

All these problems set the focus on the same paradigm, cybersecurity issues affects IoT ecosystem in enterprise network, and need to be prevented and solved. There are some technologies which can help to avoid most of these problems, or at least complicate it.

The authors suggested in a conference paper the utility to group sensors and actuators in small clusters, which can be closed groups and controlled with a more powerful controller limiting some of those problems [5, 7]. The clusters can be included in a cluster of clusters creating a bigger one, making a scalable net of systems like a human body. This idea is shared between most of the people in the IoT industry helping them to classify and minimise the impact of this features in the enterprise ecosystem. A. Dorri et al., call controller for this small clusters as *Cluster Head*, establishing a practical point to home IoT environments [3].

3 Blockchain Main Concepts and Cybersecurity Problems

Blockchain approach was developed in 1991 to secure the signature and the content of engineering drawings which became to be shared through internet, via e-mail, as a method which allows receiver to check that the non-encrypted drawing is valid and has been signed by the persons which are registered in. This method of validation requires a big amount of processing capacity, because of the Proof of Work (POW) inherent to the blockchain process [8].

After a while, in 2008, with the appearance of the Bitcoin as a crypto currency which doesn't require a bank or any authority to assure that the transactions made in the system are valid, due to everybody has a copy of all transactions perform in the system and preventing double spending the same "virtual coin". This reborn was possible with the rise of processing capacity of computers and its small portable siblings, the smartphones [8].

Blockchain offers a platform in which any modification is multi-validated, and this set a greater challenge in security-break actions, overcoming the disruption of nonvalid actors (as simulated sensors) in the network.

Main Blockchain concepts are, which are necessary to understand it:

1. *Operation/transaction*: each single change made in the items managed by the Blockchain. If it is cryptocurrency based, each expense of the "coins". In our case, device based, each request made, like: get data, save data, access to data, set action, etc.
2. *Block*: changes are collected in groups, these are called blocks. It contains a header with at least: hash off the previous block, miners address and creation time. Body includes a list with all transactions. Other fields can be added to the header like: software version, validation test, and any other blockchain implementer will add.
3. *Clients*: agents which can connect to the Blockchain only as viewers, with no other valid operation.
4. *Miners*: are agents with operation/transaction and validation capabilities. These blockchain agents have a double work, create operations/transactions which are recorded in a block, and validate all other miners suggested blocks to be added to the chain.
5. *Chain*: collection of valid and validated blocks.
6. *Proof-of-Work (POW)*: test perform to validate block contain. Sometimes, it is replaced by a simple check, depending on the implementation and the scope of the blockchain solution. This check can be performed by the use of a smart contract, which is a piece of code running in our blockchain.
7. *Mining process (validation process)*: when a block is full, by time or capacity, it is sent to be validated by all the miners. If the response of the majority of the miners is positive, block is appended to the main chain. Otherwise is rejected and all information recorded in is lost, because it could be malicious or corrupt data.

8. *Consensus protocol*: mining/validation operation is launched by a miner, and the rest of the miners can accept or reject the block. In order to not overload blockchain, some consensus should be adopted to approve a block. If miner number is low, Practical Byzantine Fault Tolerance can be used, it set a maximum value of failures of 1/3 of the miners (f), if this value is raised, and block is rejected. On the other hand, if ($f+1$) value is raised, block is considered as valid, the value which is shown first set the final state of the block. For environments with great amount of miners, other consensus protocols can be used.
9. *Fork*: when two different valid blocks are sent for validation, a division of the chain can be done. There are soft-forks and hard-forks. In first ones, both streams can be validated with the previous blockchain blocks. These kinds of forks are forbidden in cryptocurrency blockchains. Hard-forks are produced by a change in software, and with the new version previous blocks in the chain cannot be validated, creating two streams.
10. *Smart contract*: second generation blockchain allows to create pieces of scripting which run inner of the blockchain generating operations inside. To validate the contract, miners should create a block which includes it inside. If the block is approved, smart contract begins to work. It is running till it is valid to continue performing its tasks. This tool helps to automatise some operations and checks. This tool when is validated cannot be modified, creating a secure programmable method out of the standard blockchain behaviour.

Blockchain paradigm helps to make each transaction unique and secure, avoiding encryption of all the transaction data, some can be public and sensitive content can be encrypted, making it valid in raw based on its mechanism. M. A. Khan et al. and X. Li et al., shows another vulnerabilities in the blockchain use: "*Despite providing robust approaches for securing IoT, the blockchain systems are also vulnerable* [9]. *The consensus mechanism depending upon the miner's hashing power can be compromised, thereby allowing the attacker to host the blockchain. Similarly, the private keys with limited randomness can be exploited to compromise the blockchain accounts. Effective mechanisms yet need to be defined to ensure the privacy of transactions and avoid race attacks which may result in double spending during transactions*" [4], which sets us in the path of making our blockchain robust implies use a fast but strong enough consensus mechanism (POW) as well as set a hash generating mechanism which allows us to grow almost limitless for our implementation, but keeping in mind that performance is as important as security.

Blockchain, can be used to: enumerate valid sensors/actuators, include software updates for our network devices, schedule them to avoid DoS in any device, validate sensor operating ranges for data sent, virtualise them in order there is no direct access to the device, or even, create a validated use history of measures and actions. Best approximation to cybersecurity, is the use of all these methods merged in a full solution.

4 IIoT + Blockchain, an Affordable Combination

Based on the IoT ecosystem requirements, there are three types of cyber-attack which can affect significantly to sensors and actuators: DDoS, MitM and eavesdropping (data sniffing); and there is one, birthday attack, which can affect to the first security layer if is based on blockchain.

Each problem in the IoT devices should be studied and check if blockchain can help in its solution:

1. To avoid direct access to devices, especially when these devices are insecure, virtualisation of them can be an effective solution. This virtualisation is controlled through blockchain, and only certified agents or applications can access to the Virtualised IoT Network. Based in M. Samaniego et al. investigations, with this decoupling of the control plane and the data plane, a new concept is shown based on the Software-Defined Networking (SDN), which is the Software-Defined IoT (SD-IoT) [10].
2. Update of devices, operating system or application layer, should be also controlled by a blockchain layer, allowing only certified updates to be included in the Update Work Stream and in the Update Blockchain. This concept, allows only certified agents set mandatory updates, schedule them in low work hours and also scale the update to avoid overload of the network if update requires a huge download of installation packages or package size. Badly planned update processes can drive to an inner DDoS attack, perform by the enterprise IT team by mistake.
3. Blockchain can be also applied to security backups of any device in the network, virtual or real. If devices allow it, a security copy of their state-of-art previous to the update can be periodically saved, registered and secured, if any update fails, the device is corrupted or has arrived to the end of its working live, based on the backup copy, can be restored, in the first case or replaced with a copy of its current state minimising the impact of this event in the network.
4. Cluster creation based in an advanced controller overcomes some of the insecure devices problems, which via a blockchain with a cluster controller, allows to connect and disconnect devices in the network. Only registered (certified) devices in a cluster controller can interchange information with other cluster devices or even with devices in the same cluster. Cluster creation can only include one device, like a smartphone, which is identified as a single device cluster with enough capability to run some of the blockchain process inside. Other devices which similar capabilities, like laptops or workstations, can be considered in the same way.
5. Data traceability, all operations can be traced in a Blockchain, and if this has also a header of permissions which can only be altered by a real agent with the corresponding rights and certified by at least two agents more, the operation blockchain helps to trace any operation which occurs in the network. These special agents are called permission miners, and should be always different from the data traceability miners. This is the only case where the change of part

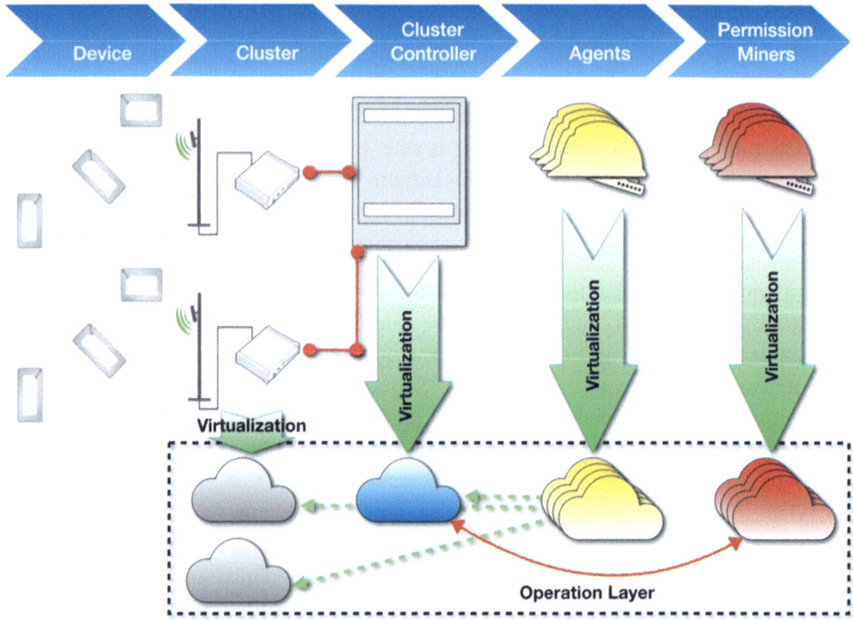

Fig. 2 Arrange of an IoT virtualised network

of the header of the blockchain should open a new branch closing the previous one.

This is basically the first layer of securitisation which can be reached based on blockchain technology. Figure 2 illustrates all these features:

Some characteristics are:

1. Each blockchain layer requires to have its own POW, different hash generation and also header contain. If it is developed in this way, a malicious attacker which breaks hash generation in a blockchain layer, birthday attack, cannot affect to the rest of layers, which can close its relation to this layer.
2. POW can be substituted in high efficient requirement and high availability environment, like IoT device action and data process, by a smart contract which is created as a validator of the blockchain content.
3. Nonpersistent devices, like smartphones, can use a smart contract to re-authenticate in the blockchain network, as agents or miners. Also, smart contracts can be used to set some decentralised authentication rules and logic to allow single or multiparty verification of any IoT Device.
4. All these contracts should always be run in the operation layer, which is the virtualised representation of the IoT device network.

5 Study Cases

5.1 Smart Home

Home automation creates a working environment based on sensors and actuators that connect to the internal network of the house using cable or via WAN. The environment generated from objects that get or receive data is under the IoT umbrella. These implementations have to be low cost, so there are insecure sensors, and with high performance, so they do not allow very complex environments.

To carry out these implementations, as stated by A. Dorri et al., we must group the insecure sensors in clusters that serve as working nodes, with a cluster header which connects with the cluster controller. The home IoT ecosystem must be based on the immutable layer paradigm, in which all devices are identified and registered. Any new device should be added by the Smart Home Manager [3].

There are three challenges to be addressed with this case of study are: Resource Optimisation, Privacy and Centralisation [11].

The in-house implementation requires:

1. Devices.
2. Cluster header with acts as a controller of the devices connected to.
3. Cluster controller/Smart Home Miner. This is the only miner in the whole blockchain. POW is substituted by a permission header for validating block transactions, allowing or denying them previously to be add to the chain.
4. Local Storage System. It can be integrated with the miner or like a separate device. Store method used is First-In-First-Out (FIFO) to keep all devices data and operation linked.

With this items, we are going to build a local blockchain to control the IoT ecosystem. Characteristics of this blockchain are:

1. Use of a lightweight hash creation method, reducing check times, as proposed by A. Bogdanov et al. [12].
2. POW is not required.
3. Header of each block is divided in proper block header and the permission header.
4. Any operation is validated against a permission header, which is a small set of valid operations/transactions to be performed by the different agents in the Blockchain, like devices and users.
5. Any transaction is validated against blockchain, and recorded in a block. If it is valid, blockchain sets a shared key with a valid time interval in both cluster headers in order the devices can communicate directly. Using this method eliminates the delay in continuous checking with the miner.
6. When validity of the key ends, an end of transaction operation is sent to the miner.
7. Any addition of a new device requires the Smart Home Manager to be added to one cluster node, generating a genesis transaction to be stored by sharing a key with the device using a generalised Diffie-Hellman [13].

8. Cluster nodes can contain as many devices as is required from one-to-many.
9. Smartphones, as valid devices, can connect to the blockchain as consumers generating request data operations.
10. Smart devices should be included in the permission header.
11. Only Smart Home Manager can validate new devices and modify this header.
12. Permission header modification closes current block and open a new one in the miner.
13. Local miner can be connected to other smart houses in order to create an external network which can act as a coordinated one.
14. Also, local miner can be connected to cloud services to offer the smart home information to allowed devices over the cloud services.

This is an example of an implementation of the Blockchain + IoT for a cyber-secured environment maintaining the three pillars of the challenges: Resource Optimisation, Privacy and Centralisation [11].

Also, it keeps the CIA security requirements: Confidentiality, Integrity and Availability [2].

5.2 *Smart Home Cluster for Security Enterprises*

Some security enterprises offers also home automation for customers, which can be integrated with its own anti-theft system, but some house use data also, needs to be shared in order to check if someone has broken into our property, when we are not at home.

This use case establishes a special paradigm due to some data needs to be uploaded to the security enterprise network.

Previous implementation case set the bases of an implementation of this type, creating a valid ecosystem, but we need to change three of the requirements: permission header, security cluster management, and multi-cloud data sharing [14].

Permission header needs to be divided in three segments, security enterprise header permissions, home devices shared access permissions and smart home manager access permissions. First one can only be modified by the security enterprise manager over its enterprise cloud, where customer needs to have a secured access [14]. Second one requires a double agreement digitally signed, security enterprise manager and smart home owner, which should be the smart home manager. And third one can only be modified by the home owner. This requires to implement a special control layer in the blockchain miner.

Security devices needs to be also connected to the smart home, but its management in the smart home can only perform by the security company.

Shared devices, such as door open information, blinds, water consumption, and others which indicates movement in the house, can be parametrised in order to send data to security enterprise if an abnormal operation is detected. This second group of devices needs to upload data to both cloud services, smart home owner and security enterprise.

Due to security enterprise cloud service should run a blockchain to control, classify and store encrypted all owner data, a smart contract can be activated for each customer to check if shared data is out of common use parameters. For this contract signature, smart home owner, via the smart home miner needs to validate each time the smart contract needs to be updated, allowing the smart home miner to be one miner in the security enterprise Blockchain.

5.3 Smart Updates for IoT Devices

IoT devices require that the operating system software and applications are up-to-date to avoid security holes. The firmware of devices also has to be updated, but this step is less common and usually requires a face-to-face action.

Software update like application update in a highly distributed system is a nightmare, and in this process, also blockchain can help.

First step is to create a virtual representation of the IoT environment, creating two blockchain layer, one to host the real IoT devices and the second to host the virtual representation.

The virtual resources are going to be focused on all the maintenance management of the real devices, with this the software update command will be scheduled so that it is done outside of business hours and will be launched when that time is reached, as long as the device is without load. This requires several steps:

1. An incremental copy of the current information of the IoT device as a backup copy, which will be stored until two more copies are done, discarding it when it is not necessary.
2. The update process will then launch the update download on the device.
3. Next step is the update installation.
4. Verification process applied to device should be composed by software verification, procedure validation and device verification performing a unit test in each one.
5. When all verification are marked as correct, a mark for software released is updated in the update control blockchain layer.
6. If one of the verifications fails, a rollback is applied to the sensor, installing the image backup. In this case is marked as unreleased and the verification error message is stored in the blockchain.

6 IIoT + Blockchain, Sum-Up Table

All these features are summed up in Tables 1 and 2. Values are authors' suggestion, which can be modified:

Table 1 Blockchain definition to complete an enterprise network

Blockchain type	Requires strong POW	Hash generation	Header content	Read access to other blockchain
Cluster controller blockchain	✓		Previous block hash BC software version Cluster hash Devices hash	
Virtualization blockchain	✓	✓	Previous block hash BC software version Cluster controller hash Cluster hash Devices hash	Cluster controller blockchain
Software updating blockchain	✓	✓	Previous block hash BC software version Software update hash Backup block hash Affected clusters hash Affected devices hash	Virtualization blockchain + Devices backup blockchain
Devices backup blockchain	✓	✓	Previous block hash BC software version Cluster controller hash Cluster hash Devices hash	Cluster controller blockchain + Virtualization blockchain
Operation blockchain		✓	Previous block hash BC software version Permission policy hash Cluster data limits	Virtualization blockchain + Permission blockchain
Permission blockchain	✓	✓	Previous block hash BC software version Cluster controller hash	

7 Conclusion

IoT has increased its popularity due to its simplicity, low cost and great results with a little effort, in both fields, home and industry. But IoT devices have an open set of vulnerabilities, which requires a costly implementation to solve in origin, a high energy consumption and processing overhead.

Blockchain is a highly proved technology in the cryptocurrency environment, which sets a trusted way for checking operation and data.

When both technologies work together, IoT and Blockchain, most of the vulnerabilities of both are overcome, generating a trustable environment implementation, with not high costs associated and really scalable. These are two technologies which work perfectly together.

Table 2 Block creation and blockchain relations

Blockchain type	Header modification opens a new branch	Can modify?			Read access to other blockchain
		Agents	Permission miners	Installation miners	
Cluster controller blockchain				✓	
Virtualization blockchain	✓		✓		Cluster controller blockchain
Software updating blockchain	✓		✓✓ Requires a double check confirmation, because could affect to IoT ecosystem		Virtualization blockchain + Devices backup blockchain
Devices backup blockchain				✓	Cluster controller blockchain + Virtualization blockchain
Operation blockchain	✓	✓	✓		Virtualization blockchain + Permission blockchain
Permission blockchain	✓		✓		

8 Future Research

After enhancing cybersecurity and enterprise network reliability, common operation can be mined using Artificial Intelligence (AI) and Machine Learning (ML) to study normal working patterns, explore function anomalies and prevent IoT failures.

In the end, all possible layers of Industry 4.0 must be incorporated into the company's implementation to ensure that we effectively and efficiently cover all the improvement needs that this paradigm can bring to perform an automation of business solution processes.

References

1. Benayas-Ayuso, A., & Pérez, R. (2019). What should shipbuilding expect from the CAD/CAM systems of the future? *The Naval Architect. April Magazine*.
2. Komninos, N., Philippou, E., & Pitsillides, A. (2014). Survey in smart grid and smart home security: Issues, challenges and countermeasures. *IEEE Communications Surveys & Tutorials, 16*(4), 1933–1954.

3. Dorri, A., Kanhere, S. S., Jurdak, R., & Gauravaram, P. (2017). *Blockchain for IoT security and privacy: The case study of a smart home*. https://doi.org/10.1109/PERCOMW.2017.7917634.
4. Khan, M. A., & Salah, K. (2017). IoT security: Review, blockchain solutions, and open challenges. *Future Generation Computer Systems*. https://doi.org/10.1016/j.future.2017.11.022.
5. Benayas-Ayuso, A., & Pérez, R. (2018). Automated/controlled storage for an efficient MBOM process in the shipbuilding managing the IoT technology. *SMART SHIP, 23 and 24 January*.
6. Banafa, A. (2017, January). IoT and blockchain convergence: Benefits and challenges. *IEEE Internet of Things*. Retrieved from https://iot.ieee.org/newsletter/january-2017/iot-and-blockchain-convergence-benefits-and-challenges.html.
7. Pérez, R., & Benayas-Ayuso, A. (2018). Data management for smart ship or how to reduce machine learning cost in IoS applications. *SMART SHIP, 23 and 24 January*.
8. Nakamoto, S. (2009). *Bitcoin: A peer-to-peer electronic cash system*. Cryptography Mailing list at https://metzdowd.com.
9. Li, X., Jiang, P., Chen, T., Luo, X., & Wen, Q. (2017). A survey on the security of blockchain systems. *Future Generation Computer Systems*. https://doi.org/10.1016/j.future.2017.08.020.
10. Samaniego, M., & Deters, R. (2016). Hosting virtual IoT resources on edge-host with blockchain. In *2016 IEEE international conference on computer and information technology*. https://doi.org/10.1109/CIT.2016.71.
11. Dorri, A., Kanhere, S. S., & Jurdak, R. (2017, April). Towards an optimised blockchain for IoT. *IoTDI 2017, Pittsburgh, PA, USA*. https://doi.org/10.1145/3054977.3055003
12. Bogdanov, A., Knezevic, M., Leander, G., Toz, D., Varici, K., & Verbauwhede, I. (2011). *A lightweight hash function* (pp. 312–325). Springer.
13. Delfs, H., Knebl, H., & Knebl, H. (2002). *Introduction to cryptography* (Vol. 2). Springer.
14. Shafagh, H., Hithnawi, A., Burkhalter, L., & Duquennoy, S. (2017). Towards blockchain-based auditable storage and sharing of IoT data. *CCSW'17, November 3, 2017, Dallas, TX, USA*. https://doi.org/10.1145/3140649.3140656.

A Data-Driven Traffic-Responsive Signal Control for a Smart City Road Network Under Uncertainty

Suh-Wen Chiou

1 Introduction

For area wide traffic control in road networks, the main objective of period-dependent signal decision support system (PDSS) is to mitigate protracted traffic congestion effectively over multiple periods of travel demand [1, 2]. In the presence of period-dependent traffic flows, severe traffic congestion and stochastic travel delay can be incurred by all road users as a result of insufficient provision of link capacity. As regards variability of periodic traffic flow over multiple periods, it can make PDSS task substantially more complicated. In order to better control system performance against uncertainty, a data-driven stochastic programming [3, 4] has long been considered a good alternative [5–10]. In the presence of stochastic travel demand, a few of data-driven signal decisions have been proposed with various prospective. In particular, taking account of traffic dynamic within urban road networks, [7] presented a multi-period system optimal signal control (MSO) to minimize total travel time for all road users. A data-driven stochastic program is proposed for system optimum under uncertain period-dependent travel demand. Using a macroscopic traffic flow model to capture vehicular movement, MSO can be regarded as a lower bound for PDSS under uncertainty since users' route choice is not fully considered. As it reported, MSO can achieve comparable results in vehicle delay, total throughput, and vehicle queue lengths than those did the deterministic ones under uncertain traffic flow. However, when applies to a real city road network with road users' route choice being considered, MSO can be practically restrictive due to highly intensive computational overheads.

S.-W. Chiou (✉)
Department of Information Management, National Dong Hwa University, Hualien County, Taiwan
e-mail: chiou@mail.ndhu.edu.tw

F. P. García Márquez, B. Lev (eds.), *Introduction to Internet of Things in Management Science and Operations Research*, International Series in Operations Research & Management Science 311,
https://doi.org/10.1007/978-3-030-74644-5_6

In the presence of high consequence of uncertainty due to stochastic travel delay, a renewed interest in robust optimization seeking to optimize performance against the worst-case scenario has received growing interest [11, 12]. While robust optimization being considered a good alternative against high-consequence realization of uncertainty, it may trade off too much efficiency and optimality of solutions [13]. On the other hand, a number of hybrid strategies of stochastic programming and robust optimization have been developed [14]. Among which a scenario approach [15, 16] is used to provide a probabilistic performance guarantee without knowledge of probability distribution. Considering PDSS, a few recent data-driven approaches following robust optimization have been widely noticed [9, 17–19] in the literature. In particular, [18] presented a multi-period set-based robust model (MSR) to minimize uncertain link queue over entire road networked system. In order to effectively support decision makers, a predictive model in [18] is proposed to determine signal splits. The weighted link queues in [18] are minimized for uncertain travel demand. A constrained minimax optimization model is proposed to robustly determine green splits against the worst-case uncertainty in travel demand and stochastic delay. Numerical experiments using real-world traffic data are carried out to demonstrate effectiveness and computational feasibility of proposed green splits. As compared to nominal signal control under various traffic conditions, as expected, MSR achieved relatively better performance against worst-case scenarios. Due to restriction of traffic flow in a norm-bounded uncertainty set, the solutions of MSR, however, can be overly conservative for a general road networked system against high consequence of uncertainty.

In most recent development for PDSS like MSO [7] and MSR [18], road user' route choice has not been yet fully considered. As it has been commented in the literature [20, 21], ignoring users' choice may consequently undermine practical effectiveness of PDSS particularly when applies to real-time implementations. In order to fully understand the effectiveness of proposed approach for PDSS while allowing for road users' response, a new approach can be proposed as illustrative Figs. 1 and 2 for urban area wide traffic control. As it can be seen in Fig. 2, the period-dependent decisions made at upper level, and network flow distribution at the lower level can be optimally determined with period-dependent response from road users. In order to optimize period-dependent decisions at both sides, a novel two-stage approach in Fig. 3 is proposed in this chapter. The contribution and novelty made to the field of Internet of Things in the Management Science and Operations Research can be summarized as follows.

1. A period-dependent signal decision support system (PDSS) is proposed, and can be formulated as a stochastic mathematical program with equilibrium constraints (SMPEC).
2. Since SMPEC is notoriously difficult to solve [22], a new SMPEC2 model using smoothing function is proposed. As it can be seen in Fig. 3, two period-dependent optimization problems under stochastic travel delay are respectively presented.
3. A novel two-stage solution approach for SMPEC2 is proposed in Fig. 3 to approximately solve the SMPEC2 with stochastic travel delay.

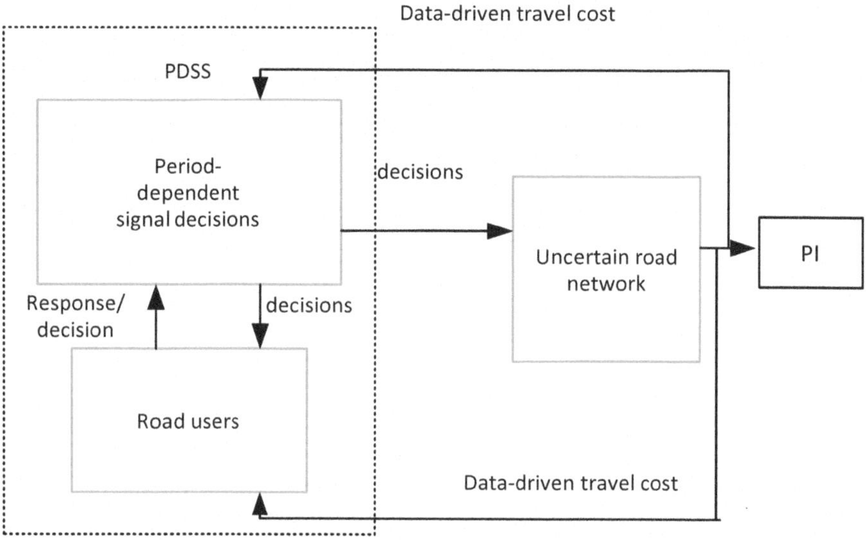

Fig. 1 Period-dependent signal decision support system (PDSS)

4. In order to demonstrate feasibility of proposed model, numerical experiments at a real-data city road network [23] are performed. In order to understand computational effectiveness of proposed model, numerical comparisons are made with existing the state-of-the-art data-driven signal controls.
5. In order to investigate feasibility robustness and loss of proposed model under uncertainty, numerical experiments and comparisons are made with recently proposed alternatives like MSO and MSR. These results obviously indicate that proposed model can achieve reliably better performance than did recently proposed ones while attenuating sub-optimality effectively.

The rest of the chapter is organized as follows. Section 2 presents preliminary results for period-dependent user equilibrium with stochastic travel delay. Section 3 presents a PDSS traffic-responsive signal control with stochastic travel delay. Section 4 presents a novel solution approach for the proposed model. A novel two-stage solution method is presented. In Sect. 5, numerical computations using a real-data Sioux Falls city road network [23] are performed. Numerical comparisons with recently proposed data-driven signal controls such as MSO and MSR are also made. Section 6 concludes this chapter and proposes future extension to topics of interest.

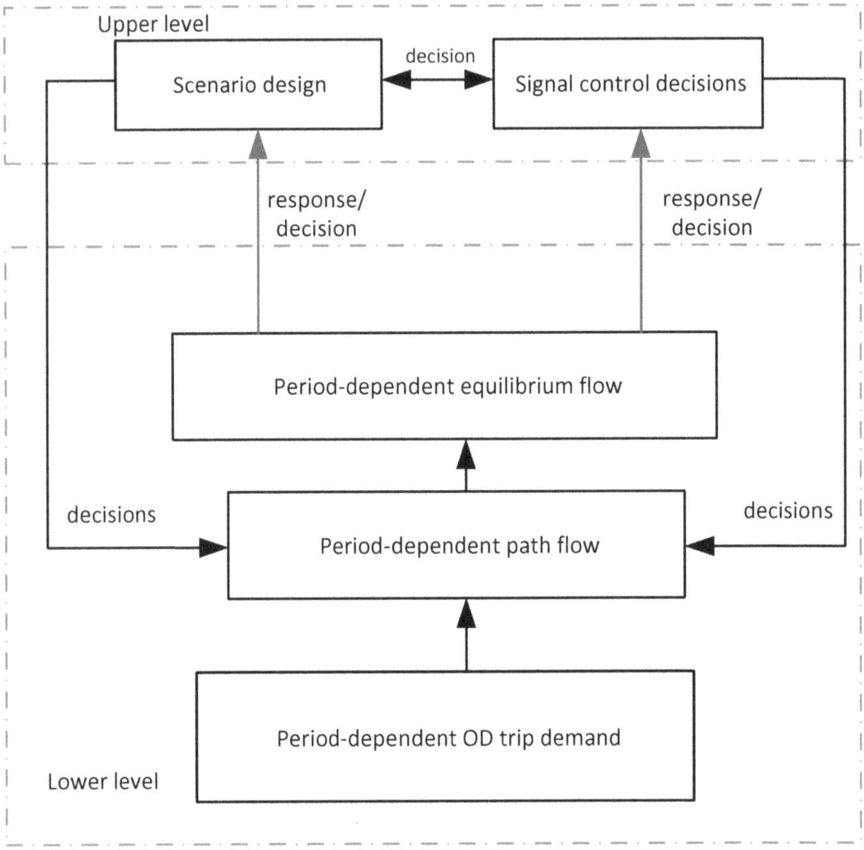

Fig. 2 Architecture of PDSS

2 A Period-Dependent User Equilibrium with Stochastic Travel Delay

For period-dependent signal decision system (PDSS), a user equilibrium following Wardrop's principle with stochastic travel delay can be presented as a complementarity problem. For PDSS subject to stochastic travel delay on links, a data-driven travel cost model is proposed to regulate stochastic link travel times. Despite robust optimization is generally regarded as a good alternative against high-consequence realization of uncertain link delay, it can lead to overly conservatism in practice. In order to attenuate sub-optimality of stochastic traffic flow, a data-driven travel cost is proposed in this section. Notation used throughout this chapter is introduced first.

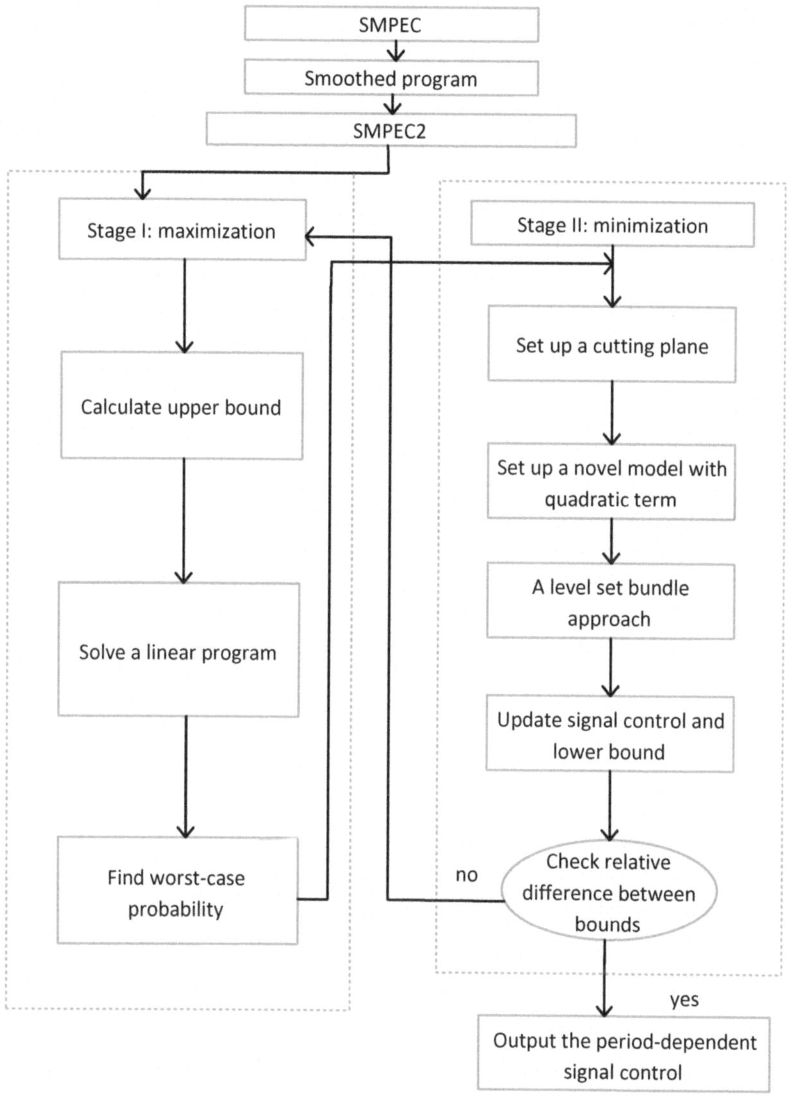

Fig. 3 A two-stage solution approach

2.1 Notation

Let $G(N, L)$ denote a directed road network, where N represents a set of signal-controlled junctions and L represents a set of links denoted by (i,j), $\forall\ (i, j) \in L$, $\forall\ i, j \in N$.

C—a set of origin-destination (OD) pairs.

Ξ—a set of scenarios with index s, $s = 1, 2, \ldots, |\Xi|$.

T—a set of multiple periods.

ζ^t—the reciprocal of common cycle time during t period, $\forall\ t \in T$.

$\tilde{\zeta}, \hat{\zeta}$—the minimum and maximum reciprocals of common cycle time.

$\theta^t = \left[\theta^t_{am}\right]$—the vector of starts of green as proportions of cycle time during t period where θ^t_{am} is start of next green for signal group a at junction m.

$\varphi^t = \left[\varphi^t_{am}\right]$—the vector of durations of green as proportions of cycle time during t period where φ^t_{am} is the duration of green for signal group a at junction m.

γ_{abm}—the clearance time between the end of green for signal group a and the start of green for incompatible signal group b at junction m.

$\Psi^t = (\zeta^t, \theta^t, \varphi^t)$—the set of signal setting variables during t period, respectively for the reciprocal of common cycle time, start and duration of greens.

$g^t_{(i,j)}$—link effective green during t period, $\forall\ (i,j) \in L$.

$\tilde{g}$—the minimum green.

$T_m(a, b)$—collection of numbers 0 and 1 for each pair of incompatible signal groups at junction m, where $T_m(a, b) = 0$ if the start of green for signal group a precedes that of b and 1, otherwise.

$\rho^t_{(i,j)}$—maximum degree of link saturation during t period, $\forall\ t \in T, \forall\ (i,j) \in L$

$\mu^t_{(i,j)}$—saturation link flow during t period, $\forall\ t \in T, \forall\ (i,j) \in L$.

$Q^t = \left[Q^t_w\right]$—OD trip demand matrix during t period, $\forall\ t \in T, \forall\ w \in C$.

$\overline{d}^t_{(i,j)}$—average link delay during t period, $\forall\ t \in T, \forall\ (i,j) \in L$.

$\sigma^t_{(i,j)}$—upside perturbation in link delay during t period, $\forall\ t \in T, \forall\ (i,j) \in L$.

$d^{s,t}_{(i,j)}$—a data-driven link delay during t period under scenario s, $\forall\ s \in \Xi$, $\forall\ t \in T, \forall\ (i,j) \in L$.

$D^t_{(i,j)}, E^t_{(i,j)}$—respectively denote link delay rate and number of stops per unit time during t period, $\forall\ t \in T, \forall\ (i,j) \in L$.

W_D—weighting factor for rate of delay D.

W_E—weighting factor for number of stops E.

M_D—monetary factor associated with D.

M_E—monetary factor associated with E.

α—converting factor from delay rate D to number of stops E.

(continued)

Γ^t—uncertainty budget during t period for stochastic delay, $\forall\ t \in T$.
$p^{s,t}_{(i,j)}$—probability of occurrence of stochastic link delay under scenario s during t period, $\forall\ s \in \Xi, \forall\ t \in T, \forall\ (i,j) \in L$.
$f^t_{(i,j)}$—link flow during t period, $\forall\ t \in T, \forall\ (i,j) \in L$.
λ—link-path incidence matrix.
Λ—OD-path incidence matrix.
h^t—path flow vector during t period, $\forall\ t \in T$.
$c^0_{(i,j)}$—link cruise travel time, $\forall\ (i,j) \in L$.
$c^t_{(i,j)}, c^{s,t}_{(i,j)}$—respectively denote mean and data-driven link travel time during t period under scenario s, $\forall\ s \in \Xi, \forall\ t \in T, \forall\ (i,j) \in L$.
τ^t_i—minimum node arrival time during t period, $\forall\ t \in T, \forall\ i \in N$.
$\pi^t_{(i,J)}$—minimum link travel time during t period, $\forall\ t \in T, \forall\ (i,j) \in L$.

2.2 A Data-Driven Period-Dependent Travel Delay

For period-dependent decisions at downstream traffic signals $\Psi^t = (\zeta^t, \theta^t, \varphi^t)$, a data-driven link delay $d^{s,t}_{(i,j)}$ lying in $\left[d^t_{(i,j)}, \overline{d}^t_{(i,j)} + \sigma^t_{(i,j)}\right]$ can be introduced in this section.

Let Δ^t denote a link flow distribution for period-dependent demand Q^t such that

$$\Delta^t = \{ f^t : f^t = \lambda h^t, \Lambda h^t = Q^t, h^t \geq 0\} \tag{1}$$

Also, let $\omega^{s,t}_{(i,j)}$ denote a link scaled deviation constrained by a period-dependent budget Γ^t for data-driven delay $d^{s,t}_{(i,j)}$ such that for every period-dependent flow $f^t \in \Delta^t$,

$$\begin{aligned} d^{s,t}_{(i,j)} &= d^{s,t}_{(i,j)}(\Psi^t, f^t) = \overline{d}^t_{(i,j)} + \omega^{s,t}_{(i,j)} \cdot \sigma^t_{(i,j)}, \quad \forall\ (i,j) \in L \\ \text{with} \quad & \sum_{s=1}^{|\Xi|} \omega^{s,t}_{(i,j)} \leq \Gamma^t \\ \text{and} \quad & \omega^{s,t}_{(i,j)} \in \{0,1\}, \quad \forall\ s \in \Xi, \quad \forall\ (i,j) \in L \end{aligned} \tag{2}$$

A data-driven link travel delay for every period t can be defined as follows. For every data-driven probability $p^{s,t}_{(i,j)}$ over all scenarios on links according to Eq. (2), it implies

$$d^t_{(i,j)}(\Psi^t, f^t) = \sum_{s=1}^{|\Xi|} p^{s,t}_{(i,j)} \cdot d^{s,t}_{(i,j)}(\Psi^t, f^t)$$
$$\text{with} \quad \sum_{s=1}^{|\Xi|} p^{s,t}_{(i,j)} = 1, \quad \forall\ (i,j) \in L \tag{3}$$

Since a period-dependent link travel time can be calculated as a sum of cruise travel time $c^0_{(i,j)}$, and data-driven delay Eq. (2), a period-dependent link travel time can be expressed as follows.

$$c^{s,t}_{(i,j)}(\Psi^t, f^t) = c^0_{(i,j)} + d^{s,t}_{(i,j)}(\Psi^t, f^t) \tag{4}$$

According to Eq. (3), Eq. (4) can be re-expressed:

$$c^t_{(i,j)}(\Psi^t, f^t) = c^0_{(i,j)} + d^t_{(i,j)}(\Psi^t, f^t) \tag{5}$$

Or in a vector form:

$$c^t(\Psi^t, f^t) = c^0 + d^t(\Psi^t, f^t) \tag{6}$$

2.3 A User Equilibrium Expressed as a Complementarity Problem

According to Wardrop's first principle, a user equilibrium for period-dependent demand constraint Eq. (1) over multiple periods can be expressed as a complementarity problem. For period-dependent link flow $f^t_{(i,j)}$ subject to Eq. (1), according to Eq. (5), it implies

$$\begin{aligned} & f^t_{(i,j)} \cdot \left(c^t_{(i,j)}(\Psi^t, f^t) + \tau^t_i - \tau^t_j \right) = 0 \\ & c^t_{(i,j)}(\Psi^t, f^t) + \tau^t_i \geq \tau^t_j \\ & f^t_{(i,j)} \geq 0, \quad \forall\ (i,j) \in L \end{aligned} \tag{7}$$

According to Eq. (5), it implies that for every link with positive flow, i.e., $f^t_{(i,j)} > 0$, the minimum node arrival time τ^t_j equals those minimum node arrival time τ^t_j, plus a period-dependent link travel time $c^t_{(i,j)}$ Eq. (5). By definition, for $\forall\ (i, j) \in L, \ \forall\ i, j \in N$, it holds that

$$\pi^t_{(i,j)} = \tau^t_j - \tau^t_i \tag{8}$$

The complementarity Eq. (7) can be re-expressed as a following vector form:

$$\begin{aligned} &f^t \cdot (c^t(\Psi^t, f^t) - \pi^t) = 0 \\ &c^t(\Psi^t, f^t) \geq \pi^t \\ &f^t \geq 0 \end{aligned} \tag{9}$$

3 A PDSS Traffic-Responsive Signal Control

As shown in Fig. 2, a PDSS with equilibrium constraints Eq. (9) under stochastic delay can be formulated as a stochastic mathematical program with equilibrium constraints (SMPEC). Consider data-driven travel time in Eqs. (2) and (3). A data-driven SMPEC can be presented to minimize total traffic queue for all users while occurrence of uncertainty being maximized.

3.1 *Constraints for Period-Dependent Traffic Signals*

For signal-controlled junctions, the constraint set Π for period-dependent signal control variables $\Psi^t = (\zeta^t, \theta^t, \varphi^t)$ can be represented according to [24]. First, the cycle time constraint can be expressed as

$$\widetilde{\zeta} \leq \zeta^t \leq \widehat{\zeta}, \quad \forall \ t \in T \tag{10}$$

For each signal-controlled junction m, the phase a green time for all signal groups at junction m can be expressed as

$$\widetilde{g} \cdot \zeta^t \leq \varphi^t_{am} \leq 1, \quad \forall \ a, m \tag{11}$$

The period-dependent link capacity for all links leading to junction m can be expressed as

$$f^t_{(i,j)} \leq \rho^t_{(i,j)} \cdot \mu^t_{(i,j)} \cdot g^t_{(i,j)}, \quad \forall \ (i,j) \in L \tag{12}$$

The clearance time γ_{abm} for incompatible signal groups a and b at junction m can be expressed as

$$\theta^t_{am} + \varphi^t_{am} + \gamma_{abm} \cdot \zeta^t \leq \theta^t_{bm} + T_m(a,b), \quad \forall\ a,b \tag{13}$$

3.2 A Mathematical Program with Equilibrium Constraints (MPEC)

According to [24], a period-dependent performance index (PI) taken as a following weighted sum of period-dependent rate of delay and period-dependent number of stops per unit time can be expressed.

$$P^t(\Psi^t, f^t) = \sum_{(i,j)\in L} D^t_{(i,j)}(\Psi^t, f^t) \cdot W_D \cdot M_D + E^t_{(i,j)}(\Psi^t, f^t) \cdot W_E \cdot M_E \tag{14}$$

A period-dependent mathematical program with equilibrium constraints (MPEC) can be therefore expressed as follows.

$$\begin{aligned} \underset{\Psi^t\in\Pi,\ f^t\in\Delta^t}{\text{Min}} \quad & \sum_{t\in T} P^t(\Psi^t, f^t) \\ \text{subject to} \quad & f^t(c^t(\Psi^t, f^t) - \pi^t) = 0 \\ & c^t(\Psi^t, f^t) \geq \pi^t \\ & f^t \geq 0 \end{aligned} \tag{15}$$

3.3 A Stochastic MPEC (SMPEC)

Consider period-dependent link delay with data-driven decision at downstream signal-controlled junction via Eqs. (2) and (3). By definition, it implies

$$D^t_{(i,j)}(\Psi^t, f^t) = f^t_{(i,j)} \cdot d^t_{(i,j)}(\Psi^t, f^t) \tag{16}$$

and

$$E^t_{(i,j)}(\Psi^t, f^t) = \alpha \cdot D^t_{(i,j)}(\Psi^t, f^t) \tag{17}$$

According to Eq. (3), a period-dependent link delay for all data-driven scenarios during period t can be expressed as follows.

$$d^t_{(i,j)}(\Psi^t, f^t) = \sum_{s=1}^{|\Xi|} p^{s,t}_{(i,j)} \cdot d^{s,t}_{(i,j)}(\Psi^t, f^t) \tag{18}$$

Substitute Eq. (14) with Eqs. (16)–(18). According to [23], a period-dependent PI for all data-driven delays can be expressed. For every period t, according to Eq. (14), the period-dependent PI for all data-driven decisions can be expressed.

$$\begin{aligned} P^t(\Psi^t, f^t) = & \sum_{(i,j)\in L} \sum_{s=1}^{|\Xi|} p^{s,t}_{(i,j)} \cdot f^t_{(i,j)} \cdot d^{s,t}_{(i,j)}(\Psi^t, f^t) \cdot W_D \cdot M_D \\ & + \alpha \cdot \sum_{s=1}^{|\Xi|} p^{s,t}_{(i,j)} \cdot f^t_{(i,j)} \cdot d^{s,t}_{(i,j)}(\Psi^t, f^t) \cdot W_E \cdot M_E \end{aligned} \tag{19}$$

By definition, the period-dependent delay rate on link with scenarios can be expressed as follows.

$$D^{s,t}_{(i,j)}(\Psi^t, f^t) = f^t_{(i,j)} \cdot d^{s,t}_{(i,j)}(\Psi^t, f^t), \quad \forall\ (i,j) \in L, \quad \forall\ s \in \Xi \tag{20}$$

A period-dependent PI for all data-driven scenarios in Eq. (19) can be accordingly expressed as follows.

$$\begin{aligned} P^t(\Psi^t, f^t) = & \sum_{(i,j)\in L} \sum_{s=1}^{|\Xi|} p^{s,t}_{(i,j)} \\ & \cdot \left(D^{s,t}_{(i,j)}(\Psi^t, f^t) \cdot W_D \cdot M_D + E^{s,t}_{(i,j)}(\Psi^t, f^t) \cdot W_E \cdot M_E\right) \end{aligned} \tag{21}$$

A stochastic mathematical program with equilibrium constraints (SMPEC) Eq. (15) for all data-driven scenarios can be expressed as a following period-dependent stochastic optimization.

$$\begin{aligned} \underset{\Psi\in\Pi, f\in\Delta}{\text{Min}}\ \underset{p}{\text{Max}} \quad & P(\Psi, f, p) = \sum_{t\in T} P^t(\Psi^t, f^t, p^t) \\ \text{subject to} \quad & f^t(c^t(\Psi^t, f^t) - \pi^t) = 0 \\ & c^t(\Psi^t, f^t) \geq \pi^t \\ & f^t \geq 0 \\ & \sum_{s=1}^{|\Xi|} p^{s,t}_{(i,j)} = 1, \quad \forall\ (i,j) \in L \end{aligned} \tag{22}$$

Let

$$\Pi_p^t = \left\{ p^{s,t}; \quad \sum_{s=1}^{|\Xi|} p^{s,t} = 1, \quad 0 \le p^{s,t} \le 1 \right\}, \quad \forall\ t \in T \tag{23}$$

It implies that the solution for SMPEC Eq. (22) subject to complementarity Eq. (9) have the following properties:

Proposition 1 For SMPEC Eq. (22), the objective function from domain set to $(-\infty, +\infty)$, then

$$\underset{p \in \Pi_p^t}{\text{Max}} \underset{\Psi \in \Pi, f \in \Delta}{\text{Min}} P(\Psi, f, p) \le \underset{\Psi \in \Pi, f \in \Delta}{\text{Min}} \underset{p \in \Pi_p^t}{\text{Max}} P(\Psi, f, p) \tag{24}$$

□

Let a solution set for SMPEC Eq. (22) denoted by Ω_Ψ if $\Psi^* \in \Omega_\Psi$ solves Eq. (22).

Proposition 2 Let the objective function in Eq. (22) from domain set to $(-\infty, +\infty)$. According to Proposition 1. It implies

$$\underset{p \in \Pi_p^t}{\text{Max}} P(\Psi^*, f^*, p) \le P(\Psi^*, f^*, p^*) \le \underset{\Psi \in \Pi, f \in \Delta}{\text{Min}} P(\Psi, f, p^*) \tag{25}$$

A triple point (Ψ^*, f^*, p^*) is a saddle point of $P(\Psi, f, p)$ if and only if the maximum in Eq. (22) is achieved at p^*, and the minimum in Eq. (22) is achieved at (Ψ^*, f^*), and the equalities are hold in Eq. (25). That is,

$$\underset{p \in \Pi_p^t}{\text{Max}} P(\Psi^*, f^*, p) = P(\Psi^*, f^*, p^*) = \underset{\Psi \in \Pi, f \in \Delta}{\text{Min}} P(\Psi, f, p^*) \tag{26}$$

If (Ψ^*, f^*, p^*) is a saddle point to SMPEC Eq. (22), the saddle-value is P^*. □

4 Solution Method

As it is widely known from the literature [22], the MPEC Eq. (15) and SMPEC Eq. (22) cannot be solved efficiently by classical non-linear programming methods and software due to the complementarity problem in Eq. (9) that may fail to satisfy some qualification constraint at every feasible point. In order to solve the period-dependent SMPEC Eq. (22) over multiple periods, a smoothed program is proposed. The solutions satisfying Propositions 1 and 2 for SMPEC Eq. (22) can be approximately found by a two-stage solution approach proposed as follows.

4.1 A Smoothed SMPEC

In order to effectively solve SMPEC Eq. (22), a smoothing function [25] is used to solve the SMPEC approximately with good convergence. The SMPEC Eq. (22) can be re-formulated as a following smoothed SMPEC (SMPEC2). According to [25], let $\Sigma_\varepsilon(x, y)$ denote a smoothing function such that

$$\Sigma_\varepsilon(x, y) = x + y - \left(x^2 + y^2 + \varepsilon\right)^{\frac{1}{2}} \tag{27}$$

When $\varepsilon > 0$, a smoothing function satisfies

$$\Sigma_\varepsilon(x, y) = 0 \Leftrightarrow x > 0, \quad y > 0, \quad x \cdot y = \frac{\varepsilon}{2} \tag{28}$$

and is smooth with respect to (x, y). A smoothed program for complementarity Eq. (9) with respect to some period t can be therefore expressed as follows:

$$\Sigma_\varepsilon^t(f^t, c^t - \pi^t) = f^t + (c^t - \pi^t) - \left((f^t)^2 + (c^t - \pi^t)^2 + \varepsilon\right)^{\frac{1}{2}} = 0 \tag{29}$$

Proposition 3 (Non-singularity of SMPEC2) For a smoothed program Eq. (29) when $\varepsilon > 0$, the smoothed Jacobian matrices $\nabla_{f^t}\Sigma_\varepsilon^t(f^t, c^t - \pi^t)$ are not singular and can be expressed as follows.

$$\begin{aligned}\nabla_{f^t}\Sigma_\varepsilon^t(f^t, c^t - \pi^t) = {} & \left(1 - f^t \cdot \left((f^t)^2 + (c^t \quad \pi^t)^2 + \varepsilon\right)^{\frac{-1}{2}}\right) \\ & + (\nabla_{f^t} c^t(\Psi^t, f^t))\left(1 - (c^t - \pi^t)\left((f^t)^2 + (c^t - \pi^t)^2 + \varepsilon\right)^{\frac{-1}{2}}\right)\end{aligned} \tag{30}$$

□

The period-dependent SMPEC Eq. (22) over multiple periods can be re-expressed as a following smoothed SMPEC (SMPEC2):

$$\begin{aligned} \underset{\Psi\in\Pi, f\in\Delta}{\text{Min}} \ \underset{p\in\Pi_p^t}{\text{Max}} \quad & P(\Psi, f, p) = \sum_{t\in T} P^t(\Psi^t, f^t, p^t) \\ \text{subject to} \quad & \Sigma_\varepsilon^t(f^t, c^t - \pi^t) = 0 \end{aligned} \tag{31}$$

4.2 Sensitivity Analysis

The sensitivity analysis for SMPEC2 Eq. (31) can be carried out as follows.

$$\nabla_{\Psi^t}\Sigma_\varepsilon^t \cdot \partial\Psi^t + \nabla_{f^t}\Sigma_\varepsilon^t \cdot \partial f^t = 0 \tag{32}$$

Provided with non-singular Jacobian matrices by Proposition 3, a sensitivity analysis for period-dependent flow with respect to period-dependent decisions in Eq. (31) can be obtained below.

$$\begin{aligned}\nabla_{\Psi^t} f^t &= \left(-\nabla_\Psi c^t(\Psi^t, f^t)\right)\\ &\cdot\left(1-(c^t-\pi^t)\left((f^t)^2+(c^t-\pi^t)^2+\varepsilon\right)^{\frac{-1}{2}}\right)\left(\nabla_{f^t}\Sigma_\varepsilon^t\right)^{-1}\end{aligned} \tag{33}$$

The period-dependent SMPEC2 Eq. (31) can be expressed as a following period-dependent single-level optimization problem over multiple periods.

$$\underset{\Psi\in\Pi}{\mathrm{Min}}\,\underset{p\in\Pi_p^t}{\mathrm{Max}} P_1(\Psi, p) = \sum_{t\in T} P_1^t(\Psi^t, p^t) \tag{34}$$

The sensitivity analysis for period-dependent PI in Eq. (34) denoted by P_1^t can be of the following form.

$$\begin{aligned}\nabla_\Psi P_1^t = \sum_{s=1}^{|\Xi|} p^{s,t} \cdot &\left(\left(\left(\nabla_\Psi D^{s,t} + \nabla_{f^t} D^{s,t}\cdot\nabla_\Psi f^t\right)\cdot W_D\cdot M_D\right)\right.\\ &\left.+\left(\left(\nabla_\Psi E^{s,t} + \nabla_{f^t} E^{s,t}\cdot\nabla_\Psi f^t\right)\cdot W_E\cdot M_E\right)\right)\end{aligned} \tag{35}$$

In Eq. (35), the first order derivatives for traffic flow can be found in Eq. (34). The derivatives for period-dependent PI can be found in [24].

4.3 Two-Stage Solution Approach

In order to effectively solve the period-dependent single-level optimization Eq. (34), a two-stage solution approach as shown in Fig. 3 can be performed as follows. For every period t, an effective lower bound for period-dependent PI in Eq. (34) can be defined.

$$P_{\mathrm{LB}}^t = \underset{\Psi^t\in\Pi}{\mathrm{Min}} P_1^t(\Psi^t, p^t) \tag{36}$$

Similarly, an effective upper bound for period-dependent PI in Eq. (34) can be defined below.

$$P^t_{\mathrm{UB}} = \underset{p^t \in \Pi^t_p}{\mathrm{Max}} P^t_1(\Psi^t, p^t) \tag{37}$$

Find mutually optimal solutions (Ψ^{t*}, p^{t*}) to mitigate period-dependent PI bounds between Eqs. (36) and (37) such that

$$\Psi^{t*} = \underset{\Psi^t \in \Pi}{\mathrm{ArgMin}} P^t_{\mathrm{UB}} \tag{38}$$

and

$$p^{t*} = \underset{p^t \in \Pi^t_p}{\mathrm{ArgMax}} P^t_{\mathrm{LB}} \tag{39}$$

when the following condition holds:

$$P^t_{\mathrm{LB}} \leq P^{t*} = P^{t*} \leq P^t_{\mathrm{UB}} \tag{40}$$

4.3.1 Stage I: A Linear Program for Period-Dependent PI Maximum

In order to determine an effective upper bound for period-dependent PI in Eq. (37) with respect to all scenarios, a linear maximization program with respect to the occurrence of probability can be expressed as follows. According to Eq. (21), a period-dependent PI maximum for Eq. (37) can be detailed below.

$$P^t_{\mathrm{UB}} = \underset{p^t \in \Pi^t_p}{\mathrm{Max}} \sum_{s=1}^{|\Xi|} p^{s,t} \cdot \left(D^{s,t}(\Psi^t) \cdot W_D \cdot M_D + E^{s,t}(\Psi^t) \cdot W_E \cdot M_E \right) \tag{41}$$

4.3.2 Stage II: A Bundle-Like Approach for Period-Dependent PI Minimum

In order to determine an effective lower bound for period-dependent PI in Eq. (36) with respect to period-dependent signal control decisions, a bundle-like minimization program can be formulated as follows. For every period t, according to Eq. (14), a period-dependent PI minimum for Eq. (36) can be detailed below.

$$P_{\mathrm{LB}}^{t} = \underset{\Psi^{t}\in\Pi}{\mathrm{Min}} D^{t}(\Psi^{t}) \cdot W_{D} \cdot M_{D} + E^{t}(\Psi^{t}) \cdot W_{E} \cdot M_{E} \tag{42}$$

According to Eq. (41), by definition it implies

$$P_{\mathrm{LB}}^{t} = \underset{\Psi^{t}\in\Pi}{\mathrm{Min}} P_{\mathrm{UB}}^{t} \tag{43}$$

Moreover, according to Rademacher's theorem [26], it implies

$$\partial P_{\mathrm{LB}}^{t} = \mathrm{co}\left\{ \lim_{k\to\infty} \nabla P_{\mathrm{UB}}^{t,k} : \Psi^{t,k} \to \Psi^{t*}, \nabla P_{\mathrm{UB}}^{t,k} \text{ exists} \right\} \tag{44}$$

In Eq. (44), the gradient $\nabla P_{\mathrm{UB}}^{t,k}$ at iterate k can be expressed as follows.

$$\begin{aligned} \nabla P_{\mathrm{UB}}^{t,k} = {} & \left(\nabla_{\Psi^{t}} D^{t,k} + \nabla_{f^{t}} D^{t,k} \cdot \nabla_{\Psi^{t}} f^{t}\right) \cdot W_{D} \cdot M_{D} \\ & + \left(\nabla_{\Psi^{t}} E^{t,k} + \nabla_{f^{t}} E^{t,k} \cdot \nabla_{\Psi^{t}} f^{t}\right) \cdot W_{E} \cdot M_{E} \end{aligned} \tag{45}$$

For a period-dependent PI minimum in Eq. (43), a linear approximation of P_{UB}^{t} can be established using a bundle of sub-gradients $\left\{\nabla P_{\mathrm{UB}}^{t,i} = \nabla P_{\mathrm{UB}}\left(\Psi^{t,i}\right);\ 1 \le i \le k\right\}$. Let $\overline{P}^{t,k}$ denote a linear approximation of $P_{\mathrm{UB}}^{t,k}$ close to $\Psi^{t,\,k}$ at iteration i, $1 \le i \le k$, it implies

$$\overline{P}^{t,k} = \underset{1\le i\le k}{\mathrm{Max}} \left\{ \nabla P_{\mathrm{UB}}^{t,i} \left(\Psi^{t} - \Psi^{t,i}\right) + P_{\mathrm{UB}}^{t,i} \right\} \tag{46}$$

Let

$$e_{i,k}^{t} = P_{\mathrm{UB}}^{t,k} - \left(P_{\mathrm{UB}}^{t,i} + \nabla P_{\mathrm{UB}}^{t,i}\left(\Psi^{t,k} - \Psi^{t,i}\right)\right) \tag{47}$$

denote an error bound for a linear approximation of $P_{\mathrm{UB}}^{t,k}$. A linear approximation of $P_{\mathrm{UB}}^{t,k}$ can be expressed in terms of sub-gradients.

$$\overline{P}^{t,k} = \underset{1\le i\le k}{\mathrm{Max}} \left\{ \nabla P_{\mathrm{UB}}^{t,i} \left(\Psi^{t} - \Psi^{t,k}\right) - e_{i,k}^{t} \right\} + P_{\mathrm{UB}}^{t,k} \tag{48}$$

A period-dependent cutting plane for Eq. (43) can be expressed.

$$\underset{\Psi^{t}\in\Pi}{\mathrm{Min}} \overline{P}^{t,k} = \underset{\Psi^{t}\in\Pi}{\mathrm{Min}} \underset{1\le i\le k}{\mathrm{Max}} \left\{ \nabla P_{\mathrm{UB}}^{t,i} \left(\Psi^{t} - \Psi^{t,k}\right) - e_{i,k}^{t} \right\} + P_{\mathrm{UB}}^{t,k} \tag{49}$$

Since a cutting plane model Eq. (49) for the period-dependent minimum of $\overline{P}^{t,k}$ may incur slow convergence, a bundle model using a quadratic stabilized term via a predetermined parameter m_k can be presented to reliably solve the period-dependent minimum of $\overline{P}^{t,k}$.

$$\begin{aligned} \underset{\Psi^t \in \Pi}{\text{Min}} \quad & \overline{P}^{t,k} = z + \frac{1}{2}\left(\Psi^t - \Psi^{t,k}\right) m_k \left(\Psi^t - \Psi^{t,k}\right) \\ \text{subject to} \quad & \nabla P_{\text{UB}}^{t,i}\left(\Psi^t - \Psi^{t,k}\right) - e_{i,k}^t + P_{\text{UB}}^{t,k} \le z, \quad 1 \le i \le k \end{aligned} \tag{50}$$

4.4 A Level Set Bundle (LSB) Method

In order to attenuate iterative period-dependent PI bounds in Eqs. (41) and (42), a level set bundle (LSB) method can be developed in this section. Let $\widehat{\Psi}^{t,k}$ solve Eq. (50) and let $\delta^{t,\ k}$ denote a period-dependent decision bound (PDB) between PI bounds in Eqs. (41) and (42) such that

$$\delta^{t,k} = P_{\text{UB}}^{t,k} - P_{\text{LB}}^{t,k} \tag{51}$$

Introduce a period-dependent level set for Eq. (51):

$$\mathrm{X}^{t,k} = \left\{\Psi^t \in \Pi, \overline{P}^{t,k} \le P_{\text{LB}}^{t,k} + l\delta^{t,k}\right\} \tag{52}$$

with $l \in [0, 1]$. Let $\text{Pr}_{\mathrm{X}^{t,k}}\left(\widehat{\Psi}^{t,k}\right)$ denote the projection of $\widehat{\Psi}^{t,k}$ on a level set $X^{t,\ k}$ such that

$$\left\|\widehat{\Psi}^{t,k} - \text{Pr}_{\mathrm{X}^{t,k}}\left(\widehat{\Psi}^{t,k}\right)\right\| = \inf_{x \in \mathrm{X}^{t,k}} \left\|\widehat{\Psi}^{t,k} - x\right\| \tag{53}$$

A tentative solution for Eq. (50) can be presented.

$$\widetilde{\Psi}^{t,k} = \text{Pr}_{\mathrm{X}^{t,k}}\left(\widehat{\Psi}^{t,k}\right) \tag{54}$$

A sequence of period-dependent iterates $\{\Psi^{t,\ k}\}$ with step length $\beta \in (0, 2)$ that minimizes period-dependent $\overline{P}^{t,k}$ in Eq. (50) can be decided accordingly by a following period-dependent decision operator (PDO):

$$\Psi^{t,k+1} = \text{Pr}_{\Pi}\left(\Psi^{t,k} + \beta\left(\widetilde{\Psi}^{t,k} - \Psi^{t,k}\right)\right) \tag{55}$$

4.5 Solution Scheme

A two-stage approach for PDSS against uncertainty in data-driven link delay can be determined in the following steps.

Step 1. Start with initial period-dependent decisions $\Psi^{t,\ k}$ and $p^{t,\ k}$. Set iteration index $k = 1$, and a stopping threshold $\gamma^{t,\ k}$.

Step 2. Solve a linear maximization Eq. (41) in *Stage I* for a period-dependent PI maximum $P_{\mathrm{UB}}^{t,k}$ with respect to data-driven probability decisions $p^{t,\ k}$ over all scenarios.

Step 3. Solve a period-dependent minimization Eq. (42) in *Stage II* for a period-dependent PI minimum $P_{\mathrm{LB}}^{t,k}$ with respect to period-dependent signal decisions $\widehat{\Psi}^{t,k}$.

Step 4. Calculate a period-dependent decision bound (PDB) defined by Eq. (51), and construct a period-dependent level set via Eq. (52).

Step 5. Find new period-dependent decisions $\Psi^{t,\ k+1}$ by period-dependent decision operator (PDO) Eq. (55).

Step 6. Bound check: if the PDB $\delta^{t,\ k}$ is within a threshold $\gamma^{t,\ k}$ then stop, and period-dependent signal decisions $\Psi^{t,\ k+1}$ are optimal solutions for PDSS. Otherwise, move iteration k to $k + 1$ and continue Step 2.

5 Numerical Experiments and Results

In order to understand feasibility and effectiveness of proposed model for PDSS under stochastic delay, numerical computations using a real-data city road network [23] are performed over multiple periods of travel demand. In order to investigate computational efficiency for period-dependent decisions at downstream junctions, numerical comparisons are also made with those did by data-driven signal controls such as MSO [7] and MSR [18].

5.1 Input Data

To investigate feasibility of proposed model with stochastic travel delay as shown in Fig. 1, numerical computations are carried out using a real-data Sioux Falls city network [23] with 11 signal-controlled junctions as shown in Fig. 4. The initial data set for Sioux Falls city road network is given in Table 1. To understand feasibility of proposed approach, numerical comparisons are also made with recently proposed data-driven signal controls: MRO [7] and MSR [18]. Computational results for proposed model are briefly summarized in Tables 1 and 2. Comparison results for proposed approach LSB (in this chapter), MSO [7], and MSR [18] are also

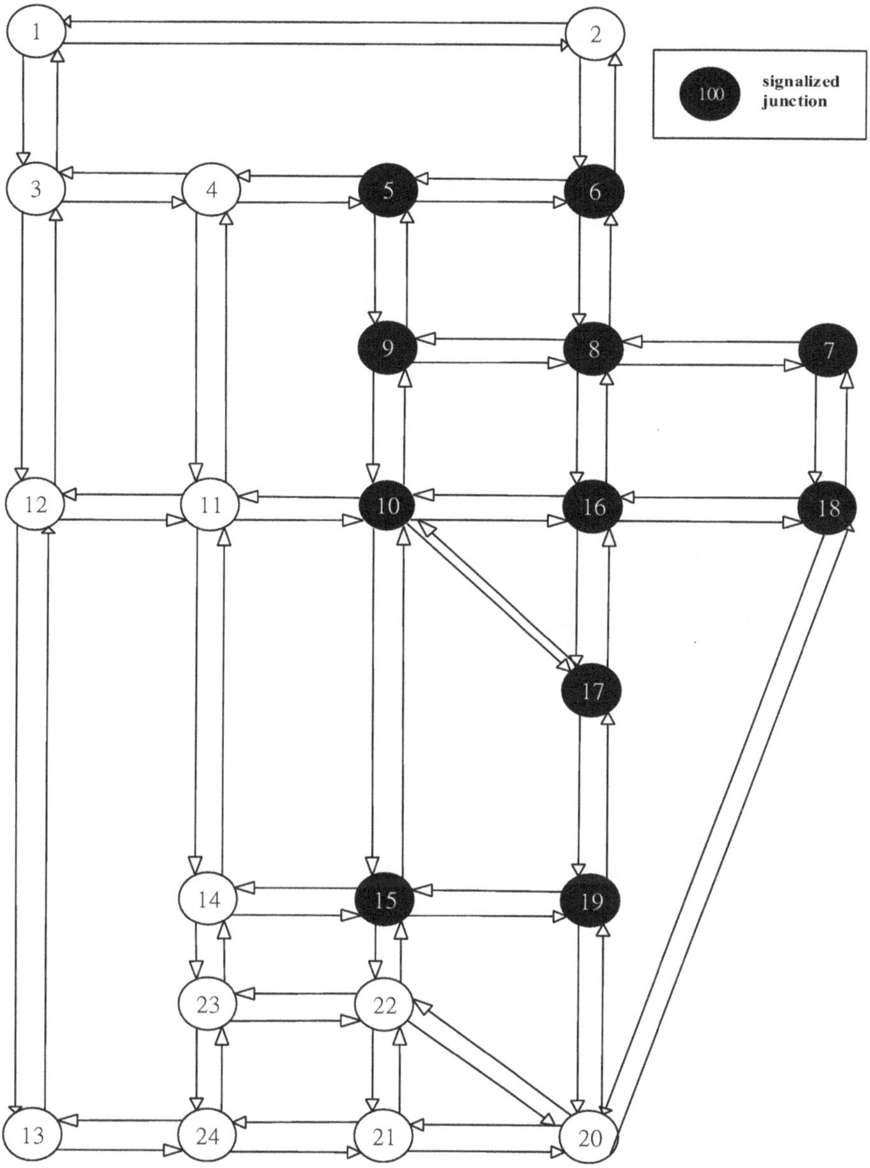

Fig. 4 Sioux Falls network with 11 signalized junctions

summarized in Figs. 5 and 6. In the following, the minimum green time for each group is 7 s using typical value found in practice, and the clearance times are 5 s between incompatible signal groups. The maximum cycle time is set at 180 s. The stopping criterion used in solution scheme is set when the relative gap ratio for PDB in Eq. (57) over PI maximum in Eq. (47) is less than 0.15%. Implementations for

Table 1 Initial data and results for Sioux Falls city real-data network

Signal settings	Initial data	Results
$1/\zeta$	90	120
φ_{15}/ζ	40	56
φ_{25}/ζ	40	54
φ_{16}/ζ	40	55
φ_{26}/ζ	40	55
φ_{17}/ζ	40	55
φ_{27}/ζ	40	55
φ_{18}/ζ	40	54
φ_{28}/ζ	40	56
φ_{19}/ζ	40	55
φ_{29}/ζ	40	55
$\varphi_{1,\ 10}/\zeta$	40	55
$\varphi_{2,\ 10}/\zeta$	40	55
$\varphi_{1,\ 15}/\zeta$	40	56
$\varphi_{2,\ 15}/\zeta$	40	54
$\varphi_{1,\ 16}/\zeta$	40	52
$\varphi_{2,\ 16}/\zeta$	40	58
$\varphi_{1,\ 17}/\zeta$	40	55
$\varphi_{2,\ 17}/\zeta$	40	55
$\varphi_{1,\ 18}/\zeta$	40	53
$\varphi_{2,\ 18}/\zeta$	40	57
$\varphi_{1,\ 19}/\zeta$	40	62
$\varphi_{2,\ 19}/\zeta$	40	48
PI (in $)	775	351

Table 2 LSB optimal solutions for Sioux Falls city real-data network

Ψ^k	P^k_{UB} (in $)	P^k_{LB} (in $)	$100\% * \left(\frac{\delta^k}{P^k_{\mathrm{UB}}}\right)$	∇P^k_1
Ψ^1	775	151	80.52	−121.6
Ψ^2	763	162	78.77	−102.8
Ψ^3	719	178	75.24	−89.5
Ψ^4	685	196	71.39	−71.5
Ψ^5	612	219	64.22	−63.4
Ψ^6	578	238	58.82	−51.3
Ψ^7	521	261	49.90	−39.8
Ψ^8	485	287	40.82	−27.5
Ψ^9	423	318	24.82	−19.6
Ψ^{10}	388	335	13.66	−11.2
Ψ^{11}	363	347	4.41	−7.1
Ψ^{12}	356	348	2.25	−4.1
Ψ^{13}	353	350	0.85	−1.8
Ψ^{14}	351	351	0.00	−0.6
Ψ^{15}	351	351	0.00	0

carrying out computations are made on DELL 7810, Intel Xeon 2.5 GHz processor with 32 GB RAM under Windows 10 using C++ compiler.

5.2 Computational Results

As it can be seen in Table 1, the proposed LSB makes considerable reduction in PI from initial value of \$775 to \$351 with improvement rate of 54.71%. As it can be seen in Fig. 5, the system optimal signal control MSO, as expected, achieves the least PI value of \$328 with improvement rate of 57.68% while being incurred intensive computational overheads. On the other hand, another data-driven signal control (MSR) using set-based robust model achieves relatively higher PI value of \$450 with improvement rate of 42%. In order to understand effectiveness of proposed LSB, detailed computations for decisions over iterations are also summarized in Table 2. As it can be seen in Table 2 and also in Fig. 6, the proposed LSB successfully mitigates the relative gap ratio for the period-dependent decision bound (PDB) in Eq. (51) over the PI maximum in Eq. (41) as computation proceeds. The corresponding gradients for LSB in column 5 are progressively increased from iteration to iteration. As it can be seen in Table 2, LSB takes around 15 iterations to obtain solutions.

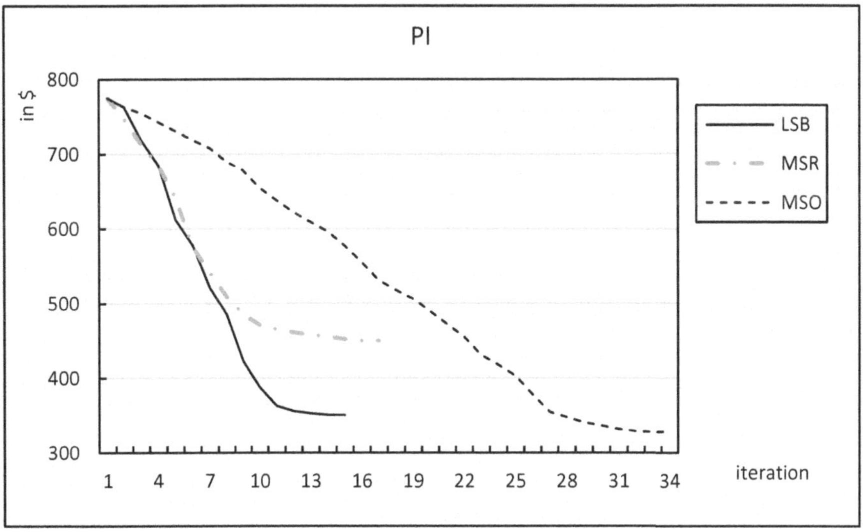

Fig. 5 Comparisons of Performance Index (PI) with alternatives

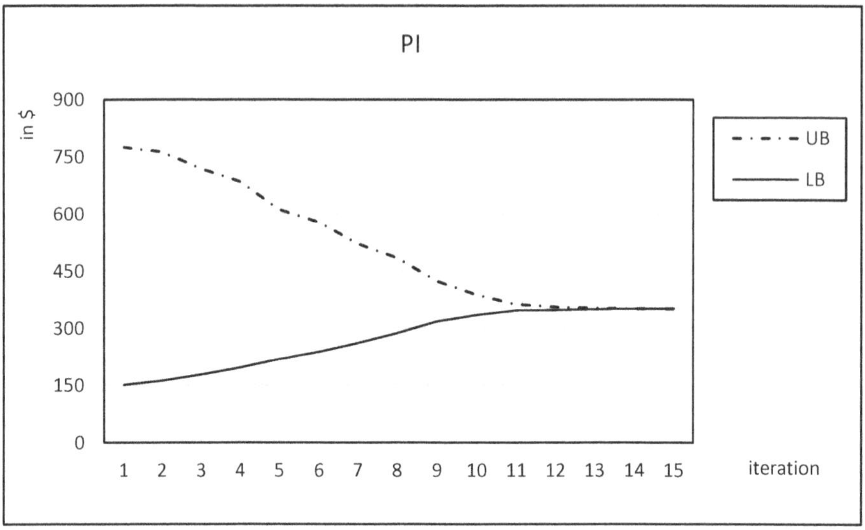

Fig. 6 Performance Index (PI) for LSB over iterations

5.3 Numerical Comparisons with Data-Driven Signal Controls

To investigate feasibility of proposed LSB under uncertainty, numerical comparisons are made with recently proposed MSO and MSR. Let P_R^t and Z_R^t respectively denote robust and nominal solutions under stochastic travel delay for period-dependent travel demands. A period-dependent robustness ratio in percentage over that did a nominal one can be given as follows:

$$G_R^t = 100 * \left(\frac{Z_R^t - P_R^t}{P_R^t} \right) \% \tag{56}$$

Next, let P_N^t and Z_N^t denote robust and nominal solutions in deterministic scenarios. A period-dependent loss ratio in percentage over that did in nominal situation can be given as follows:

$$L_N^t = 100 * \left(\frac{P_N^t - Z_N^t}{Z_N^t} \right) \% \tag{57}$$

The feasibility gain ratio between Eqs. (56) and (57) can be defined below.

$$\text{GAP} = G_R^t - L_N^t \tag{58}$$

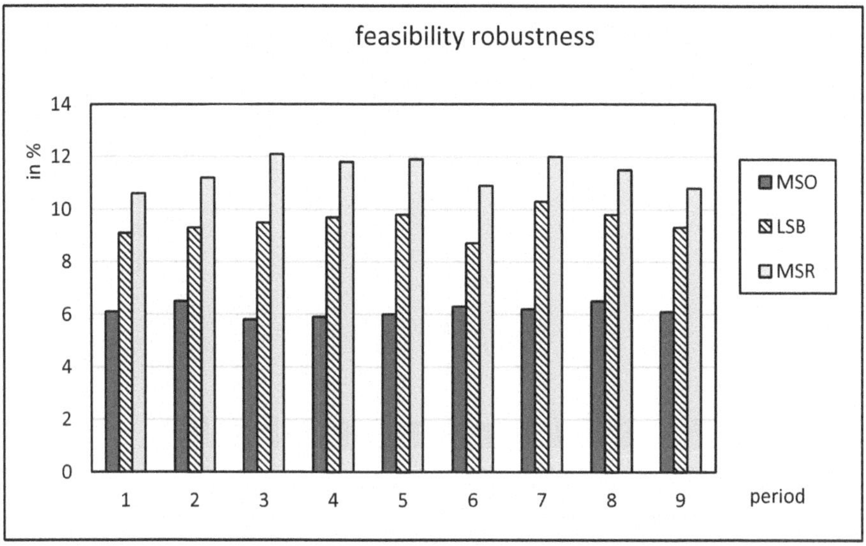

Fig. 7 Robustness for PDSS under uncertainty budget with $\Gamma = 10$

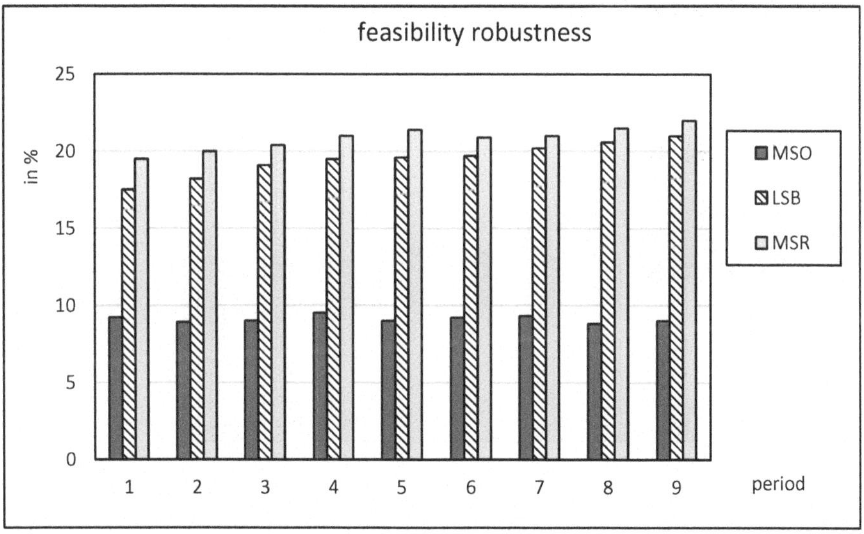

Fig. 8 Robustness for PDSS under uncertainty budget with $\Gamma = 20$

Numerical results for MSO, MSR, and LSB are accordingly summarized in Figs. 7, 8, 9, 10, 11 and 12 with varying budget of uncertainty. Computational results for feasibility robustness by MSO, MSR, and LSB under stochastic delay budget with $\Gamma = 10$ can be summarized in Fig. 7. As it can be seen in Fig. 7, the set-based robust data-driven signal control MSR achieves most robust feasibility of

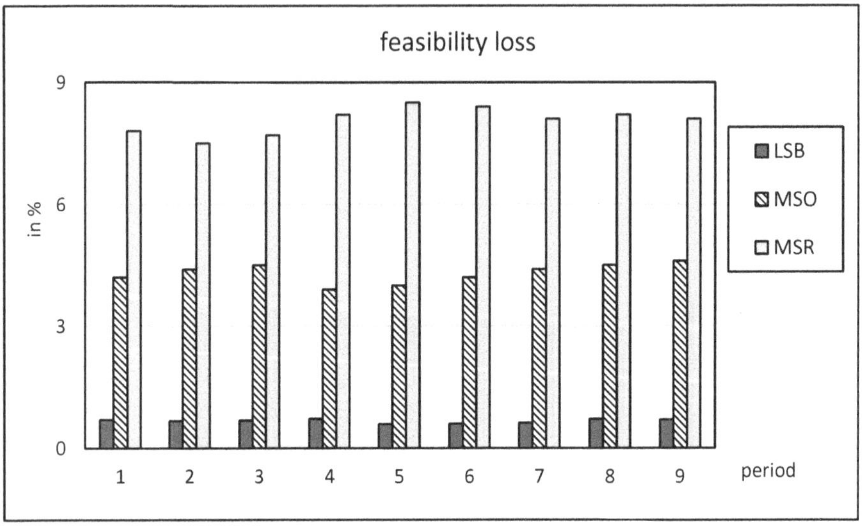

Fig. 9 Feasibility loss of PDSS under uncertainty budget with $\Gamma = 10$

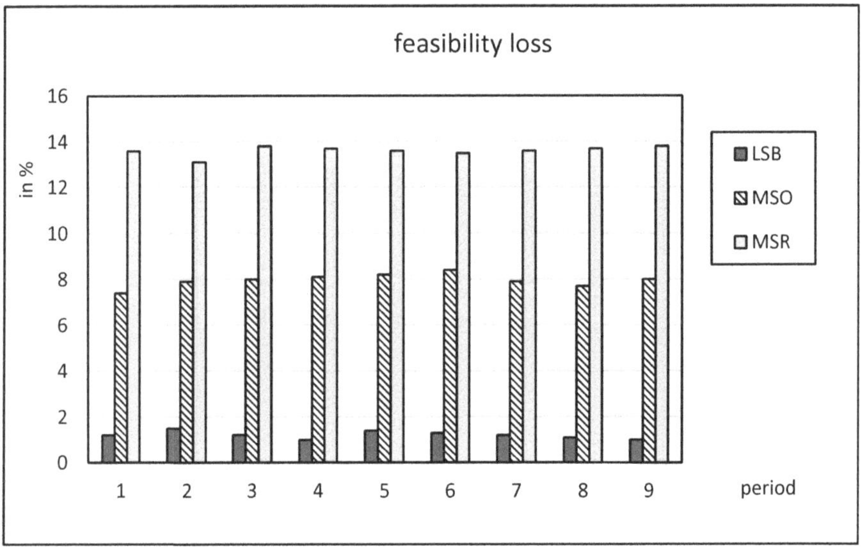

Fig. 10 Feasibility loss of PDSS under uncertainty budget with $\Gamma = 20$

all in successive 9-period travel demand. The proposed LSB achieves relatively high robustness in successive 9-period travel demand. Without considering any period-dependent response from road users, a system optimum data-driven signal control MSO achieves least high robustness under stochastic delay in 9-period travel demand. Computational results for feasibility robustness by MSO, MSR, and LSB

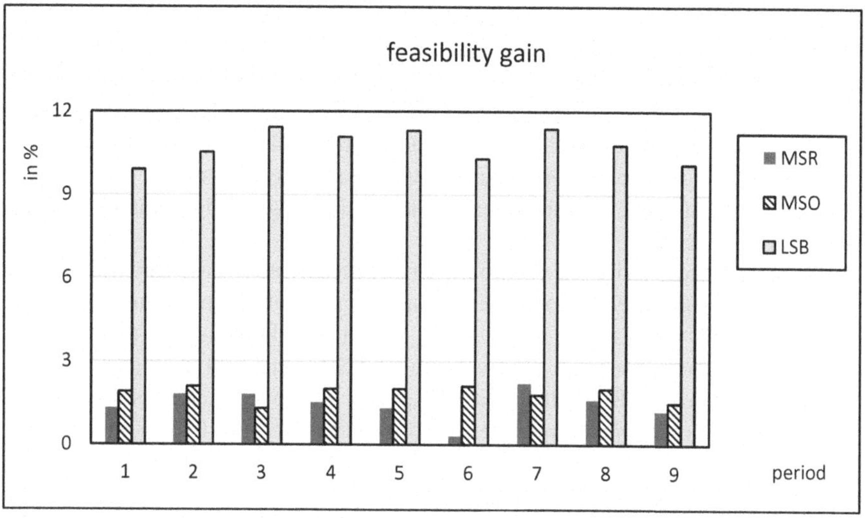

Fig. 11 Feasibility gain of PDSS under uncertainty budget with $\Gamma = 10$

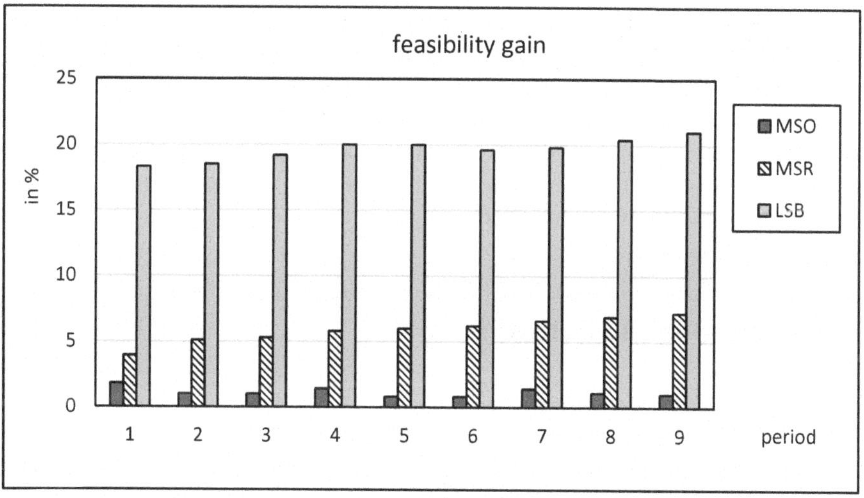

Fig. 12 Feasibility gain of PDSS under uncertainty budget with $\Gamma = 20$

under stochastic delay budget with $\Gamma = 20$ can be also summarized in Fig. 8. As it can be seen in Fig. 8, similarly, LSB achieves reliably high robustness as those did the MSR over successive 9-period travel demand.

Computational results for feasibility loss by MSO, MSR, and LSB under stochastic delay budget with $\Gamma = 10$ can be summarized in Fig. 9. As it can be seen in Fig. 9, as expected, taking full account of period-dependent response from road users under stochastic delay, LSB incurs least feasibility loss as compared to those did by recently proposed signal controls. MSR using a norm-bounded set incurs most high feasibility loss of nearly 9%. Computational results for feasibility loss by MSO, MSR, and LSB under stochastic delay budget with $\Gamma = 20$ can be also summarized in Fig. 10. Again, as expected, LSB considering period-dependent response from road users incurs least feasibility loss in 9-period travel demand. As noticed in the literature, a set-based robust optimization MSR can be overly conservative under nominal condition, and can accordingly incur fairly high sub-optimality loss as uncertainty budget rises.

The relative feasibility gain ratio in Eq. (58) between feasibility robustness in Eq. (56) and loss in Eq. (57) under stochastic travel delay can be summarized in Figs. 11 and 12 respectively with various uncertainty budgets. As it is seen in Fig. 11, the period-dependent relative gain of LSB can be of as high as nearly 12% while those of MSR gradually vanishing over multiple periods. As it is seen in Fig. 12, the period-dependent relative gain of LSB can be of as high as nearly 20% while those of MSO being nearly zeros over multiple periods of travel demand. As expected, again, LSB exhibits a most high period-dependent feasibility gain under stochastic travel delay in 9-period travel demands for growing budgets.

As it can be also shown in Figs. 11 and 12, LSB achieves a most high gain ratio of all for multi-period travel demand, and thus exhibits a best advantage of all. MSO taking account of probability of uncertainty a priori can incur a least positive gain ratio in PDB against high consequence of stochastic travel delay. MSR considering a norm-bounded set against the worst case of uncertain periodic queue, however, can also incur a least positive gain ratio in all cases. As the level of uncertainty budget increases, as seen in Fig. 12, MSO even incurs a barely zero margin of positive gain ratio while LSB exhibiting a reliably high advantage in 9-period of travel demand when compared to those did by others.

6 Conclusions and Remarks

In this chapter, a period-dependent decision support for information system with area wide traffic signal control has proposed. A period-dependent signal decision support system (PDSS) was presented to decrease stochastic travel delay under uncertain traffic congestion. Allowing for period-dependent response from road users, a stochastic mathematical program with equilibrium constraints (SMPEC) can be proposed. In order to solve SMPEC more efficiently, a computational scheme SMPEC2 has been presented. A two-stage novel solution approach is also proposed to approximately solve the SMPEC2.

In order to investigate feasibility of proposed model, numerical experiments have been performed using a real-data Sioux Falls city road network with selected signalized junctions. As it reported, the proposed LSB (Level Set Bundle method) achieved reliably better performance when compared to those did the system optimum MSO for period-dependent traffic signal control. Moreover, in order to investigate effectiveness of proposed LSB, numerical comparisons are made with recently the state-of-the-art data-driven traffic signals like MSO [7] and MSR [18] with successive periods of travel demand. As it reported, LSB can exhibit a relatively high feasibility gain over other options against high consequence of stochastic travel delay while attenuating sub-optimality effectively.

Consider recent developments for decision support on time-dependent traffic-responsive signal control system in real-time implementations [2, 20, 21]. A time-varying PDSS to entirely enhance networked information system resilience can be furthermore extended from this paper in the presence of time-dependent traffic congestion. The proposed model can be readily applied to time-dependent decision support on real-time traffic-responsive signal control where traffic dynamics and network loading for time-dependent traffic flow are taken into account.

For practical issues about empirical implementations, in this paper, we only consider a novel heuristic to solve SMPEC approximately for moderate instances. For large-sized general road networked information system with hundreds of decisions and instances, time-dependent polynomial-type algorithms for PDSS need to be furthermore investigated from the perspective of computational complexity. Numerical comparisons using a variety of large-size road networks with time-dependent OD trips can be accordingly made with other alternatives for these issues of interest, and we will discuss these points in subsequent papers.

Acknowledgments The author is grateful to anonymous reviewers and Prof. Fausto Pedro García Márquez for their helpful comments on earlier version of this paper. Many thanks also go to Taiwan MOST for financial support via grant 108-2221-E-259-001.

References

1. Heydecker, B. G. (2004). Objectives, stimulus and feedback in signal control of road traffic. *Intelligent Transportation Systems, 8*, 63–76.
2. Papageorgiou, M., Diakaki, C., Dinopoulou, V., Kotsialos, A., & Wang, Y. (2003). Review of road traffic control strategies. *Proceedings of the IEEE, 91*, 2043–2067.
3. Birge, J. R., & Louveaux, F. V. (2011). *Introduction to stochastic programming*. Springer.
4. Shapiro, A. (2008). Stochastic programming approach to optimization under uncertainty. *Mathematical Programming, 112*, 183–220.
5. Hu, C., Liu, X., & Lu, J. (2017). A bi-objective two-stage robust location model for waste-to-energy facilities under uncertainty. *Decision Support Systems, 99*, 37–50.
6. Tong, Y., Zhao, L., Li, L., & Zhang, Y. (2015). Stochastic programming model for oversaturated intersection signal timing. *Transportation Research Part C, 58*, 474–486.
7. Ukkusuri, S. V., Ramadurai, G., & Patil, G. (2010). A robust transportation signal control problem accounting for traffic dynamics. *Computers and Operations Research, 37*, 869–879.
8. Willing, C., Klemmer, K., Brandt, T., & Neumann, D. (2017). Moving in time and space—Location intelligence for carsharing decision support. *Decision Support Systems, 99*, 75–85.
9. Yin, Y. (2008). Robust optimal traffic signal timing. *Transportation Research Part B, 42*, 911–924.
10. Zhang, X., & Mahadevan, S. (2017). Aircraft re-routing optimization and performance assessment under uncertainty. *Decision Support Systems, 96*, 67–82.

11. Ben-Tal, A., El Ghaoui, L., & Nemirovski, A. (2009). *Robustness optimization*. Princeton University Press.
12. Bertsimas, D., Brown, D. B., & Caramanis, C. (2011). Theory and applications of robust optimization. *SIAM Review, 53*, 464–501.
13. Bertsimas, D., & Sim, M. (2004). The price of robustness. *Operations Research, 52*(1), 35–53.
14. Alamo, T., Tempo, R., Luque, A., & Ramirez, D. R. (2015). Randomized methods for design of uncertain systems: Sample complexity and sequential algorithms. *Automatica, 52*, 160–172.
15. Calafiore, G., & Campi, M. (2006). The scenario approach to robust control design. *IEEE Transactions on Automatic Control, 51*, 742–753.
16. Tempo, R., Calafiore, G., & Dabbene, F. (2013). *Randomized algorithms for analysis and control of uncertain systems, with applications*. Springer.
17. Li, J.-Q. (2011). Discretization modeling, integer programming formulations and dynamic programming algorithms for robust traffic signal timing. *Transportation Research: Part C, 19*, 708–719.
18. Tettamanti, T., Luspay, T., Kulcsár, B., Peni, T., & Varga, I. (2014). Robust control for urban road traffic networks. *IEEE Transactions on Intelligent Transportation Systems, 15*, 385–398.
19. Zhou, H., Bouyekhf, R., & Moudni, A. E. L. (2015). Constrained H∞ control of urban transportation network. *Journal of Advanced Transportation, 49*, 434–456.
20. Meneguzzer, C. (2012). Dynamic process models of combined traffic assignment and control with different signal updating strategies. *Journal of Advanced Transportation, 46*, 351–365.
21. Smith, M., Liu, R., & Mounce, R. (2015). Traffic control and route choice: Capacity maximisation and stability. *Transportation Research Part B, 81*, 863–885.
22. Luo, Z. Q., Pang, J. S., & Ralph, D. (1996). *Mathematical programs with equilibrium constraints*. Cambridge University Press.
23. Chiou, S.-W. (2017). Robust stochastic design of signal-controlled road network under uncertain travel demands. *IEEE Transactions on Automatic Control, 62*, 3152–3164.
24. Chiou, S.-W. (2003). TRANSYT derivatives for area traffic control optimisation with network equilibrium flows. *Transportation Research: Part B, 37*, 263–390.
25. Kanzow, C. (1996). Some noninterior continuation methods for linear complementarity problems. *SIAM Journal on Matrix Analysis and Applications, 17*, 851–868.
26. Clarke, F. (1983). *Optimization and nonsmooth analysis*. Wiley.

Utilization of Consumer Appliances in Smart Grid Services for Coordination with Renewable Energy Sources

Miloš Radenković, Zorica Bogdanović, Snežana Popović, Marijana Despotović-Zrakić, and Aleksandra Labus

1 Introduction

Tight regulations and vertical integration have long been synonymous with the energy sector, but with the rise of emerging technologies and current trends of deregulation, this is bound to change. The energy sector must evolve its primary business models that have been unchanged for decades, and embrace new technological advancements and innovation. The first step in this transition is deregulation, whose goal is often seen in forming more energy markets and exchanges for various services. Participation in these markets often requires the use of new information technologies and business models. Power grids that have embraced the importance of these new technologies and services are called "Smart grids" [1, 2]. One of these new services that seek to modernize both the grid and the business models is demand response.

The focus of this chapter is on designing innovative business models that support smart grid services, and utilization of Internet of Things technologies (IoT) as a basis for future demand response implementations [3, 4]. Through the use of IoT-enabled devices embedded in power outlets, we can turn cheap regular appliances into smart devices capable of basic decision-making and coordination. Coordination between these devices is done over the users' LAN networks. In order for thousands of devices to coordinate and communicate together, the system needs to be distributed

M. Radenković · S. Popović
School of Computing, Union University, Belgrade, Serbia
e-mail: mradenkovic@raf.rs; spopovic@raf.rs

Z. Bogdanović (✉) · M. Despotović-Zrakić · A. Labus
Faculty of Organizational Sciences, University of Belgrade, Belgrade, Serbia
e-mail: zorica@elab.rs; maja@elab.rs; aleksandra@elab.rs

F. P. García Márquez, B. Lev (eds.), *Introduction to Internet of Things in Management Science and Operations Research*, International Series in Operations Research & Management Science 311,
https://doi.org/10.1007/978-3-030-74644-5_7

in nature. For this purpose, we have decided on using a blockchain as the basis for most coordinative activities. In addition, by utilizing open-source hardware as a base for smart plugs we can remove any monetary and technological restrictions, allowing the consumers to focus purely on the ecological incentives and social responsibility.

Finally, the focus of the chapter is on considerations of the possibilities of harnessing blockchain infrastructure for the implementation of core demand response services, as well as building advanced customer services, such as loyalty programmes.

The rest of the chapter is organized as follows. In Sect. 2, we have described the theoretical background regarding the participation of individual consumers in smart grid and demand response. We have considered the ecological aspects of demand response. In addition to elaborating on the positive effects of replacing fossil fuels for electricity production by engaging renewable sources, the results of research on the negative impact of wind farms on ecology and the environment were also discussed. Section 3 presents business models for household participation in demand response based on smart plugs and blockchain. Section 4 gives the results of a pilot study on the readiness of consumers for accepting the proposed business model in the context of a developing smart grid market. Section 5 presents the conclusions and future work directions.

2 Theoretical Background

2.1 Unit Commitment and Renewable Power Sources

Unit commitment (UC) combines the dominant processes of planning and operational dispatch control of the power system. The purpose of UC is to provide a secure and reliable power supply to all energy consumers while meeting technical and business constraints. The added complexity of UC is the constraints imposed by uncertainties, such as sudden changes in consumer load, operability, and available power of generators, as well as the availability of primary energy sources [5]. Due to the technical and financial importance, methods for more precise and reliable UC [6] are always in development.

The growing relative share of renewable sources in total power production, especially the share of wind farms, can be considered from several aspects. The contribution of renewable energy sources to reduce the consumption of nonrenewable, fossil fuels primarily, and thus their negative impact on ecology and the environment, is evident. The effective involvement of renewable sources has aggravated the solution to the already complex technical and financial tasks of UC [7]. The new power system structure requires that UC methods, in the processes of planning the operational work of power systems, include the uncertainty of the availability of primary energy. Due to the stochastic occurrence of wind, short-term

UC is less uncertain, so a period of 24 h in advance and hourly planning is recommended [5, 6].

In the past, the dominant production and management of energy consumption took place at a high voltage level, starting from 110 kV and higher. Existing conventional generators, especially thermal generators, are inert and do not allow short-term and rapid power changes. The inertia and the large difference in voltage levels have left individual energy users, such as households, out of power control loops. Today, changes in energy regulations, decentralization of power control, and the establishment of new energy markets have provided the preconditions for controlling power even on the level of an individual consumer.

2.2 Consumer Participation in Smart Grid Services and Demand Response

Conventional dispatch control systems consider the restrictions of electrical energy consumption a valid approach to combating severe operating scenarios [8]. In contrast to this conventional approach, demand response technology offers an alternative in the form of active consumer engagement in order to provide situational controllable load in the form of their electrical appliances [9]. By accepting remote control of their appliances (on /off), energy users partially lose comfort but, by contributing to the operation of the system, gain some benefits, such as reduced bills for example. Two dominant models are available. In the first case, named as the curtailment method, the devices are just switched off, and so reduced power is not shifted to the following periods. The more flexible method is called shifting. Depending on the power system's operating states; the required power and energy of dedicated home appliances are shifted from peak periods to off-peak periods. Such shifting contributes to control of the security and stability of the power system and supports energy market balancing activities [10, 11].

Considering and solving problems of decarbonization in power production processes is a long-term goal of European energy plans and includes, among others, demand response technology [12]. Currently, despite its importance and benefits, demand response technology is seen as a market resource only in several European countries.

A conventional demand response implementation uses smart household devices or household smart meters. The lack of smart devices and the high prices of smart meters make it difficult to consider a conventional demand response system in Serbia. In order to counteract this, we considered the use of IoT technologies. We concluded that IoT, more precisely smart plugs, could upgrade various common plugs to dedicated demand-response-able devices at affordable prices and with minimal infrastructural requirements.

Participation in the energy market is regulated by numerous technical, economic, and legal acts, which must be incorporated into a functional business model. For this reason, as well as the fact that most energy markets have monetary barriers of entry, households practically cannot be independent subjects on the energy market. To ensure the full functionality of demand response, a demand response aggregator model was introduced [13]. Aggregators are companies that act as market participants and perform intermediary activities for the households that wish to be involved in demand response. Some of these activities include the measurement and calculation of energy consumption and validation of each households' contributions.

2.3 Ecological and Environmental Aspects of Demand Response

When comparing the share of wind and solar energy, it can be concluded that the share of wind energy is significantly higher [14]. Therefore, it is useful to review the positive and negative impacts of wind turbines on ecology and the environment. The main advantage of substituting thermal energy with wind energy is the reduction of non-renewable, fossil fuels, and the resulting pollution of the thermal power plant's surroundings.

However, some negative impacts, especially of wind turbines on ecology and the environment are possible. The main parameters of the research of such issues are the electromagnetic field of the wind turbine, dynamic movement of blades and noise, the building of the wind turbine, occupation of the land, etc. [15]. Objects of research are birds and insects, as well as nearby citizens.

Results of the published research show that wind farms occasionally change the routes of migratory birds, but the birds' mortality, due to collisions with the blades of wind turbines, is not significantly observed [16]. The possible impacts on bees are especially significant due to their irreplaceable contribution to pollination. Regarding the extremely complex nature of a bee and swarm, the assumption is that bees avoid locations of wind farms due to the magnetic field, rotation of turbine blades, and air turbulence. At the time of writing this article, apart from some individual opinions, we did not find the results of relevant researches yet. Land occupation by wind farms plants is one of the critical factors. Therefore, turbine manufacturers are trying to increase the power density of the wind turbine per unit of required land [17]. The additional negative effect of operating wind turbines is the noise whose sources are rotors and blades of turbines. Some research has shown that this noise is unpleasant to residents when wind turbines are located close to urban areas [18]. Results of measuring the electromagnetic field near the wind turbines show smaller values when compared to the values of the electromagnetic field in the proper residential areas, so it is considered that the negative impact on people and animals is negligible [19].

By acknowledging the potential public relations impact of some of these claims, the energy company hosting the turbines could implement plans to lessen the generation in parts of the grid, when for example a flock of migratory birds is near. These events are hard to predict in advance, and would greatly impact the monetary penalties imposed for breaching the scheduled generation of the wind park. For this reason, an internal demand response market could be utilized to make up for reductions in generation. The demand response services purchased for this purpose would be much lower in cost with respect to the monetary penalties imposed by the market operators for breaching the scheduled generation. Through the utilization of internal demand response markets, companies could avoid bad publicity altogether, and show that they are taking steps to avoid or lessen their potential negative impact on the environment.

The ecological aspect of demand response services primarily lies in the new role of the balancing market. Due to solar plants and wind farms constantly deviating from their "goal" energy production, the stability of the grid can be negatively affected. In order to offset these deviations, other types of generators must make up for their lacking or overproducing energy, by selling it on the balancing market. Due to this, it is often the case that in order to cover for the wind deviations, a non-renewable plant must be utilized for balancing purposes.

The approach that we propose hopes to change this fact by making the majority of the balancing market into a controllable load that can be shed or utilized in order to balance the grid. In this way, renewable plants can cover their deviations with household devices, rather than conventional power plants, the result being a green system, where there is less need for conventional plants in the balancing market.

In order to make any notable change to the environment and the energy sector as a whole, we have recognized that end-users are fast becoming a driving factor in many environmental programs [20, 21]. By focusing on the end-users, and thorough acceptance studies, a better understanding of the driving factors behind the end-users decisions can be obtained, and their eventual stance toward demand response as a technology.

Previous researches have shown that consumers' attitudes toward green energy and environmental protection are becoming important incentives for the acceptance of new consumer-centric business models in the energy sector. However, the 'green gap' between consumer attitudes to the environment and the adoption of green behavior has been identified [22] and should be taken into account during the model development in order to achieve a better acceptance.

3 A Model of Household Participation in Demand Response

3.1 Business Model

The business model that we propose offers demand response services to the consumers in the Serbian electricity market. The model is based on a system for distributed control of IoT-enabled household devices, through the use of smart plugs. Three distinct business models can be made, based on the current state of regulation. The first approach is the more conservative one, where demand response

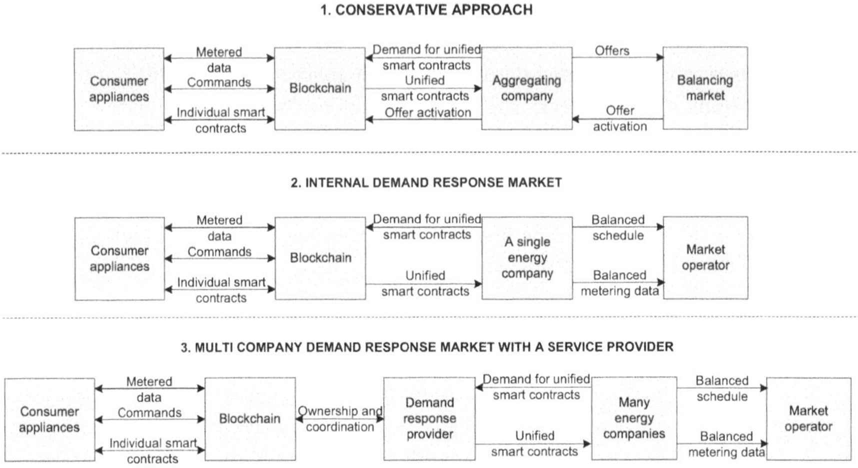

Fig. 1 Summary of the three proposed business models

activities are strictly monitored and coordinated by a single company, who acts as a single participant in the balancing market. The second approach seeks to innovate but has some regulative barriers. In this approach, all coordination is similarly done by a single company, but the company owns renewable energy generation, which in turn uses the households to balance their net energy against the fluctuations in renewable generation. The third approach is the variation of the second approach, where the goal is to maximize the benefits of blockchain technology. In the third approach, there is an only loose association with the generation company, in the form of hundreds of smart contracts made directly between a company and appliance owners. For this approach, a new actor is required in the form of an intermediary company that owns the blockchain and acts as a broker for smart contracts between the owners and the companies. A summary of all three models can be seen in Fig. 1.

The conventional purpose of all proposed business models can be surmised in providing balancing activities, either independently or on the Serbian balancing market. This demand-side load can also be used to balance the variability of certain renewable power plants by filling the gaps in the generation, or utilizing excess energy. This approach is based on the idea of utilizing individual consumer devices and aggregating their load in order to provide large amounts of energy required for balancing purposes [23, 24]. By aggregating similar devices into a single controllable load, we can use statistical models to make accurate predictions of available capacity. This is a stark change from the aggregation of entire households, where predictions can be more unpredictable, and harder to finely control. This aggregated load of individual devices can then be bundled into a single offer to the balancing market. Upon the activation of the offer, any device whose capacity was offered would coordinate with other devices, in order to work out an accurate time schedule for the curtailment of their energy usage. This curtailment is not very strict in the sense that if possible, user comfort will always take precedence. The comfort of

Table 1 Business canvas model for the proposed platform

Key partners:	Key activities:	Value proposition:	Customer relationships:	Customer segments:
– Energy companies – Non-energy companies – Utility companies – Government	– Platform development – Smart contract creation – Point schemes development	– A demand response platform for incentivizing participation and social responsibility – The infrastructure of a collaborative loyalty system for a smart grid	– Mobile app – Web platform – Recognition of the most valued customers by assigning green badges	– Citizens with controllable load – Small-scale companies
	Key resources: – Developers – The platform – The mobile app – Integration APIs		Distribution channels: – Mobile app – Social media – Partner marketing	
Cost structure: – Platform maintenance – Subventions (in accordance with the national strategy and budgets)		Revenue streams: – Transaction fees per realized MW – Partner company subscription – In-app marketing – Demand response transactions reduced costs in other related activities		

users is perhaps the key component of the business model, as their satisfaction is critical to its success, for this reason coordination of devices must be done on a very fine level, even if it results in the reduction of overall available system capacity. Once settlement of the activated offer is completed, any earnings made by the company can be used for compensation of appliance owners for their brief loss of comfort.

The business model for the proposed platform is given in Table 1. The model is presented using the well-known business canvas template developed by Osterwalder et al. [25]. The template allows a clear and brief presentation of value proposition, infrastructure (key partners, activities, and resources), customers (relationships, channels, and segments), and finances (costs and revenues).

Additionally, an alternative mode of operation for the proposed demand response network is possible; this mode puts a particular focus on interaction with renewable generation companies. Rather than placing their demand response services on the balancing market or exchange, a new autonomous "market" can be made. This new market would be based around the proposed demand response network, where the load reduction/increase services could be sold. The clients in such a network would primarily be renewable companies who are looking to buy those services, in order to balance out the unpredictability of their renewable generation. Due to the distributed nature of the demand response network, the implementation of such a market can be a straightforward affair through the use of blockchain technology, in particular the smart contracts. Through these smart contracts, the renewable company would post a certain number of contracts and user devices could bid individually or collaborate in order to meet the criteria. Once this criterion is met, a smart contract is scheduled to activate an agreement between the company and potentially thousands of user devices. By making formalized agreements between individual household users and companies, we are cutting out the intermediaries such as aggregating companies who traditionally intercede in the place of household users. This direct collaboration between users and energy companies lends many benefits such as increases in monetary incentives for users and an overall higher level of involvement of household users in the energy sector. Household user involvement is perhaps the most important factor for the continued evolution of the business model, as it is directly dependant on a large number of users and their continued participation in providing renewable companies with consistently performing controllable load.

In addition to the benefits provided by smart contracts, the fact that the network is based on the blockchain can provide some additional benefits, such as extensions that allow for further functionalities. One of these functionalities, which seek to further incentivize household users, is the capability of the blockchain to host its own loyalty program. Loyalty programs have been an industry standard for many years, and collaborative loyalty programs where many companies participate in a single loyalty program have proven to have many increased benefits for the users of such programs. The blockchain can host its own loyalty program, facilitated by smart contracts, where non-energy companies can offer discounts or services to users who are devoted to saving the environment through demand response. A non-energy company can reap positive marketing that comes with association with such environmentally friendly initiatives, in addition to potentially increasing their own revenue by reaching more potential customers.

The alternative model is not tied to the balancing market, and having its own independent market has some drawbacks. The greatest drawback is in the fact that when it comes to regulation of balancing activities, most system operators demand that all such activities be done through a single official balancing market, in a centralized fashion. The proposed model seeks to decentralize the balancing process, by allowing individual companies to balance their own energy consumption/generation by trying to keep their scheduled and actual energies to a net-zero, through an external controllable load. By allowing and demanding each company to manage their own balancing activities, rather than managing the system balance as a whole, the power grid can become more flexible. The model can be adapted to fit into the current regulatory framework, but it would have to be limited in scope in the sense that all companies that wish to participate in the demand response network would have to manage their energy net balance as a single whole, rather than individually. For this reason, this approach under current regulation could be suitable for a single renewable energy company that wishes to balance its generation/load through the use of a private demand response market.

3.2 IoT Infrastructure

By relying on IoT as a backbone for our infrastructure, we can connect disparate household devices into a single controllable system. To achieve this, we are proposing the use of smart plugs. Smart plugs are convenient hardware that acts as a proxy between the power plug and the appliance, with the added luxury of a microcontroller logic and wireless connectivity. Through intelligent control of these smart plugs, we aim to provide a controllable demand-side load for the purpose of balancing the Serbian power grid [26]. In order to provide this much needed controllable load, it has to be done through the designated energy market, which is the Serbian Balancing Energy market. One of the chief constraints we have set before us is the affordability and sustainability of the system as a whole, as it needs to be able to provide energy with minimal investment and setup time. To fulfil the limitations of these constraints, we do not rely on the complex and expensive metering infrastructures that are a common sight in the current industry standard for demand response. In addition, as modernization of the power grid is a slow process in the developing countries, advanced metering infrastructures are a luxury and are generally not available. Instead of focusing on these advanced metering infrastructures, we can focus on the utilization of widely available LAN-enabled microcontrollers that can be connected to the power outlets. Through them, we can control and coordinate the load of hundreds of thousands of appliances at a time [27]. By using a microcontroller, we can turn any individual appliance, no matter how old, into a smart device capable of basic decision making and adapting their energy use to the needs of the grid as a whole. Today microcontrollers come in many varieties, but through the use of open-source hardware, we can effectively remove any monetary and technological limitations that are common in the energy industry. Open-Source hardware results in a system that is easily understood and hardware that is widely available for any future researchers that are looking to improve and understand demand response.

The concept of the smart plug is shown in Fig. 2. Arduino Microcontrollers are widely available and affordable, for this reason, we have chosen them to be the basis for our smart plugs. Arduino-enabled smart plugs are wirelessly connected to the internet and the blockchain network where most communication and coordination take place. The communication protocols suitable for this purpose are TCP/IP alongside Restful services on the applicative layer. The use of RESTful services affords us additional flexibility and scalability due to their easily distributed nature.

In this context, smart contracts are defined and used to implement the energy demand flexibility of smart plugs, rules for participation in the proposed model, incentives, and penalties. A smart contract is made at the level of each smart plug. For each value provided by the smart plug, the corresponding smart contract is evaluated [28], and if needed, the actions are taken (turn the device on or off).

The industry-standard approach relies on calculating the base load of the household and taking any deviations from it as a result of a successful demand response. By focusing on the individual device, rather than the smart meter for the household,

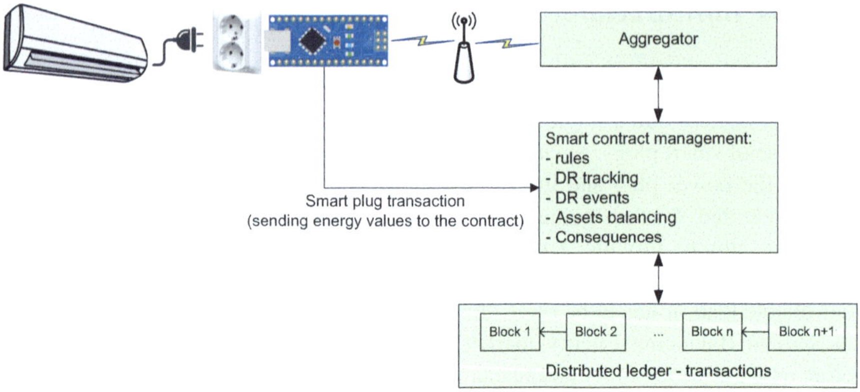

Fig. 2 The concept of a smart plug

we can simplify the calculations and the business logic entirely. The calculations regarding the "baseload" of a single device and its usage patterns are easily isolated, and as such can be grouped together with similar neighboring devices. Devices grouped in such a way are easily clustered into groups with similar characteristics and can be further analyzed and utilized for the purposes of more intelligent demand response practices. By grouping these devices into a single whole through the use of a blockchain we can make the whole system scalable with minimal investment, which is a stark contrast to conventional smart grid projects that require a sizable investment.

In order to better facilitate the collaboration between nodes, a standardized infrastructure is preferable to a custom-made distributed network, for this reason, we have decided on a blockchain infrastructure, which is the most utilized distributed network today with well-known performance and functionalities. Perhaps the most promising functionality of the blockchain is that of smart contracts that can run off the blockchain. These contracts allow for easier abstraction of business rules and make transactions between nodes possible. In this blockchain every node also serves as a storage node for the current state of the chain it is a part of, this state is achieved via consensus between nodes and is used for telling how much demand response capacity that segment of the chain can commit, for the purposes of fulfilling a smart contract. In this way, many segments of the blockchain can band together in order to fulfil a smart contract requirement for a much greater capacity than any single segment can commit to. The decision to work in segments rather than one huge blockchain is mostly due to the potential size of the network, and the limited storage on IoT devices that act as nodes.

In the sense of a traditional demand response business model, the blockchain network serves as a replacement for the aggregating companies and aims to do the aggregation of load in an automated manner. The blockchain contains the business logic which allows for communication with external companies, in the form of smart contracts. In the sense of demand response, this external communication via smart

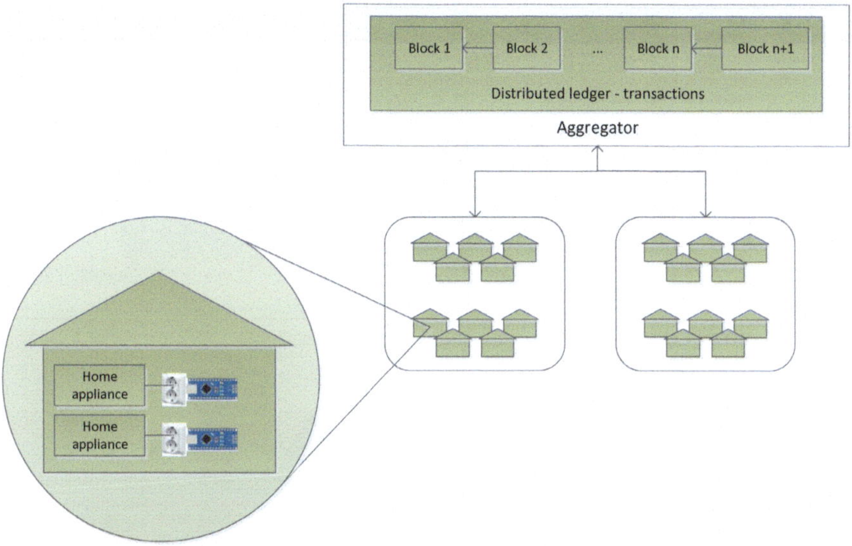

Fig. 3 Control infrastructure for aggregation of smart plugs

contracts involves B2B and possibly B2C in a market environment. The architecture of the aggregation aspect of the proposed model is shown in Fig. 3.

Every participant can use a web application for monitoring the electricity consumption of each device connected to a smart plug (Fig. 4).

3.3 Blockchain Infrastructure and Loyalty Management

In this chapter, we propose a demand response platform based on IoT and blockchain. Each smart plug represents a node in the blockchain and is capable of basic blockchain actions, storage of blocks, consensus, and participation in smart contracts. When participating in a traditional balancing market, blockchain can function at a reduced functionality where blocks can store distinct states of the network and vote on who gets priority for fulfilling activation requests. In the extended mode of operation, where blockchain is used as a basis for an independent market, the network would utilize smart contracts between companies and individual devices. These smart contracts wouldn't require advanced functionalities and would function similarly to any other system based on smart contracts. The only difference to the conventional smart contracts would be that in order to fulfill a request for demand response, hundreds of devices would need to post a unified offer in order to meet all the conditions of the contract.

As blockchain is an infrastructure that is easily extended with additional functionalities, it is possible to add a loyalty platform on top of the already existing base

Fig. 4 An example of a report on electricity consumption [3]

functions. Basing the loyalty program on the blockchain allows for a high level of transparency, trust, and the capability of trading of loyalty points between users themselves as each node is aware of the loyalty points in the network. In order to provide all these functionalities, the platform needs to become collaborative in nature and connect energy companies, non-energy companies, governments, and consumers into a single network. The goal of this platform is to provide a traditional point-based loyalty program with the added concepts of social responsibility, crowdsourcing, and participation. With the end product being to enable the consumers to obtain loyalty points by acting in a socially and environmentally responsible manner. Figure 5 shows the main stakeholders in the proposed model.

In order to achieve a collaborative platform, where points can be freely used in different companies, the platform requires proper management concerning membership. Keeping in spirit with the lack of intermediaries in the process, we propose a consensus-based system where users themselves can vote to accept, decline, or remove any non-energy companies that are looking to join the loyalty program. Non-energy companies can use this platform for integrating their existing loyalty

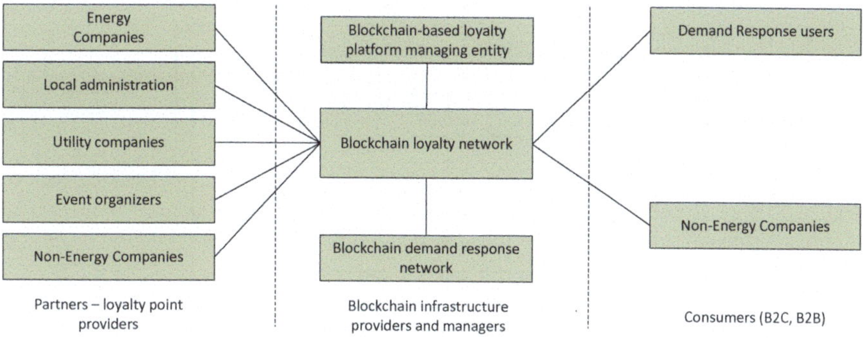

Fig. 5 Stakeholders in the loyalty platform for demand response

programs or for providing different loyalty schemes. The consumers will be provided with a mobile application as the main channel for monitoring their points and transactions. In addition, the system can be integrated with mobile wallets applications and with the demand response controlling applications for increased ease of use.

Companies that wish to join the loyalty network can do so by applying for approval over the blockchain management application. Once approved, the companies agree on rules of participation. The main goal of the presented platform is to further incentivize users and not to make a profit. In order to provide for upkeep costs, the platform can be maintained by in-app marketing and partner subscriptions, donations, and government subsidies. Partner companies can post smart contracts that are not for demand response services but serve to dictate additional steps needed in order to utilize their loyalty points. The platform takes care of a variety of services, such as membership management, subscriptions, and notifications, identity management, privacy, and data protection [29]. The communication with participants is automated, so when a participant performs an action, the platform matches the performed action with the corresponding smart contract. Depending on the scenario, one or more contracts are executed. A communication and architecture workflow for the utilization of loyalty points can be seen in Fig. 6 [30].

The prototype of the loyalty scheme of the proposed blockchain infrastructure was implemented using the Hyperledger platform [31]. Information about devices, consumers, partners, loyalty points, and performed transactions are kept within the Hyperledger Fabric [32, 33]. Figure 7 shows an example of a list of transactions for one participant.

The prototype can serve for future smart contract implementations, once a suitable IoT infrastructure capable of running demand response services is complete.

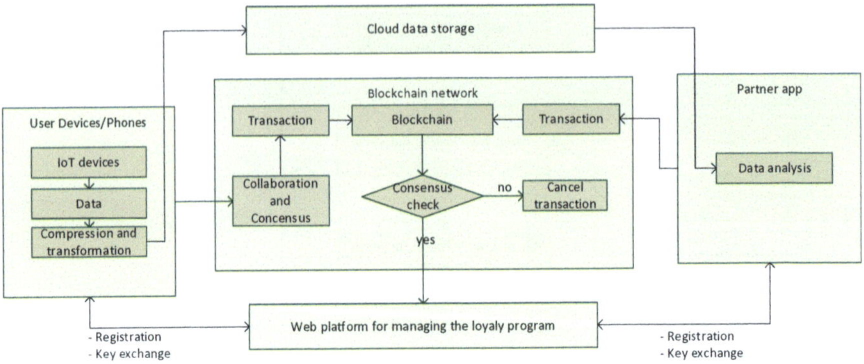

Fig. 6 The software architecture and communication workflow

Fig. 7 An example of a list of transactions

4 Assessing Readiness for Participation in Demand Response

4.1 Design, Procedure and Methods

The context of this research is the Serbian electricity market, where the participation of individual households or devices in the smart grid is not available at the time of writing this chapter. Therefore, the analysis is focused on surveying the consumers and determining their readiness to participate in demand response services once they become available. The survey was based on UTAUT2 model [34] for assessing the acceptance of technology, with modifications of this model, so as to include only a set of variables of interest. As the dependent variable, "readiness to use demand response services" was chosen, with respect to behavioral intention variable from UTAUT2. As independent variables, we considered "the attitude toward green energy" and "the attitude toward environmental protection" based on the Social influence variable from UTAUT2. Age, income, and employment status of

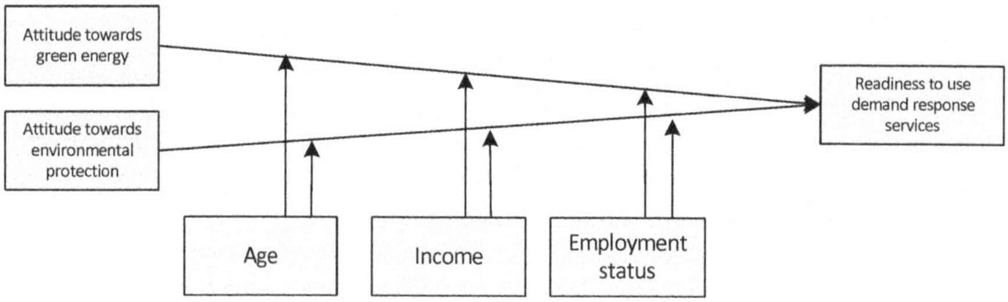

Fig. 8 Research model

Table 2 Demographic data

Age		Employment status		Income	
<30	39%	Employed	56%	Up to 250€	10%
31–40	16%	Retired	8%	250€–500€	35%
41–50	18%	Student	34%	>500€	17%
>50	27%	Unemployed	2%	No answer	38%

respondents were considered moderating effects (Fig. 8). The customers' attitudes regarding the green energy and environmental aspects were evaluated as a part of a larger study on general customers' readiness to accept smart grid and demand response services [35]. The following hypotheses were set:

- H1.1: The attitude of consumers toward green energy impacts their readiness to use demand response services, with age, income, and employment status as moderating effects.
- H1.2: The attitude of consumers toward environmental protection impacts their readiness to use demand response services, with age, income, and employment status as moderating effects.

Before taking the survey, each respondent was given details about the proposed services and the aspects of the application of the proposed services regarding environmental protection and green energy. The demographic data of 244 participants are shown in Table 2.

For the analysis of results, the following methods were used:

1. For general analysis of the attitudes and incentives for participation the proposed demand response business model, we have used standard statistical measures (means and standard deviations), and we have visualized the distributions of the data using the Tableau software [36].
2. Testing of statistical hypotheses and post-hoc analysis were done using the PLS-SEM method and SmartPLS 3.0 software tool [37]. The obtained value of the R^2 coefficient for the model is 0.337, which is generally considered as a low effect, but acceptable in the contexts such as social sciences, business research, user behavior and technology acceptance analysis [38, 39].

4.2 Results

Table 3 shows the incentives for participation in the proposed demand response services. The results indicate that respondents generally favor environmental protection (4.33) to green energy (4.12), but both aspects represent significant incentives that should be taken into further consideration.

Table 3 shows that the general attitudes of consumers are positive, but when it comes to participation in specific demand response services which cause a certain discomfort, such as turning the AC off in the summer period (regulation down) or turning the storage heaters on in the winter period (regulation up), the average readiness to participate is significantly lower (around 3.5).

Figure 9 shows the attitudes toward green energy and environmental protection moderated by age. In accordance with the results in Table 3, consumers prefer environmental protection to green energy support. Age groups 31–40 and 41–50 are more incentivized by these aspects comparing to younger or older respondents.

Figure 10 shows the distributions of the attitudes toward green energy and environmental protection by employment status. The number of unemployed participants was low, so this group was not considered. Respondents from all employment statuses (students, employed, and retired) value environmental protection more than green energy. However, green energy gets higher support from employed and retired respondents, then from students.

Table 3 Incentives for participation in demand response

	Incentive	Mean	Std. dev.
General attitude	Attitude toward environmental protection	4.33	0.89
	Attitude toward green energy	4.12	0.97
Regulation up	Contribution to environmental protection	3.54	1.35
	Contribution to green energy	3.58	1.32
Regulation down	Contribution to environmental protection	3.57	1.37
	Contribution to green energy	3.58	1.32

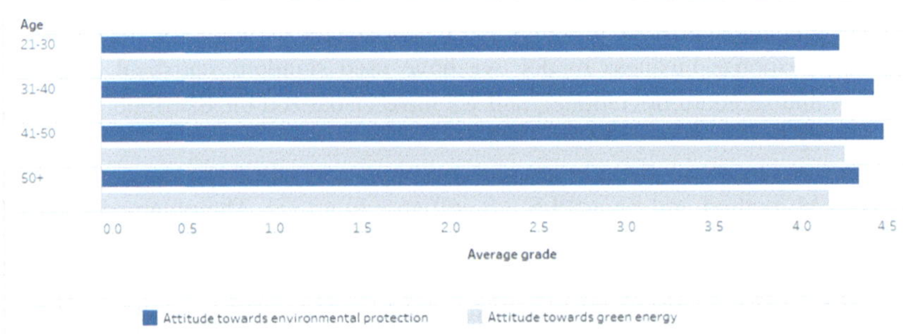

Fig. 9 Distribution of attitudes toward green energy and environmental protection by age

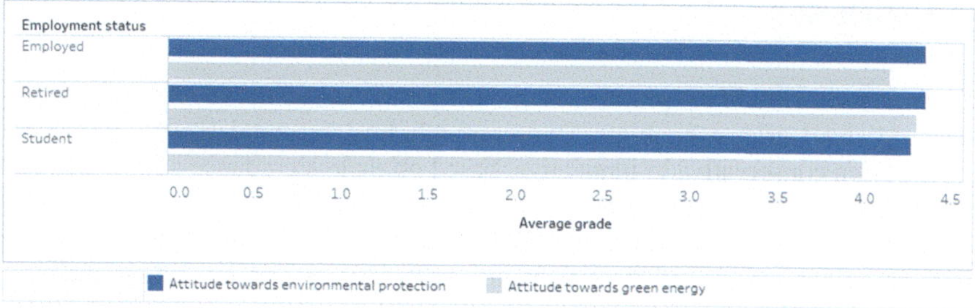

Fig. 10 Distribution of attitudes toward green energy and environmental protection by employment status

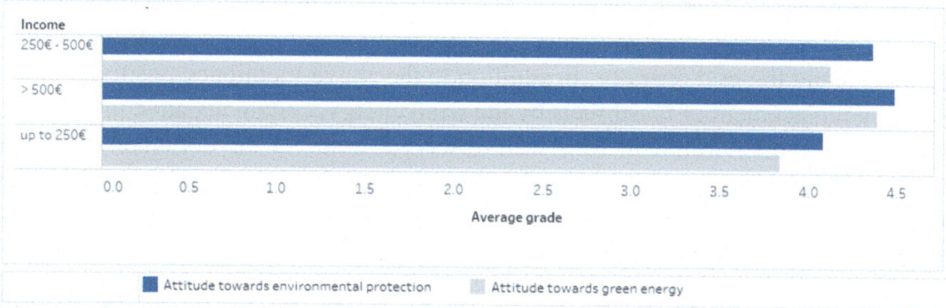

Fig. 11 Distribution of attitudes toward green energy and environmental protection by income

Figure 11 shows that the respondents with the highest incomes value green energy and environmental protection more than consumers with lower incomes. Expectedly, the lowest support to both aspects is given by respondents with low incomes.

Statistical hypotheses testing and post-hoc analysis lead to the following conclusions:

- For the age group 50+, there is a statistical significance of the influence of Attitudes toward green energy on Readiness to participate in the demand response services ($\beta = 0.625$, $p < 0.05$).
- For the employed participants, the influence of the Attitudes toward environmental protection on Readiness to participate in the demand response services is statistically significant ($\beta = 0.348$, $p < 0.05$).
- For the participants with income 250€–500€, the impact of Attitudes toward environmental protection on Readiness to participate in the demand response services is statistically significant ($\beta = 0.628$, $p < 0.05$).

5 Conclusion

The implementation of the proposed approach should result in a novel system for an advanced smart grid technology. Three possible business models were proposed, ranging from conservative to innovative, based on their accordance with regulation and market rules. All three models seek to offer flexible demand-side energy as an alternative to non-renewable power plants. The models are market-based, either in the form of balancing market participation with tertiary and secondary ancillary services being sold as a product, or an adaption of the model for purposes of private demand response oriented markets. Any solutions resulting from this approach would result in less coal use in the energy sector. With the end goal of all models being the added flexibility of demand response for finer balancing of renewable generators, such as wind power plants. The fulfilment of this goal would improve the quality of the grid, modernize it, and offer potential new business practices to both the market and the grid operator. In addition to the above-mentioned positive effects of partial replacement of fossil fuels by the wind energy, certain negative impacts on ecology and the environment were also observed. Some of the dominant ones are land occupation, impact on the animal world, generated noise, and its impact on the surrounding population. Some of these negative impacts can be lessened or negated altogether by utilizing an internal demand response market, to compensate for the lost energy generation.

Additionally, by informing the public of demand response as a technology, as well as by promoting the consumers who participated the most, we can hopefully change the stance of the end-users into a pro-active one in regards to energy consumption and environment.

Internet of Things in conjunction with blockchain technologies can be used to offer a modern solution to a problem of demand response coordination and management. By relying on individual devices connected to IoT controllers rather than household smart meters we can simplify the business logic, and allow the devices to formulate their own decisions, based on minimal outside input. Device coordination is managed through the blockchain technology, where outside parties can post smart contracts for demand response, and individual devices coordinate with each other in order to meet all the contract requirements. Since we have recognized that demand response programs are heavily dependent on user participation, we propose a loyalty program be added to the business model. This loyalty program will also be blockchain-based and will serve to award user participation with loyalty points that can be redeemed at partner companies, in the form of discounts and other incentives. The proposed loyalty model is collaborative in nature allowing many partner companies to join the program, in order to improve their environmental image.

As the results of the survey show, consumers are generally motivated to participate in new smart grid services by their attitudes toward environmental protection and green energy. The results show that attitude toward environmental protection is generally more important than the attitude toward green energy. Although these concepts can be perceived as similar, the obtained results can be of high importance for marketing purposes. Further, the obtained results can be used for adjusting the business model with respect to users' preferences, and more precise market segmentation, based on age, income, and employment status. The results of the post-hoc analysis suggest that attitudes toward green energy and environmental protection can be strong incentives for early adoption of the proposed demand response services for participants who are in age group 50+, who are employed, and who are with income 250€–500€, so the pilot projects and the first implementations can be directed toward these groups. Still, further analysis is needed to fully understand the perceptions of different consumer groups and to take a step toward designing personalized demand response services.

Acknowledgments Authors are thankful to Ministry of education, science and technological development, Republic of Serbia, grant 174031.

References

1. Ipakchi, A., & Albuyeh, F. (2009). Grid of the future. *IEEE Power & Energy Magazine, 7*, 52–62. https://doi.org/10.1109/MPE.2008.931384.
2. Farhangi, H. (2010). The path of the smart grid. *IEEE Power & Energy Magazine, 8*, 18–28. https://doi.org/10.1109/MPE.2009.934876.
3. Radenković, M., Bogdanović, Z., Despotović-Zrakić, M., et al. (2020). An IoT approach to consumer involvement in smart grid services: A green perspective. In *Advances in intelligent systems and computing* (pp. 539–548). New York: Springer.
4. Mashima, D., & Chen, W. P. (2016). Residential demand response system framework leveraging IoT devices. In *2016 IEEE international conference on smart grid communications, SmartGridComm 2016* (pp. 514–520). New York: Institute of Electrical and Electronics Engineers Inc..
5. Abedi, S., Riahy, G. H., Hosseinian, S. H., & Alimardani, A. (2011). Risk-constrained unit commitment of power system incorporating PV and wind farms. *ISRN Renew Energy, 2011*, 1–8. https://doi.org/10.5402/2011/309496.
6. Zheng, Q. P., Wang, J., & Liu, A. L. (2015). Stochastic optimization for unit commitment – A review. *IEEE Transactions on Power Apparatus and Systems, 30*, 1913–1924. https://doi.org/10.1109/TPWRS.2014.2355204.
7. Abujarad, S. Y., Mustafa, M. W., & Jamian, J. J. (2017). Recent approaches of unit commitment in the presence of intermittent renewable energy resources: A review. *Renewable and Sustainable Energy Reviews, 70*, 215–223. https://doi.org/10.1016/j.rser.2016.11.246.
8. Kundur, P., Paserba, J., Ajjarapu, V., et al. (2004). Definition and classification of power system stability. *IEEE Transactions on Power Apparatus and Systems, 19*, 1387–1401. https://doi.org/10.1109/TPWRS.2004.825981.
9. Rahimi, F., & Ipakchi, A. (2010). Demand response as a market resource under the smart grid paradigm. *IEEE Transactions on Smart Grid, 1*, 82–88. https://doi.org/10.1109/TSG.2010.2045906.
10. Zhao, L., & Zeng, B. (2012). Robust unit commitment problem with demand response and wind energy. In *IEEE power and energy society general meeting*.
11. Albadi, M. H., & El-Saadany, E. F. (2008). A summary of demand response in electricity markets. *Electric Power Systems Research, 78*(11), 1989–1996.

12. ENTSO-E. (2017). Guideline on electricity balancing. Retrieved May 23, 2017, from https://www.entsoe.eu/Documents/Network%20codes%20documents/NC%20EB/Informal_Service_Level_EBGL_16-03-2017_Final.pdf.
13. Mahmoudi, N., Heydarian-Forushani, E., Shafie-khah, M., et al. (2017). A bottom-up approach for demand response aggregators' participation in electricity markets. *Electric Power Systems Research, 143*, 121–129. https://doi.org/10.1016/J.EPSR.2016.08.038.
14. Eurostat (2020) Renewable energy statistics. Retrieved September 15, 2020, from https://ec.europa.eu/eurostat/statistics-explained/index.php/Renewable_energy_statistics.
15. Saidur, R., Rahim, N. A., Islam, M. R., & Solangi, K. H. (2011). Environmental impact of wind energy. *Renewable and Sustainable Energy Reviews, 15*, 2423–2430.
16. Marques, A. T., Santos, C. D., Hanssen, F., et al. (2020). Wind turbines cause functional habitat loss for migratory soaring birds. *The Journal of Animal Ecology, 89*, 93–103. https://doi.org/10.1111/1365-2656.12961.
17. Rinne, E., Holttinen, H., Kiviluoma, J., & Rissanen, S. (2018). Effects of turbine technology and land use on wind power resource potential. *Nature Energy, 3*, 494–500. https://doi.org/10.1038/s41560-018-0137-9.
18. Hanning, C. D., & Evans, A. (2012). Wind turbine noise. *BMJ, 344*.
19. McCallum, L. C., Whitfield Aslund, M. L., Knopper, L. D., et al. (2014). Measuring electromagnetic fields (EMF) around wind turbines in Canada: Is there a human health concern? *Environmental Health: A Global Access Science Source, 13*, 9. https://doi.org/10.1186/1476-069X-13-9.
20. Shuqin, W., Ang, T., & Jancenelle, V. E. (2018). Willingness to pay more for green products: The interplay of consumer characteristics and customer participation. *Journal of Retailing and Consumer Services, 45*, 230–238. https://doi.org/10.1016/j.jretconser.2018.08.015.
21. Vand, B., Hast, A., Bozorg, S., et al. (2019). Consumers' attitudes to support green energy: A case study in Shanghai. *Energies, 12*. https://doi.org/10.3390/en12122379.
22. Gupta, S., & Ogden, D. T. (2009). To buy or not to buy? A social dilemma perspective on green buying. *Journal of Consumer Marketing, 26*, 378–393. https://doi.org/10.1108/07363760910988201.
23. Schuitema, G., Ryan, L., & Aravena, C. (2017). The consumer's role in flexible energy systems: An interdisciplinary approach to changing consumers' behavior. *IEEE Power & Energy Magazine, 15*, 53–60. https://doi.org/10.1109/MPE.2016.2620658.
24. Abi Ghanem, D., & Mander, S. (2014). Designing consumer engagement with the smart grids of the future: Bringing active demand technology to everyday life. *Technology Analysis and Strategic Management, 26*, 1163–1175. https://doi.org/10.1080/09537325.2014.974531.
25. Osterwalder, A., Pigneur, Y., Clark, T., & Smith, A. (2010). *Business model generation: A handbook for visionaries, game changers, and challengers*. Hoboken, NJ: John Wiley & Sons.
26. Kiviluoma, J., Heinen, S., Qazi, H., et al. (2017). Harnessing flexibility from hot and cold: Heat storage and hybrid systems can play a major role. *IEEE Power & Energy Magazine, 15*, 25–33. https://doi.org/10.1109/MPE.2016.2626618.
27. Pipattanasomporn, M., Feroze, H., & Rahman, S. (2009). Multi-agent systems in a distributed smart grid: Design and implementation. IEEE/PES power syst conf expo 2009. PSCE '09 1–8. https://doi.org/10.1109/PSCE.2009.4840087.
28. Pop, C., Cioara, T., Antal, M., et al. (2018). Blockchain based decentralized management of demand response programs in smart energy grids. *Sensors (Switzerland)*, 18. https://doi.org/10.3390/s18010162.
29. Zyskind, G., Nathan, O., & Pentland, A. S. (2015). Decentralizing privacy: Using blockchain to protect personal data. In *Proceedings – 2015 IEEE security and privacy workshops, SPW 2015* (pp. 180–184). New York: Institute of Electrical and Electronics Engineers Inc..
30. Zheng, X., Mukkamala, R. R., Vatrapu, R., & Ordieres-Mere, J. (2018). Blockchain-based personal health data sharing system using cloud storage. In *2018 IEEE 20th international conference on e-health networking, applications and services*. Czech Republic: Healthcom 2018.

31. Ertemel, A. (2018). Implications of Blockchain technology on marketing. *Journal of International Trade, Logistics and Law, 4*, 35–44.
32. Thakore, M. (2020). Blockchain can save Customer Loyalty Programs from becoming Unfruitful! Retrieved June 28, 2020, from https://hackernoon.com/blockchain-can-save-customer-loyalty-programs-from-becoming-unfruitful-3992c6bc6053.
33. Yang, M., Zhu, T., Liang, K., et al. (2019). A blockchain-based location privacy-preserving crowdsensing system. *Future Generation Computer Systems, 94*, 408–418. https://doi.org/10.1016/j.future.2018.11.046.
34. Venkatesh, V., Thong, J. Y. L., & Xu, X. (2012). Consumer acceptance and use of information technology: Extending the unified theory of acceptance and use of technology. *MIS Quarterly, 36*(1), 157–178.
35. Radenković, M., Bogdanović, Z., Despotović-Zrakić, M., et al. (2020). Assessing consumer readiness for participation in IoT-based demand response business models. *Technological Forecasting and Social Change, 150*, 119715. https://doi.org/10.1016/j.techfore.2019.119715.
36. Tableau. Retrieved January 10, 2021, from https://www.tableau.com/.
37. SmartPLS. Retrieved January 10, 2021, from https://www.smartpls.com/.
38. Zikmund, W., Babin, B., Carr, J., & Griffin, M. (2013). *Business research methods* (9th ed.. South-Western Cengage Learning). Mason, OH.
39. Urbach, N., & Ahlemann, F. (2010). Structural equation modeling in information systems research using partial least squares. *Journal of Information Technology Theory and Application, 11*(2).

Application of Internet of Things (IoT) to Demand-Side Management in Smart Grids

Armin Hosseini Rezaei Asl, Mir Mahdi Safari, Morteza Nazari-heris, and Behnam Mohammadi-Ivatloo

1 Introduction

Electricity is the principal motivation for the development of human societies. Nowadays, emerging digital-based technologies are entering the market [1]. These devices require sustainable electricity for having a continuous operation. So, the power system has to provide available, stable, high reliability, high resiliency, flexibility, high quality, high-efficiency services. Most rate of the power is generated by thermal power plants all around the world. The process of ending fossil fuels in the upcoming years, alongside their low efficiency and environmental problems, caused optimal and economic operation crucial. So, electricity generation utilities move to incorporate more rate of renewable energy sources (RES) for supplying clean and cheap electrical energy. Europe plans to produce 100% of the power demand from these sources until 2050 [2]; however, renewable sources are unpredictable [3]. On the other hand, for supplying consumers with electricity demand, it passes over long distances from generation sides to the consumption parts. Planning and controlling this system is difficult. So, the power system has moved toward becoming smart [4]. The smart grid provides a system able to control, monitoring, and protection in an intelligent way. An intelligent way can decide and interact with the system. The use of distributed generation (DG), especially RES integration on the demand side, has speeded up [5]. In addition to RES, demand-side

A. Hosseini Rezaei Asl (✉) · M. M. Safari · B. Mohammadi-Ivatloo
Faculty of Electrical and Computer Engineering, University of Tabriz, Tabriz, Iran
e-mail: a.hosseini98@ms.tabrizu.ac.ir; safari@tabrizu.ac.ir; bmohammadi@tabrizu.ac.ir

M. Nazari-heris
Department of Architectural Engineering, Pennsylvania State University, State College, PA, USA
e-mail: m.nazari@ieee.org

F. P. García Márquez, B. Lev (eds.), *Introduction to Internet of Things in Management Science and Operations Research*, International Series in Operations Research & Management Science 311,
https://doi.org/10.1007/978-3-030-74644-5_8

management (DMS) has been developed for helping peak clipping, valley filling, load shifting, and flexible load shape [6]. DSM covers some of the uncertainty of RES. Managing this system with constraints is one of the challenges. Each technology can be connected to the internet via the internet of things (IoT). IoT fills the gap between the physical and digital worlds. IoT can define as a system able to listen, think, and talk that uses sensors and actuators to gather data. Internet gateways and data acquisition systems send data to the datacenter and cloud. Datacenter and cloud analyze and process data to choose the optimal decision in a short time.

2 Demand-Side Management

The electrical energy load in the world is growing every day, for which buildings are large consumers of this energy type, especially by considering air conditioners [7]. Such significant growth needs an investment in developing and building new plants and grids. On the other hand, the operating point of power generation equipment is continuously changing. The imbalance of supply and demand causes fluctuations in system frequency. For a quick response to frequency fluctuations, the spinning reserve is used in [8]. The use of spinning reserve costs to customers. DSM can play a role in affecting the system. One of the accepted definitions for DSM is "the planning, implementation, and monitoring of those utility activities designed to influence customer use of electricity in ways that will produce desired changes in the utility's load shape, i.e., changes in the time pattern and magnitude of a utility's load" [9]. For planning and implementation of DSM, the system operator should be able to develop end-use demand forecasting, recognize consumption patterns and market barriers, find target customers and measures, identify sources of financing, perform DSM cost/benefit investigations, and define local socioeconomic and environmental effects.

DSM includes four cases of energy savings, energy efficiency, strategic demand increase, and demand response programs (DR) [10]. The classification of DSM is shown in Fig. 1. Energy savings is known as measuring reduced energy consumption like fuel switching. Energy efficiency is the usage of new technologies and a review of the process that aims to reduce consumption to provide the same services. Strategic load growth programs enhance the level of demand within electricity supply in a strategic state by using different programs like involving demand to increase market share. According to the definition of the USA Federal Energy Regulatory Commission, DR is "changing in electric usage by end-use customers from their normal consumption patterns in response to changes in the price of electricity over time, or to incentive payments designed to induce lower electricity use at times of high wholesale market prices or when system reliability is jeopardized" [11].

Incentive-based (IB) and price-based (PB) programs are the two main programs of DR. PB programs involve customer payments over a specific period. Time of use (TOU), real-time pricing (RTP), and critical peak pricing (CPP) are included in the

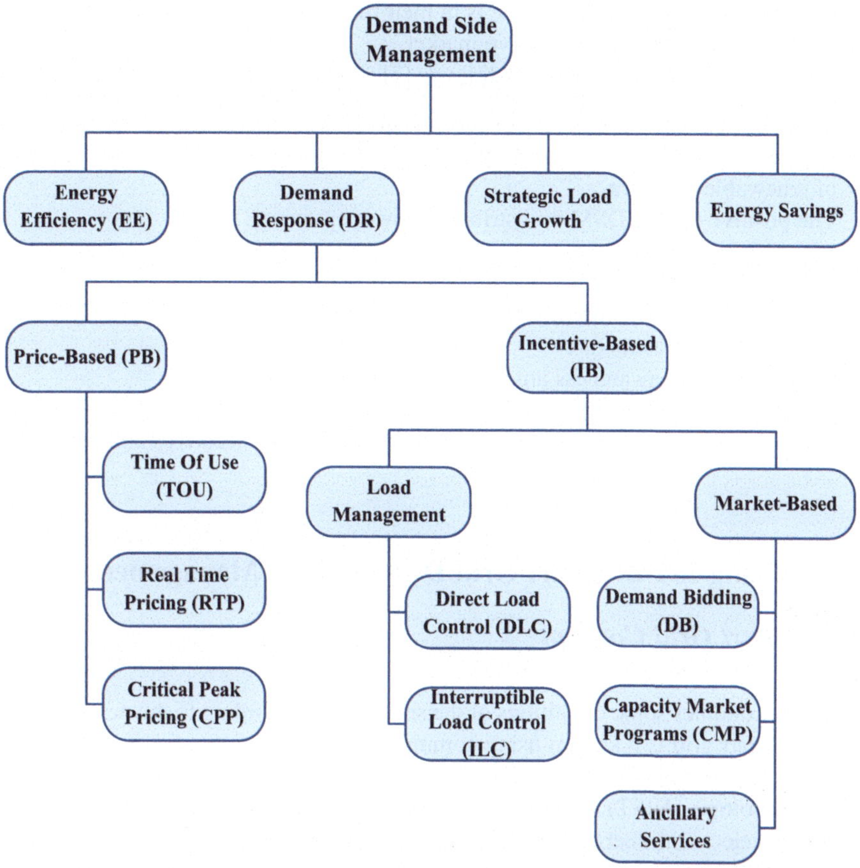

Fig. 1 Classification of DSM

programs of PB. TOU is used for different pricing for various periods, and RTP is based on an hourly price that can be daily or day ahead. CPP is used in critical peak days that usually happen in summer. IB is based on direct payments or motivation to customers, which aims to decrease load when necessary, and it includes load management and market-based programs. Direct load control (DLC) allows the utility to shuts down electrical equipment on the demand-side (e.g., air conditioner, electric stove) for a short time. The ILC pays an incentive or gives a discount on the bill if the customer decreases load when the operator requested. If customers reject the operator's request, they will have to pay a predetermined penalty. In demand bidding, customers send an offer to the market that includes load decries and price. In the capacity market program, the operator considers the customer as a system capacity to replace conventional generation. The customer receives a fixed amount for the preparation and a fee for the performance time. Ancillary service looks like demand bidding, but their difference is in their market. Ancillary service allows the customer to participate in the reserve market.

DSM has significant benefits, as follows [7].

- Improving the efficiency of investment in the system, especially in operation.
- Improving the balance between supply and load in the system with the presence of renewable resources.
- The positive role of DSM in distributed power systems.

DSM has some challenges, as follows [7, 8].

- Lack of customers familiarity with DSM.
- Lack of ICT infrastructure.
- Lack of creating awareness among consumers about DSM.
- Lack of suitable structure to motivate consumers to use energy-efficient devices.
- Lack of a proper framework in the electricity market to incentives and penalty.

3 Utilizing IoT in Smart Grid Demand-Side Management

3.1 Smart Grid Concept

This part examines some definitions of the smart grid. According to the definition of IEEE, a smart grid is a system using communication and information technologies for the improvement of end-use applications [9]. The National Institute of Standards and Technology (NIST) describes the smart grid as the integration of the last traditional electrical energy network with information and communication equipment [10]. The smart grid is a network that can prepare a two-way flow of information and electricity. It participates in generators up to consumers to increase system stability, reliability, flexibility, economics, and secure electricity supplies [11]. The smart grid is a system that includes bidirectional communication infrastructure using information and communication technologies (ICTs) in all players [12]. A smart grid develops the traditional system by adding communication infrastructures [13]. Smart gird uses information communication technologies to control processes [14]. All the above definitions refer to the telecommunications platform that IoT is one of them.

3.2 Smart Grid Challenges

There is some motivation to move from the traditional to the intelligent grid. Some of these are providing available, stable, high reliability, high resiliency, flexibility, high quality, high efficiency, clean, and low economic service to customers. The ways to achieve smart grid goals are as follows.

- Demand-side management (DSM).
- Distributed energy resources (DER): DER includes different technologies, such as photovoltaic, wind turbines, fuel cells, diesel engines. DER allows the customer to optimize their energy strategies.
- Monitoring and Controlling: Monitoring makes the system real time. Operators maneuver faster because of getting notified nodal voltages, circuit loading conditions, and faults. Phasor Measurement Units (PMU) is one of the key sensors. PMUs sample power flows and voltage profiles. PMUs used in strategic locations.
- Efficient communication system: The communication system is the soul of ICT that all the processes depend on its operation. Data is used for load forecasting, optimal power flow, and running market. It gathers data from generation to customer and then it sends the gathered data to the control center. Equipment, algorithms, telecommunications platform, and cyber protocols are needed for proper operation.
- Advanced metering infrastructure (AMI): AMI is one of the devices to operate DSM. It is one way to reduce demand, increase supply management efficiently, and optimize the management of existing resources [15]. It is also used to gain load shape and customer company validation and power change rate.

3.3 IoT in Smart Grid

In the traditional electrical system, electricity flows from power generation to customer by transmission and distribution lines. The smart grid makes customers active such as distributed energy resources, advanced metering infrastructure, dynamic behavior loads, and demand-side management. Gathering and analyzing data are generally used in optimal design and online operation control of power systems. IoT can be an economical solution [16], but it needs more sensors, bandwidth communication, and cybersecurity. The structure of a smart grid can be as Fig. 2 [17].

In the following, different players and domains are introduced briefly.

- Customer: The smart grid provides to use advanced measurement, DSM, smart home (SH), electric vehicles (EVs), and distributed generation (DG) on the consumption side. With the advantages of IoT, customers can manage energy consumption and cost.
- Market: Price spikes are one of the market problems. IoT operates in real time and reacts faster to power fluctuations, which can happen in four platforms. Device centric communication/connectivity centric, industry-centric, and cloud-centric.
- Operations: In the power system, supply and demand should have balance. Blackout is the worst possible situation. Load forecasting, unit commitment, transmission limits, and transmission losses should be optimal. IoT is receiving

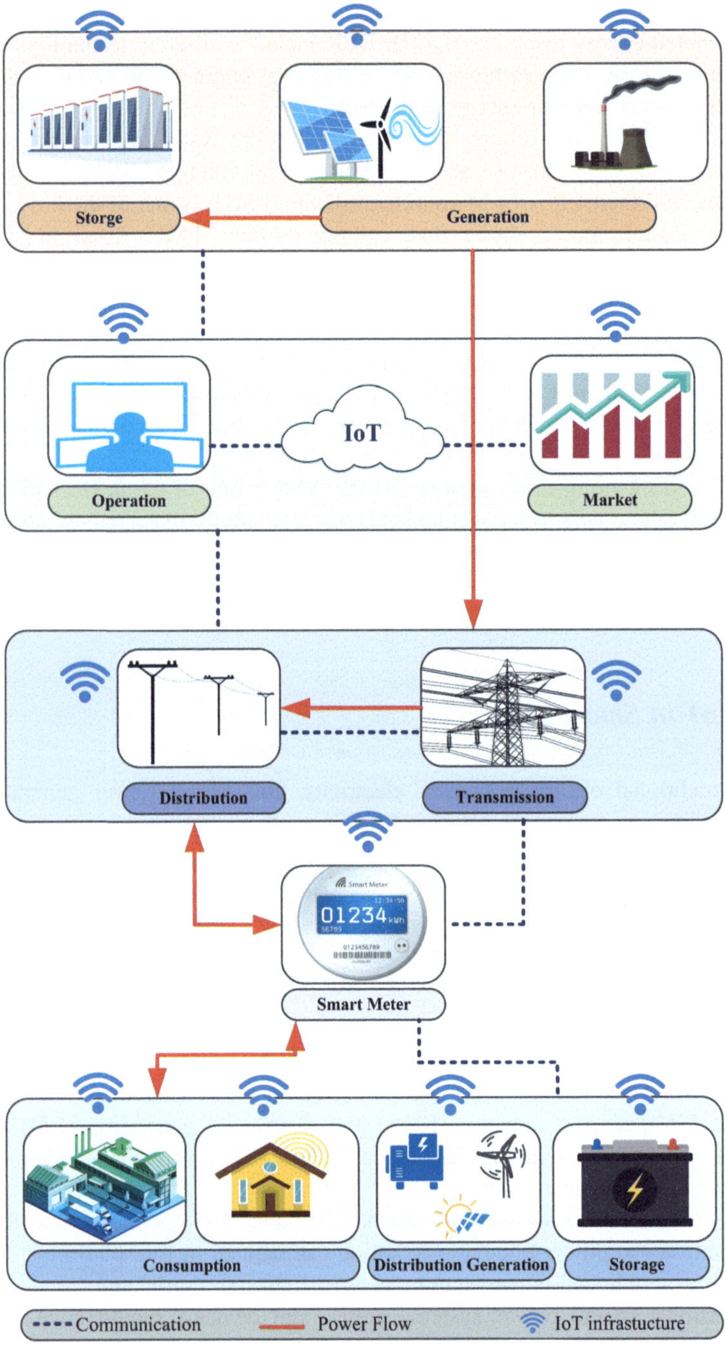

Fig. 2 Sample of IoT in the smart grid

high priority and importance for power system operators. Accuracy and speed are too significant to operators.

- Generation: Controlling reactive and active power, output voltage, changing transformer tap changer, checking equipment health level are some examples for the generation part. But one of the advantages of IoT for the generation part is a virtual power plant.
- Transmission: IoT sends parameters needed from different parts of the lines, which helps operators to decide fast and correctly. These parameters can be voltage, current, phase, and tower leaning. On the other hand, IoT can recognize fault and its area. Most faults happen because of the weather, such as wind deviation, conductor temperature, and icing.
- Distribution: DER, DSM, and plug-in EVs (PEVs) are new challenges of distribution networks. Renewable sources are unpredictable. On the other hand, customers want to earn more profit by selling or participating in the DR program. Both of these reasons make managing different. IoT can monitor and call customers to answer to change in the network.

3.4 Smart Home

IoT-based smart home (SH) technology has changed human life by providing communication for all devices seamlessly, at any time and place. SHs are intelligent buildings that have tracking and control devices such as cleaning, cooling, and heating, ventilation, lighting, and privacy systems [18]. These advanced technologies are managed by IoT, which includes sensors for gathering and communicating with the use of a personal computer (PC), tablet, or mobile phone [19]. Figure 3 shows an SH structure [20].

IoT-based SH has many benefits, which are summarized as [21]:

- Energy conservation (i.e., logical use of appliances, reduce energy wastage).
- Increasing reliability while reducing cost (i.e., check and control the equipment remotely).
- Healthcare (i.e., remote control of the elderly, patients and children, medical services).

SHs encounter many challenges, such as concerns of marketing, device connectivity, security and privacy, data management, and energy consumption. Controlling and managing the power consumption related to the appliances through IoT is one of the most important steps of energy consumption concern. Energy demand for SHs is increasing rapidly. The energy transactive system (TE) used with Internet technology is a good option for managing power networks [22]. Obtaining the consumption pattern of each electrical device in the load disaggregation [23] and recognizing the features allows consumers to be informed of their power consumption pattern at any time. Residential consumers need information about power consumption patterns to manage energy consumption. One of the appropriate solutions is non-intrusive load

Fig. 3 SH structure

monitoring to extract consumption patterns from the collected data measured in meters. For a more accurate understanding of home appliance consumption, load analysis methods include three steps: data analysis and feature extraction, home appliance consumption modeling, and identification of home appliances in terms of different signatures [24].

4 IoT-Enabled SHs Algorithms Targeting DSM

This chapter has provided an introduction to algorithms applied for enabling IoT is SHs to perform DSM. The operation of SGs based on IoT is considered as one of the modern systems, which has a prominent task in keeping a balance between supply and demand by utilizing the DR program. HEM system has engrossed a lot of

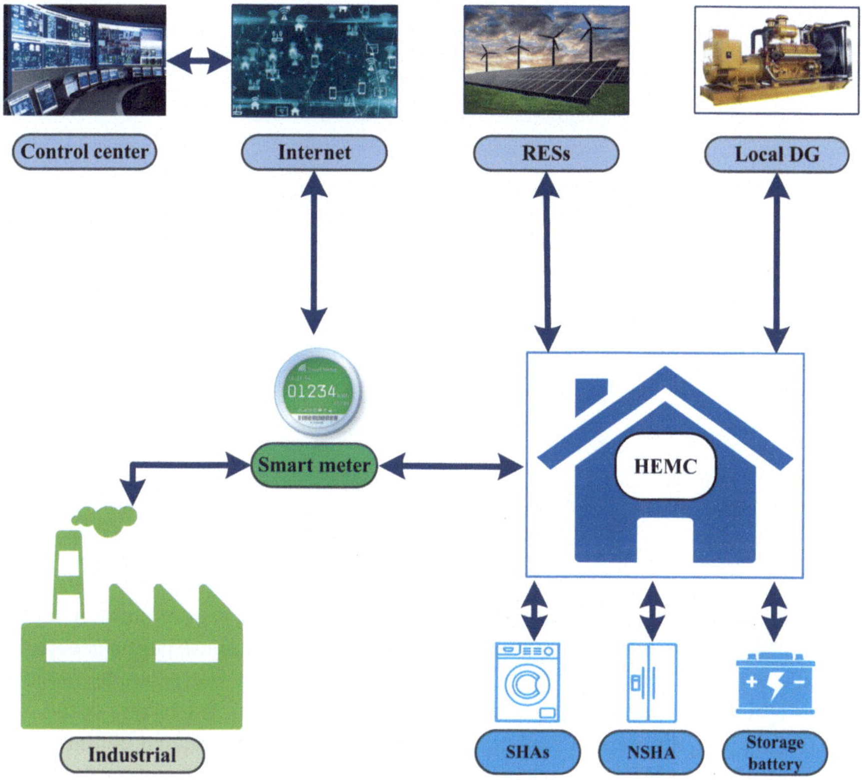

Fig. 4 HEMS technology for an SH

attention in SG, which is called DSM. In recent years, significant research has been done on developing an algorithm for optimal performance of home energy management systems (HEMSs). A common HEMS structure is illustrated in Fig. 4 [25]. The HEMS controller has a prominent role. It is in a control algorithm that includes all the computational intelligence needed for the best HEMS performance.

In DR-based HEMS, the controller usually calculates the best schedules for the shiftable home appliance, whereas for a DR synergized with energy storage (ESS) and renewable energy sources system (RESs) optimal dispatch (DRSREOD)-based HEMS, it calculates the best schedules with the optimal transmission for the RESs, the ESS and the grid to get the HEMS objectives.

DRSREOD-based HEMS mainly consists of smart meters, home area networks, Has, RESs, an ESS, a HEMS controller [25]. Researchers all over the world work to propose an efficient algorithm that optimally schedules the appliances' power demand in SHs to benefit the consumers reliably. Optimization problem methods are utilized for solving the power scheduling problem in an SH that can be controlled through IoT technology. In Fig. 5, the optimization methods are summarized [26].

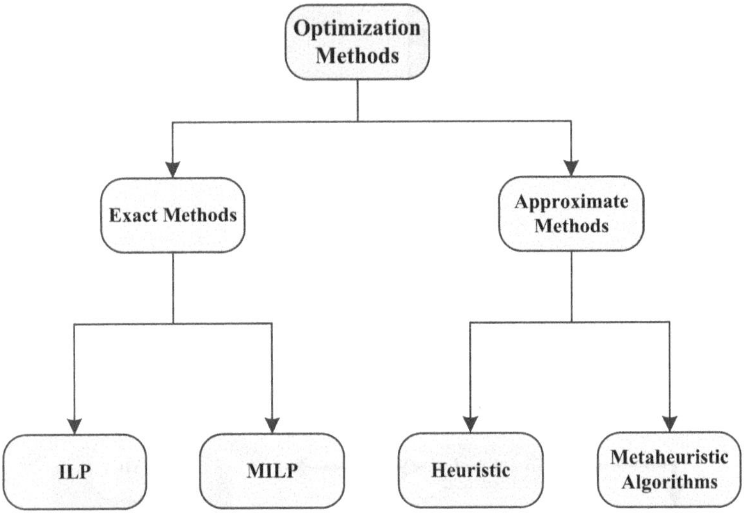

Fig. 5 Optimization methods

In the past, many exact algorithms, including integer linear programming (ILP) [27], mixed-integer linear programming (MILP) [28], and heuristic/metaheuristic algorithms have been studied for solving practical problems. For example, particle swarm optimization (PSO) [29], genetic algorithm (GA) [30], ant colony optimization (ACO) [31], differential evolution (DE) [32], Backtracking search optimization algorithm (BSA) [33], artificial fish swarm algorithm and genetic algorithm [34] Harris-hawks [35]. Some of these algorithms are reviewed in Table 1.

5 Conclusions

This chapter aimed at providing a review on the usage of IoT for DSM application. Also, a comprehensive assessment of algorithms for IoT enabled smart homes targeting demand-side management has been discussed. An increase in power demand and becoming complex systems make problems to maintain reliability. So, the smart grid has been introduced as a potential solution for such issues. A smart grid uses the end-to-end power grid through some technologies and applications. Smart grids are connected to political, environmental, and socioeconomic factors that provide replaced bulky and polluting power stations with distributed and cleaner ones especially renewable energy resources. On the other hand, it prepares motivation to make customers active. DSM has a considerable effect on consumption by using new technologies to increase efficiency or change the demand pattern. Appropriate mechanisms must be in place for implementation. Developing AMI, smart home, and communication systems make DSM easy to run. Finding the right algorithms based on programs makes it easy to run on time and monitor.

Table 1 Review of algorithms applied to smart home scheduling

References	Algorithm	Objective	Brief description
[36]	Quadratic programming (QP)	Peak to average ratio	Focus on the shiftable appliance
[37]	HSDE algorithm	Maximum capacity of electricity consumers	HSDE algorithm that is a hybrid HSA and EDE method [38, 39]
[40]	Using the GA optimization method	Cost of energy pursuit from the grid	Day-ahead pricing/inclining block rate (IBR) model
[41]	HEM scheme, RTP, CPP, TOU, DAP	Energy consumption	RTP, CPP, TOU, and day-ahead pricing (DAP), and energy consumption are mentioned as a HEM scheme in detail
[26]	Heuristic algorithm for a DRSREOD-based HEMS	Minimize the cost of energy and time-base discomfort with conflicting tradeoffs	Propose a new heuristic algorithm for a DRSREOD-based HEMS targeting parallel operation of the PV system
[42]	WDO-DE	Increasing convergence rate of traditional WDO and DE	Increased convergence speed causes some local optimum information lost
[43]	Distributed algorithm	Robust algorithm	Fast convergence and scalability
[44]	TLBO and shuffled frog leaping (SFL)	Reduce cost	TLBO and SFL algorithms are utilized to lessen the payment costs in SG
[45]	GA, BPSO, WDO, HGPO	Peak to average ratio and cost	OHEMS by integrating RES and ESS
[46]	IIS method	The coverage ratio of HAS [47]	Has a better convergence time in comparison with normal and improved GA. Complex with respect to EDE
[33]	Binary backtracking search algorithm (BBSA)	Cost of energy pursuit from the grid	TOU and HAS. Using MILP/CPLEX optimization method
[48]	HAMS algorithms with GA, BPSO, and ACO	Peak to average ratio and cost of energy pursuit from grid	Elastic and photovoltaic as well as TOU and HAS and IBR
[49]	HSA, IHS, BBO	Cost minimization	Economic dispatch problem
[50]	Greedy iterative algorithm	Optimization of consumers energy consumption pattern	RTP signal is used
[51]	Multi-objective evolutionary algorithm	Delay and cost	Proposing a threshold policy
[52]	Using HAS optimization problem	Net present value in cash	Dispatchable generator, photovoltaic and fixed load
[53]	DWS-PSO-based algorithm	Cost of energy	PDDR-and PDDR-RED-based HEMSs are discussed

(continued)

Table 1 (continued)

References	Algorithm	Objective	Brief description
[54]	GWCSO algorithm	Peak to average ratio	A new has scheduling framework has been discussed based on the GWCSO algorithm for efficient DR
[29]	BPSO	Peak to average ratio and cost	DERs and storage is considered for HEMS
[55]	Hybrid Multi-objective algorithm	Cost and peak to average ratio	Tradeoffs between residential privacy and energy costs
[56]	Classic, Hybrid	Cost and end user's comfort	Overview of existing HEMS and their feasibilities

References

1. Noorollahi, Y., Yousefi, H., & Mohammadi, M. (2016). Multi-criteria decision support system for wind farm site selection using GIS. *Sustainable Energy Technologies and Assessments, 13*, 38–50.
2. Child, M., Kemfert, C., Bogdanov, D., & Breyer, C. (2019). Flexible electricity generation, grid exchange and storage for the transition to a 100% renewable energy system in Europe. *Renewable Energy, 139*, 80–101.
3. Tummuru, N. R., Mishra, M. K., & Srinivas, S. (2015). Dynamic energy management of renewable grid integrated hybrid energy storage system. *IEEE Transactions on Industrial Electronics, 62*(12), 7728–7737.
4. Hossain, M., Madlool, N., Rahim, N., Selvaraj, J., Pandey, A., & Khan, A. F. (2016). Role of smart grid in renewable energy: An overview. *Renewable and Sustainable Energy Reviews, 60*, 1168–1184.
5. Tuballa, M. L., & Abundo, M. L. (2016). A review of the development of Smart Grid technologies. *Renewable and Sustainable Energy Reviews, 59*, 710–725.
6. Logenthiran, T., Srinivasan, D., & Shun, T. Z. (2012). Demand side management in smart grid using heuristic optimization. *IEEE Transactions on Smart Grid, 3*(3), 1244–1252.
7. Strbac, G. (2008). Demand side management: Benefits and challenges. *Energy Policy, 36*(12), 4419–4426.
8. Kumar, D., & Singh, H. (2016). A review on industry challenges in smart grid implementation. In *2016 7th India international conference on power electronics (IICPE)* (pp. 1–5). Washington, DC: IEEE.
9. Photovoltaics, D. G., & Storage, E. (2011). *IEEE guide for smart grid interoperability of energy technology and information technology operation with the electric power system (EPS), end-use applications, and loads*. Washington, DC: IEEE.
10. Gungor, V. C., Sahin, D., Kocak, T., Ergut, S., Buccella, C., Cecati, C., & Hancke, G. P. (2011). Smart grid technologies: Communication technologies and standards. *IEEE Transactions on Industrial Informatics, 7*(4), 529–539.
11. Buchholz, B. M., & Styczynski, Z. A. (2020). Vision and strategy for the electricity networks of the future. In *Smart grids* (pp. 1–17). New York: Springer.
12. Kabalci, E., & Kabalci, Y. (2019). Introduction to smart grid architecture. In *Smart grids and their communication systems* (pp. 3–45). New York: Springer.
13. Al-Shaer, E., & Rahman, M. A. (2016). Smart grids and security challenges. In *Security and resiliency analytics for smart grids* (pp. 3–13). New York: Springer.

14. Dalipi, F., & Yayilgan, S. Y. (2016). Security and privacy considerations for IoT application on smart grids: Survey and research challenges. In *2016 IEEE fourth international conference on future internet of things and cloud workshops (FiCloudW)* (pp. 63–68). Washington, DC: IEEE.
15. Barai, G. R., Krishnan, S., & Venkatesh, B. (2016). Smart metering and functionalities of smart meters in smart grid – A review. In *2015 IEEE electr. power energy conf. smarter resilient power syst.* (pp. 138–145). Bengaluru: EPEC 2015.
16. Liu, J., Li, X., Chen, X., Zhen, Y., & Zeng, L. (2011). Applications of Internet of things on smart grid in China. In *13th international conference on advanced communication technology (ICACT 2011)* (pp. 13–17). Washington, DC: IEEE.
17. Shahinzadeh, H., Moradi, J., Gharehpetian, G. B., Nafisi, H., & Abedi, M. (2019). IoT architecture for smart grids. In *2019 international conference on protection and automation of power system (IPAPS)* (pp. 22–30). Washington, DC: IEEE.
18. Samuel, S. S. I. (2016). A review of connectivity challenges in IoT-smart home. In *2016 third MEC international conference on big data and smart city (ICBDSC)* (pp. 1–4). Washington, DC: IEEE.
19. Galinina, O., Mikhaylov, K., Andreev, S., Turlikov, A., & Koucheryavy, Y. (2015). Smart home gateway system over Bluetooth low energy with wireless energy transfer capability. *EURASIP Journal on Wireless Communications and Networking, 2015*(1), 178.
20. Sovacool, B. K., & Del Rio, D. D. F. (2020). Smart home technologies in Europe: A critical review of concepts, benefits, risks and policies. *Renewable and Sustainable Energy Reviews, 120*, 109663.
21. Alaa, M., Zaidan, A. A., Zaidan, B. B., Talal, M., & Kiah, M. L. M. (2017). A review of smart home applications based on Internet of Things. *Journal of Network and Computer Applications, 97*, 48–65.
22. Daneshvar, M., Pesaran, M., & Mohammadi-ivatloo, B. (2019). Transactive energy in future smart homes. In *The energy internet* (pp. 153–179). Amsterdam: Elsevier.
23. Moradzadeh, A., Sadeghian, O., Pourhossein, K., Mohammadi-Ivatloo, B., & Anvari-Moghaddam, A. (2020). Improving residential load disaggregation for sustainable development of energy via principal component analysis. *Sustainability, 12*, 3158.
24. Zeinal-Kheiri, S., Shotorbani, A. M., & Mohammadi-Ivatloo, B. (2020). Residential load disaggregation considering state transitions. *IEEE Transactions on Industrial Informatics, 16*, 743–753.
25. Makhadmeh, S. N., Khader, A. T., Al-Betar, M. A., Naim, S., Abasi, A. K., & Alyasseri, Z. A. A. (2019). Optimization methods for power scheduling problems in smart home: Survey. *Renewable and Sustainable Energy Reviews, 115*, 109362.
26. Hussain, B., Hasan, Q. U., Javaid, N., Guizani, M., Almogren, A., & Alamri, A. (2018). An innovative heuristic algorithm for IoT-enabled smart homes for developing countries. *IEEE Access, 6*, 15550–15575.
27. Zhu, Z., Tang, J., Lambotharan, S., Chin, W. H., & Fan, Z. (2012). An integer linear programming based optimization for home demand-side management in smart grid. In *2012 IEEE PES innovative smart grid technologies (ISGT)* (pp. 1–5). Washington, DC: IEEE.
28. Wang, J., Sun, Z., Zhou, Y., & Dai, J. (2012). Optimal dispatching model of smart home energy management system. In *IEEE PES innovative smart grid technologies* (pp. 1–5). Washington, DC: IEEE.
29. Abid, S., Zafar, A., Khalid, R., Javaid, S., Qasim, U., Khan, Z. A., & Javaid, N. (2017). Managing energy in smart homes using binary particle swarm optimization. In *Conference on complex, intelligent, and software intensive systems* (pp. 189–196). Cham: Springer.
30. Nadeem, Z., Javaid, N., Malik, A. W., & Iqbal, S. (2018). Scheduling appliances with GA, TLBO, FA, OSR and their hybrids using chance constrained optimization for smart homes. *Energies, 11*(4), 888.
31. Wang, J., Jiayi, C., Bin, L., Sungyoung, L., & Sherratt, R. S. (2015). Bio-inspired ant colony optimization based clustering algorithm with mobile sinks for applications in consumer home automation networks. *IEEE Transactions on Consumer Electronics, 61*(4), 438–444.

32. Essiet, I. O., Sun, Y., & Wang, Z. (2019). Optimized energy consumption model for smart home using improved differential evolution algorithm. *Energy, 172*, 354–365.
33. Ahmed, M. S., Mohamed, A., Khatib, T., Shareef, H., Homod, R. Z., & Abd Ali, J. (2017). Real time optimal schedule controller for home energy management system using new binary backtracking search algorithm. *Energy and Buildings, 138*, 215–227.
34. Talha, M., Saeed, M. S., Mohiuddin, G., Ahmad, M., Nazar, M. J., & Javaid, N. (2017). Energy optimization in home energy management system using artificial fish swarm algorithm and genetic algorithm. In *International conference on intelligent networking and collaborative systems* (pp. 203–213). Cham: Springer.
35. Mouassa, S., Bouktir, T., & Jurado, F. (2020). Scheduling of smart home appliances for optimal energy management in smart grid using Harris-hawks optimization algorithm. *Optimization and Engineering*, 1–28.
36. Liu, Y., Yuen, C., Huang, S., Hassan, N. U., Wang, X., & Xie, S. (2014). Peak-to-average ratio constrained demand-side management with consumer's preference in residential smart grid. *IEEE Journal of Selected Topics in Signal Processing, 8*(6), 1084–1097.
37. Kazmi, S., Javaid, N., Mughal, M. J., Akbar, M., Ahmed, S. H., & Alrajeh, N. (2017). Towards optimization of metaheuristic algorithms for IoT enabled smart homes targeting balanced demand and supply of energy. *IEEE Access, 7*, 24267–24281.
38. Arafa, M., Sallam, E. A., & Fahmy, M. (2014). An enhanced differential evolution optimization algorithm. In *2014 fourth international conference on digital information and communication technology and its applications (DICTAP)* (pp. 216–225). Washington, DC: IEEE.
39. Moon, S., & Lee, J.-W. (2016). Multi-residential demand response scheduling with multi-class appliances in smart grid. *IEEE Transactions on Smart Grid, 9*(4), 2518–2528.
40. Zhao, Z., Lee, W. C., Shin, Y., & Song, K.-B. (2013). An optimal power scheduling method for demand response in home energy management system. *IEEE Transactions on Smart Grid, 4*(3), 1391–1400.
41. Patel, K., & Khosla, A. (2015). Home energy management systems in future smart grid networks: A systematic review. In *2015 first international conference on next generation computing technologies (NGCT)* (pp. 479–483). Washington, DC: IEEE.
42. Bao, Z., Zhou, Y., Li, L., & Ma, M. (2015). A hybrid global optimization algorithm based on wind driven optimization and differential evolution. *Mathematical Problems in Engineering, 2015*, 389630.
43. Mhanna, S., Chapman, A. C., & Verbič, G. (2016). A fast distributed algorithm for large-scale demand response aggregation. *IEEE Transactions on Smart Grid, 7*(4), 2094–2107.
44. Derakhshan, G., Shayanfar, H. A., & Kazemi, A. (2016). The optimization of demand response programs in smart grids. *Energy Policy, 94*, 295–306.
45. Ahmad, A., Khan, A., Javaid, N., Hussain, H. M., Abdul, W., Almogren, A., Alamri, A., & Azim Niaz, I. (2017). An optimized home energy management system with integrated renewable energy and storage resources. *Energies, 10*(4), 549.
46. Effatnejad, R., Hosseini, H., & Ramezani, H. (2014). Solving unit commitment problem in microgrids by harmony search algorithm in comparison with genetic algorithm and improved genetic algorithm. *International Journal on Technical and Physical Problems of Engineering (IJTPE), 21*, 61–65.
47. Geem, Z. W., Kim, J. H., & Loganathan, G. V. (2001). A new heuristic optimization algorithm: Harmony search. *Simulation, 76*(2), 60–68.
48. Rahim, S., Javaid, N., Ahmad, A., Khan, S. A., Khan, Z. A., Alrajeh, N., & Qasim, U. (2016). Exploiting heuristic algorithms to efficiently utilize energy management controllers with renewable energy sources. *Energy and Buildings, 129*, 452–470.
49. Karthigeyan, P., Raja, M. S., Hariharan, R., Prakash, S., Delibabu, S., & Gnanaselvam, R. (2015). Comparison of harmony search algorithm, improved harmony search algorithm with biogeography based optimization algorithm for solving constrained economic load dispatch problems. *Procedia Technology, 21*, 611–618.

50. Chavali, P., Yang, P., & Nehorai, A. (2014). A distributed algorithm of appliance scheduling for home energy management system. *IEEE Transactions on Smart Grid, 5*(1), 282–290.
51. Muralitharan, K., Sakthivel, R., & Shi, Y. (2016). Multiobjective optimization technique for demand side management with load balancing approach in smart grid. *Neurocomputing, 177*, 110–119.
52. Askarzadeh, A. (2017). Distribution generation by photovoltaic and diesel generator systems: Energy management and size optimization by a new approach for a stand-alone application. *Energy, 122*, 542–551.
53. Hussain, B., Khan, A., Javaid, N., Hasan, Q. U., Malik, S., Ahmad, O., Dar, A. H., & Kazmi, A. (2019). A weighted-sum PSO algorithm for HEMS: A new approach for the design and diversified performance analysis. *Electronics, 8*(2), 180.
54. Waseem, M., Lin, Z., Liu, S., Sajjad, I. A., & Aziz, T. (2020). Optimal GWCSO-based home appliances scheduling for demand response considering end-users comfort. *Electric Power Systems Research, 187*, 106477.
55. Chang, H.-H., Chiu, W.-Y., Sun, H., & Chen, C.-M. (2018). User-centric multiobjective approach to privacy preservation and energy cost minimization in smart home. *IEEE Systems Journal, 13*(1), 1030–1041.
56. Rajendhar, P., & Jeyaraj, B. E. (2019). Application of DR and co-simulation approach for renewable integrated HEMS: A review. *IET Generation, Transmission & Distribution, 13*(16), 3501–3512.

Understanding the Factors Influencing Consumers' Behaviour Towards Autonomous Vehicles Adoption

Patrice Seuwou

1 Introduction

For several years, IT users' acceptance has been a very important area of study by social scientists and management information system scholars. They have been analysing the behaviour of technology users at an individual level and within organisational settings [1]. With the fast pace of technological innovation in the transportation industry, vehicles are becoming more and more intelligent. Many are being equipped with advanced technologies allowing them to move commuters with no driving capabilities or with disabilities from one place to another. Autonomous Vehicles (AVs) will be here sooner than most people expect. These technologies are equipped with radar systems, camera, LiDAR, GPS systems, and other smart devices, controlled by powerful AI programmes allowing these vehicles to sense their environment, navigate independently without the need of human intervention. These AVs also learn from their mistakes and improve their accuracy faster than any probable human driver. Today, it is recognised that more than 50% of innovations in vehicles are on electronic components [2]. Most cars are now equipped with some level of automation to assist drivers when parking their vehicles or following other vehicles. Indeed, latest generations of cars have the capabilities of detecting, anticipating and correcting drivers' manoeuvres accurately and autonomously. Certainly, AV can be considered as a disruptive technology as it will completely change the way most people live their lives, it will affect parking spaces, insurance industry, the taxi industry and many other businesses. New car sharing schemes will be introduced and fewer people may own their private cars in the future.

P. Seuwou (✉)
Northampton University, Northampton, UK
e-mail: patrice.seuwou@northampton.ac.uk

F. P. García Márquez, B. Lev (eds.), *Introduction to Internet of Things in Management Science and Operations Research*, International Series in Operations Research & Management Science 311,
https://doi.org/10.1007/978-3-030-74644-5_9

Throughout history, not all innovative technologies predicted by the media have been immediately welcomed by the society and looking at all the changes this emerging technology may bring, AV may be rejected by a proportion of the population not ready to alter their habits. In the past few decades, several models and theories have been proposed to predict people use behaviour of technology. But in the literature, there is still a gap as most of the proposed models are still not able to fully capture the complexity brought by AVs. So, there is still a need to explore the key factors that will influence consumers' behavioural intention to adopt AV [1, 3, 4]. For several years, UTAUT (Unified Theory of Acceptance and Use of Technology) and later UTAUT2 were models that have been used extensively in the past to assist researchers in understanding the main factors influencing use behaviour of various technologies [5].When analysing most existing models and theories, including the latest car technology acceptance research model, it becomes evident that several factors not previously considered will have to be explored in this AV scenario. The rest of the paper is organised as follows: Sect. 2 gives a state of art review on AV acceptance, Sect. 3 discusses the main constructs identified for the proposed AVTAM model with the hypothesis, Sect. 4 provides the methods and techniques used to test the proposed research model, the results are presented in Sect. 5 followed by a brief conclusion with future work in Sect. 6.

2 State of the Art Review

2.1 Brief History and Background of Autonomous Vehicles

Since Norman Bel Geddes envisioned autonomous vehicles in the 1939 World's Fair General Motors exhibit Futurama, autonomous vehicle technology has come a long way. The idea of robotic vehicles and intelligent highways in the middle of the twentieth century was mostly debated by futuristic and science fiction fanatics. The thought of automating the driver of the vehicle became a possibility only few decades after the first Model T Ford was introduced. During the subsequent decades, technology magazines predicted and documented the prospects of vehicles that could drive themselves becoming a reality [6]. The Defense Research Advanced Projects Agency (DARPA) Grand Challenge that took place in 2004, 2005, and 2007 (Urban challenge), were some of the most prestigious developments in federal support for the industry. The prize for the winning team with the best AV technology was $1 million [7]. During the first competition in 2004, none of the robot vehicles finished the race, but during the second race, five vehicles successfully completed. The third competition of the DARPA Grand Challenge rules included obeying all traffic regulations while negotiating with other traffic and obstacles and merging into traffic. These activities brought several teams to the US coming from all over the world including Japanese and European car manufacturers and universities. Many of the participants are still working as AV engineers or researchers, committed at making the deployment of this technology a reality in their lifetime [8].

For decades, researchers claimed the breakthrough was imminent and now, it appears, it has finally arrived. Assuming the diversity of the main parties involved in the achievement of the same goal, it is evident that the names given to the technology are not the same. In some texts, it is referred to as self-driving car, driverless car, connected and autonomous vehicle (CAV), robot-car, robotic car or autonomous vehicle (AV) which is the choice selected for this paper. They all mean that the vehicle is capturing large amount of data from its environment, processing it and driving the passengers with a considerable level of autonomy. The advances made in the last 40 years can be understood in terms of three successive waves of development. *Phase 1*: Foundational research, from 1980 to 2003 dominated by university research centres, sometimes in partnership with transportation agencies and automotive companies, they undertook basic studies of autonomous transportation, *phase 2*: from 2003 to 2007, DARPA held three "Grand Challenges" that decidedly accelerated advancements in AV technology and reignited the public's imagination. *Phase 3*: from 2007 till now, commercial development. Table 1 shows the chronological listing of some important events and projects in the history of autonomous vehicle systems.

2.2 Autonomous Vehicles as a Disruptive Technology

Disruptive technology as coined by Christensen in [9] is an innovation that significantly changes the way that industries, businesses or consumers do things. It sweeps away or alters the systems or habits it replaces because it has characteristics that are observably superior. Christensen argues that when these technologies appear on the market, they may increase emerging market niches, get better very quickly with time and eventually overtake traditional products from established markets [9, 10]. Even a startup with restricted resources can aim at technology disruption by inventing an entirely new way of getting something done. There are supporting technologies with capability of improving the performance of existing products or services. Most markets appreciate, adopt and use them without delay [3]. At the same time, there are innovations that drastically challenge or change habits and the current state of affairs in the market. At the beginning, these products underachieve in the market, but after some time, few users value them, sooner or later the products become so convincing that all customers give up the old habits and flocks to the new way of doing things.

Globally, the transportation industry is inseparably connected to the energy industry and it is worth about $4 trillion [11]. The internal combustion engine technology is currently been disrupted and this will also provoke a massive reaction through the oil industry. The first level of disruption of the hundred-year-old car manufacturing industry would be electric vehicles (EVs), which is currently happening. The next wave of disruption will be AV technologies, and this will affect the market even before EV disruption has ended. Nothing will ever be the same again [3, 12, 13]. Indeed, societies as well as most cities in the western world and other

Table 1 Important events and projects in the history of AVs

Date	Events and projects	Info
1977	The first AV was built by Tsukuba Mechanical engineering lab	This vehicle was able to reach 20 miles per hour by following some white street markers on a distance of up to 50 m
1980s	The work of the pioneer Ernst Dieter Dickmanns on dynamic computer vision and his team in Germany, equipped Mercedes-Benz van with camera and other sensors	The 5-ton van was re-engineered in such a way that it was possible to control steering wheel, brakes and throttle, through computer commands based on real-time evaluation of image sequences. The van could achieve 60 miles per hour on streets without traffic
1987–1995	Pan-European PROMETHEUS Project also recognised as the largest ever funded project on autonomous vehicle	This project defined the state of the art of autonomous vehicles. The prototype car was able to exceed 110 miles per hour on the German Autobahn. Numerous universities and car manufacturers participated in this Pan-European project. Unlike the early AVs it drove in traffic and was capable of accomplishing manoeuvres to pass other cars
1995	CMU Navlab "No Hands Across America Project". The vehicle was semi-autonomous	The vehicle was 98.2% autonomous and made almost 3000 miles. Brakes and throttle needed human input
1997	AHS Demo'97 (Automated Highway System)	On a highway in San Diego, CA, more than 20 fully automated vehicles were operated
2000–2002	CARSENSE	This prototype was equipped with a variety of sensors, lasers, radar system, and camera vision. The project focused on more complex scenarios such as traffic jams
2000	AHSRA Demo 2000 (Japan)	This was an automated system able to operate with magnetic sensors on the road. In this demo, 38 cars, trucks and buses showed the ideal system for reducing accidents on the road based on accurate information provided to drivers and control assist systems
2000–2003	CHAMELEON	The system was made up of a processing module for crash prediction (control unit) and a sensor module for obstacle detection (vision system, medium range radar, laser scanner, laser, short-range radar). Output was intended to be used by an advanced passive safety system on board
2001	DARPA Demo III	This demo showed the ability of unmanned ground vehicles to navigate

(continued)

Table 1 (continued)

Date	Events and projects	Info
		miles of tough off-road terrain, avoiding obstacles such as trees and rocks
2001–2004	ARCOS (Research Action for Secure Driving) (France)	This project main objective was to reduce accidents by 30%. The key functions were: – controlling inter-vehicle distances; – avoiding lane departure; – avoiding collisions with fixed or slowly moving objects; – alerting other vehicles of accidents
2001–2004	CarTALK 2000	This European project focused on the new driver assistance systems, which are based upon vehicle to vehicle communication
2001–2005	INVENT (intelligent traffic and user-oriented technology) (Germany)	The prototypes were tried in the city of Magdeburg, Germany in April 2005. The main purpose of this project was to enhance the traffic flow and safety by using intelligent and user-friendly systems
2004–2008	PREVENT (EU)	This project is aiming to develop and test safety-related applications, using existing devices that can be integrated into on-board systems for driver assistance. PREVENT will alert the car driver of hazard situations and take necessary measures if the driver is not reacting
2004	DARPA (The Defense Advanced Research Projects Agency) Grand Challenge	The first competition of the DARPA Grand Challenge was held in March 2004 in the Mojave Desert region of the United States. No winner was declared, and the cash prize was not given
2005	DARPA Grand Challenge II	It was designed to be a race in the desert environment with no traffic. The course was predefined by GPS points and obstacle types were known in advance. Stanford University was the team that won the competition
Nov. 2007	DARPA Grand Challenge III	The third DARPA Grand Challenge race featuring autonomous ground vehicles in an urban environment took place in November 2007, at the site of the now-closed George Air Force Base
Jan. 2009	Google Car	The project was launched by Sebastian Thrun, the former director of the Stanford Artificial Intelligence Laboratory (SAIL) and Anthony Levandowski.

(continued)

Table 1 (continued)

Date	Events and projects	Info
		Google's development of self-driving technology began on January 17, 2009, at the company's secretive X lab run by co-founder Sergey Brin
2011	WildCat Project	Oxford University's WildCat Project created a modified Bowler Wildcat which is capable of autonomous operation using a flexible and diverse sensor suite
2013	RobotCar UK project	In February 2013, Oxford University unveiled the RobotCar UK project. An inexpensive autonomous car capable of quickly switching from manual driving to autopilot on learned routes
2015	Project Titan	Apple Inc. developed an electric car prototype (iCar) as part of their autonomous vehicle scheme
Dec. 2016	Waymo	In December 2016, the Google car unit was renamed Waymo and spun-off into a new division in Alphabet. The name Waymo was derived from its mission, "a new way forward in mobility"

parts of the globe will face massive transformation. Major technology giants and car manufacturers such as BMW, Mercedes-Benz, Tesla, Bosch, General Motors, Ford, Nissan, Waymo, Apple, Uber are already testing AV prototypes. Vehicles with some degree of autonomy are already been sold on the market. These innovations (EV, AV) are set to become a large part of our fleet. They will bring great opportunities such as new types of jobs, an increase in employees productivity, less accidents, cheaper and easier commute with fewer fatalities, less congestion, reduction in environmental emissions, therefore, reducing the billions of pounds the government spend on infrastructures etc. but in turn this will also create job losses, disruption in various industries which will have to reinvent themselves or disappear altogether and many other problems not currently identified. AV is a truly disruptive technology and we cannot predict the future by simply deducing from the past. All the above issues will change the forecasts for standard infrastructure and major transportation projects.

2.3 Concept Underlying User Acceptance

Generally, the term "acceptance" refers to "agreeing, acknowledging or approving". This is the action of consenting to receive or use something [5]. For decades, IT

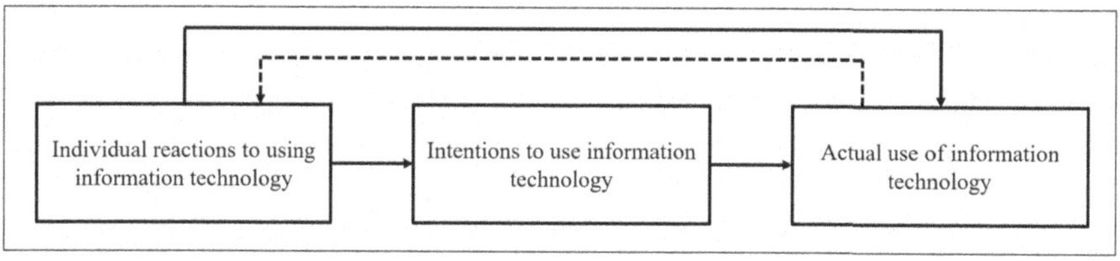

Fig. 1 Basic concept underlying user acceptance models [15]

acceptance has been an area of intense study by academics and practitioners investigating and proposing various models and theories attempting to explain and predict people behaviours towards various technologies [1]. In their struggle to clarify and give a rationale to system use, they developed a tool to measure computer user satisfaction. In order to do that, they first consulted the psychologists who have had a tracked record of studying user satisfaction [14]. In this paper, user acceptance will be defined as the demonstrable willingness within a group of users to employ a form of technology for the tasks it is intended to support. Thus, the term will not be employed in conditions consumers claimed to have used it in or for reasons unintended by the originators or creators. In reality, there are always possibilities that the actual usage deviates from the intended purpose. The main idea behind acceptance theory is that these types of deviation are not observed on a large scale, therefore not significant and that it can be modelled and predicted. In some instances, users are reluctant to use technologies in the event that their usage will result in massive performance gain. This is another reason why user acceptance is regarded as a pivotal factor when determining whether a new information technology or information system is a failure or a success on the market. Most technology acceptance models and theories proposed in the past follow a similar concept despite having their own specific attributes. Figure 1 illustrates the fundamental concept underlying user acceptance models.

In recent years, technologies linked to the automation of transportation systems has fascinated audiences around the world, from the stakeholders to the media. Car manufacturers and other stakeholders such as technology companies are joining forces to develop automated systems that will resolve the increasing demand of mobility around the world. On one hand, the recent deployment of electric vehicles by companies such as Tesla has exposed the public to a new form of energy-powered vehicles, slowly gaining momentum and trust. Despite the problems related to the limited number of charging stations in major cities, several car manufacturers all over Europe and other parts of the world are currently running tests and pilot programs as prerequisites to make sure that such investments pay off in the future. On the other hand, many are convinced that consumer acceptance will be the most challenging problem for AV penetration [1, 3, 12]. A survey conducted in the UK and the US has identified that several passengers will be reluctant to have faith on robots by putting their lives in their hands. There is a split opinion whether people would like to have various levels of automation in their vehicles. Many car drivers enjoy the experience of driving, owning their own vehicles and believe that their independence and freedom to go where ever they please may be taken away from them once this technology is deployed all over the world. Citizens may only be able to go to places authorised by the government. In the past few decades, the world has experienced massive changes related to driving experiences. These rapid changes have been introduced by car manufacturers in terms of technological advancement. For instance, a typical middle-class classic vehicle has standard features such as electronic stability program, automatic gearbox, and power windows [5]. More expensive class of vehicles are equipped with more intelligent features such as self-parking technology, active lane assistance, and automatic startup framework. These new features have made driving more comfortable, however, these vehicles still need human interaction to perform some other complex tasks [16]. More and more AV manufacturers are investing massively on these technologies to make them fully autonomous; able to operate without any human intervention; allowing the vehicle to control the acceleration, steering and braking while the passengers may be focusing their energies on other activities [10].

There is a variety of factors people must consider when thinking about purchasing a vehicle such as psychological factors, personal attitudes, situational factors including the regulatory environmental bodies or agencies. According to [5] environmentally conscious behaviours are influenced by several factors. These include personal values, environmental concerns depicting the fact that a difference can be made in the world and the environment by using the appropriate vehicles that generate less pollution. This contributes to individuals purchase decision for alternative eco-friendly forms of energy, reduction of air pollution, reduction of maintenance and better handling. It is evident that environmentalists and people who prefer cleaner energy sources will be more attracted to hybrid electric vehicles. According to [17], research shows that the most important attributes for car buyers are vehicles' price, reliability and the fuel economy. According to the unified theory of acceptance, different cultures around the world have distinct characteristics with regards to their behaviour towards AV technologies. For example, Hong Kong citizens give priority to the benefits related to the technology and the environment, followed by economic advantages and social benefits. In most developed societies, several limitations to AV and EV technologies have been identified. These include the lack of AV and EV infrastructure, the limitations in terms of variety of EV technologies available and the possibility of electrical rates being increased as a result of EV and AV mass adoption. In [4] the researchers have identified four key factors influencing potential buyers purchase behaviour. These include short battery capacity, high buying costs, psychological factors and charge inconvenience. Other findings in China highlighted further issues such as overall cost of operations, and possible speeds. A study in [13] also demonstrates that personal norms, perceived behavioural control, attributes, as well as the planning abilities will influence consumers' decisions to purchase AV. It is evident that potential advantages such as safety benefits, time saving, and fuel savings will always be in peoples' minds.

2.4 Key Challenges to Autonomous Vehicles Acceptance

The century old car manufacturing industry used to be the area of mechanical engineering. Today, due to significant progress in computing and electronics achieved in the past few decades, more and more software and technology firms are joining the race. One of the main purposes of developing AV was to decrease the number of accidents on the road and increase safety [18]. It appears that over 90% of road accidents are somehow due to bad driving habits and human errors, whether it is dangerous driving or driving under the influence of alcohol [19]. Some initial studies conducted on car safety few decades ago produced the introduction of vehicles to vehicles communication (V2V) and Vehicles to Infrastructure (V2I) communication also referred to as VANET (Vehicular Ad-hoc NETwork) generated a lot of attraction in the past. Today, the goal of AV is making road accident be something of the past. Despite all the obvious positive reasons AV will bring to humanity, there are several challenges these technologies will also be facing. These vehicles will be developed with massive computing capabilities with internet connection, therefore very likely to be compromised by cyber criminals. Furthermore, in today digital world, our data is the new gold, the new oil, the new currency; these vehicles will generate large amount of data (passenger location, speed, record of the places it has been to) opening a whole pandora box for privacy concerns and ethical concerns. Other concerns will be legal, jobs losses. In the following sections, some of the key barriers to AV will be explored.

2.4.1 Safety

Most governments in the developed world are actively planning the deployment of AV technologies. At the beginning, people may be reluctant to hand over their lives to robots. There are surveys conducted in the past showing a split in opinion regarding making AV technology available in their vehicles [16]. It appears that mass adoption will surely take time, particularly there has been instances when these vehicles despite their technology superiority, have been involved in accident [20]. For example, in 2016, Google car (Waymo) was involved in several collisions, in March 2018, an autonomous car operated by Uber during real-world testing with a human emergency driver behind the wheel, struck and killed Elaine Herzberg in what is believed to be the first recorded pedestrian fatality involving an Autonomous car. This type of accident could generate fear from consumers particularly if they happen to take place early on in the adoption phase whether it is the vehicle system's fault or not.

2.4.2 Legal Implications

Countries introducing AVs technologies to their respective populations will also have to develop laws that allow these cars to be driven on the street with vulnerable people. At the moment, there are suitable laws that determine liability when there is an accident involving traditional vehicles and other vehicles with some level of autonomy. Although it is being debated in various countries, many countries around the world are still behind on laws regulating vehicle accidents where one of the parties is fully autonomous. The general vehicle safety rules that govern car design assume that a human sits behind the steering wheel of each vehicle. In fact, they assume each vehicle has a steering wheel. Now those rules may begin to change [21]. In this scenario, it is difficult to identify who to blame [2]. Is it the car owner, or the AV manufacturer? The adjusted standards would nix some rules related to rider safety for AVs that carry goods like groceries, but no people. They would address the protections needed when steering wheels and steering columns have gone the way of the dodo. They would reexamine how airbags might work in a car newly configured to drive itself and consider barring children from the front left seat of a vehicle, where the steering wheel traditionally lives [21]. The rules would also clarify the definition of “driver”, which the agency has now decided it will not change within the standards. Instead, it will clarify within each mention whether “driver” refers to a fleshy human, or the advanced driver systems that might 1 day operate cars all on their own. There is a need for more clarity on civil and criminal laws [20, 22]. Some other implications of this would be when disable people or passengers unable to drive could “get behind the wheel” of an AV, or when these vehicles move from one location to another without passengers. What then happens if there is an accident? Who will be to blame in this instance. For semi-autonomous car, when there is a driver behind the wheel, the ultimate liability remains on the driver even if at this stage it may be intensely debatable. With Brexit underway, the UK Government has started consultation in allowing autonomous driving—self-driving—modes up to 70mph, with the potential for legislation as early as spring 2021, bringing UK law and standards in line with UNECE targets [23].

2.4.3 Social and Ethical Issues

Two kinds of ethical questions are raised by autonomous vehicles.

(a) Large fleets of AV are being tested every day in roads all around the world. These technologies are equipped with advanced machine learning capabilities. When one vehicle makes an error, other vehicles with the same algorithm from a specific car manufacturer also learn from that mistake and avoid it next time around. Technology firm developing these vehicles are spending huge sums on the development, therefore their programmes and source codes are secretly guarded. Now, is it possible to really programme these vehicles to respond to every conceivable road scenarios? Particularly in cases when the vehicle must disregard the law in order to save someone's life in a dangerous situation or break the law related to speed limit when taking someone to the hospital (A&E)? In some cases, the vehicle may have to choose between different options in a dangerous situation (either killing a young child crossing the road, a young adult, another old and disable person or heading towards a tree or a wall possibly killing the passengers of the vehicle). How would it make the selection?

(b) It is undeniable that AV introduction will deliver considerable social and economic benefits to the world, at the same time, it will make several existing jobs become obsolete. Today, when using your smartphone, you have the right to opt in or opt out when sharing your personal data. In the future, although that rule may still apply, it may be mandatory to share limited personal data by law, which will impact on people privacy right.

2.4.4 Technology

It appears that the mass adoption of AV technologies may face some practical technological hurdles. Vehicular Ad-hoc NETworks, (VANETs) were created by applying some of the key principles of Mobile Ad-hoc NETworks (MANETs). Although research on this technology remained mainly in the academic world, some of their principles are likely to be implemented soon where vehicles will be equipped with short-range radios capable of communicating with other vehicles or with highway infrastructures at distances of at least 1 km [24]. The IEEE 802.11p was initially considered as the de facto standard that will support Intelligent Transportation Systems (ITS) applications in VANETs and connected autonomous vehicles (CAVs). This technology has scalability issues, unbounded delays, and lack of deterministic quality of service (QoS) guarantees. While many research partnerships have had this as a focus topic during Horizon 2020 [25], a problem with fragmentation has slowed progress. Although 5G is just getting started, and yet to be deployed nationwide in the UK, 6G network technologies is expected to bring autonomous vehicles to their full potential, more so than 5G could [26]. With AVs and CAVs connected to the web, they will also be a component of the Internet of Things (IoT), allowing vehicles to share data on the road. This will include the actual path, traffic information, and how to navigate around any obstacles. With the IoT, and big data, data privacy and security will also be a concern [27].

2.4.5 Infrastructure

Even though AV built today will have some level of autonomy with less dependence of dedicated infrastructure compared to early prototypes, a minimum level of infrastructure will still be necessary. These may include road markings and signage, GPS mapping, strong telecom networks [2, 28]. For V2X communication, the government and other dedicated transportation authority will still need to install important infrastructures such as Road side base stations and road side units (RSUs), intelligent traffic light systems particularly for smart cities allowing communication between vehicles (V2V) or with other infrastructures (V2I) [29]. The automaker might also facilitate delivery of some traffic-specific information through such infrastructure. The infrastructure is managed by infrastructure operators. The information is then used by the driver to generate situational awareness of the car and its surroundings and make appropriate decisions while driving [30]. Situational awareness will include an understanding of the cars own driving status (such as its velocity, acceleration, location, etc.) called the self-awareness, and an understanding of the car's surroundings (objects nearby, their state of motion, traffic signals, other road signs, etc.) called the contextual awareness [2, 28, 30].

2.4.6 Cost

The technologies to build this type of vehicle are very expensive. The cost of AVs will be the biggest barrier to their adoption [31]. Indeed, these vehicles will be equipped with advanced technologies such as sensors, camera, LiDAR, which is a method for measuring distances (ranging) by illuminating the target with laser light and measuring the reflection with a sensor used to make digital 3-D representations of the target [2]. It is not only about the cost of AV, it is about the difference between the cost of traditional cars and AV [32]. In early adoption stages, possibly only wealthy people will be able to afford these vehicles but gradually, the cost of the components may be reduced later on with concepts such as the Moore's Law, the price of the vehicle components may become cheaper making vehicles affordable to the public. There would be cost related to maintenance and software updates. First cost estimates of future transport services with AVs were proposed by [31]. For three different cases (small to medium town, suburban and urban), they calculated the cost, per trip, of a centrally organised system of shared AVs (medium sedans with AV technology), which would replace existing transport services. Their estimates are based on different cost categories, which capture fixed and variable costs. They concluded that such systems could provide "better mobility experiences at radically [up to ten times] lower cost". In a second approach, [33] considered the external costs (e.g., crash or congestion cost) of today's private transport system to calculate AVs' potential benefits, which they found to be substantial. In a following paper, [34] focused on possible prices for users of a centrally organised, shared AV system. By assuming an investment cost of 70,000 US$ and operating costs of 0.50 US$ per mile for AVs only, they found that a fare of 1.00 US$ per trip-mile for an AV taxi could still produce a profit for the operator. This is a higher price level than in [31] but still very competitive compared to today's transport options.

2.4.7 Cyber Security

It is largely acknowledged that AVs as well as CAVs will be part of the internet of things (IoT) and the internet of Everything (IoE), therefore it will raise numerous cyber security concerns [2]. Indeed, these vehicles will be vulnerable and subject to cyber-attacks by hackers and cybercriminal with the objective of taking over the control of their target vehicles, thus undermining vehicle safety. Furthermore, personal data could also be harvested for malicious intent [35] particularly when sensitive data are transmitted when accessing the public network. As such, cybersecurity for AVs is important to win and maintain consumers' trust which will ultimately have a large influence on mass deployment and the rate of adoption [36].

2.5 Existing Studies of User Acceptance of AVs

Automation of vehicles and driverless technology has attracted a lot of people from the stakeholders to the media. Stakeholders have been yearning to develop and take the automated driving technology a notch higher and meet the increasing demands of consumers. Public exposure to the different forms of electric vehicles has slowly gained momentum in recent years with various manufacturers carrying out test runs and pilot programs in Europe [16]. Such programs help towards examining the user acceptance of these modern vehicles and act as prerequisites to ensure such investment pay off. Many authors believe that customer acceptance is likely to be the biggest obstacle to autonomous vehicle penetration [1, 3, 12]. According to [5], there are different factors that influence and motivate the environmentally conscious behaviours. The elements encompass the personal values; environmental concerns as well as the belief that one can make a difference in the use of such vehicles. Also, these factors contribute towards an individual's purchase intentions for the alternative fuel vehicles. Gas prices significantly impact the individual's interest in buying hybrid electric cars. There are other customer preferences such as reduced air pollution, reduced maintenance and better handling. There is no doubt that environmentalists and people that have strong preferences for energy security will automatically adopt the hybrid electric cars. Results of the study by [4] highlighted four determinant factors affecting purchasing behaviours of the potential buyers: high costs, charge inconvenience, psychological factors and short battery range. A study in China also revealed some deterministic factors or concerns when purchasing autonomous vehicles such as the cost of operations, overall buying cost, possible speeds and battery capacity. In the USA, the potential buyers considered the charge time and range as concerns other than the value of the hybrid vehicles. Findings by [13] also show that the attributes, personal norms, the perceived behavioural control as well as the planning abilities influenced the decision to buy an autonomous vehicle. Customers will always be concerned about the potential advantages as well as the promises as indicated below:

2.5.1 Safety Benefits

According to the National Highway Traffic Safety Administration (NHTSA) annual reports, most car accidents are linked with human error as a result of distractions, sickness or fatigue [10, 37]. Thus, autonomous cars are capable of increasing traffic safety as all the critical functions of the driver are system oriented. Hence, a guarantee of safety for the users is a consideration when purchasing autonomous vehicles [38].

2.5.2 Time Savings

Hybrid electric cars are considerate and time efficient. They can optimise the choice of routes based on their ability to collect updated traffic information and thus a person can reach their desired destination faster compared to human-driven vehicles. Automated vehicles also reduce congestion through minimised road accidents and shortened travel times for the users. The Internet of Things (IoT) will significantly influence the adoption of automated cars. Self-parking functionalities continue to be advanced with major improvements expected to be rolled out in the coming years to reduce damages because of parking accidents.

2.5.3 Fuel Savings

The V2V and V2I communication increases the fuel economy by a considerable percentage when automated vehicles are used. Fuel savings are also enhanced through high utilisation of highways and the ability for the vehicles to travel closely together. The use of AVs significantly lessens the environmental degradation due to reduced greenhouse emissions. Additionally, the reduction of these pollutants also minimises the social costs associated with human health [16, 38]. Autonomous technology will improve the productivity levels of the individuals. The passengers of the autonomous cars participate in other social activities such as resting (sleeping), reading, watching movies or working.

3 Formulating the Autonomous Vehicles Technology Acceptance Model (AVTAM)

This study was conducted in the UK using two surveys. The initial survey was developed to identify other important factors previously neglected by existing models and theories. The second survey was used to test the proposed model. Using a convenience sampling technique, a questionnaire (survey 1) was distributed to participant largely students and academic staffs from several British universities

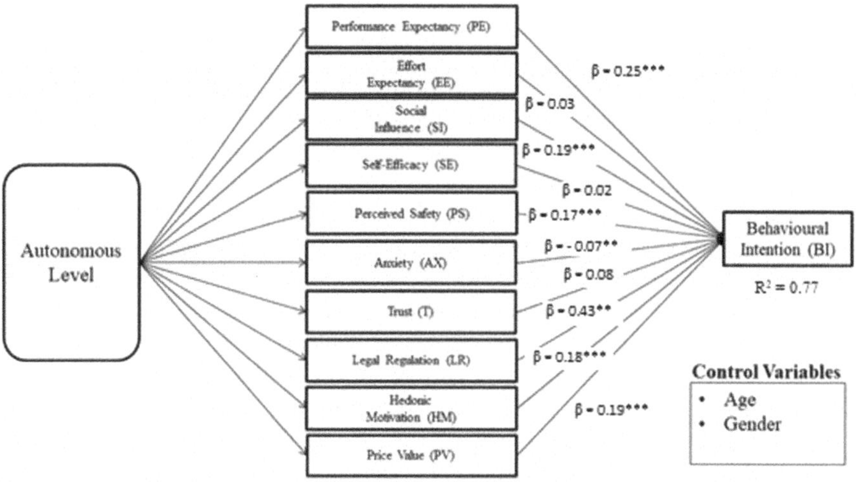

Fig. 2 Research model for measuring consumers' behavioural intention to adopt autonomous vehicles: Autonomous Vehicle Technology Acceptance Model (AVTAM)

and other random users. The target population was any potential users of commercial AV and the sample size was 408 participants. In-depth interviews were also conducted with 25 experts including academics and practitioners in the fields of sociology, psychology and computer science. Data was collected from both sources together with extensive literature analysis to help generate the AVTAM model proposed in Fig. 2.

During the study, the following factors and hypotheses were identified as key to the mass adoption of this emerging technology.

3.1 *Performance Expectancy (PE)*

In this context, *PE* is the extent to which an AV user will have confidence that the technology meets his/her expectation and would be able to improve individual daily life activities, while increasing productivity, safety, trust, privacy protection and decreasing accidents on the road. In other words, doing what it is supposed to do. Gender and age are theorised to play a moderating role in this case, such that the effect will be stronger for men and specifically for younger men [39–44].

H1: *Performance Expectancy will be positively related to behavioural intention of using autonomous vehicles.*

3.2 Effort Expectancy (EE)

In this scenario, EE is referred to as the degree of ease related to learning how to operate this type of technology safely. It appears that the influence of EE on people intention or use behaviour will be moderated by gender, age and previous experience of using the technology. The clarity of the instructions from AV manufacturers and the simplicity of the interaction with these vehicles. The influence of effort expectancy on behavioural intention will be moderated by gender, age and experience. It is suggested that effort expectancy is more salient for women than for men. The gender differences predicted here could be driven by cognitions related to gender roles. It has also been showed that the further someone is older, the harder it is to process complex information. Thus, the study proposes that effort expectancy will be most noticeable for women, particularly those who are older and with relatively little experience with autonomous vehicles. The influence of effort expectancy on behavioural intention will be moderated by gender, age and experience, such that the effect will be stronger for women, particularly younger women and mostly at early stages of experience [39, 42, 43].

H2: *Effort Expectancy will be positively related to behavioural intention of using autonomous vehicles.*

3.3 Social Influence (SI)

In this setting, SI could be understood as the degree to which someone would perceive that people who are important to him or her would appreciate him or her using the technology. Your friends, family members, Journalists, expert reviewers and the media have a strategic position to influence your opinions, emotions or behaviours. This construct can be seen taking several forms; socialisation, conformity, review of information, persuasion, peer pressure obedience, sales and marketing. The impact of social influence on behavioural intention will be moderated by gender, age and experience, such that the effect will be stronger for women, particularly older women, particularly older women in mandatory stages of experience [42].

H3: *Social Influence will be positively related to behavioural intention of using autonomous vehicles.*

3.4 Self-Efficacy (SE)

In this scenario, the construct self-efficacy is defined as someone's belief in his/her abilities and competence to use a piece of technology and accomplish a specific task.

Generally, self-perception and external experiences play a key role on how someone approach a goal or a task. In the AV context, people with high self-efficacy - those who believe they can perform well are more likely to view a tough task as something to be learned rather that something to be avoided.

H4: *Self-Efficacy will be positively related to behavioural intention of using autonomous vehicles.*

3.5 Perceived Safety (PS)

PS in this scenario is defined as the degree to which an individual believes that using a specific technology will threaten his or her safety. Within AV, this also comprises the judgement of one's own driving capabilities and safety feeling in relation to other drivers. The impact of perceived safety is assumed as critical in the process of predicting the behavioural intention to use, as the user will evaluate the potential effect of safety-related consequences through using the technology on public road and dangerous surroundings. The following concepts are included in this factor: Vehicle security and safety,. cyber security concerns.

H5: *Perceived Safety will be positively related to behavioural intention of using autonomous vehicles.*

3.6 Anxiety (AX)

In this scenario, AX is defined as the degree to which an individual reacts to a circumstance with uneasiness. The construct AX and Behavioural Anxiety differ as per their origin, as Anxiety was borrowed from the computer anxiety determinant proposed within the Social Cognitive Theory (SCT) and was also used in the Unified Theory of Acceptance and Use of Technology (UTAUT) validation. Behavioural Anxiety otherwise reflects anxiety in a more general understanding towards the autonomous vehicle or system behaviour which addresses e.g., the fear to lose control of the car [45, 46].

H6: *Anxiety will be negatively related to behavioural intention of using autonomous vehicles.*

3.7 Trust (T)

In the past few years, some car manufacturers have misled the public and some other government authorities about their real engine CO^2 emission. This kind of behaviours can largely damage consumer trust. Today, it may be difficult to accept statements from car manufacturers without evidence or proof. In this scenario, trust is defined as the belief in the reliability, truth, or ability of the car. The belief that consumers can trust the car and the system to function as presented while protecting users' personal data.

H7: *Trust will be positively related to behavioural intention of using autonomous vehicles.*

3.8 Legal Regulation (LR)

In this AV scenario, LR is defined as the rule of order having the force of law made and maintained by an authority and transportation regulatory bodies. The following elements are included in this construct:

Effort by the government and car manufacturers to better support users, regulations, policies, legislation, liability, law.

H8: *Legal Regulation will be positively related to behavioural intention of using autonomous vehicles.*

3.9 Hedonic Motivation (HM)

HM in this context refers to the influence of a person's pleasure and pain receptors on their willingness to move towards a goal or away from a threat. The fun or pleasure derived from using a technology, it has been shown to play an important role in determining the rate of technology acceptance and use. Therefore, the influence of HM on behavioural intention will be moderated by age, gender and experience.

H9: *Hedonic Motivation will be positively related to behavioural intention of using autonomous vehicles.*

3.10 Price Value (PV)

Consumers' technology may be influenced largely by the cost of these technologies, and the pricing structure of their maintenance. In marketing studies, it is accepted that the quality of a product or service is also theoretically related to the price. PV is positive when the benefits of using a technology are perceived to be superior to the monetary cost and such price value has a good impact on behavioural intention. Thus, price value has been added as a predictor of BI to use AV [47]. The following elements are included in this factor: Cost of the vehicle, operational cost and maintenance cost, cost related to the network protocols and standards being used.

H10: *Price Value will be positively related to behavioural intention of using autonomous vehicles.*

3.11 Behavioural Intention (BI)

BI in this context can be defined as a person's aim to perform a given act which can predict corresponding behaviours when an individual acts voluntarily. Besides that, BI is the subjective probability of carrying out behaviour and also the cause of certain usage behaviour [48]. Thus, intentions show the motivational factors that influence behaviour and are indicators of how hard people are willing to try and the effort they put in to engage in a behaviour. Also, it was found that behavioural intention is to be the main factor of individual AV usage and that usage intentions are rational indicators of future system use.

4 Method

In this study, UTAUT2 has been used as a base model to better understand behavioural intention to accept AV. UTAUT2 [49] was expanded as illustrated in Sect. 3 to develop the AVTAM. After creating the proposed research model, it was necessary to test and validate the constructs. For the second survey, the population selection was similar to the first survey, also conducted in the UK. The participants were people who used car as passengers or drivers and they didn't have to have had experience riding an AV in the past. Questions were developed using the free tool Google Forms and administered online and via email whenever possible using social media network. Indeed, by creating our questionnaire using Google Forms, the system generated a unique link that could be shared electronically. The questionnaire had an introductory paragraph included at the beginning explaining what self-driving cars were about. The introductory paragraph also clarified the purpose of the study and explaining to participants how all information collected would be anonymous and confidential. At the same time, participants had to confirm that they were at least 18 years of age. Before anyone could start answering the question there was a very short YouTube video demonstrating to participants how self-driving cars (Google Car) worked and what could be the benefits of this technology to future road users.

To test the hypothesis and validate the proposed model, the researcher designed series of questions (Observable Variables) to help us measure our constructs (Independent Variables) (PE, EE, SI, SE, PS, AX, T, LR, HM, PV) which are variables that are not directly observed but are rather inferred [49]. The researcher has developed a series of Likert scale questions. All items of the model were measured using a seven-point Likert scale, [50–52] with the anchors being "strongly disagree" and "strongly agree". 482 valid responses were analysed using the Structured Equation Modelling (SEM) techniques with the R Studio and the Statistics Package for Social Science (SPSS) software. The following statistical tests were applied to the data.

4.1 Reliability Analysis

Reliability analysis is a measure to define the degree to which measurements are free from error, that is how closely related a set of items are as a group and therefore yield consistent results [49]. In this study, Cronbach's Alpha was used to examine the internal consistency of each measure. As recommended by [53], a minimum cut off of 0.7 for Cronbach's Alpha reliability coefficients was employed. The result of this test is shown in Table 3. Below, for conceptual purposes, (1) shows the formula for the Cronbach's Alpha [53]:

$$\alpha = \frac{N\overline{c}}{\overline{v} + (N-1)\overline{c}} \tag{1}$$

Here N is equal to the number of items, $\overline{c}$ is the average inter-item covariance among the items and $\overline{v}$ equals the average variance.

4.2 Correlation Analysis

Correlation analysis is a measure of the degree to which a change in the independent variable will result in a change in the dependent variable. This test is a bivariate analysis that measures the strength of association between variables and the direction of the relationship. In terms of the strength of relationship, the value of the correlation coefficient varies between +1 and −1. A value of ±1 indicates a perfect degree of association between the two variables. As the correlation coefficient value goes towards 0, the relationship between the two variables will be weaker. The result of this test is shown in Table 4.

4.3 Regression Analysis

Regression analysis includes any techniques for modelling and analysing several variables, with a focus on the relationship between a dependent variable and one or more independent variables.

4.4 *Structure Equation Modelling (SEM)*

Structure Equation Modelling (SEM) is a "multivariate technique combining aspects of factor analysis and multiple regression that enables the researcher to simultaneously examine a series of interrelated relationships among the measured variables and latent constructs as well as between latent constructs" [54] SEM examines interrelated relationships among multiple dependent and independent variables [54, 55]. In this study, Exploratory Factor Analysis (EFA) was used to summarise information from many variables in the proposed research model into a smaller number of factors. The Confirmatory Factor Analysis (CFA) was also used to assess unidimensionality, reliability and validity of the constructs used in the model. In the process, this path analysis (SEM) was used to examine the hypothesised relationships between the latent constructs in the proposed model. According to [53], critical ratio (CR) estimates value $\geq$1.96 suggests significance of the causal path between latent constructs. The results of the original structural model are illustrated in Table 5.

5 Results

Sample characteristics were analysed using frequency distributions (Table 2). The analysis of the data collected shows gender groups are evenly represented with 56.4% males and 43.6% females. The most represented age groups are 45–54 years (22%), 35–44 years (21.6%). With respect to levels of education, 78.8% of respondents had achieved a higher educational degree, with 13.7% PhD holders.

In this section, we use Cronbach's Alpha (see Table 3) to measure the internal consistency that is, how closely related set of items are as a group. All the values are greater than 0.7, which clearly shows the reliability of the scale/research instrument. Dillon-Goldstein rho should be higher than 0.8, as the minimum is 0.91 this is satisfactory.

Table 4 below presents the correlation matrix showing the correlation coefficients between different constructs part of the proposed model. The most correlated variables are PE & BI (0.81), so with the higher performance expectancy there is higher behavioural intentions, and PE & PS (0.73) and the least correlated variable is the Age. The anxiety is negatively correlated and that is good, the maximum is for Perceived safety (−0.74), which corresponds to what could be expected, as higher Perceived Safety implies less Anxiety.

Both the goodness of fit indices and parameter estimates coefficients were examined to check whether the hypothesised structural model fitted the data and to test the hypotheses. The fit indices indicated that the hypothesised structural model provided the good fit to the data. All hypotheses were supported (see Table 5).

Table 2 Demographic breakdown of respondents

Demographic aspect		U.K. ($N = 482$)	Percentage (%)
Age group	18–24	89	18.5%
	25–34	82	17%
	35–44	104	21.6%
	45–54	106	22%
	55–64	75	15.6%
	65 and over	15	3.11%
	Prefer not to say	11	2.3%
Gender	Male	272	56.4%
	Female	210	43.6%
Level of driving experience	No driving experience	51	10.6%
	Novice	42	8.7%
	Intermediate	80	16.6%
	Experienced	296	61.4%
	Expert	13	3.7%
Education	No formal qualifications	1	0.2%
	GCSE or equivalent	10	2.1%
	A level or equivalent	91	18.9%
	Bachelor's degree	148	30.7%
	Master's degree	151	31.3%
	PhD	66	13.7%
	Other	15	3.1%

Table 3 Cronbach's alpha

#	Measure	Cronbach's alpha
1	Performance expectancy	0.91
2	Effort expectancy	0.93
3	Social influence	0.82
4	Self-efficacy	0.86
5	Perceived safety	0.80
6	Anxiety	0.88
7	Trust	0.85
8	Legal regulation	0.90
9	Hedonic motivation	0.96
10	Price value	0.87
11	Behavioural intention	0.92

Table 6 illustrates that a total of ten research hypotheses were tested to examine if the independent variables significantly explained the dependent variables.

The summary of the research hypotheses test; also, a reflection of the hypotheses relating to proposed conceptual model the performance of the said proposed model.

Table 4 Correlations matrix

Measure	PE	EE	SI	SE	PS	AX	T	LR	HM	PV	BI	Age	Gdr
PE	1												
EE	0.66	1											
SI	0.73	0.62	1										
SE	0.55	0.62	0.6	1									
PS	0.68	0.6	0.48	0.42	1								
AX	0.51	−0.5	0.38	0.33	0.74	1							
T	0.64	0.57	0.55	0.53	0.6	0.45	1						
LR	0.55	0.48	0.54	0.46	0.43	−0.3	0.72	1					
HM	0.58	0.45	0.53	0.42	0.36	−0.3	0.5	0.45	1				
PV	0.56	0.49	0.5	0.4	0.51	0.43	0.54	0.5	0.42	1			
BI	0.81	0.63	0.72	0.55	0.7	0.57	0.66	0.55	0.64	0.66	1		
Age	−0.0.5	−0.4	−0.3	−0.2	−17	0.06	0.40	0.03	0.26	0.23	0.5	1	
Gender	0.08	−0.5	−0.4	0.22	0.12	0.11	0.18	0.21	0.02	0.13	0.29	0.29	1

Table 5 Results of the original structural model

Construct	Code name	Hypotheses	Relationship (positive)	Standardised regression weights (β)	Supported
Performance expectancy	PE	H1	PE→BI	0.256	Yes***
Effort expectancy	EE	H2	EE→BI	0.038	YES
Social influence	SI	H3	SI→BI	0.199	Yes***
Self-efficacy	SE	H4	SE→BI	0.020	YES
Perceived safety	PS	H5	PS→BI	0.176	Yes***
Anxiety	AX	H6	AX→BI	−0.077	Yes**
Trust	T	H7	T→BI	0.084	YES
Legal regulation	LR	H8	LR→BI	0.043	Yes**
Hedonic motivation	HM	H9	HM→BI	0.184	Yes***
Price value	PV	H10	PV→BI	0.193	Yes***

***Significant at 0.001 level (two tailed). **Significant at 0.01 level (two tailed)

Table 6 Summary of research hypotheses

HN	Research hypotheses	Results
H1	Performance expectancy will be positively related to behavioural intention of using autonomous vehicles	Supported
H2	Effort expectancy will be positively related to behavioural intention of using autonomous vehicles	Supported
H3	Social influence will be positively related to behavioural intention of using autonomous vehicles	Supported
H4	Self-efficacy will be positively related to behavioural intention of using autonomous vehicles	Supported
H5	Perceived safety will be positively related to behavioural intention of using autonomous vehicles	Supported
H6	Anxiety will be negatively related to behavioural intention of using autonomous vehicles	Supported
H7	Trust will be positively related to behavioural intention of using autonomous vehicles	Supported
H8	Legal regulation will be positively related to behavioural intention of using autonomous vehicles	Supported
H9	Hedonic motivation will be positively related to behavioural intention of using autonomous vehicles	Supported
H10	Price value will have a significant influence on behavioural intention of using autonomous vehicles	Supported

It is possible to compare the predictability of the Autonomous Vehicle Technology Acceptance Model with previous study.

Table 7 illustrates the comparison of previous studies for the adjusted R^2 obtained for both behavioural intention and actual behaviour. The comparison clearly

Table 7 Comparison of intention and behaviour in terms of adjusted R^2

Study	Theory	Adjusted R^2	
		Behavioural intention	Actual behaviour
Davis et al. (1989)	TAM	–	0.45
Davis et al. (1989)	TRA	–	0.32
Davies (1989)	TAM	–	0.51
Taylor and Todd (1995)	DTP	0.57	0.34
Taylor and Todd (1995)	TBP	0.57	0.34
Taylor and Todd (1995)	TAM	0.52	0.34
Karahanna et al. (1999)	TRA ± TAM	0.38	–
Agarwal and Karahanna (2000)	TAM and cognitive absorption	0.50	–
Gefen and Straub (2000)	TAM	0.20	–
Brown et (2002)	TAM	0.52	–
Koufaris (2002)	TAM ± flow theory	0.54	–
Current study	AVTAM	0.77	–
Recommended level (Straub et al., 2004)		0.40 or above	0.40 or above

demonstrates that the AVTAM performed as well as the previous studies. With regards to the behavioural intention value of adjusted R^2 varied between 0.20 [56] and 0.57, the adjusted R^2. For this study is found to be 0.77, which suggests that the model has a very high predictability power [57, 58].

Living in the twenty-first century, technology often overtakes our ability as a civilisation to come up with accepted rules of how it can be used. AV is one of these technologies that would disrupt the way how almost everything works in our society. Recent predictions that AVs will be here sooner than most people expect is progressively being acknowledged and becoming a reality. In the UK, the government's strategic policy plans are very favourable for research and investments in intelligent transportation systems. The following are some of the main recommendations surfaced and questions that still require answers:

- The impact AV deployment will have on the type of future road infrastructures should be investigated by researchers and professionals in the department of transport UK. Immediate studies will be required to reassure the public.
- The unpredictable and unknown element of future regulation subject to be imposed also appears to be one of the greatest barriers to innovation. In fact, despite all simulation and tests taking place now all around the world, it is difficult to know the rules that will be applied in their final forms. Therefore, questions remain about how fast tests can be endorsed and the length of the application process.
- Due to the life-threatening nature of this technology, it will be necessary to have policies, protocols and standards in place that would allow AV manufacturers to

share their data with other car manufacturers to better understand each other mistake therefore reducing possible instance where these mistakes are duplicated.

- In a future world where AVs bring multiple travel advantages, it may be necessary to implement some form of road pricing that will play a crucial task in avoiding the rise of traffic volumes and congestion.
- It is predicted that AV deployment will provide more freedom and flexibility to people with disabilities such as passengers with mobility problems. This is likely to be available at a lower cost than the on-demand transport system which is presently offered.
- These vehicles may be supplementing bus services, so should the public transport authorities manage their operation? Tests conducted on existing prototypes demonstrate that AV will be generating large amount of data. Should the government own and manage people private information? Wouldn't it give considerable powers to authorities? Should it be administered by private parties? So, it is still unclear who will own the data generated and how it would be managed.

6 Conclusion and Future Work

Throughout this study, technology acceptance literature shows the scarcity of empirical research of the determinants of the individuals' behavioural intention to use AV, especially in UK. This study examined the viability of the UTAUT2 model, which was established in developed economy settings for information systems, in explaining a similar behaviour within emerging technologies settings. Thus, the results of the present research contributions fill this important gap as AVTAM has been identified as a useful model to better understand consumers' behavioural intention to adopt AV. Most governments around the developed world are urgently working on sustainable transport policies and strategies to resolve key problems like environmental degradation, social inequity, congestion, road accidents and public health. In this paper, AV as a disruptive technology has been identified as a potential innovative transportation option for smart cities in an attempt to create a more sustainable productive development. It has been observed that consumers' acceptance is likely to be one of the most challenging aspect of AV deployment. Constructs influencing user behavioural intention to accept the technology have been identified and tested. The findings suggest that safety of these vehicles, trust, privacy protection and legal requirement and price value will play a crucial role and the proposed research model has a considerable predictive power. Findings of this research study have many marketing, managerial and customer service implications for different stakeholders such as car manufacturers and emerging technology designers. Future studies could focus in exploring the effect of factors such as cultural influence and socio-economic status on technology adoption, it is also important to evaluate various age groups behaviour such as senior citizens intention towards AV and the challenges they will face after the mass adoption.

References

1. Becker, F., & Axhausen, K. W. (2017). Literature review on surveys investigating the acceptance of autonomous vehicles. *Transportation, 44*, 1293–1306.
2. Seuwou, P., Chrysoulas, C., Banissi, E., & Ubakanma, G. (2020). Measuring consumer behavioural intention to accept technology: Towards autonomous vehicles technology acceptance model (AVTAM). In *WorldCIST 2020 conference*. New York: Springer.
3. Stanley, M.. (2013). *Autonomous cars: Self-driving the new auto industry paradigm*. s.l. Morgan Stanley Blue Paper.
4. Cho, Y., Park, J., Park, S., & Jung, E. S. (2017). Technology acceptance modeling based on user experience for autonomous vehicles. *Journal of the Ergonomics Society of Korea, 36*(2).
5. Fraedrich, E., & Lenz, B. (2016). Societal and individual acceptance of autonomous driving. *Springer Journal on Autonomous Driving*, 621–640.
6. Lari, A., Douma, F., & Onyiah, I. (2014). Self-driving vehicles: Current status of autonomous vehicle development and Minneasota policy implications. *Minnesota Journal of Law, Science & Technology, 16*(2), 5.
7. Toth, C. K., Paska, E., Chen, Q., Zhu, Y., Redmill, K., & Ozguner, U. (2006). Mapping support for the OSU DARPA grand challenge vehicle. In *Proc. IEEE ITS conf., Toronto, ON, Canada* (pp. 1580–1585). Washington, DC: IEEE.
8. Bilger, B. Auto correct. *The New Yorker*. Retrieved July 24, 2020, from http://www.newyorker.com/reporting/2013/11/25/131125fa_fact_bilger?currentPage=all.
9. Christensen, C. M. (1997). *The innovator's dilemma: How new technologies cause great firms to fail*. Boston: Harvard Business School Press.
10. 2025ad.com: 2025AD I 2025AD. (2020). The automated driving community [Online]. Retrieved July 24, 2020, from https://www.2025ad.com/categories/latest/technology/.
11. Seba, T. (2014). *Clean disruption of energy and transportation*. UK: Milton Keynes.
12. ERTRAC. (2015).Automated driving roadmap: status 3rd draft for public consultation.
13. Niculescu, A. I., Dix, A., & Yeo, K. H. (2017). Are you ready for a drive?: User perspectives on autonomous vehicles. In *Proceedings of the 2017 CHI conference extended abstracts on human factors in computing systems* (pp. 2810–2817). New York: ACM.
14. Bailey, J., & Pearson, S. (1983). Development of a tool for measurement and analyzing computer user satisfaction. *Management Science, 29*(5), 530–575.
15. Venkatesh, V., Morris, M. G., Davis, G. B., & Davis, F. D. (2003). User acceptance of information technology: Toward a unified view. *MIS Quarterly, 27*(3), 425–478.
16. Sheela, P., & Mannering, F. (2019). The effect of information on changing opinions toward autonomous vehicle adoption: An exploratory analysis. *International Journal of Sustainable Transportation*. https://doi.org/10.1080/15568318.2019.1573389.
17. Rödel, C., Stadler, S., Meschtscherjakov, A., & Tscheligi, M. (2014). Towards autonomous cars: the effect of autonomy levels on acceptance and user experience. In *Proceedings of the sixth international conference on automotive user interfaces and interactive vehicular applications* (pp. 1–8). New York: ACM.
18. Connor, M. (2019). In M. Connor (Ed.), *Automobile sensors may usher in self-driving cars*. N. p., Retrieved July 9, 2019, from http://www.edn.com/design/automotive/4368069/ Automobile-sensors-may-usher-in-self-driving-cars.
19. Olarte, O. (2019). Human error accounts for 90% of road accidents. *Driver Risk Management Solutions*. Retrieved September 9, 2019, from http://www.alertdriving.com/home/fleet-alert-magazine/international/human-error-accounts-90-road-accidents/.
20. KPMG. (2015). Connected and autonomous vehicles—The economic opportunity, s.l. SMMT Driving the motor industry.
21. Marshall, A. (2020). *New rules could finally clear the way for self-driving cars*. WIRED. https://www.wired.com/story/news-rules-clear-way-self-driving-cars/. Last retrieved 2020/09/29.
22. McChristian, L., & Corbett, R. (2016). Regulation issues related to autonomous vehicles. *Journal of Insurance Regulation, 35*(7).

23. Kilpatrick, R. (2020). Autonomous driving set to become legal in the UK. https://www.carmagazine.co.uk/car-news/motoring-issues/lane-keeping-self-driving-uk-law/#:~:text=With%20Brexit%20underway%2C%20the%20UK,in%20line%20with%20UNECE%20targets. Last retrieved 2020/09/29.
24. Schoch, E., Kargl, F., Leinmuller, T., Schlott, S., & Papadimitratos, P. (2006). Impact of pseudonym changes on geographic routing in VANETs. In *Proc. of the European workshop on security and privacy in ad hoc and sensor networks (ESAS)* (pp. 43–57).
25. U2b.com. (2019). Self-driving cars & 6G: How European scientists will spend €100 billion, https://u2b.com/2019/05/29/self-driving-cars-6g-how-european-scientists-will-spend-e100-billion/. Last retrieved 2021/09/29.
26. Dyton, J. (2020). 6G? Already? Are you serious? *Connected Real Estate Magazine*. https://connectedremag.com/das-in-building-wireless/6g-already-are-you-serious/.
27. Parno, B., & Perrig, A. (2005). Challenges in securing vehicular networks. In Proceedings of the workshop on hot topics in networks (HotNets-IV).
28. Seuwou, P., Banissi, E., & Ubakanma, G. (2019). *The future of mobility with connected and autonomous vehicles in smart cities, digital twin technologies and smart cities, Internet of Things (IoT)*. New York: Springer International Publishing.
29. Seuwou, P., Patel, D., Protheroe, D., & Ubakanma, G. (2012). Effective security as an ill-defined problem in vehicular ad hoc networks (VANETs). In *IET and ITS conference on road transport information and control (RTIC 2012).*, E-ISBN: 978-1-84919-674-1. Washington, DC: IEEE.
30. Gopalswamy, S., & Rathinam, S. (2018). Infrastructure enabled autonomy: A distributed intelligence architecture for autonomous vehicles. arXiv preprint. arXiv:1802.04112.
31. Burns, L. D. (2013). Sustainable mobility: A vision of our transport future. *Nature, 497*, 181–182.
32. Haboucha, C., Ishaq, R., & Shiftan, Y. (2017). User preferences regarding autonomous vehicles. *Transportation Research Part C, 78*, 37–49.
33. Fagnant, D., Kockelman, K., & Bansal, P. (2015). Dynamic ride-sharing and optimal fleet sizing from a system of shared autonomous vehicles. In *Paper presented at the 94th annual meeting of the transportation research board, Washington, DC.*
34. Bosch, P. M., Becker, F., Becker, H., & Axhausen, K. W. (2018). Cost-based analysis of autonomous mobility services. *Transport Policy, 64*, 76–91.
35. The Telegraph. (2019). *Autonomous cars in smart cities*. retrieved July 10, 2019, from https://www.telegraph.co.uk/business/risk-insights/autonomous-cars-in-smart-cities/
36. Lim, H. S. M., & Taeihagh, A. (2018). Autonomous vehicles for smart and sustainable cities: An in-depth exploration of privacy and cybersecurity implications. *Energies, 11*(5), 1062. https://doi.org/10.3390/en11051062.
37. Mannering, F. (2018). Temporal instability and the analysis of highway accident data. *Analytic Methods in Accident Research, 17*, 1–13.
38. Barbour, N., Menon, N., Zhang, Y., & Mannering, F. (2018). *Shared autonomous vehicles: A statistical analysis of consumer use likelihoods and concerns*. Working Paper, Department of Civil and Environmental Engineering, University of South Florida, Tampa.
39. Davis, F. D. (1989). Perceived usefulness, perceived ease of use of users acceptance of information technology. *MIS Quarterly, 13*(3), 319–340.
40. Davis, F. D., Bagozzi, R. P., & Warshaw, P. R. (1992). Extrinsic and intrinsic motivation to use computers in the workplace. *Journal of Applied Social Psychology, 22*(14), 11.
41. Davis, F., Bagozzi, R., & Warshaw, P. (1989). User acceptance of computer technology: A comparison of two theoretical models. *Management Science*. https://doi.org/10.1287/mnsc.35.8.982.
42. Thompson, R. L., Higgins, C. A., & Howell, J. M. (1991). Personal computing: Toward a conceptual model of utilisation. *MIS Quarterly, 15*(1), 124–143.

43. Moore, G. C., & Benbasat, I. (2001). Development of an instrument to measure the perceptions of adopting an information technology innovation. *Information Systems Research, 2*(3), 192–222.
44. Compeau, D. R., Higgins, C. A., & Huff, S. (1999). Social cognitive theory and individual reactions to computing technology: A longitudinal study. *MIS Quaterly, 23*(2), 145–158.
45. Dwivedi, Y. K., Rana, N. P., Jeyaraj, A., Clement, M., & Williams, M. D. (2019). Re-examining the unified theory of acceptance and use of technology (UTAUT): Towards a revised theoretical model. *Information Systems Frontiers, 21*(3), 719–734.
46. Rana, N. P., Dwivedi, Y. K., Williams, M. D., & Weerakkody, V. (2016). Adoption of online public grievance redressal system in India: Toward developing a unified view. *Computers in Human Behavior, 59*, 265–282.
47. Zeithaml, V. A. (1988). Consumer perceptions of price, quality, and value: A means–end model and synthesis of evidence. *Journal of Marketing, 52*(3), 2–22.
48. Yi, M. Y., Jackson, J. D., Park, J. S., & Probst, J. C. (2006). Understanding infor-mation technology acceptance by individual professionals: Toward an integrative view. *Information & Management, 43*, 350–363.
49. Venkatesh, V., Thong, J. Y. L., & Xu, X. (2012). Consumer acceptance and use of information technology: Extending the unified theory of acceptance and use of technology. *MIS Quarterly, 36*(1), 157–178.
50. Venkatesh, V. (2000). Determinants of perceived ease of use: Integrating perceived behavioral control, computer anxiety and enjoyment into the technology acceptance model. *Information Systems Research, 11*(4), 342–365.
51. Venkatesh, V., & Davis, F. D. (2000). A theoretical extension of technology acceptance model: Four longitudinal field studies. *Management Science, 46*(2), 186–204.
52. Venkatesh, V., Thong, J., Y.,L & Xu, X. Unified theory of acceptance and use of technology: A synthesis and the road ahead. Journal of the Association for Information Systems (2016) 17 (5):328–376.
53. Hair Joseph, F., Jr., Black William, C., Babin Barry, J., Anderson Rolph, E., & Tatham Ronald, L. (2006). *Multivariate data analysis* (6th ed.). Upper Saddle River, NJ: Pearson Prentice Hall, Pearson Education, Inc..
54. Hair Joseph, F., Jr., Black William, C., Babin Barry, J., Anderson Rolph, E., & Tatham Ronald, L. (2006). *Multivariate data analysis* (6th ed.). Upper Saddle River, NJ: Pearson Prentice Hall, Pearson Education, Inc..
55. Cohen, E., & Cohen, S. A. (2012). Current sociological theories and issues in tourism. *Annals of Tourism Research*. [Online]. https://doi.org/10.1016/j.annals.2012.07.009.
56. Gefen, D., & Straub, D. (2000). The relative importance of perceived ease of use in IS adoption: A study of E-commerce adoption. *Journal of the Association for Information Systems, 1*(8), 1–30.
57. Taylor, S., & Todd, P. (1995). Assessing its usage: the role of prior experience. *MIS Quarterly, 19*(4), 561–570. Last retrieved 2020/10/01.
58. Taylor, S., & Todd, P. (1995). Understanding information technology usage: a test of competing models. *Information Systems Research, 6*, 144–176. Last retrieved 2020/10/01.

Development Path, Experience and Implications of the Internet of Things Industry in Wuxi, Jiangsu Province, China

Yuhong Wang, Wuyong Qian, and Yong Liu

1 Introduction

Internet of things (IoT) has been launched in Wuxi, Jiangsu Province, China since 2009; up to now, it has grown energetically and boomingly. Establishing a deep foundation and also constantly progressing forward, the IoT in Wuxi has transitioned from an initial concept to the sound industrial ecology. At present, the IoT industry in Wuxi is booming and speeds up developing toward scale, agglomerated, ecological, and commercial modes, and has become a new engine for the development of Wuxi city [1].

As a pioneer city developing China's IoT industry, Wuxi keeps up with science and technological progress, swiftly grasps the huge potential and market opportunity along with the development of the IoT industry. Relying on its industrial advantages in software, integrated circuit (IC), etc., Wuxi municipal government takes the development opportunity, makes development strategies, designs the development path of the IoT industry, and constantly drives the development of the IoT industry according to the thought of policy guidance, technological innovation, industrial cultivation, and application demonstration. Through persistent exploration and practice, a series of remarkable development achievements have been realized in this city.

At present, there are over 2000 IoT enterprises in this city, which have formed an IoT industry chain covering various fields such as chips, sensing devices, network communication, and application service. Moreover, the integration between the IoT industry and traditional industries develops steadily. The IoT technology has been

Y. Wang (✉) · W. Qian · Y. Liu
School of Business, Jiangnan University, Wuxi, Jiangsu Province, China
e-mail: yuhongwang@jiangnan.edu.cn

F. P. García Márquez, B. Lev (eds.), *Introduction to Internet of Things in Management Science and Operations Research*, International Series in Operations Research & Management Science 311,
https://doi.org/10.1007/978-3-030-74644-5_10

widely applied in various fields including industry, agriculture, finance, environmental protection, logistics, transportation, security and health care. Unique experience with Taihu Lake characteristics has shaped with the development of the IoT industry in Wuxi. Therefore, exploring the development path and summarizing the development experience and implications from the IoT industry in Wuxi are important for investigating the development theory and practice of the regional IoT industry. This can provide reference for developing the IoT industry in the other cities.

2 Analysis of the Development Path of the IoT Industry in Wuxi

The IoT industry in Wuxi has experienced three stages since its emergence, i.e., initiation, development, and rapid growth.

2.1 Initiation Stage (2009–2012)

2.1.1 Determination of the Development Orientation

In 2005, the International Telecommunication Union (ITU) released a report on IoT. With the rapid development of the new generation of information technology, countries all over the world highly concern the development of the IoT industry and successively formulate the development strategies of the IoT industry. In the end of 2008, the United States government declared a national development strategy for the IoT industry, that is, *Smart Planet*; in 2009, the European Union (EU) launched the *2020 milestone plan (I-Europe)* for the IoT industry; in 2009, the Japanese government implemented the *U-Japan* strategy based on the ubiquitous network; in 2009, the Chinese government put forward the development strategy of *Sensing China* and established the center thereof in Wuxi. In the same year, the State Council of the People's Republic of China officially approved to build a National Demonstration Area of Sensor Networks in Wuxi. Therefore, Wuxi city has become the only Innovative National Demonstration Area of Sensor Networks, which means that the development of the IoT industry in Wuxi is supported by national strategies.

2.1.2 Actively Taking Actions

After determining the development orientation of the IoT industry in Wuxi, Wuxi municipal government starts to actively plan the development strategy for driving the IoT industry and take effective actions: on one hand, Wuxi municipal government strives for some policy resources from relevant national ministries; on the other hand, the government initiatively carries out cooperation with different organizations such as Chinese Academy of Sciences (CAS) and telecom operators in attempt to seek for the breakthrough of developing the IoT industry and fully promote the development of the IoT industry. By doing so, some remarkable achievements are achieved. The details are displayed in the following aspects:

1. Leading the industrial development based on plans: In May 2010, Wuxi municipal government announced the *Outline of the Development Plan for the Internet of Things Industry (2010–2015)*. It was explicitly pointed out in the outline to seize the development opportunity of the IoT industry aiming to lead the development of China's IoT industry under the driving of innovation and promotion of applications; with enterprises as the subject and according to the industrial layout of one core and multiple key areas, it stated to build an Innovative National Demonstration Area of Sensor Networks, which is influential nationwide. It is expected to enable the IoT industry to be the endogenous power of economic growth in Wuxi [2]. In August 2012, the State Council officially approved the *Outline of Development Plan of Innovative National Demonstration Area of Sensor Networks in Wuxi*, which explicitly pointed out that through prior trials, an Innovative Demonstration Area of Sensor Networks which is globally influential should be energetically built to promote the healthy and sustainable development of China's IoT industry [3]. The announcement of these plans clarifies a direction for the development of the IoT industry in Wuxi, which is significant for leading the development of the IoT industry in Wuxi.
2. Promoting technological innovation with carrier cultivation: Starting from constructing the Innovative National Demonstration Area of Sensor Networks, Wuxi municipal government actively cultivates the carrier construction for IoT technological innovation and drives the IoT technological innovation and industrial development by strengthening the carrier cultivation. In the period of 2009–2012, Wuxi municipal government had been approved for constructing ten major carriers, including the National Sensor Network Research and Development (R&D) Center for Engineering Technology, National Professional Incubator for Sensor Networks, National High-tech Industrial Base of Sensor Networks, National Application Display Center of Sensor Networks, National Demonstration Base for Newly Industrialized Industries and National Pilot Demonstration City for Service Innovation And Development of Cloud Computing. They play an important role in promoting the technological innovation, industrial cultivation and application demonstration of the IoT industry in Wuxi.
3. Integrating development resources through industry–university–research cooperation: To drive the development of the IoT industry and improve the technology R&D capability of the industry, the IoT industry in Wuxi initiatively strengthens its cooperation with some universities and scientific research institutions. The top universities (such as Peking University, Tsinghua University, Fudan University and Shanghai Jiao Tong University) in China have established R&D with Wuxi municipal government, as well as the Jiangsu R&D Center for Internet of Things. By carrying out the industry–university–research cooperation, some remarkable

achievements have been made in resource integration, talent cultivation, and industrial cultivation.

4. Promoting the industrial cultivation based on policies and applications: the relevant national ministries have issued a series of policies and application demonstration projects for driving the development of the IoT industry to support the development of this industry in Wuxi. Moreover, Wuxi municipal government also launched relevant policies for boosting the industrial development; it also deployed demonstration projects in fields such as transportation, environmental protection, medical care and security and promoted the cultivation of the IoT industry through applications.

2.2 Development Stage (2013–2015)

The IoT industry in Wuxi steps into a steady development stage in the period of 2013–2015 after the accumulation in the initiation stage. In this period, the policy effect in the early stage continued to emerge; the technological innovation system constantly improved and the market demand also grew. The IoT industry experienced a progressive transition from the cultivation stage dominated by the government to an independent development stage promoted by the market. Wuxi city has been selected as the application demonstration construction sites for the IoT industry, which include the national pilot city for smart tourism, pilot city for TD-LTE network, national pilot for smart city construction, national demonstration city for public security applications of IoT, national pilot city for information benefit and national next-generation internet city. As the only Asian city, Wuxi city has also been included in the IEEE global pilot program of smart cities. The IoT industry in Wuxi healthily and sustainably developed as a whole and made some achievements.

2.2.1 Forming Industrial Layout of IoT with One Core and Multiple Key Areas

Based on original supporting industries (e.g., IC, intelligent computing, wireless communication, sensor, software and information service industry), Wuxi municipal government constantly strengthens the system planning of the spatial layout of the IoT industry to persistently optimize the spatial layout of the industry. This follows the thought (scientific planning, overall design, taking advantages, reasonable layout, breakthrough at key points and demonstration application) of the industrial planning, supported by the national and provincial governments, national key scientific research institutions and key enterprises [4]. At present, the spatial layout of the industry with one core and multiple key areas has been preliminarily formed in Wuxi; the core and key areas concentrate on Xinwu, Binhu, and Liangxi Districts of the city: Wuxi National Sensing Information Center (Wuxi Taihu International Tech-Park), Wuxi Binhu Economic and Technical Development Area and Liangxi

High-tech Park of Sensor Networks, covering a total of 15 km^2, intensively develop the generic technologies and products; these key districts focus on developing products and technologies in the application profile; the other districts (such as Huishan and Xishan Districts) are called the extended areas, which offer the supporting for industrial development [5]. In the end of 2015, the IoT R&D carriers over 3×10^6 m^2 were built in the core area: six IoT parks (including the Sensor Network Innovation Park, Sensor Network Information Service Park and Sensing China Windows) were constructed in Xinwu District; Wuxi (Nanchang) National Sensing Information Center was established in Liangxi District; Wuxi (Binhu) National Sensing Information Center was built in Binhu District; in addition, Wuxi (National) Intelligent Transportation Industrial Park was also established to fully play the technological and data advantages of Traffic Management Research Institute of the Ministry of the Public Security and speed up the layout of intelligent transportation and some subdivisions such as internet of vehicles. Additionally, various districts in Wuxi also further define their own key fields, for example, intelligent environmental protection in Yixing, intelligent energy in Jiangyin, intelligent manufacturing in Huishan District, intelligent agriculture in Xishan District, and intelligent sensor and intelligent health in Xinwu District. In this way, a relatively stable industry chain has preliminarily taken shape in Wuxi.

2.2.2 Constantly Improving Support by R&D Institutions and Public Service Platforms

Over the period of 2013–2015, Wuxi municipal government attached much importance to strengthening the close cooperation with universities and scientific research institutions to accelerate the technological innovation of the IoT industry; moreover, they highly concerned the construction of public service platforms to fully play the supporting role of R&D institutions and public service platforms in the development of the industry. A batch of institutions (including Jiangsu R&D Center for IoT, Wuxi Research Institute for IoT Industry, China Electronics Technology Group Corporation (CETC) and China Aerospace Science and Technology Corporation (CASC)) focusing on IoT technology R&D have settled in Wuxi and played an important role in many aspects such as technology R&D and industrial cultivation for IoT; in addition, some key universities (e.g., Tsinghua University, Peking University and Fudan University) also successively set up a R&D center for IoT in Wuxi. Universities and enterprises continue to extend the scope and deepen the fields of cooperation, persistently showing some cooperation achievements. Moreover, some multinational corporations also set the R&D centers (including Intel Joint Innovation Center, Siemens IoT Innovation Center, IBM China Systems and Technology (Wuxi) Lab (CSTL) and Microsoft Customer Service and Support, Asia Pacific and Greater China Region (APGC, CSS)) in various industrial parks in succession. In order to increase the public service capacities (such as technology R&D, application popularization and industrial development) of IoT, the public service platforms for the IoT industry have been energetically developed in Wuxi to form a relatively complete public service system (including public cloud platform for IoT, inspection and testing service platform, intermediary service platform for technologies, service platform for standards and intellectual properties and application popularization platform) for the IoT industry. Oriented by demands for core and generic technologies of the IoT industry and targeted to the development, application, and sharing of these technologies, the basic structure of technological innovation service platform of the IoT industry has been built. The structure contains several layers, including public decision-making, support platform and innovation subject layers and its construction takes the technology market of the IoT industry as the carrier based on collaborative innovation of different subjects, e.g., the government, enterprises, research institutions and agencies (see Fig. 1).

2.2.3 Constantly Expanded Application Demonstration Fields

Over the period of 2012–2015, being promoted by the IoT technology application and starting from the application demonstration projects, the application fields were constantly expanded and levels of the IoT industry improved. A batch of major IoT application demonstration projects (including electronic logos of vehicles, residents' health information management, meteorological IoT and finance and taxation) were successively implemented in Wuxi; a series of key technologies and industrial standards emerged. Some IoT standards including *General Rules on Sensor Networks, Nomenclature*, *Technical Specification for Low Speed Wireless Sensor Network Layer and Application Support Sub-layer*, *Signal Interface Specification*, *General Technical Specification for Information Security*, and *Coding Specification for Identification and Sensing Nodes*, providing the pilot demonstration for the national scale application of IoT.

2.3 Rapid Growth Stage (2016–2019)

After experiencing the initiation and development in the early stages, the IoT industry in Wuxi has progressively rapidly grown since 2016 to step into a new stage characterized by attention focusing, integration across industries, integrated innovation and scale development, showing a favorable development trend. The IoT technology was extensively applied in many industrial fields such as transportation, automobiles, environmental protection and physical education. IoT has been deeply integrated across industries and brought about a changing new industrial atmosphere. In this development stage, Wuxi city was becoming the development center of global IoT revolution [6].

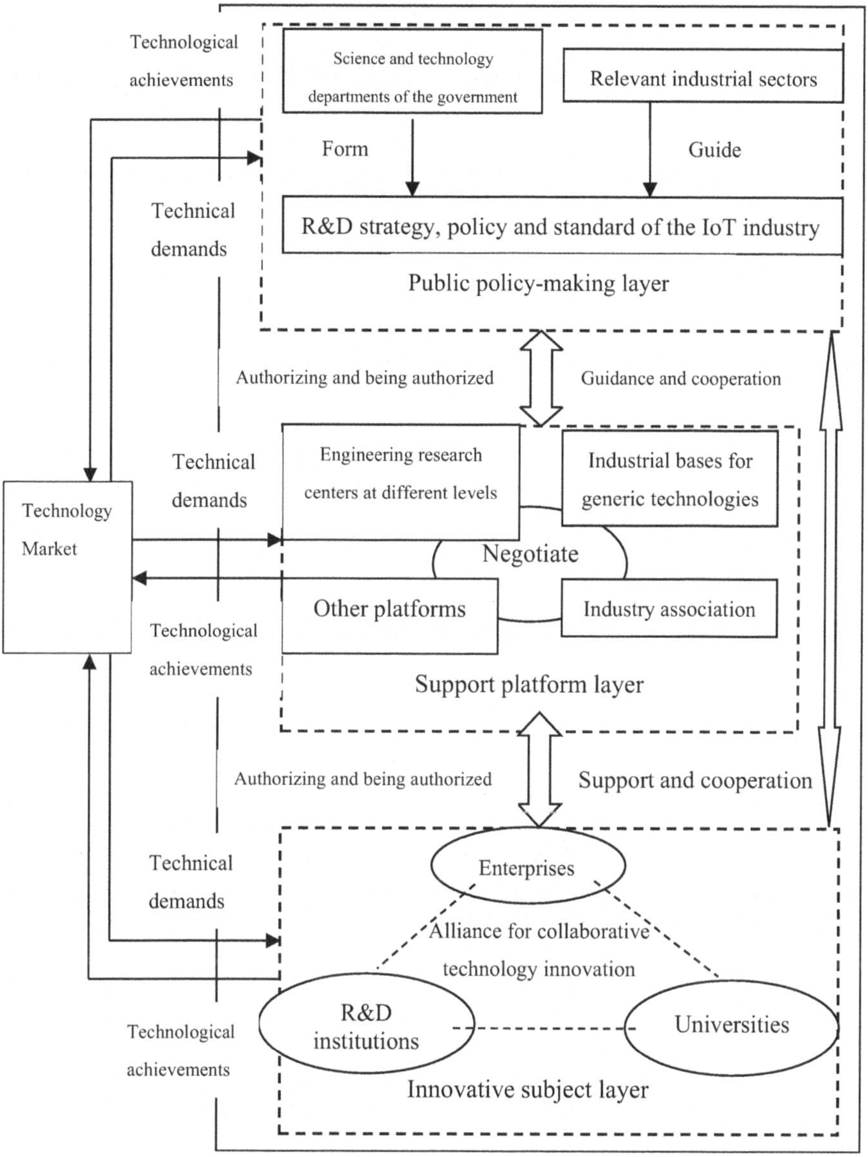

Fig. 1 Structure of the technological innovation service platform of the IoT industry

2.3.1 Agglomerative Development Stage of the IoT Industry

During 2016–2019, the IoT industrial scale rapidly increased and agglomeration effect constantly appeared in Wuxi. Up to 2019, the revenue from the IoT industry was more than 300 billion CNY in Wuxi; during 2016–2019, the annual average growth rate of scales of the IoT and related industries there reached over 30%, fostering a complete industry chain covering various industry chains (e.g., associated chips, sensing devices, network communication, intelligent hardware and application scene) and supplementary services. In 2019, there were 1678 IoT enterprises and more than 2000 ubiquitous IoT enterprises, absorbing more than 180,000 employees to IoT and related industries. The number of scale enterprises kept increasing and more than 20 enterprises gained the annual revenue of over one billion CNY. At present, the agglomerate advantage of the IoT industry in Wuxi in various aspects (including basic supporting industries, R&D of key and generic technologies, application demonstration projects, innovative resource aggregation, standard formulation, industry chain cultivation, and supporting policy-making) is constantly enhanced (see Table 1). Up to now, Wuxi city has become the region with the fastest development of China's IoT industry and the most concentrated resources. In particular, this city has established a certain foundation and advantages in terms of policy resources, industrial scale, etc. The industrial agglomeration effect continues to show and the scale and cluster effects of Wuxi's IoT industry are highlighted unceasingly [7].

2.3.2 Transition from Government-Dominated to Market-Dominated Application Mode

With the gradual popularization of the pilot application of the IoT industry, a transition occurs from the government-dominated to the market-oriented application mode in this stage. Market demand is the key to the development of emerging industries. In contrast to some local governments that introduce the previous preferential policies, Wuxi municipal government is more willing to provide back-end market for IoT enterprises, allowing Wuxi to be a base for trial and error of enterprises; by using the technology and market operation, high-quality products are produced and more competitive enterprises fostered; subsequently, these enterprises and their services are popularized nationwide and even in the world. The IoT projects undertaken by enterprises in Wuxi have spread to more than 700 cities in over 60 countries and 31 provinces and cities in China, promoting the popularization of IoT technology and boosting the optimization and upgrading of traditional industries. Moreover, several projects have been successfully applied to international cities such as Houston (the U.S.), London (Britain), Tokyo (Japan), Aarhus (Denmark), and Buenos Aires (Argentina). Envision Energy, which pioneered the Wind OS™ management system, has become the first Chinese enterprise to provide wind field management services for American companies; Wishen Innovation Ltd., which developed the safety monitoring system for engineering structures, has become the first Chinese enterprise to occupy the safety inspection of various structures such as London subway and Thames water conservancy and sewerage project.

Table 1 Development status of Wuxi's IoT industrial agglomeration

Number	Major field	Development status
1	Development of basic supporting industries	National Industrialization Base for IC Design and National High-tech Industrial Base are built in Wuxi; IC sales, IC capacity, and manufacturing technology all rank the top in China; there is a complete industrial system in IC, intelligent computing, wireless communications, sensors, software, information services, etc., with a promising development trend
2	R&D of key and generic technologies	Having a batch of key enterprises and important scientific research institutions, including the CAS, CETC, AstraZeneca, CETHIK, Alibaba Group, Inspur Co., Ltd., Huawei, MEMSIC, JCET Group, China Resources Microelectronics Limited, Jiangnan University, Jiangsu IoT R&D Center and Wuxi Research Institute for IoT Industry, Wuxi city shows strong R&D strength in many aspects such as R&D of key and generic technologies; there are over 2000 R&D projects, with over 2500 invention patents approved
3	Application demonstration projects	IoT application services have been provided in electric power, transportation, agriculture, environmental protection, etc. and application demonstration projects in 76 fields including industry, agriculture and electric power have been carried out; the city has been approved for implementing 17 application demonstration projects by national ministries; it actively promotes the construction of IoT towns, such as Hongshan, Xuelang and Huihaiwan IoT towns, and launches major projects such as IoT healthcare of AstraZeneca and Alibaba entrepreneurship and innovation center
4	Innovative resource aggregation	With 180,000 employees engaged in the IoT industry, more than 3000 top-level IoT talents introduced, 41 major IoT R&D institutions gathered and 19 scientific research institutions (CAS R&D center for IoT, Perking and Tsinghua) established, Wuxi has presented the superiority in gathering funds, technologies, talents, etc.
5	Standard formulation	More than 60 international and national standards and 25 industrial standards have been formulated for the IoT industry, 4 of the 9 national standards for smart cities are undertaken, and 54 IoT public platforms are built; 11 international standards and 49 national standards have been set in terms of the formulation of the IoT architecture standards; in the International Sensor Network Standardization Working Group WG10, one editor-in-chief and two co-editors-in-chief for the system architecture project group are from Wuxi
6	Cultivation of industry chain	The IoT industry chain at the perception layer, network layer, platform layer and application layer has basically taken shape; a related industry system covering the four links and four fields of key technologies in the IoT industry chain has been established, in which the industrial cluster of intelligent sensing system is considered to be formed first in China
7	Supporting policies	The supporting policies in various aspects (including industrial planning, technology R&D, pilot application, standardization construction, talent cultivation and service system) are increasingly improved

2.3.3 Rapid Development of Key Enterprises

By the end of 2019, there were more than 2000 IoT enterprises in Wuxi; several growing enterprises with technology, market and scale emerged; more than 400 enterprises showed the annual sales revenue exceeding 20 million CNY. As for IoT device development and design, key enterprises such as China Key System & Integrated Circuit Co., Ltd. and Wuxi Si-Power Microelectronics Co., Ltd., which mainly develop and design IoT devices, are based in Wuxi; in terms of device production, the world-leading key enterprises (including MEMSIC, Wuxi Arixin Electronics Co., Ltd. and Connasenk) have been built in Wuxi; in terms of system integration, Wuxi city holds many key enterprises, such as SK Hynix, China Resources, and JCET Group, which deliver a strong industrial advantage in IC manufacturing, packaging and testing, chip packaging and testing, etc. The related industries lay a solid foundation and information industry serves as the important basis for supporting the development of the IoT industry. More than 600 manufacturing enterprises for electronic information products above designated size are resided in Wuxi, with the sales revenue of over 200 billion CNY. For example, the application software and embedded software development enterprises (such as Tsinghua Unigroup and JSETC) are able to develop downstream value-added IoT services, which has laid a solid foundation for the application of the downstream value-added IoT services.

3 Development Experience and Implications of the IoT Industry in Wuxi City

Over the past 11 years, Wuxi city has formed special Wuxi intelligence and Wuxi experience when it makes efforts to grow, fostering the enlightening mode and path in the initiation, cultivation and development processes of the IoT industry.

3.1 Adhering to the Coordinated Driving to Foster the Development Mode Under the Coupling Driving of the Government and Market

The initiation and growth of the IoT industry will be affected by many uncertain factors and therefore the government needs to offer the support in policy, fund, etc.; moreover, it is necessary for the IoT industry to experience the market test during its initiation and cultivation in order to healthily grow. Wuxi municipal government launches many policies supporting the industrial development in the startup stage of the IoT industry. By setting up diversified supporting systems (including various preferential policies, project support and capital guidance), Wuxi city appeals to a batch of innovation platforms and factors (such as IoT R&D institutions, enterprises and innovative talents) with core competitiveness, thus fostering the original driving force for the development of the IoT industry in this city. The innovation subjects give play to their initiative through various innovation platforms and application demonstration projects, which enhances the deep integration between the innovation chain and industry chain of IoT. Furthermore, it solves the market failure of key and generic technologies to constitute the external impetus and original driving force promoting the development of the IoT industry, thus powerfully guaranteeing the development of the industry. After the IoT industry gradually steadily develops, it is necessary to play the market's role in resource allocation. Promoted by the market demand, the whole advancement mechanism of the market-oriented IoT industry is established by longitudinally promoting the extension of upstream and downstream IoT industry chains and horizontally driving the integrative development between IoT technology and traditional industries. In this way, it is possible to form the endogenous power and core power influencing the development of the IoT industry.

3.2 *Adhering to Taking Well-Targeted Steps and Building an Open, Collaborative and Sharing Industrial Ecology*

The IoT industry is considered as a strategic emerging industry with complex core technology, broad application field and long innovation chain and industry chain. It is impossible for a city to take all things into account if it expects to make achievements in the IoT industry and related fields. The city should be selectively engaged in something to intensively make breakthroughs in the key fields conforming to the city's development demand. In the processes of formulating the development strategy of the IoT industry and advancing the development of IoT industry, Wuxi municipal government has fully considered the industrial foundation and advantages. By taking the construction of the Innovative National Demonstration Area of Sensor Networks as the carrier and the construction of the IoT innovation platform as the starting point and focusing on application demonstration, industrialization and industrial ecosystem construction, the government is committed to creating the platform with technological innovation, industrial agglomeration and application demonstration. In the process of guiding and supporting the development of the IoT industry, it is necessary to persistently avoid the industrial cultivation mode with the over dispersed characteristic. Instead, it is suggested to implement the targeted cultivation for some key technologies and industries. By doing so, it can be realized to effectively guarantee the centralized breakthrough and rapid development of Wuxi's IoT industry in key fields. Additionally, a favorable industrial ecology is required for the sound development of the IoT industry. The mutual promotion of related industries and cooperative innovation between enterprises are prompted to intensively build an open, collaborative and sharing industrial ecology by concentrating on improving the IoT industry chain and creating the IoT industrial eco-chain. This is evinced in two aspects: on the one hand, it improves the spatial integration between IoT and the related industries by setting up the R&D center, science parks, industrial bases and public service platforms and aggregating high-quality innovation resources; on the other hand, it drives the development of supporting industries and related industries by core industries (such as IC and cloud computing), thus forming an integrated and coordinated development pattern between traditional superior industries and the IoT industry.

3.3 Persisting Demand Guidance and Cultivating the Innovation Culture of Fault Tolerance, Trial and Error and Error Correction

The IoT industry develops and extends by depending on a large number of back-end applications; the industrialization of many technologies needs to rely on application promotion and breakthrough in key core technologies. In the process of cultivation, the IoT industry explores the breakthrough of technologies and strengthens the integrated innovation during the basic research by being promoted by applications and taking enterprises as the subject. Thus, it opens up the technical path, develop core products and explore the business model, forming the industrial advantages. In addition, guided by the transformation and upgrading demands of local enterprises in Wuxi, the integrative development between the IoT industry and traditional industries is actively explored; a great number of local traditional enterprises are initiatively transformed and upgraded based on the IoT technology to constantly develop toward the advanced industrial value chain. As a strategic emerging industry, the IoT industry is affected by many uncertain factors in the development process; it is inevitable for the industry to encounter failure in the development process while a good innovation culture can provide a powerful support for industrial innovation. An innovation culture of fault tolerance, trial and error and error correction has taken shape in Wuxi, as the pilot zone of developing the IoT industry in China, in the process of promoting the development of the IoT industry. It provides a good guarantee mechanism for the innovation of key and generic technologies and the transformation and application of innovation achievements of the IoT industry. In the process of continuous practice, trial and error and error correction, it has opened up a technical path, formed a number of competitive technologies, products and services, and created a good atmosphere for boosting the sustainable development of the IoT industry in Wuxi.

4 Existing Problems in the Development Process of the IoT Industry in Wuxi

4.1 Intensively Dominated by the Government and Still in the Partially Market-Dominated Stage

In terms of the IoT industry in Wuxi in the transition process from the initiation to the gradual development, the government plays a dominant role in the cultivation process of the industry both from the perspectives of the top-level design and the development path and track. At present, no matter from the perspective of the industrialization of the IOT technology or the application of the IOT technology and the marketization of products, a clear commercial application and profit model has not been formed in the development process of the IoT industry in Wuxi yet. There is still a certain gap from the mass commercialization and the R&D and application of the IoT technology and products are still locally led by the market. How to give full play to the dominant role of the market and construct the market-dominated development mechanism is one of the problems facing the development of the IoT industry in Wuxi.

4.2 Being Urgent to Make Breakthroughs in Core Technologies and Strengthening the Standardization Construction

It is still an urgent need to make breakthroughs in key core technologies in Wuxi city, even if the city is taken as the pilot zone and demonstration area of developing China's IoT industry. It is mainly reflected as follows: key generic technologies (e.g., core chip, high-side sensor, basic system, intelligent processing and basic architecture of cloud computing) are highly dependent on foreign technologies; it remains to improve the R&D capability of key generic and core technologies; the enterprises capable of realizing the end-to-end large-scale system integration of hardware, software, network, platform, application and business process are lacking. In addition, breakthroughs are urgent to be made in key core technologies. Most technical systems and product interfaces from the core IoT architecture to each layer have not been standardized, so the standardization construction needs to be strengthened. The core architecture of the IoT industry and technical systems and product interfaces at various layers are basically not standardized and thus standardization construction remains to be enhanced.

4.3 *Impeded Connection Between Technologies and the Market and Weak Driving Force of Key Enterprises*

Although there have been over 2000 ubiquitous IoT enterprises in Wuxi, these IoT enterprises exhibit some problems (small, dispersed, weak profitability and weak sustainable development ability on the whole) from the perspectives of the overall revenue scale and status of profit. The main reason is that the technologies of these enterprises fail to be effectively marketized, showing a series of problems including grasping few core technologies and finding it difficult to realize the technology marketization and application and popularization. Although tens of leading IoT enterprises are built in Wuxi, the majority presents a small enterprise size and there is lack of key upstream enterprises able to drive the industrial development. In terms of the sensor, only a small number of key enterprises with independent intellectual property rights are built; as for the system integration, there are only a handful of leading enterprises with high-end integration and service ability. Additionally, existing leading enterprises perform unsatisfactorily in driving and leading the development of the IoT industry.

5 Countermeasures for Promoting the Sustainable Development of the IoT Industry in Wuxi

5.1 *Establishing a Dual Mechanism of Combining the Government Regulation with the Market Regulation*

It is necessary to give full play the role of the market regulation in the initial development stage of the IoT industry; it should play the fundamental role of the market allocation of resources when the IoT industry develops into a certain stage. By giving full play to the market effect, it is possible to realize the product industrialization and implementation of the IoT technologies; through reasonable market allocation of various resources, it is expected to promote the factor mobility across industries and facilitate the healthy development of the IoT industry. It also needs to play the role of the market mechanism, speeds up building a business model achieving the win-win of multiple parties and drives the integration between the IoT industry and traditional industries. By doing so, IoT can truly become a driving force for the business, to allow the subjects taking part in the construction of the IoT industry to attain the commercial gain.

5.2 *Building a Dual Driving Mechanism of Combining Technological Innovation and Financial Innovation*

It is expected to promote the technological innovation and breakthrough of key generic technologies of the IoT industry and facilitate the transformation and application of technological achievements through the following aspects: establishing the industry–university–research technological innovation alliance of the IoT industry; building the IoT technological innovation network coordinated by multiple subjects; designing the innovation mechanism and benefit sharing mechanism coordinated by multiple subjects; constructing a collaborative innovation platform for the IoT key generic technologies; and integrating and embedding the high-quality innovation resources into the innovation network and platform. While promoting the technological innovation, financial innovation should also be actively driven: formulating and issuing related policies that can encourage the IoT industry and provide the financial support for the industry to improve the financial guarantee mechanism for the IoT industry; constructing multiple financing modes led by the financial fund by taking the venture capital as the subject; increasing the financial support for the infrastructures, important platforms and carriers, and key generic technology projects of the IoT industry and offering the credit guarantee for these projects; establishing a multi-subject sharing mechanism of the investment risk of IoT technologies and encouraging to set up the equity investment fund and venture angel funding of the IoT industry; strengthening the effect of investment guidance of the government-owned venture capital fund on the development of the IoT industry; encouraging to construct the venture capital institutions and the industrial investment fund and attracting the venture capital and social investment at home and abroad to the IoT industry.

5.3 *Building a Dual-Chain Integration Mechanism of the Innovation and Industry Chains*

The internal integration mechanism of the innovation and industry chains of the IoT industry should be analyzed by combining the structural characteristics of the innovation and industry chains of the IoT industry. Furthermore, the integration mechanism of the innovation and industry chains needs to be built to amplify the booming effect of the dual-chain integration, promote the technological innovation, improve the technological innovation achievements and accelerate the transformation of innovation achievements of the IoT industry. Additionally, it is essential to explore the value-added mechanism of the dual-chain integration and construct the dynamic mechanism of driving the dual-chain integration.

References

1. Remarkable achievements have been made in the innovative development of Jiangsu Internet of Things industry. Available online: http://www.most.gov.cn/dfkj/js/zxdt/201211/t20121130_98179.htm.
2. Outline of development planning of internet of things industry in Wuxi (2010–2015).
3. Outline of development planning of Wuxi national innovative demonstration area of sensor networks (2012–2020).
4. Internet under industrial competition—Acceleration of the development of the Internet of things industry to form a new advantage in Wuxi (Part 1). Available online: http://epaper.wxrb.com/paper/wxrb/resfiles/2017-09/08/rbA01A01C0908.pdf.
5. Opening up the IoT world through prior trials—Acceleration of the development of the Internet of things industry to form a new advantage in Wuxi (Part 2). Available online: http://epaper.wxrb.com/paper/wxrb/resfiles/2017-09/09/rbA01A01C0909.pdf.
6. The development of China's internet of things industry led by Wuxi. Available online: http://news.cqnews.net/html/2013-10/31/content_28449266.htm.
7. Dong, X. (2011). *Internet of things and its industrial development*. Beijing: China Social Sciences Press.

Use of Convolutional Neural Networks for Quality Control in Automotive Industry

Diego Ortega Sanz, Carlos Quiterio Gómez Muñoz, and Fausto Pedro García Márquez

1 Introduction

The chain of suppliers in the automobile industry has a hierarchical structure. This structure includes the Original Manufacturing Equipment (OEM). Within the OEM, Tier 1 companies are usually the most technically capable companies in the supply chain. They have the resources and know-how to provide the key components required by equipment manufacturers, and have established processes for managing suppliers below them. In addition, it is common in the automotive industry that Tier 1 companies offer a manufacturing service for the OEM, allowing the OEM to focus on final assembly. Supply chains feed each other, which means that a failure in any one point of the chain directly affects the rest, including the OEM. In addition, the manufacturing processes of these companies are usually massive, due to the high volume of monthly demand from the OEM. It generally involves manufacturing by batches marked by the raw material.

A defect in the material or in the manufacturing process, would imply that the entire lot that is manufactured will be defective. This can be extrapolated to all the manufacturing processes of a component, from its raw material to its delivery to the OEM. Therefore, quality control plays a fundamental role in the detection of defects.

D. Ortega Sanz · C. Q. Gómez Muñoz (✉)
Universidad Europea de Madrid, Villaviciosa de Odón, Spain
e-mail: carlosquiterio.gomez@universidadeuropea.es

F. P. García Márquez
Ingenium Research Group, University of Castilla-La Mancha, Ciudad Real, Spain
e-mail: FaustoPedro.Garcia@uclm.es

F. P. García Márquez, B. Lev (eds.), *Introduction to Internet of Things in Management Science and Operations Research*, International Series in Operations Research & Management Science 311,
https://doi.org/10.1007/978-3-030-74644-5_11

Digital images analysis techniques are within the field of digital image processing [1]. Deep Learning or Deep Neural Network are Artificial Neural Networks (ANN) with multi layers. The interest of these neural networks has increased, by increasing their number of hidden layers, they have improved performance and precision in different fields, for example in pattern recognition [2]. One of the neural networks that provide the best results and one of the most popular is Convolutional Neural Network (CNN). CNN have multiple layers, including convolutional layer, nonlinearity layer, pooling layer, and fully connected layer. The convolutional and fully connected layers have parameters, unlike to pooling and nonlinearity layers. The CNN have a high precision and performance especially in applications where the input information is an image, so their possibilities grow exponentially in the field of computer vision, and natural language processing [3–5].

Traditional methods of inspecting parts during their manufacture can be ineffective in detecting dynamic failures such as tool degradation. In addition, the processing speed also becomes critical in this type of process [6]. Another problem with traditional methods is their lack of connectivity. An industrial camera with embedded hardware uses information from machine vision algorithms to send a binary signal. Depending on the trained neural network the part will be good or defective.

The use of intermediate hardware between the camera and the machine allows the processing of all the information. In order to achieve this connectivity, the Internet of Things (IoT) is considered as the solution for this approach [7].

Internet of Things emerges as the natural evolution of a part of the Internet that needs to communicate with the real world. It can be understood like a large interconnection of devices that can interact with each other and share data with networks of other levels. It can work in a similar way to the automation pyramid where the devices at the base of the pyramid provide valuable information to the higher levels. Then these data are analyzed either by classical techniques or by using ANN as proposed in this chapter [8].

There are several definitions of IoT, and it is instructive to examine these definitions to see the similarities and differences, for example, IBM defines the Internet of Things as "the concept of connecting any device (physical object) to the Internet and to other connected devices" [9]. Gartner defines it as "the network of physical objects that contain embedded technology to communicate and sense or interact with their internal states or the external environment." Oxford Dictionary summarizes IoT technology as "a proposed development of the Internet in which everyday objects have network connectivity, allowing them to send and receive data" [10].

When the Internet of Things exists in an ecosystem there are four major components: things, data, people, and process. Figure 1 shows how all these concepts are related to each other.

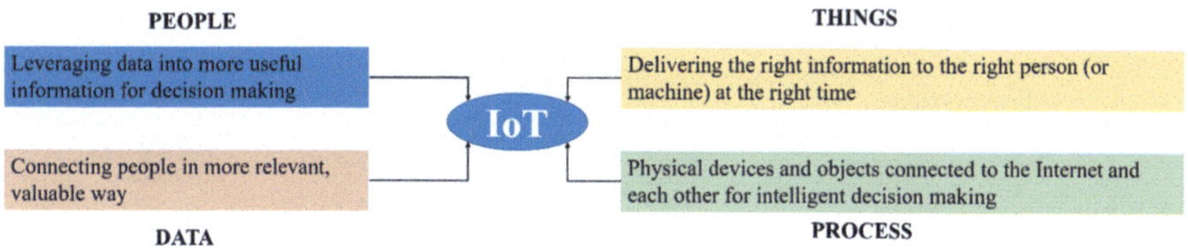

Fig. 1 IoT ecosystem network connection

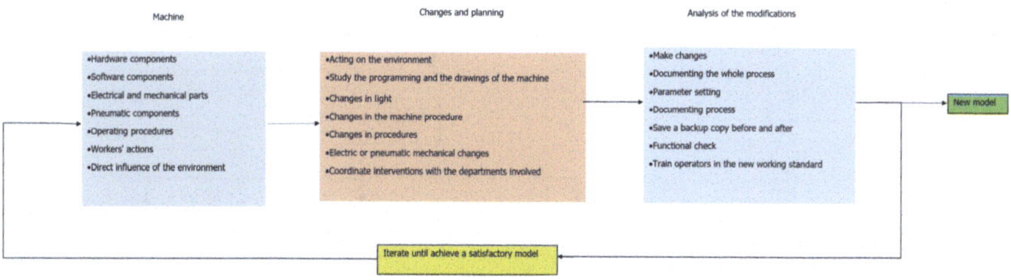

Fig. 2 Workflow

2 Modeling and Approach

It is necessary to consider all those variables that may affect the correct classification of images such as working conditions, lighting, machine vibrations, etc. Figure 2 shows the workflow of the proposed system.

Figure 3 shows the flowchart of the presented approach for industrial pieces inspection. The illumination and image acquisition process provide feedback to adjust the parameters according to the precision of the obtained results. The images are acquired to prepare a classified dataset to train the neural network. The model is trained through iterations modifying the parameters of the network until reaching a stabilization of the results without reaching overtraining.

The generation of a correct Dataset and its preprocessing is vital for a correct training of neural networks. CNN are vulnerable and sensitive to an adverse example which can lower the accuracy of the entire network considerably [11].

Figure 4 shows the flowchart of the system implemented on the industrial pc and connected to the visual computer system.

The final architecture deployment will involve different phases associated in blocks (Fig. 5). Not achieving the final objectives will imply the revision of each block until a suitable model is achieved.

Different neural network architectures have been analyzed and tested to determine the one that yields the highest precision for the training Dataset. Different options have been considered and tested, under the premise of achieving real-time video processing and being able to deploy the solution on industrial equipment [12]. *AlexNet* [13] contained eight layers; the first five were convolutional layers, some of them followed by max-pooling layers, and the last three were fully

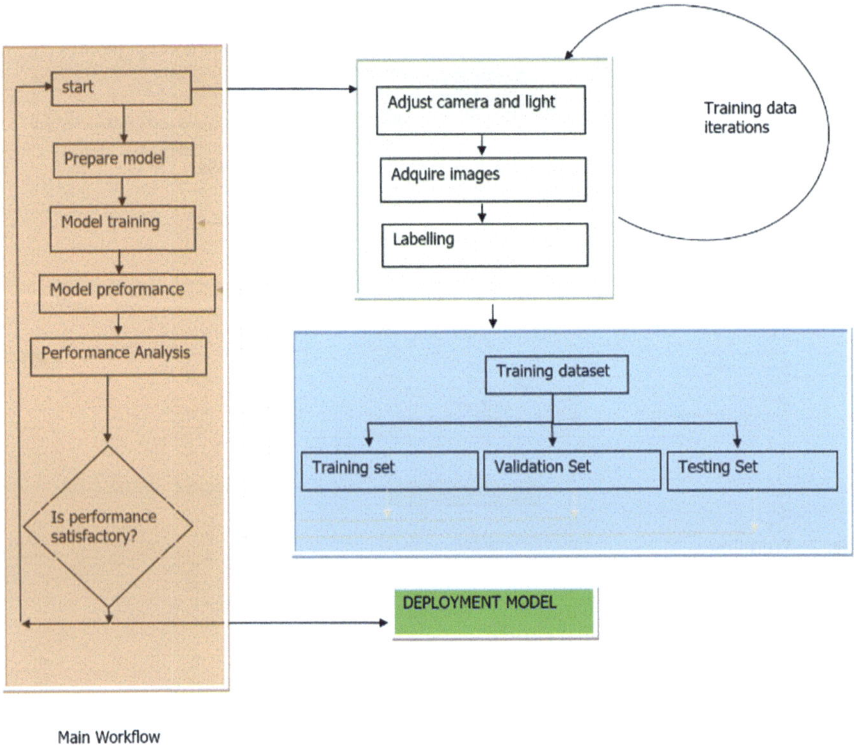

Fig. 3 Chart flow for CNN deployment

connected layers. It used the non-saturating ReLU activation function, which results in a lower computational cost than the sigmoid function [6, 14]. *SqueezeNet* is a similar CNN to *AlexNet* which achieved similar accuracy in the tests performed [13, 15, 16].

One of the goals, is to achieve real time. *MobileNet* is an architecture designed mainly for mobile vision applications. Therefore, it is mainly focused on reducing as much as possible the computational power required for the processing. It is a simpler architecture that sacrifices some precision and performance. This is largely achieved through the use of separable convolutions by depth [17].

Finally, another CNN architecture who combined low computational power and good precision in classifying objects, was *Darknet. Darknet* is an open-source neural network framework written in C language and *CUDA*. It is fast, easy to install, and supports CPU and GPU computation. *Darknet* is mainly designed for Object Detection and have different architecture and features than other deep learning frameworks. It is faster than many other CNN architectures [1, 18, 19].

Finally, *You Only Look Once* (*YOLO*) architecture [20], which is based on Darknet architecture [1, 21, 22]. The *YOLO* algorithm classifies and locates the object in only one step. In the output layer is given the position and category. This

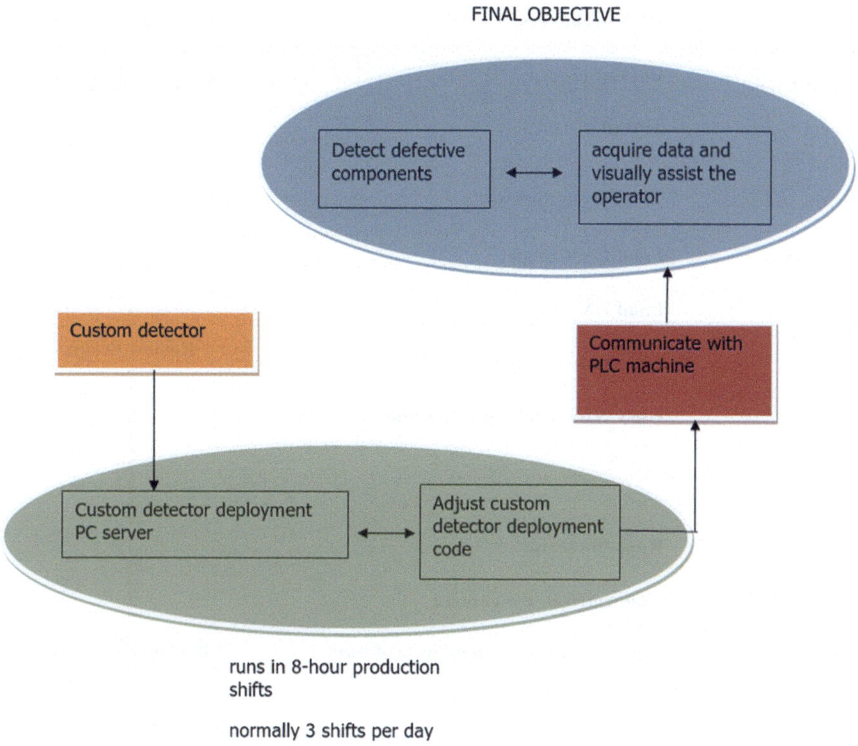

Fig. 4 Overall process diagram

approach improves processing speed to address requirements in real time for object detection [23]. The Single Shot multibox Detector integrates the end-to-end approach of the *YOLO* and the anchor boxes mechanism of the Faster RCNN. In older versions of *YOLO* less information about small objects is saved in the high-level feature map, and the detection result was not as accurate. The *YOLO v3* uses the network adapting features on the basis of Darknet-53, and the Logistic loss instead of SoftMax loss, which has advantages for small object detection [24]. One of the objectives is to achieve real time processing [20]. *YOLO v3* can detect multiple objects with a single inference, and its detection speed is therefore extremely fast; in addition, by applying a multi-stage detection method, it can complement the low accuracy of *YOLO* and *YOLO v2* [25–27].

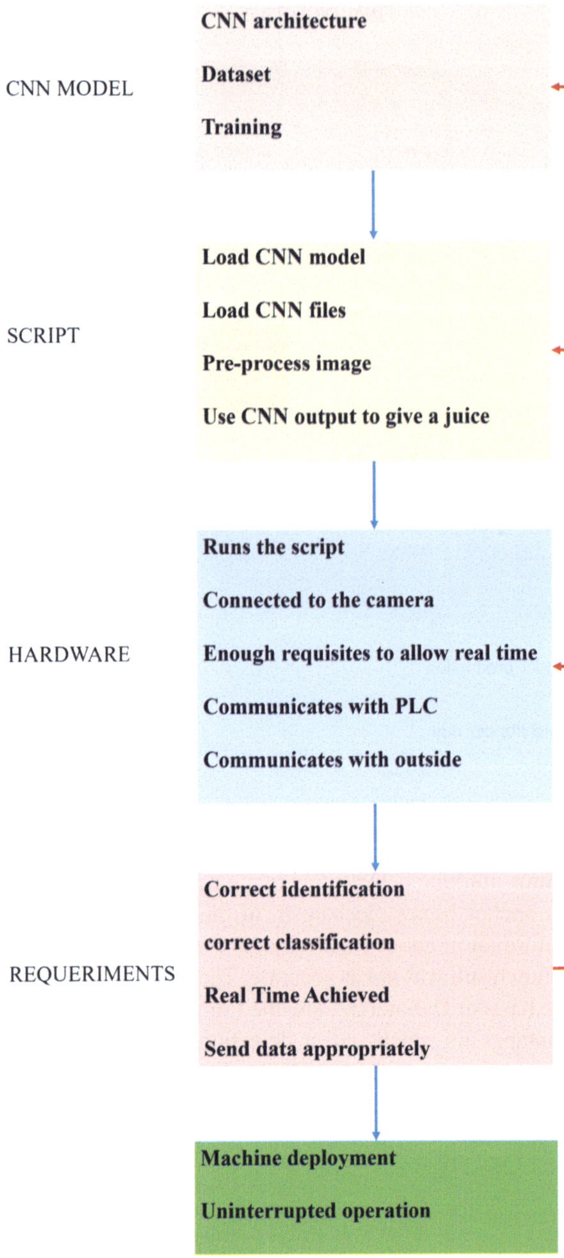

Fig. 5 Basic flow chart

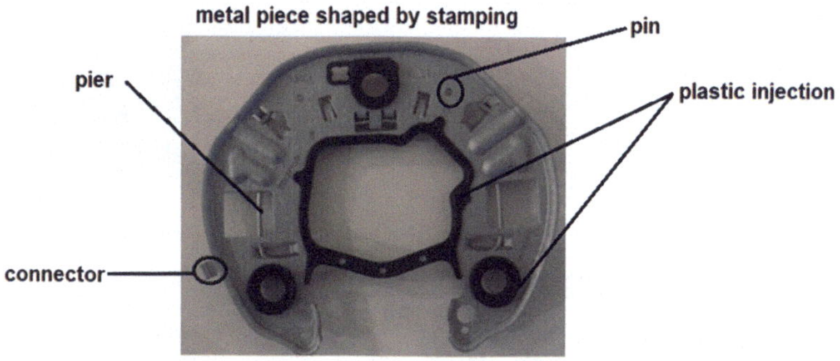

Fig. 6 Component parts

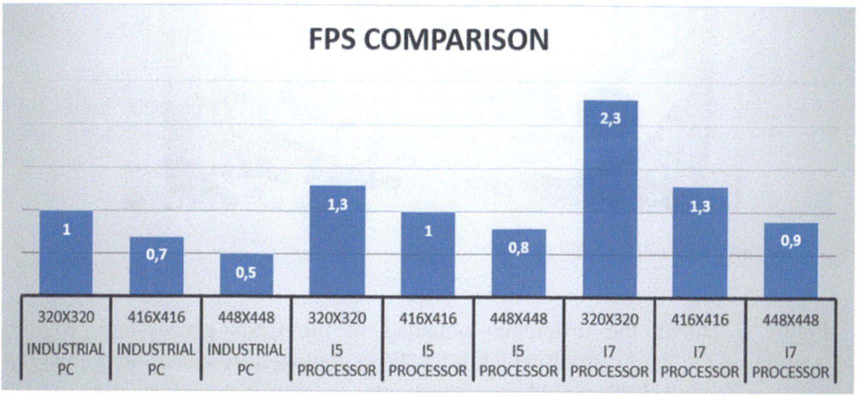

Fig. 7 CNN speed depending on processing hardware (processor and resolution)

3 Case Study

A test has been performed under real conditions on a machine that places the pins into the component. Figure 6 explains the components of the final piece. The piece is produced by stamping, then, is over-molding by plastic injection and placement of the spring, and finally, four pins by stamping.

The manufacturing process is as follows. The machine takes a piece from the entry zone and places it in an intermediate tool. Then, the piece is checked in a spring force testing zone. If the piece passes the test, it is placed in the pressing tool. The part is placed in the press and the pins are stamped in the component.

The verification system based on neural networks will determine if the part is in good condition or defective and the machine will perform a series of actions depending on this result. Due to the camera does not have internal processing, it is performed in an industrial PC that will control the entire system and communications with the PLC.

Fig. 8 Varifocal camera USB output

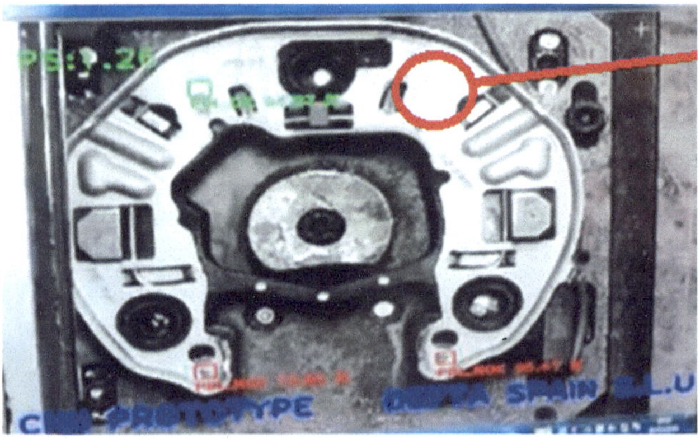

Fig. 9 Negative effect of ambient light

Figure 7 shows the difference obtained in the CNN processing program depending on the hardware on which it has been deployed. A speed lower than 0.6 Frames per Second (FPS) would compromise the sending of the information in time to the rest of the machine and could lead to a malfunction of the system. It has been verified that for this application to correctly work a framerate higher than one FPS must be obtained.

The chosen camera is a varifocal with a 50 mm focal lens and USB connectivity (Fig. 8).

The system is designed to operate 24 h a day, so the ambient and light conditions will change. The network will be trained with images taken in different exposures and environmental conditions to increase its robustness. Figure 9 shows an image with ambient light that has a negative effect since it does not allow to detect some areas of the piece. The pins in the image can be hardly distinguished.

To solve this problem, a new lighting system has been built. The new design covers an area of the camera to minimize the influence of outside light and adds a new light system of 1320 lumens to provide more constant and homogeneous light conditions.

Figure 10 shows the position of the old system light, and the position of the new one. The component now has an accurate lighting.

The images for the dataset were acquired and verified during the manufacturing. The next step was to perform a preprocessing with the aim of reducing noise, highlighting contours, and equalizing the histogram. The new image dataset is

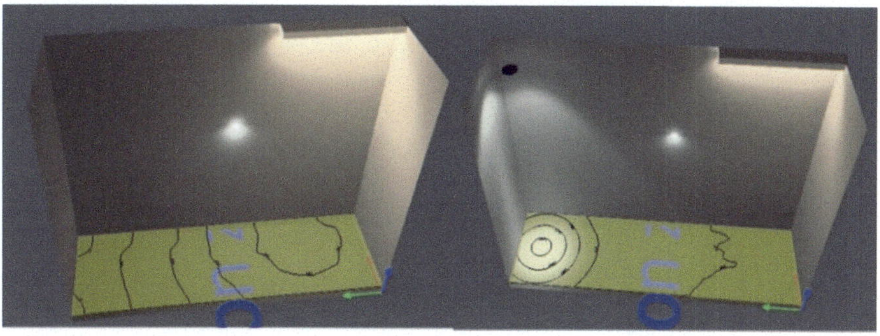

Fig. 10 Study of light influence in order to add a new light

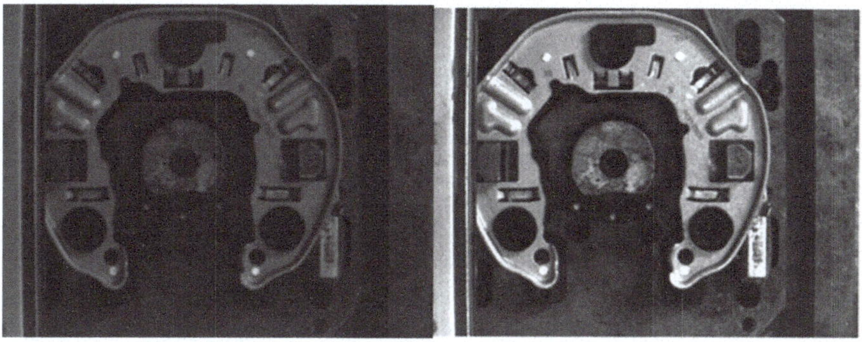

Fig. 11 Image preprocessing

more homogenized and can be introduced to the convolutional neural network (Fig. 11).

The network is based on the following structure (Fig. 12): The initial convolutional layers of the network are responsible for extracting features from the image, while the full connection layers predict the output probability and the coordinates of the object.

The network has 24 convolutional layers followed by 2 full connection layers; it makes use of 1×1 reduction layers followed by 3×3 convolutional layers.

4 Results

Different neural network architectures have been compared, confirming that the architecture chosen, *YOLO v3* is the right one for this work, as shown in Fig. 13. Although the algorithm and architecture of *YOLO v3*, a comparative study has been carried out with the accuracy achieved with other networks in training and validation.

	Type	Filters	Size	Output
	Convolutional	32	3 x 3	256 x 256
	Convolutional	64	3 x 3 / 2	128 x 128
1 x	Convolutional	32	1 x 1	
	Convolutional	64	3 x 3	
	Residual			128 x 128
	Convolutional	128	3 x 3 / 2	64 x 64
2 x	Convolutional	64	1 x 1	
	Convolutional	128	3 x 3	
	Residual			64 x 64
	Convolutional	256	3 x 3 / 2	32 x 32
8 x	Convolutional	128	1 x 1	
	Convolutional	256	3 x 3	
	Residual			32 x 32
	Convolutional	512	3 x 3 / 2	16 x 16
8 x	Convolutional	256	1 x 1	
	Convolutional	512	3 x 3	
	Residual			16 x 16
	Convolutional	1024	3 x 3 / 2	8 x 8
4 x	Convolutional	512	1 x 1	
	Convolutional	1024	3 x 3	
	Residual			8 x 8
	Avgpool		Global	
	connected		1000	
	Softmax			

Fig. 12 YOLO V3 architecture diagram

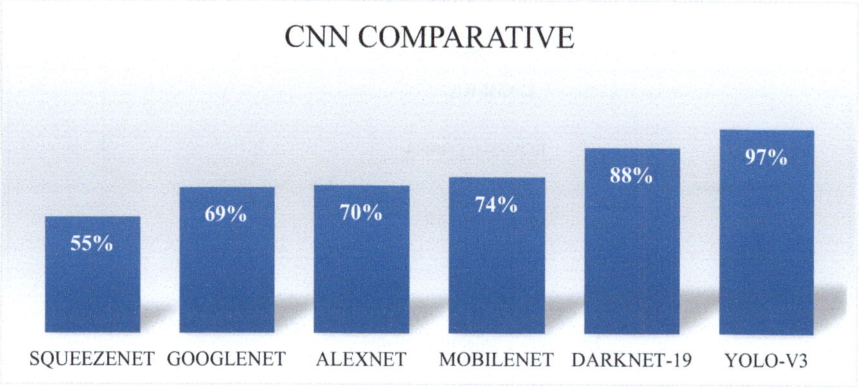

Fig. 13 CNN comparisons

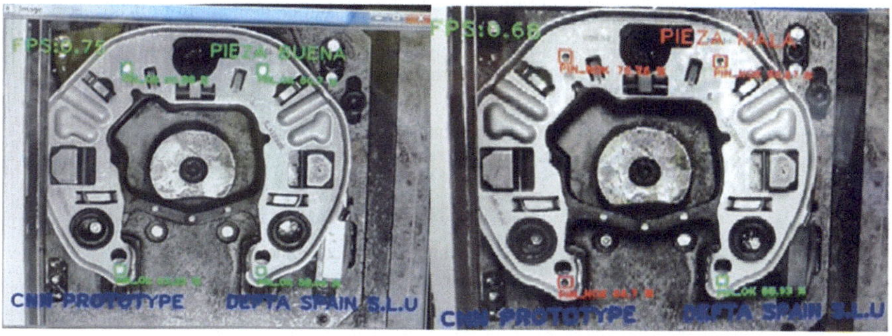

Fig. 14 Results of part without defect (left) and defective component (right)

It can be observed that the networks designed to work in embedded hardware are the ones that achieve the best results. *Darknet-19* achieves a higher speed, but at the cost of sacrificing too much precision, so that during the tests, when faced with slight changes in lighting or brightness focused on the area of interest, CNN was not able to detect the four zones correctly.

YOLO V3 (based on *Darknet-53*) manages to remain stable and achieve good accuracy and low computational cost. It is observed that the network used is the one that achieves the higher accuracy (97%).

Figure 14 shows two images with the result determined with the neural network.

The part on the left has been considered as a good part since it has found all four pins successfully, however the part on the right has found three faulty pins. The existing system shown in Fig. 15 was a very simple model and not very tolerant to failures, the camera acquired the image and processed it, giving a single output that was transmitted to the PLC. The PLC was the element that communicated with the outside. The information collected was very limited and not very useful.

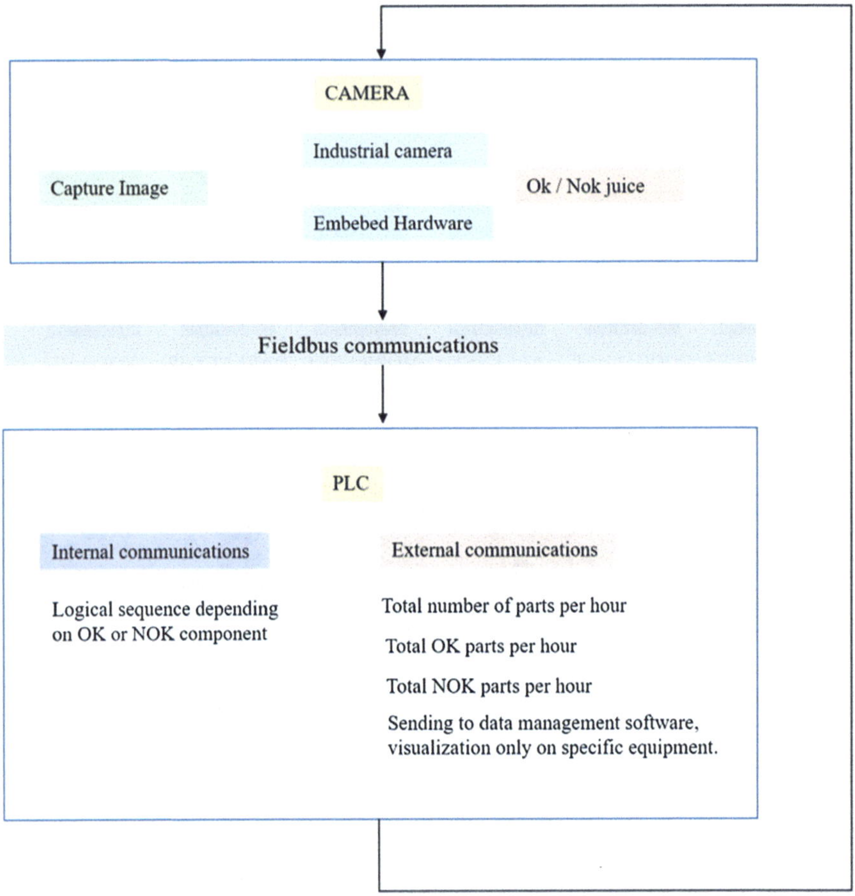

Fig. 15 Standard system

The new model shown in Fig. 16 is more complex, but more fault-tolerant and versatile. This approach has implemented direct communication with the PLC in addition to the possibility of storing data.

5 Conclusion

A convolutional neuronal network has been designed, implemented, and tested in working conditions for fault detection. Different architectures were tested to obtain those with higher accuracy. The algorithm has been developed to optimize resources and minimize computational cost.

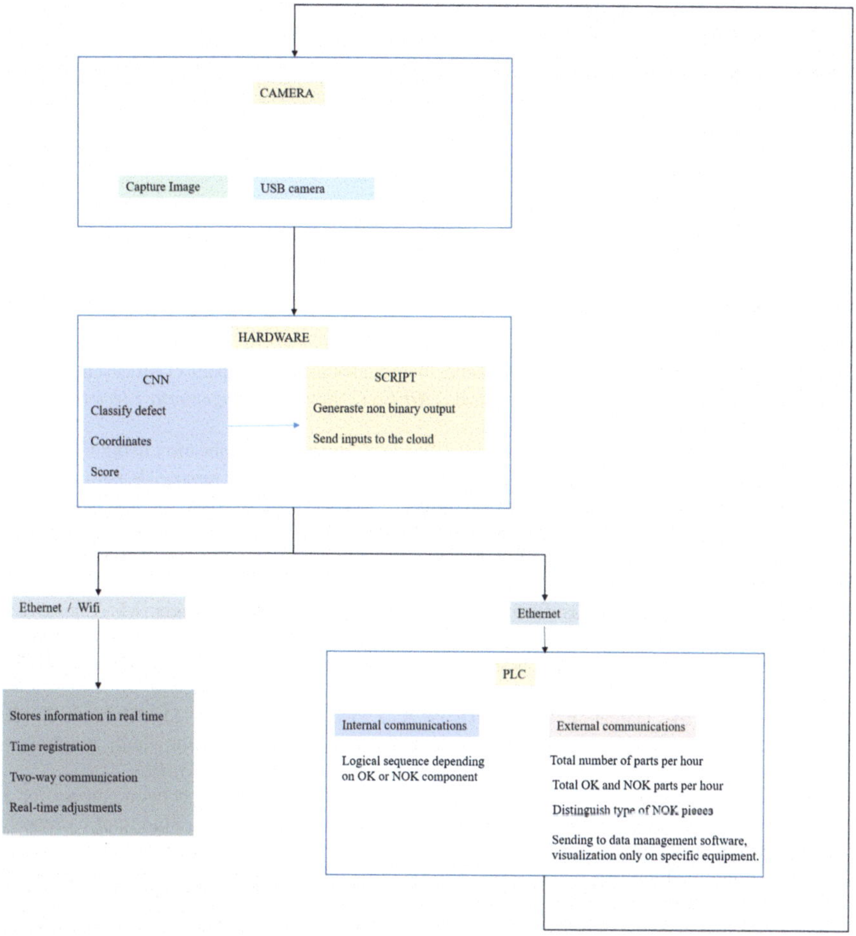

Fig. 16 IoT and CNN model approach

It has been concluded that *YOLO V3 CNN* yields a performance for processes where real-time use prevails. This approach has proven to be robust in different environmental conditions of light and brightness and has achieved a prediction accuracy of 97%. Definitely, *YOLO V3* has presented a balance between precision and computational cost suitable for this type of application very demanded in the industry. This type of approach adds great value to the process of obtaining relevant information, compared to traditional pattern recognition algorithms.

The proposed approach increases the amount of information that can be collected and analyzed with a real time response, which is very useful to give the system feedback and act immediately. The model based on IoT allows a robust control of the inputs and outputs of the system, while providing full connectivity with the rest of the plant. The corrections can be performed in the same process, or in previous or subsequent processes, decreasing the number of defective pieces. The evaluation of all the collected data can be processed using Big Data and cloud computing techniques, to obtain statistics, trends and forecasting of condition of parts and wear of tools.

Acknowledgments The authors are thankful to Defta Spain S.L.U. company.

References

1. Juan, R. Q., & Mario, C. M. (2011). Redes neuronales artificiales para el procesamiento de imágenes, una revisión de la última década. *RIEE&C, Revista de Ingeniería Eléctrica, Electrónica y Computación, 9*(1), 7–16.
2. Kawahara, M., Inoue, T., & Nishio, Y. (2010). Image processing application using CNN with dynamic template. In *2010 12th international workshop on cellular nanoscale networks and their applications*, CNNA 2010 (pp. 1–6). https://doi.org/10.1109/CNNA.2010.5430330.
3. Albawi, S., Mohammed, T. A., & Al-Zawi, S. (2017, August). Understanding of a convolutional neural network. In *2017 international conference on engineering and technology (ICET)* (pp. 1–6). Washington, DC: IEEE.
4. Gómez Muñoz, C. Q., Arcos Jiménez, A., García Márquez, F. P., Kogia, M., Cheng, L., Mohimi, A., & Papaelias, M. (2018). Cracks and welds detection approach in solar receiver tubes employing electromagnetic acoustic transducers. *Structural Health Monitoring, 17*(5), 1046–1055.
5. Gómez, C. Q. M., García, F. P. M., Arcos, A. J., Cheng, L., Kogia, M., Mohimi, A., & Papaelias, M. A. (2017). A heuristic method for detecting and locating faults employing electromagnetic acoustic transducers. *Eksploatacja i Niezawodność, 19*(4), 493.
6. Fukushima, K., Miyake, S., & Ito, T. (1983). Neocognitron: A neural network model for a mechanism of visual pattern recognition. *IEEE Transactions on Systems, Man, and Cybernetics, 5*, 826–834.
7. Xia, F., Yang, L. T., Wang, L., & Vinel, A. (2012). Internet of things. *International Journal of Communication Systems, 25*(9), 1101.
8. Firouzi, F., Farahani, B., Weinberger, M., DePace, G., & Aliee, F. S. (2020). IoT fundamentals: Definitions, architectures, challenges, and promises. In *Intelligent internet of things* (pp. 3–50). Cham: Springer.
9. Scuotto, V., Ferraris, A., Bresciani, S., Al-Mashari, M., & Del Giudice, M. (2016). Internet of things: Applications and challenges in smart cities. A case study of IBM smart city projects. *Business Process Management Journal, 22*(2).
10. Gershenfeld, N., Krikorian, R., & Cohen, D. (2004). The internet of things. *Scientific American, 291*(4), 76–81.
11. Carlini, N., & Wagner, D. (2017, May). Towards evaluating the robustness of neural networks. In *2017 IEEE symposium on security and privacy (sp)* (pp. 39–57). Washington, DC: IEEE.
12. Szegedy, C., Vanhoucke, V., Ioffe, S., Shlens, J., & Wojna, Z. (2016). Rethinking the inception architecture for computer vision. In *Proceedings of the IEEE conference on computer vision and pattern recognition* (pp. 2818–2826).
13. Han, X., Zhong, Y., Cao, L., & Zhang, L. (2017). Pre-trained alexnet architecture with pyramid pooling and supervision for high spatial resolution remote sensing image scene classification. *Remote Sensing, 9*(8), 848.
14. Krizhevsky, A., Sutskever, I., & Hinton, G. E. (2017). Imagenet classification with deep convolutional neural networks. *Communications of the ACM, 60*(6), 84–90.

15. Lee, H. J., Ullah, I., Wan, W., Gao, Y., & Fang, Z. (2019). Real-time vehicle make and model recognition with the residual SqueezeNet architecture. *Sensors, 19*(5), 982.
16. Iandola, F. N., Han, S., Moskewicz, M. W., Ashraf, K., Dally, W. J., & Keutzer, K. (2016). SqueezeNet: AlexNet-level accuracy with 50× fewer parameters and <0.5 MB model size. arXiv preprint. arXiv: 1602.07360.
17. Howard, A. G., Zhu, M., Chen, B., Kalenichenko, D., Wang, W., Weyand, T., Andreetto, M. & Adam, H. (2017). Mobilenets: Efficient convolutional neural networks for mobile vision applications. arXiv preprint. arXiv:1704.04861.
18. Vasavi, S., Priyadarshini, N. K., & Vardhan, K. H. (2020). Invariant feature based darknet architecture for moving object classification. *IEEE Sensors Journal, 21*(5), 11417–11426.
19. Gómez Muñoz, C. Q., García Marquez, F. P., Hernandez Crespo, B., & Makaya, K. (2019). Structural health monitoring for delamination detection and location in wind turbine blades employing guided waves. *Wind Energy, 22*(5), 698–711.
20. Choi, J., Chun, D., Kim, H., & Lee, H. J. (2019). Gaussian yolov3: An accurate and fast object detector using localization uncertainty for autonomous driving. In *Proceedings of the IEEE international conference on computer vision* (pp. 502–511).
21. Shafiee, M. J., Chywl, B., Li, F., & Wong, A. (2017). Fast YOLO: A fast you only look once system for real-time embedded object detection in video. arXiv preprint. arXiv:1709.05943.
22. Redmon, J., & Farhadi, A. (2017). Yolo9000: Better, faster, stronger. In *Proceedings of the IEEE conference on computer vision and pattern recognition* (pp. 7263–7271).
23. Mao, Q. C., Sun, H. M., Liu, Y. B., & Jia, R. S. (2019). Mini-YOLOv3: Real-time object detector for embedded applications. *IEEE Access, 7*, 133529–133538.
24. Zhang, X., Yang, W., Tang, X., & Liu, J. (2018). A fast learning method for accurate and robust lane detection using two-stage feature extraction with YOLO v3. *Sensors, 18*(12), 4308.
25. Redmon J., & Farhadi, A. (2018). YOLOv3: An incremental improvement, ArXiv, 2018.
26. Redmon, J., Divvala, S., Girshick, R., & Farhadi, A. (2016). You only look once: Unified, real-time object detection. In *Proceedings of the IEEE conference on computer vision and pattern recognition* (pp. 779–788).
27. Ramirez, I. S., Muñoz, C. Q. G., & Marquez, F. P. G. (2017). A condition monitoring system for blades of wind turbine maintenance management. In *Proceedings of the tenth international conference on management science and engineering management* (pp. 3–11). Singapore: Springer.

Using Other Multi-Attribute Decision-Making Techniques to Measure Efficiency When Data Envelopment Analysis Fails

William P. Fox, Ethan Buck, John Morris, Oliver Stein, Simon Sun, Rebecca Rousseau, and Asanah Teneng

1 Introduction

The Internet of Things (IOT) is a broad area. Examples of objects that can fall into the scope of Internet of Things include connected security systems, thermostats, cars, electronic appliances, lights in household and commercial environments, alarm clocks, speaker systems, vending machines and more. The Internet of Things (IoT) describes the network of physical objects—"things"—that are embedded with sensors, software, and other technologies for the purpose of connecting and exchanging data with other devices and systems over the internet.

Networks are also broad and might include networks very similar to Social networks within our broad definition.

This chapter initially illustrates the use of data envelopment analysis to rank order the efficiency of five Decision Making Units (DMUs) with two inputs and three outputs provided. Then, this chapter shows when data envelopment analysis fails and another ranking algorithm must be used.

W. P. Fox (✉)
College of William & Mary, Williamsburg, VA, USA
e-mail: wpfox@wm.edu

E. Buck · J. Morris · O. Stein · S. Sun · R. Rousseau · A. Teneng
Department of Mathematics, College of William and Mary, Williamsburg, VA, USA

F. P. García Márquez, B. Lev (eds.), *Introduction to Internet of Things in Management Science and Operations Research*, International Series in Operations Research & Management Science 311,
https://doi.org/10.1007/978-3-030-74644-5_12

2 Data Envelopment Analysis

We start by describing Data Envelopment Analysis (DEA).

2.1 Description and Uses

Data envelopment analysis (DEA) is a data input-output driven approach for evaluating the performance of entities called decision making units (DMUs) that convert multiple inputs into multiple outputs [1]. The definition of a DMU is generic and very flexible so that any entity to be ranked might be a DMU. DEA has been used to evaluate the relative *performance* or *efficiencies* of hospitals, schools, departments, US Air Force wings, US armed forces recruiting agencies, universities, cities, courts, businesses, banking facilities, countries, regions, SOF airbases, key nodes in networks, and the list goes on. According to Cooper [1], DEA has been used to gain insights into activities that were not obtained by other quantitative or qualitative methods.

Charnes et al. [2] described DEA as a mathematical programming model applied to observational data. It provides a new way of obtaining empirical estimates of relationship among the DMUs. It has been formally defined as a methodology directed to frontiers rather than central tendencies.

2.2 Methodology

The model, in simplest terms, may be formulated and solved as a linear programming problem [3, 4]. Although several formulations for DEA exist, we seek the most straight forward formulation in order to maximize an efficiency of a DMU as constrained by inputs and outputs as shown in Eq. (1). As an option, we might normalize the metric inputs and outputs for the alternatives if the values are poorly scaled within the data. We will call this data matrix, **X,** with entries x_{ij}. We define an efficiency unit as $E_i \, for\ i = 1, 2, \ldots, nodes$. We let E_i equal the output vectors times their weights, $O_i * t_i$. Further, we define wi be the weights or coefficients for the linear combinations of the inputs, I_j. Further, we restrict any efficiency from being larger than one. Thus, the largest efficient DMU will be 1. This gives the following linear programming formulation for single outputs but multiple inputs:

$$\text{Max } E_i$$

$$\text{subject to}$$

$$\sum_{i=1}^{n} w_i I_{ij} - O_i t_{j_i} \geq 0, j = 1, 2, \ldots \tag{1}$$

$$E_i \leq 1 \text{ for all } i$$

For multiple inputs and outputs, we recommend the formulations provided by Winston [3] and Trick [5] using Eq. (2).

For any DMU_O, let X_i be the inputs and Y_i be the outputs. Let X_0 and Y_0 be the *DMU* being modeled. Let ***w*** and ***t*** be vectors representing the weights for inputs and outputs used in the model. The DMU_o is the ratio of $\mathbf{v^TY_o/w^TX_o}$ that we want to maximize subject t

$$\mathbf{vTYo/wTXo \leq 1, j = 0, \ldots, n}$$

$$\mathbf{wT, tT \geq 0.}$$

(Source: https://mat.gsia.cmu.edu/classes/mstc/dea/node3.html.)
Maximize $\mathbf{v^TY_o/w^TX_o}$ or equivalently just $\mathbf{v^TY_o}$
Subject to:

$$\mathbf{vTYo/wTXo \leq 1, j = 0, \ldots, n} \tag{2}$$

$$\mathbf{wT \geq 0}$$

$$\mathbf{tT \geq 0}$$

2.3 *Strengths and Limitations to DEA*

DEA can be a very useful tool when used wisely according to Trick [6]. A few of the strengths that make DEA extremely useful are [6]: (1) *DEA can handle multiple input and multiple output models*; (2) *DEA doesn't require an assumption of a functional form relating inputs to outputs*; (3) *DMUs are directly compared against a peer or combination of peers*; and (4) *Inputs and outputs can have very different units. For example, X_1 could be in units of lives saved and X_2 could be in units of dollars without requiring any* a priori *tradeoff between the two.*

The same characteristics that make DEA a powerful tool can also create limitations to the process and analysis. An analyst should keep these limitations in mind when choosing whether or not to use DEA. A few additional limitations include:

1. Since DEA is an extreme point technique, noise in the data such as measurement error can cause significant problems.

2. DEA is good at estimating "relative" efficiency of a DMU but it converges very slowly to "absolute" efficiency. In other words, it can tell you how well you are doing compared to your peers but not compared to a "theoretical maximum."
3. Since DEA is a nonparametric technique, statistical hypothesis tests are difficult and are the focus of ongoing research.
4. Since a standard formulation of DEA with multiple inputs and outputs creates a separate linear program for each DMU, large problems can be computationally intensive.
5. Linear programming does not ensure all weights are considered. We find that the value for weights are only for those that optimally determine an efficiency rating. If having all criteria weighted (inputs, outputs) is essential to the decision-maker then do not use DEA.

2.4 Illustrative Examples

Example 1. Manufacturing with DEA that works well

Consider the following manufacturing process, (modified from Winston, [3]) where we have three DMUs each of which has two inputs and three outputs as shown in the data table (Table 1).

Since no units are given and the scales are similar so we decide not to normalize the data. We define the following decision variables:

t_i = value of a single unit of output of *DMU i,* for $i = 1, 2, 3$.
w_i = cost or weights for one unit of inputs of *DMU i,* for $i = 1, 2$.
$efficiency_i = DMU_i$ = (total value of i's outputs)/(total cost of i's inputs), for $i = 1, 2, 3$.

The following modeling assumptions are made:

1. No DMU will have an efficiency of more than 100%.
2. If any efficiency is less than 1, then it is inefficient.
3. We will scale the costs so that the costs of the inputs equal 1 for each linear program. For example, we will use $5w_1 + 14w_2 = 1$ in our program for DMU_1.
4. All values and weights must be strictly positive, so we use a constant such as 0.0001 in lieu of 0. This idea from Trick [5].

To calculate the efficiency of DMU_1, we define the linear program using Eq. (2) as

Table 1 Manufacturing example

DMU	Input #1	Input #2	Output #1	Output #2	Output #3
1	5	14	9	4	16
2	8	15	5	7	10
3	7	12	4	9	13

Maximize $DMU_1 = 9t_1 + 4t_2 + 16t_3$
Subject to
$-9t_1 - 4t_2 - 16t_3 + 5w_1 + 14w_2 \geq 0$
$-5t_1 - 7t_2 - 10t_3 + 8w_1 + 15w_2 \geq 0$
$-4t_1 - 9t_2 - 13t_3 + 7w_1 + 12w_2 \geq 0$
$5w_1 + 14w_2 = 1$
$t_i \geq 0.0001, i = 1, 2, 3$
$w_i \geq 0.0001, i = 1, 2$
Non-negativity

To calculate the efficiency of DMU_2, we define the linear program using Eq. (2) as

Maximize $DMU_2 = 5t_1 + 7t_2 + 10t_3$
Subject to
$-9t_1 - 4t_2 - 16t_3 + 5w_1 + 14w_2 \geq 0$
$-5t_1 - 7t_2 - 10t_3 + 8w_1 + 15w_2 \geq 0$
$-4t_1 - 9t_2 - 13t_3 + 7w_1 + 12w_2 \geq 0$
$8w_1 + 15w_2 = 1$
$t_i \geq 0.0001, i = 1, 2, 3$
$w_i \geq 0.0001, i = 1, 2$
Non-negativity

To calculate the efficiency of DMU_3, we define the linear program using Eq. (2) as

Maximize $\mathrm{DMU}_3 = 4t_1 + 9t_2 + 13t_3$
Subject to
$-9t_1 - 4t_2 - 16t_3 + 5w_1 + 14w_2 \geq 0$
$-5t_1 - 7t_2 - 10t_3 + 8w_1 + 15w_2 \geq 0$
$-4t_1 - 9t_2 - 13t_3 + 7w_1 + 12w_2 \geq 0$
$7w_1 + 12w_2 = 1$
$t_\mathrm{i} \geq 0.0001, i = 1, 2, 3$
$w_\mathrm{i} \geq 0.0001, i = 1, 2$
Non-negativity

The linear programming solutions show the efficiencies as $DMU_1 = DMU_3 = 1$, $DMU_2 = 0.77303$.

Interpretation: DMU_2 is operating at 77.303% of the efficiency of DMU_1 and DMU_3. Management could concentrate some improvements or best practices from DMU_1 or DMU_3 for DMU_2. An examination of the dual prices for the linear program of DMU_2 yields $\lambda_1 = 0.261538$, $\lambda_2 = 0$, and $\lambda_3 = 0.661538$. The average output vector for DMU_2 can be written as:

Table 2 IOT Sensors Data from five competing companies

DMU sensors	Input 1: Temperature sensor	Input 2: Humidity sensor	Output 1: Sensor hours	Output 2: Sensor total	Output 3: Total sensor successes
Unit 1	25	51	18,341	9086	63
Unit 2	15	18	8190	4049	23
Unit 3	10	23	2857	1255	31
Unit 4	33	32	22,277	6102	31
Unit 5	12	18	6830	2910	19

$$0.261538\begin{bmatrix} 9 \\ 4 \\ 16 \end{bmatrix} + 0.661538\begin{bmatrix} 4 \\ 9 \\ 13 \end{bmatrix} = \begin{bmatrix} 5 \\ 7 \\ 12.785 \end{bmatrix}$$

and the average input vector can be written as

$$0.261538\begin{bmatrix} 5 \\ 14 \end{bmatrix} + 0.661538\begin{bmatrix} 7 \\ 12 \end{bmatrix} = \begin{bmatrix} 5.938 \\ 11.6 \end{bmatrix}.$$

In our data, output #3 is 10 units. Thus, we may clearly see the inefficiency is in output #3 where 12.785 units are required. We find that they are short 2.785 units (12.785 − 10 = 2.785). This helps focus on treating the inefficiency found for output #3.

Sensitivity Analysis: Sensitivity analysis in a linear program is sometimes referred to as "what if" analysis. Let's assume that without management engaging some additional training for DMU_2 that DMU_2 output #3 dips from 10 to 9 units of output while the input 2 h increases from 15 to 16 h. We find that these changes in the *technology coefficients* are easily handled in resolving the LPs. Since DMU_2 is affected, we might only modify and solve the LP concerning DMU_2. We find with these changes that *DMU*'s efficiency is now only 74% as effective as DMU_1 and DMU_3.

Example 2. Internet of Things example that fails using DEA

We are provided data for five competing alternatives companies to provide sensors for temperatures and humidity for our new set of warehouses. Data is provided by each company on the number of sensors and output data from similar-sized warehouses shown in Table 2.

The DEA failures found include:

1. If you set up the linear programs as suggested with the constants strictly greater than 0, using w_i and $t_i \geq 0.0001$, using the Michael Trick method (2014), many of the DMU linear programs are infeasible.
2. If you allow the constants to be greater than or equal to zero, then in solving the DMU's linear programs some of the inputs and outputs are excluded by the decision variable's value being zero.

Obviously, if the decision maker provides inputs and outputs, we assume that all should be considered and used for decision analysis at non-zero levels.

To attempt a fix these failures, we decide to offer another multi-attribute decision making tool to compute the efficiency values that are used to rank alternatives.

3 Multi-Attribute Decision-Making

3.1 The Technique of Order Preference by Similarity to Ideal Solution (TOPSIS)

TOPSIS was the result of research and work done by Yoon and Hwang [7]. TOPSIS has been used in a wide spectrum of comparisons of alternatives including: item selection from among alternatives, ranking leaders or entities, remote sensing in regions, data mining, and supply chain operations. TOPSIS is chosen over other methods because it orders the feasible alternatives according to their closeness to an ideal solution [8]. Why TOPSIS? It's strength over other decision making methods is that with TOPSIS, we can indicate which metric (attributes) should be maximized and which should be minimized. In all other methods, everything is maximized. Napier [9] provided some analysis of the use of TOPSIS for the department of defense in industrial base planning and item selection.

In a business setting it has been applied to a large number of application cases in advanced manufacturing processes [10–12], purchasing and outsourcing [13, 14], and financial performance measurement [15].

3.2 TOPSIS Methodology and Efficiency Modification

We describe the TOPSIS process as it is carried out through the following steps.

3.2.1 Step 1

Create an evaluation matrix consisting of m alternatives and n criteria, with the.

intersection of each alternative and criteria given as x_{ij}, giving us a matrix $(\boldsymbol{X}_{ij})_{mxn}$.

$$D = \begin{array}{c} \\ A_1 \\ A_2 \\ A_3 \\ \vdots \\ A_m \end{array} \begin{array}{c} \begin{array}{ccccc} x_1 & x_2 & x_3 & \dots & x_n \end{array} \\ \begin{bmatrix} x_{11} & x_{12} & x_{13} & \cdots & x_{1n} \\ x_{21} & x_{22} & x_{23} & \cdots & x_{2n} \\ x_{31} & x_{32} & x_{33} & \cdots & x_{3n} \\ \vdots & \vdots & \vdots & & \vdots \\ x_{m1} & x_{m2} & x_{m3} & \dots & x_{mn} \end{bmatrix} \end{array}$$

3.2.2 Step 2

The matrix shown as $\boldsymbol{D}$ above then normalized to form the matrix $\boldsymbol{R} = (\boldsymbol{R}_{ij})_{mxn}$, using the normalization method to obtain the entries,

$$r_{ij} = \frac{x_{ij}}{\sqrt{\sum x_{ij}^2}}$$

for $i = 1, 2\ldots, m; j = 1, 2, \ldots n$.

3.2.3 Step 3

Calculate the weighted normalized decision matrix. First we need the weights. Weights can come from either the decision maker or by computation.

3.2.4 Step 3a

Use either the decision maker's weights for the attributes x_1, x_2,... x_n, pairwise comparisons method, or the entropy weighting scheme, as we use here.

$$\sum_{j=1}^{n} w_j = 1$$

The sum of the weights over all attributes must equal one regardless of the weighting method used.

3.2.5 Step 3b

Multiply the weights to each of the column entries in the matrix from *Step 2* to obtain the matrix, ***T***.

$$T = \left(t_{ij}\right)_{m\ x\ n} = \left(w_j r_{ij}\right)_{m\ x\ n}, i = 1, 2, \ldots, m$$

3.2.6 Step 4

Determine the worst alternative (A_w) and the best alternative (A_b): Examine each attribute's column and select the largest and smallest values appropriately. If the values imply larger is better (profit) then the best alternatives are the largest values and if the values imply smaller is better (such as cost) then the best alternative is the smallest value.

$$A_w = \left\{\left\langle \max\left(t_{ij}|i = 1, 2, \ldots, m \mid j \in J_-\right\rangle, \left\langle \min\left(t_{ij}|i = 1, 2, \ldots, m\right) \mid j \in J_+\right\rangle\right\}$$

$$\equiv \left\{t_{wj}|j = 1, 2, \ldots, n\right\},$$

$$A_{wb} = \left\{\left\langle \min\left(t_{ij}|i = 1, 2, \ldots, m \mid j \in J_-\right\rangle, \left\langle \max\left(t_{ij}|i = 1, 2, \ldots, m\right) \mid j \in J_+\right\rangle\right\}$$

$$\equiv \left\{t_{bj}|j = 1, 2, \ldots, n\right\},$$

where,

$J_+ = \{j = 1, 2, \ldots n|j)$ associated with the criteria having a positive impact, and.
$J_- = \{j = 1, 2, \ldots n|j)$ associated with the criteria having a negative impact.
We suggest, if possible, making all entry values in terms of positive impacts.

3.2.7 Step 5

Calculate the L2-distance between the target alternative i and the worst condition A_w.

$$d_{iw} = \sqrt{\sum_{j=1}^{n} \left(t_{ij} - t_{wj}\right)^2}, i = 1, 2, \ldots m$$

and the distance between the alternative i and the best condition A_b.

$d_{ib} = \sqrt{\sum_{j=1}^{n} \left(t_{ij} - t_{bj}\right)^2}, i = 1, 2, \ldots m$,where d_{iw} and d_{ib} are L2-norm distances from the target alternative i to the worst and best conditions, respectively.

3.2.8 Step 6

Calculate the similarity to the worst condition:

$$s_{iw} = \frac{d_{iw}}{(d_{iw} + d_{ib})}, 0 \leq s_{iw} \leq 1, i = 1, 2, \ldots, m$$

$S_{iw} = 1$ if and only if the alternative solution has the worst condition; and
$S_{iw} = 0$ if and only if the alternative solution has the best condition.

3.2.9 Step 7

Rank the alternatives according to their value from S_{iw} ($i = 1,2,\ldots,m$).

3.2.10 Step 8

Efficiency $= S_{iw}/(\text{Max } S_{iw})$, $i = 1\ldots n$.

4 Entropy Weighting Scheme

Shannon and Weaver [16] proposed the entropy concept and this concept had been highlighted by Zeleny [17] for deciding the weights of attributes. Entropy is the measure of uncertainty in the information using probability methods. It indicates that a broad distribution represents more uncertainty than does a sharply peaked distribution. To determine the weights by the entropy method the normalized decision matrix we call R_{ij} is considered. The equation used is

$$e_j = -k\sum_{i=1}^{n} R_{ij} \ln \left(R_{ij}\right)$$

where $k = 1/\ln(n)$ is a constant that guarantees that $0 \leq e_j \leq 1$. The value of n refers to the number of alternatives. The degree of divergence (d_j) of the average information contained by each attribute can be calculated as:

$$d_j = 1 - e_j.$$

The more divergent the performance rating R_{ij}, *for all i & j*, then the higher the corresponding d_j the more important the attribute B_j is considered to be.

The weights, eq. 3, are found by the equation

$$w_j = \frac{(1 - e_j)}{\sum(1 - e_j)}. \tag{3}$$

Let's assume that the criteria were listed in order of importance by a decision maker. Entropy ignores that fact and uses the actual data to compute the weights. Although homeruns might be the most important criteria to the decision maker it might not be the largest weighted criteria using entropy. Using this method, we must be willing to accept these type results in weights.

5 Illustrative Example

We return to Example 2 posed earlier which failed to give adequate results using DEA. We used the data and obtained the entropy weights. We used entropy with our data and found the weights, all non-zero, were:

Input 1	0.15284
Input 2	0.13217
Output 1	0.3095
Output 2	0.26007
Output 3	0.14542

Thus, using entropy none of the decision-makers inputs or outputs are eliminated from the decision process to calculate efficiency.

Next, we use TOPSIS with our five DMUs, we found these efficiency results:

	TOPSIS values	Rank	Efficiency
DMU 1	0.843269	1	1
DMU 2	0.281769	3	0.3341
DMU 3	0.076850	5	0.0911
DMU 4	0.717116	2	0.8506
DMU 5	0.184806	4	0.2192

6 Conclusions

We have shown two methods for ranking alternatives of things using DEA and TOPSIS. In our examples, it is shown that DEA might always work to solve the problem using all the inputs and outputs that should be considered. TOPSIS used to measure efficiency to rank order alternatives is clearly the better choice.

In our second illustrative example on sensor alternatives, we showed TOPSIS is the better mathematical process to rank the alternatives. Clearly, DMU 1 is considered 100%. This is because the largest TOPSIS divided by itself is 1. Therefore, one

DMU must be 100% in the process as is the process in DEA. In general, we would prefer to use DEA and take advantage of the powerful sensitivity analysis that it avails to the analyst. However, as seen in our example, DEA might not work and then we are forced to find an alternative method to measure efficiencies. The results indicate the Unit 1 (DMU 1) is the Sensor alternative that should be used to maximize success.

References

1. Cooper, W., Seiford, L., & Tone, K. (2000). *Data envelopment analysis*. Kluwer Academic Press.
2. Charnes, A. W., Cooper, W., & Rhodes, E. (1978). Measuring the efficiency of decision making units. *European Journal of Operations Research, 2*, 429–444.
3. Winston, W. (1995). Introduction to mathematical programming. *Duxbury Press*, 322–325.
4. Callen, J. (1991). Data envelopment analysis: Practical survey and managerial accounting applications. *Journal of Management Accounting Research, 3*, 35–57.
5. Trick, M. A. (2014). *Data envelopment analysis* (Chapter 12). Accessed April 2014. http://mat.gsia.cmu.edu/classes/QUANT/NOTES/chap12.pdf.
6. Trick, M. A. (1996). *Multiple criteria decision making for consultants*. Accessed April 2014. http://mat.gsia.cmu.edu/classes/mstc/multiple/multiple.html.
7. Hwang, C.-L., & Yoon, K. (1981). *Multiple attribute decision making: Methods and applications*. New York: Springer-Verlag.
8. Malczewski, J. (1996). GIS-based approach to multiple criteria group decision-making. *International Journal of Geographical Information Science - GIS, 10*(8), 955–971.
9. Napier, J. (1992). Industrial base program item selection indicators analytical enhancements. *Department of Defense Pamphlet*, DLA-93-P20047.
10. Agrawal, V. P., Kohli, V., & Gupta, S. (1991). Computer aided robot selection: The multiple attribute decision making approach. *International Journal of Production Research, 29*(8), 1629–1644.
11. Parkan, C., & Wu, M. (1999). Decision-making and performance measurement models with applications to robot selection. *Computers and Industrial Engineering, 36*(3), 503–523.
12. Parkan, C., & Minglu, W. (1997). On the equivalence of operational performance measurement and multiple attribute decision making. *International Journal of Production Research, 35*(11), 2963–2988.
13. Cengiz, K., Engin, O., Kubak, O., & Kaya, L. (2009). Information systems outsourcing decisions using group decision-making approach. *Engineering Applications of Artificial Intelligence, 22*(6), 832–841.
14. Shyura, H., & Shih, H. (2006). A hybrid MCDM model for strategic vendor selection. *Mathematical and Computer Modeling, 44*(7–8), 749–761.
15. Feng, C., & Wang, R. (2001). Considering the financial ratio on the performance evaluation of highway bus industry. *Transport Reviews, 21*(4), 449–467.
16. Shannon, C., & Weaver, W. (1949). *The mathematical theory of communication*. USA: University of Illinois Press. ISBN: 0-252-72548-4.
17. Zeleny, M. (1982). *Multiple criteria decision making*. New York: McGraw Hill.

Comprehensive Potential Evaluation for the Rooftop PV Development Based on IPO

Qiong Shen, Xue Wan, Wanyu Ni, Benjamin Lev, and Lu Gan

1 Introduction

At present, most cities in China have experienced rapid urbanization and economic growth. Urbanization has led to a large increase in energy use and is one of the largest contributors [1]. The construction sector including residential, commercial, and public buildings currently accounts for 31% of the world's energy demand. Therefore, building integrated photovoltaic system (BIPV) has become one of the best choices to deal with energy shortage and environmental pollution. It is an emerging technology that can save energy and reduce emissions without being limited by the geographical distribution of resources [2]. Meanwhile, a large number of rooftop surface areas and sufficient sunlight in the city provide sufficient conditions for the construction sector. And it carries out rooftop distributed solar power generation [3] to achieve sustainable urban development. Therefore, a large number

Q. Shen · X. Wan · W. Ni
College of Architecture and Urban-Rural Planning, Sichuan Agricultural University, Dujiangyan, People's Republic of China

B. Lev
Decision Sciences Department, LeBow College of Business, Drexel University, Philadelphia, PA, USA

L. Gan (✉)
College of Architecture and Urban-Rural Planning, Sichuan Agricultural University, Dujiangyan, People's Republic of China

Decision Sciences Department, LeBow College of Business, Drexel University, Philadelphia, PA, USA

Business School, Sichuan University, Chengdu, People's Republic of China
e-mail: ganlu_soarpb@sicau.edu.cn

F. P. García Márquez, B. Lev (eds.), *Introduction to Internet of Things in Management Science and Operations Research*, International Series in Operations Research & Management Science 311,
https://doi.org/10.1007/978-3-030-74644-5_13

of scholars began to study the power generation potential of rooftop photovoltaic (PV) systems. The research area has gradually evolved from the initial assessment of geographical potential and technological potential [4–6] to comprehensive potentials. It includes economic feasibility, environmental benefits, and social influences [2, 7–9] to maximize the benefits of rooftop PV.

However, the promotion process of rooftop PV faces many challenges in China as the following: (1) The property right of urban building roof is complex and the business model is not mature; (2) there are many stakeholders involved and it is difficult to coordinate; (3) the installation price is high and the public acceptance and market penetration are low; (4) the current subsidy policy is not adaptable enough to meet the actual needs of the residents. The one-way information communication mode leads to less interaction and ignores the real actual needs. In this case, fast and convenient Internet and popular smart phones can become useful tools to cope with these challenges.

The Internet of Things (IOT) has gotten more and more attention with the development of social and economy. People widely use the advantages of the Internet in production, life, and technology promotion. The Internet with its wide audience, speed, and timeliness of information transmission has become an important public platform [10]. It provides a new opportunity and approach to obtain the needs of the public [11]. Many studies highlight that the lack of public awareness is a major barrier to the acceptance of renewable energy technologies [12]. Most of the researches have focused on technical, policy, and financial challenges to renewable energy deployment [13, 14]. However, less attention has been paid on its social dimensions like public opinion. In this age of technology, opinions created by social networks provide an exceptional opportunity to mine valuable insights from them [15]. Building a bridge between the public and the construction of emerging technologies through the Internet is the deep meaning of the IOT. It is an important driving force for future development evaluation (Angelico et al., 2003). Internet Public Opinion (IPO) is about screening and obtaining a large amount of data from website through web crawler technology. It is a program technology used to filter and download web pages. It will play an important role in the development of large-scale construction projects in the future [16]. As a key participant of PV project, it is very important to grasp the needs of the investors or beneficiaries effectively. It contributes to the development of rooftop PV project. Therefore, this chapter will introduce IPO to study rooftop PV. It is helpful to collect numbers of public opinions and suggestions in a short time [17].

In general, the purpose of this study is to investigate comprehensive evaluation for the development potential of rooftop PV towards various buildings based on IPO. It reveals the root causes that hinder the development of rooftop PV industry sustainable development. Through IPO analysis and literature research, the reasonable and feasible evaluation index of rooftop PV comprehensive potential is determined. According to the development potential model, this study uses the gray relation projection method (GRPM) combined with the mean square deviation (MSD) and the Criteria Importance Though Intercriteria Correlation (CRITIC) to get the various building's potential ranking. Recently, GRPM is favored by more scholars because it can avoid the personal preference of results by distinguishing the characteristics and differences between different subjects [18]. Above all, this chapter uses the GRPM to evaluate the project comprehensively. Accordingly, the development potential and obstacles of rooftop PV are analyzed. Finally, the effectiveness of these methods is verified through the case study of Panzhihua area with real data from practice.

Nowadays, public opinions influence decision to use any new technology such as rooftop PV [19, 20]. That is because information is a key factor to influence the performance of decision makers [21]. To our best knowledge, there are rare researches using IPO for potential evaluation of rooftop PV. The novelty of this study is outlined as following. (1) It introduces text mining technology to effectively obtain numbers of IPO data for rooftop PV; (2) The attitude of stakeholders to develop rooftop PV by utilizing massive IPO data is effectively expanded through two-way communication; (3) This chapter integrates the model calculation and comprehensive evaluation of the development potential of rooftop PV. And then it explores the key influencing factors in the development.

The rest of this chapter is arranged as follows: Sect. 2 analyzes the current research; Sect. 3 introduces the modeling process and the implementation of the method in detail; Sect. 4 provides a numerical example to verify the availability and applicability of our method. Finally, Sect. 5 shows the conclusion and future research directions.

2 Background

2.1 Literature Review

The increasing demands for energy and fast depletion of fossil fuels have made cities actively develop and promote renewable energy technologies. In order to accelerate the application of rooftop PV technology in the urban and rural construction field, it is of great importance to conduct comprehensive evaluation. Therefore, this chapter divides the literature review into the following three parts: (1) Rooftop PV potential evaluation; (2) Methods of comprehensive evaluation; (3) Application of IPO.

2.1.1 Rooftop PV Potential Evaluation

As a new energy saving technology, rooftop PV is attracting people's attention. In recent years, many scholars have carried out evaluation research on the development of rooftop PV [2, 22]. It mainly evaluates and analyzes the development potential of rooftop PV from three angles of economy, technology, and environment. And then, it gradually extends to a comprehensive evaluation combining the three.

As an important guarantee for PV development, technology first received a lot of attention. Some scholars analyzed the impact of different technologies on the energy parameters of module tilt and layout [4, 23]. And they also considered the annual PV power generation whether related to the technology. The consideration is also about the distribution of modules installed on the roof and terrace of the building [6]. In addition, the calculation of the gross roof area and the PV suitable rooftop area in the city is a key issue to evaluate the utilization potential of the PV [2, 24]. With the important technical development in the field of PV, Bergamasco and Pietro [4] propose a method to estimate the potential of PV based on the existing GIS data. Subsequently, there are some studies to add economic indicators to the quantitative assessment of the economic feasibility of PV projects (Michael et al. 2020). They mainly include investment payback period, net present value, return on investment, energy level cost, and so on [25, 26]. In order to reduce the dependence of buildings on mineral energy, the energy saving benefits of solar energy were also introduced into the research scope. It considers its ability to reduce conventional energy consumption during the operation of photoelectric buildings [27, 28]. At the same time, the potential of emission reduction and their benign effects such as carbon dioxide, sulfur dioxide, and other air pollutants are also considered [26]. Subsequently, scholars begin to refine, summarize, and design different evaluation indicators based on different focuses with substantial detailed studies. They even carry out the comprehensive evaluation to different PV objects [6].

2.1.2 Methods of Comprehensive Evaluation

In recent years, there are a variety of methods for comprehensive evaluation of urban rooftop PV buildings, and they are shown in Table 1. It includes Fuzzy Analytic Hierarchy Process (FAHP) [29], Technique for Order Preference by Similarity to Ideal Solution (TOPSIS) [30], Gray Relation Analysis (GRA) [31, 32], Fuzzy Comprehensive Assessment (FAC) [33, 34], the Matter-Element Extension Theory (MEET) [35], and so on. Based on GRA and vector projection, GRPM is developed [36]. Then, some scholars start to choose the GRPM as the evaluation method [18], because it mainly distinguishes the characteristics and differences between different subjects, and can greatly reduce the loss caused by information asymmetry. The determination and comprehensive evaluation of attribute weights seriously affect the results of decision makers. The analysis shows that both the mean square deviation and entropy value can be used to represent the degree of data aggregation. So they have equal status when CRITIC method is improved [37]. Therefore, this chapter combines the MSD and CRITIC to empower the indicators. Then it chooses GRPM to evaluate the project comprehensively based on the above comprehensive evaluation methods. It further analyzes the potential of the combination of PV and urban roofs as power generation to promote rooftop PV system in the city.

In general, rare studies are concerning the development of the PV market using public opinion data, because the development of rooftop PV involves the participation of multiple stakeholders with great uncertainty and complexity. At the same time, the research mainly focuses on the potential evaluation of different objects of rooftop PV development. It has rarely appeared in previous research. This chapter is committed to exploring the potential of rooftop PV technology for buildings with different uses in cities.

Table 1 Comparison of some main evaluation methods for comprehensive evaluation

	Methodology								
Characteristics	FAHP	FCA	TOPSIS	GRA	GRPM	MEET	EM	MSD	CRITIC
It applies to the decision set of a limited and discrete scheme	✓	✓	✓	✓	✓	✓	✓	✓	✓
It can sort the alternatives	✓	✓	✓	✓	✓	✓	✓	✓	✓
It can scientifically and reasonably calculate the weight of each evaluation indicator	✓	×	✓	✓	✓	✓	✓	✓	✓
Its calculation process is not affected by subjective factors	×	×	×	✓	✓	×	✓	✓	✓
It converts qualitative information into quantitative information	×	×	×	×	×	×	×	×	×

Note: EM (Entropy Method)

2.1.3 Application of IPO

Due to the rapid development of the Internet and the popularity of smart phones, IPO is used to obtain the information, demand, and feedback of the public. For example, medicine [38], public emergencies [39], and solar PV systems [40] can be regarded as illustrations. Besides, social media can also help to analyze the development of the photoelectric industry in the future. For example, Klick [41] investigated the positive and negative views of the public on wind and solar power based on Internet to promote public support. Through the online survey, Li et al. [42] discussed the public's acceptance of the rooftop PV solar system policy. It summarizes the barriers existing in PV promotion among consumers, institutions, government, energy technology experts, and other stakeholders. It also provides useful suggestions for expanding the PV market in the future. In addition, IPO can provide rich first-hand data, grasp, and measure public views. It is to be an important driving force for future development evaluation [42]. Although there is no direct application of IPO in the potential evaluation of rooftop PV development, previous studies have shown a strong interest in network data and public opinions. Moreover, how to find the required information accurately in the massive network information resources has become the focus of scholars. Jin [43] designed and implemented a distributed network crawler system to provide high-quality data support. Since more people get to know the latest public opinion from Weibo, Du et al. [44] proposed a hot topic tracking algorithm integrating MF-LDA and HTLCM to extract and track public opinions. To summarize, the public is a decisive participant in urban building rooftop PV, so it is of great necessity to consider the public. Through IPO to collect public information, it can also better promote the development of urban building rooftop PV.

2.2 *Problem Description and Research Framework*

This chapter collects information through IPO and then abstracts and summarizes design evaluation indexes. It evaluates and sorts different types of urban buildings by using GRPM based on MSD and CRITIC method. Further it quantifies the PV potential of urban buildings and provides theoretical basis for the rapid development of urbanization in China. Consequently, the development goal of building PV is established for government departments.

A flow chart of our research framework is presented in Fig. 1.

3 Research Methodology

The chapter began with an establishment of the evaluation index system through keyword mining and extraction of IPO data and literature research. According to the development potential model, the indicator values of each evaluation object were calculated. Then, the GRPM was used to evaluate and rank the comprehensive potential of different objects based on MSD and CRITIC method. Details of each step are presented below.

3.1 *Evaluation Index System*

The establishment of the evaluation index system should be both scientific and reasonable. Therefore, this study uses IPO and literature research to collect the information. It selects the evaluation index involving economy, technology, and environment as three categories with a total of 11 sub-indicators and strives to comprehensively and truthfully reflect the potential analysis of different rooftop PV development buildings.

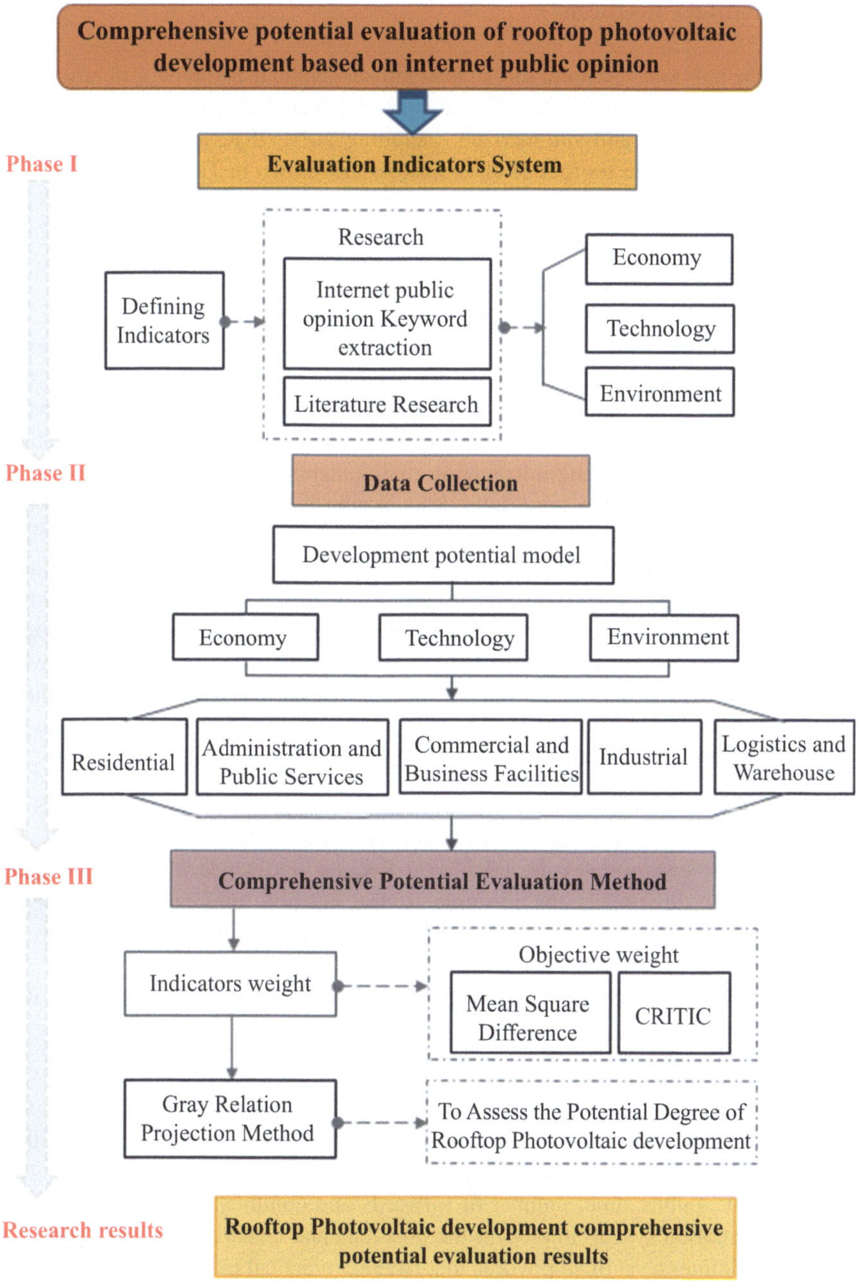

Fig. 1 The research framework

3.1.1 Literature Research

Based on the previous research, this chapter aims to evaluate and rank different types of buildings and quantifies the PV potential of urban buildings. The evaluation indexes are extracted and summarized, including NPV, IRR, and gross roof area and so on. The specific sources of all indicators are shown in Table 2 below.

3.1.2 Internet Public Opinion

More and more scholars collect information through social media. Quora, as a question and answer SNS website widely used in foreign countries, aims to dig out WIKI knowledge that is not available on the Internet and endow it with strong social media attributes. For example, Le et al. [49] analyzed the actual conversation data on Quora to explore the information that students were looking for on social media in the future. At the same time, Sina Weibo has also become an important social platform for Chinese Internet users to post comments. According to statistics, the number of monthly active users is 497 million in September 2019, so this study chooses Weibo as the other data source platform. Meanwhile, IPO is about screening and obtaining a large amount of data from website through web crawler technology. It is a program technology used to filter and download web pages. As a crawler framework, Scrapy makes the design and work of the crawler quick and easy with a high degree of scalability and robustness. So Scrapy is widely used in crawler design. The concrete principle is shown in Fig. 2.

Step 1: First, the Engine retrieves a URL from the Scheduler as the initial target of the crawl process. The crawler will start crawling from this URL.
Step 2: Engine encapsulates the URL as a Request and sends it to Downloader. Downloader downloads the resource to the machine and encapsulates it as Response.
Step 3: Spider receives Response and calls callback function.
Step 4: The Spider parses the Response to get the entity or URL. If it is an entity, it is handed to the pipeline for further processing.
Step 5: If it is a URL, the result is handed to the scheduler for processing.

This chapter uses Scrapy framework to crawl Weibo data with "solar roof" as the key word. And the collection starts from June 20, 2017, to February 24, 2020, with a total of 839 related Weibo content. Weibo data includes keyword, blogger ID, content, URL, public time, number of forwards and comments. Then, it use Jieba word segmentation system to process the post data and construct the word table. In addition, it defines a set of stop words that have no practical meaning in the context, such as determiners (a, an, the, that, those, etc.) and prepositions (of, over, under, above, etc.). Then, remove all stop words, leaving nouns, verbs, and adjectives as keywords. Finally, extract high-frequency keywords that people mainly pay attention to help design the evaluation index.

Table 2 Source of indicators

	Dimension layer B	Index layer	Source
Rooftop PV comprehensive potential A	Economy B1	NPV B11	1. Korsavi et al. [25], Mukherji et al. [28], Sun et al. [26], Bayod-Rujula et al. [23], Li [18], Spertino et al. [45] 2. IPO keyword extraction: Investment, income, value, operation, increase income
		IRR B12	1. Mukherji et al. [28], Bayod-Rujula et al. [23], Li [18], Spertino et al. [45] 2. IPO keyword extraction: Payback, benefit, response rate, rate of return, economic risk
		Energy Cost B13	1. Mangiante et al. [46], Bayod-Rujula et al. [23], Wu [34], Spertino et al. [45] 2. IPO keyword extraction: Cost, funds, electricity price, electricity bill, price, energy consumption
		Policy Subsidy B14	1. Baljit et al. [47] 2. IPO keyword extraction: Subsidy, allowances, policy, government, state subsidies
	Technology B2	Gross Roof Area B21	1. Bergamasco and Pietro [4], Jin [43], Peng and Lu [2], Hong et al. [24] 2. IPO keyword extraction: Bevel, roof, property
		The PV Suitable Rooftop Area B22	1. Jin [43], Peng and Lu [2], Sun et al. [26], Hong et al. [24]
		Power Generation B23	1. Bergamasco and Pietro [4], Mangiante et al. [46], Mukherji et al. [28], Bayod-Rujula et al. [23] 2. IPO keyword extraction: Power generation, electric power, technology, angle, installed capacity
	Environment B3	CO_2 Emission Reduction B31	1. Sun et al. [26], Li [18], Cucchiella et al. [48] 2. IPO extraction: Surroundings, resources, pollution, emission, emission reduction, energy saving, clean, green, environmental protection, renewable energy
		SO_2 Emission Reduction B32	
		NO_X Emission Reduction B33	
		Soot Emission Reduction B34	

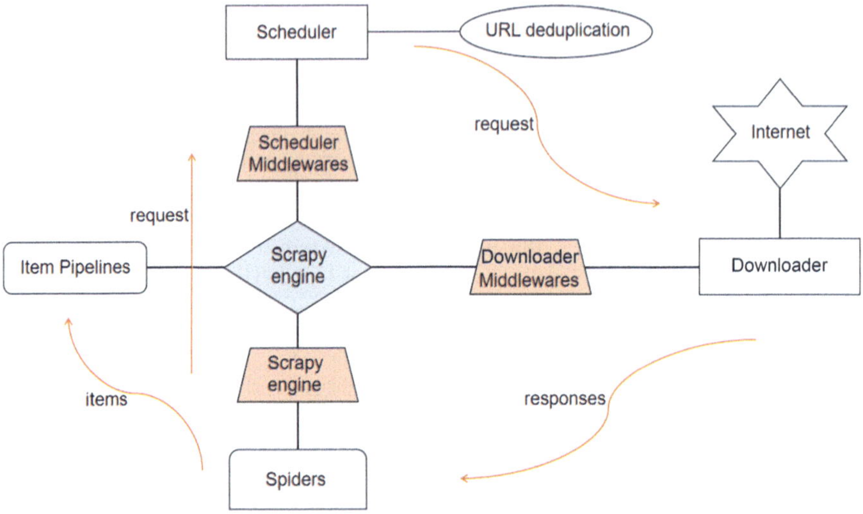

Fig. 2 Scrapy framework diagram

3.2 *Data Processing*

According to the index system established in the previous section, it obtained the initial data through statistical yearbooks, etc. In order to get the corresponding index value of each layer, the formula corresponding to the model is selected in formula (1)–(7) for calculation.

3.2.1 Economic Potential Value

In order to analyze the cost of rooftop PV power generation and the market competitiveness of PV power generation technology accurately, this chapter used net present value (NPV) and internal rate of return (IRR) to evaluate the economic potential value of rooftop PV system. And the energy cost of the power generation system was simulated by PVsyst software.

Net Present Value (NPV)

First of all, assume that all investments are rational, which means pursuing the highest return on investment. Then, the conditions for investment can be expressed as [47, 50]:

$$\mathrm{NPV} = -S + \sum_{i=1}^{N} \frac{\left(C_{\text{input}}\right)_i - \left(C_{\text{output}}\right)_i}{(1+r)^i} \tag{1}$$

where S is the initial investment; N is the life cycle; C_{input} the inflow cash value of the ith year; C_{output} is the cash outflow in the ith year; r is the discount rate.

The initial investment can be expressed as follows:

$$S = C_{\text{system}} - C_{\text{subsidy}} \tag{2}$$

where C_{system} is the initial investment of PV power generation system including PV modules, inverters, installation and construction costs, etc.; C_{subsidy} is the available investment subsidies.

The inflow part of the ith year in the system life cycle can be expressed as follows:

$$\left(C_{\text{input}}\right)_i = \left(P_{\text{buy}} \times E_{\text{PVconsume}} + P_{\text{sell}} \times E_{\text{PVinject}}\right)_i \tag{3}$$

where P_{buy} is the purchase price of electricity from the grid; E_{PVcon} is the user's own power consumption; P_{sell} is the grid electricity price of PV power generation; E_{PV} is the grid electricity.

The outflow funds in the ith year of the system life cycle can be expressed as follows:

$$\left(C_{\text{output}}\right)_i = \left(C_{\text{O\&M}} + C_{\text{loan}} + C_{\text{tax}}\right)_i \tag{4}$$

where $C_{\text{O \& M}}$ is the operation and maintenance cost of PV system; C_{loan} is the payment of loan principal and interest; C_{tax} is the taxes including income tax, urban construction tax, and education tax surcharges.

Internal Rate of Return (IRR)

IRR refers to the sum of the present value converted from the net benefit flow of each year in the calculation period of the project to the beginning of the construction period of the project. IRR is generally used to represent the anti-risk ability in the process of project operation. It is a supplement to the NPV calculation results. At the same time, it can avoid the situation that the project only produces high NPV value due to its large scale. This is helpful for investors to identify development objects with positive NPV and acceptable financial risk level. The IRR of rooftop PV system can be briefly estimated by the following equation [51]:

$$\text{FNPV}(\text{IRR}) = \sum_{i=0}^{N} \left(C_{\text{input}} - C_{\text{output}}\right)_i (1 + \text{IRR})^{-i} = 0 \tag{5}$$

where FNPV (IRR) is the financial net present value with IRR as the discount rate.

3.2.2 Technical Potential Value

The determination of rooftop area can usually be estimated by determining the per capita rooftop surface ratio or by establishing a correlation between population density and rooftop area [8]. In recent years, in order to calculate the rooftop area accurately, GIS has been continuously applied to it. However, this method requires a large amount of calculation and high data quality, which is limited to some extent [6]. Thus, a common and simple approach is chosen in this study. It uses reducing coefficients derived from literature to account for shading and other limitations. In Table 3, the utilization factors for a selection of studies are given to demonstrate the used utilization factors at the larger scale.

The above methods of the "rule of thumb" ratio (gross ground floor area to rooftop area) allow for the calculation of rooftop area in the case that ground floor area estimates are unavailable but total floor area estimates can be accessed [3]. Due to the unavailability of up-to-date cartographic information for the case study, total roof area and solar suitable rooftop area are derived from literature-informed steps.

The total active area of the rooftop PV modules can be calculated by the following equation:

$$A_{\text{act.}} = \frac{A_{\text{pot.}}}{A_{\text{occu.}}} \times A_{\text{pv}} \tag{6}$$

where A_{act} is the potential total active area of PV modules; A_{pot} is the potential PV-suitable rooftop area; A_{occu} is the installation occupancy area of a single PV module; and A_{pv} is the area of a single PV module. In this chapter, it uses PVsyst software to simulate the potential effective utilization area of PV modules which is A_{pv}/A_{occu}.

Table 3 Overview of reduction factors used in a selection of the literature

Location	Reduction factor	Source
Hong Kong	Gross roof area/ground floor area: 1.20	Peng and Lu [2]
	Architectural suitability: 0.70	
	Solar suitability: 0.55	
EU-27	Potential PV-suitable rooftop area/ground floor area: 0.40	Defaix et al. [52]
	Architectural suitability: 0.60	
	Solar suitability: 0.55	
California	Residential: 0.10	California Energy Commission [53]
	Commercial: 0.30	
USA	Residential: 0.22–0.27a	Denholm and Margolis [54], Lopez et al. [55]
	Commercial: 0.60–0.65a	
IEA (PVPS)	Architectural suitability: 0.60	Gutschner et al. [56]
	Solar suitability: 0.55	

According to the solar energy resource conditions of different cities, the best installation angle of PV module can be determined by analyzing the solar azimuth and height angle. And the radiation and effective surface area of PV module surface can be calculated based on this, so as to achieve the goal of predicting the annual power generation of PV. The potential of annual energy output of rooftop PV system can be briefly estimated by the following equation:

$$E_{\text{potential}} = A_{\text{act.}} \times G_t \times \eta \times \lambda \tag{7}$$

where $E_{\text{potential}}$ is the annual power generation of building rooftop PV system; A_{act} is the potential total active area of PV modules; G_t is the annual total solar radiation received by the PV modules installed with the optimum tilted angle, about 2256 kWh/m^2; η is the PV module's energy conversion efficiency in standard testing conditions (STC), and the efficiency is 16% declared by the manufacturer [2]; λ is the operation efficiency of PV system. This ratio considers all losses from converting solar energy into direct current electricity and then inverting the direct current into alternating current electricity. The common operating efficiency of rooftop PV is 0.75–0.80, and the most commonly used 0.75 is used in this study.

3.2.3 Environmental Potential Value

Compared with coal-fired power generation, the energy saving and environmental benefits of PV power generation are mainly reflected in the reduction of coal use and emission of CO_2, SO_2, NO_x, dust, and other pollutants. Therefore, based on the previous studies [18, 57], this study lists the energy conservation and emission reduction of the above four pollutants relative to each kilowatt hour. It aims to illustrate the specific effect of their pollution reduction and emission reduction. It is shown in Table 4 below.

3.3 Modeling Process

In this section, MSD and CRITIC were used to calculate the weight of each indicator. Then, the GRPM was used to evaluate and rank the comprehensive potential of different objects.

Table 4 Relative pollutant emissions on reduction per electricity

	CO_2	SO_2	NO_X	Dust
Emissions reduction per electricity (kg × 10^2/kwh)	88.41	00.55	00.17	00.22

3.3.1 Weight Definition

MSD mainly uses the contrast strength of index data to describe the importance of index and entropy law mainly shows the discreteness of index data. In contrast, CRITIC method is a relatively perfect objective weighting method. It not only considers the correlation (conflict) of index data but also considers the contrast strength between data. But it does not consider the discreteness between data, and MSD can effectively make up for this deficiency. The combination of the two methods can fully consider the discreteness, correlation, and contrast strength of the data.

The analysis shows that both the MSD and entropy value can be used to represent the degree of data aggregation, so they have equal status when CRITIC method is improved [58]. The following formula is combining CRITIC and MSD.

In addition, the weight of each indicator should be calculated based on the square deviation and variations of information [37, 59]. The steps are as follows:

1. A set of $X' = \left[x'_{ij}\right]$: primitive data matrix.
2. Normalize the matrix.

$$y_{ij} = \frac{x'_{ij} - \min\left(x'_{ij}\right)}{\max\left(x'_{ij}\right) - \min\left(x'_{ij}\right)}, \quad \text{If it is a benefit indicator.} \tag{8}$$

$$y_{ij} = \frac{\max\left(x'_{ij}\right) - x'_{ij}}{\max\left(x'_{ij}\right) - \min\left(x'_{ij}\right)}, \quad \text{If it is a cost indicator.} \tag{9}$$

3. Calculate the mean value of random variables E_i.

$$E_i = \frac{1}{n}\sum_{j=1}^{n} x_{ij} \tag{10}$$

4. Calculate the MSD of random variables σ_i.

$$\sigma_i = \sqrt{\frac{1}{n}\sum_{j=1}^{n}\left(x_{ij} - E_i\right)^2} \tag{11}$$

5. Calculate weight coefficient ω_i

$$\omega_i = \frac{\sigma_i}{\sum_{i=1}^{n}\sigma_i} \tag{12}$$

6. Calculate CRITIC weight

$$\omega_i = \frac{\sigma_i \sum_{j=1}^{n} (1 - r_{ij})}{\sum_{i=1}^{m} \sigma_i \sum_{j=1}^{n} (1 - r_{ij})} \quad (13)$$

where r_{ij} is the correlation coefficient between index i and j.

7. Calculate the comprehensive objective weight

$$\phi_i = \frac{(\sigma_i + e_i) \sum_{j=1}^{n} (1 - p_{ij})}{\sum_{i=1}^{m} (\sigma_i + e_i) \sum_{j=1}^{n} (1 - p_{ij})} \quad (14)$$

where ϕ_i is the weight of the index i, p_{ij} is the correlation coefficient, e_{ij} is the entropy of the index j.

3.3.2 Comprehensive Potential Evaluation

The GRPM of multiobjective decision is a new method. It combines the gray system theory of multi-objective decision with the principle of vector projection. And it evaluates by establishing the gray relation projection model of multi-objective decision. The modeling process in Tang et al. [31] is shown as follows:

1. Establish a decision-making matrix.

   Let scheme set U = {Scheme 1, Scheme 2, ..., scheme n} = $\{U_0, U_1, \ldots, U_n\}$, indicator set V = {indicator 1, indicator 2, ..., indicator m} = $\{V_1, V_2, \ldots, V_m\}$. The index value of scheme U_i to index V_j is recorded as $Y_{ij} = (i = 1, 2, \ldots, n; j = 1, 2, \ldots, m)$. Set the factor index of ideal scheme U_0 as Y_{0j}, and meet the following requirements: When V_j is a positive indicator, $Y_{0j} = \max(Y_{1j}, Y_{2j}, \ldots, Y_{nj})$; when V_j is a reverse indicator, $Y_{0j} = \min(Y_{1j}, Y_{2j}, \ldots, Y_{nj})$; the matrix $Y = (Y_{ij})_{(n+1) \times m}$ $(i = 1, 2, \ldots, n; j = 1, 2, \ldots, m)$ is the decision matrix of scheme set U to indicator set V.

2. Standardization.

   For the larger and the better the index is, the positive index processing method is used. Otherwise, the negative index processing method is used.

$$\text{Positive indicator}: x'_{ij} = (x_{ij} - \min\{x_j\})/(\max\{x_j\} - \min\{x_j\}) \quad (15)$$

$$\text{Negative indicator}: x'_{ij} = (\max\{x_j\} - x_{ij})/(\max\{x_j\} - \min\{x_j\}) \quad (16)$$

3. Mark Y' as the generation sequence of Y.

   When V_j is the benefit index, it is divided positively; when V_j is the cost index, it is divided reversely. Then Y' is the initial sequence of Y, obviously $Y_{0j} = 1$ $(j = 1, 2, \ldots, m)$, and Y'_{0j} is the ideal scheme.

$$Y'_{ij} = \frac{Y_{ij}}{Y_{0j}} \tag{17}$$

$$Y'_{ij} = \frac{Y_{0j}}{Y_{ij}} \tag{18}$$

4. Gray projection correlation.

   (S, T) is a gray correlation space, ζ is a specific correlation mapping, and r_{ij} is a sub-factor Y'_{ij} (i = 1, …, n; $j = 1, 2, \ldots, m$) on the correlation degree of the parent factor $Y'_{oj} = 1$ $(j = 1, 2, \ldots, m)$, $r_{ij} = \zeta\left(Y'_0, Y'_{ij}\right)$.

$$r_{ij} = \frac{\min\limits_{n}\min\limits_{m}\left|Y'_{0j} - Y'_{ij}\right| + \lambda\max\limits_{n}\max\limits_{m}\left|Y'_{0j} - Y'_{ij}\right|}{\left|Y'_{0j} - Y'_{ij}\right| + \lambda\max\limits_{n}\max\limits_{m}\left|Y'_{0j} - Y'_{ij}\right|} \tag{19}$$

5. In $r_{ij} = \zeta\left(Y'_0, Y'_{ij}\right)$, λ is usually called the resolution coefficient, and its function is to adjust the size of the comparison environment which means reducing and changing the comparison environment. When $\lambda = 0$, the environment disappears; when $\lambda = 1$, the environment remains intact.

$$\lambda = \frac{\frac{1}{nm}\sum_{i=1}^{m}\sum_{k=1}^{n}\left|Y'_{0j} - Y'_{ij}\right|}{\max\limits_{n}\max\limits_{m}\left|Y'_{0j} - Y'_{ij}\right|} \tag{20}$$

   And the range of ρ is

$$\Phi \le \rho \le 1.5\Phi, \quad \text{if} \quad \Phi < 1/3 \tag{21}$$

$$1.5\Phi \le \rho \le 2\Phi, \quad \text{if} \quad \Phi \ge 1/3 \tag{22}$$

6. Construct a multiobjective gray correlation degree judgment matrix F composed of r whose number is m $(n + 1)$.

$$F = \begin{vmatrix} F_{01} & F_{02} & \cdots & F_{0m} \\ F_{11} & F_{12} & \cdots & F_{1m} \\ F_{21} & F_{22} & \ldots & F_{2m} \\ \vdots & \vdots & \vdots & \vdots \\ F_{n1} & F_{n2} & \cdots & F_{nm} \end{vmatrix} \tag{23}$$

7. Gray relation projection angle.

   If each decision-making scheme is regarded as a row vector, then the angle θ between each decision-making Scheme U_i and the ideal Scheme $U*$ is called the gray relation projection value. The larger the cosine of the included angle is, the more consistent the change direction between the decision-making scheme U_i and the ideal scheme $U*$. The cosine formula of included angle is:

$$r_i = \frac{U_i \times U^*}{\|U_i\| \times \|U*\|} = \frac{\sum_{j=1}^{m}\left(W_j F_{ij} W_j\right)}{\sqrt{\sum_{j=1}^{m}\left(W_j F_{ij}\right)^2} \times \sqrt{\sum_{j=1}^{m} W_j^2}} \tag{24}$$

8. Calculate the modulus d_i of each scheme U_i where W_j (j = 1, 2, …, m) is the weight.

$$d_i = \sqrt{\sum_{j=1}^{m}\left(W_j F_{ij}\right)^2} \tag{25}$$

9. Gray relation projection value.

   Considering the size of the module and the cosine of the included angle, it can fully and accurately reflect the close degree between each decision-making scheme and the ideal scheme.

$$D_j = d_i \cdot r_i = \sqrt{\sum_{j=1}^{m}\left(W_j F_{ij}\right)^2} \cdot \frac{\sum_{j=1}^{m}\left(W_j F_{ij} W_j\right)}{\sqrt{\sum_{j=1}^{m}\left(W_j F_{ij}\right)^2} \times \sqrt{\sum_{j=1}^{m} W_j^2}}$$
$$= \sum_{j}^{m} F_{ij}\left(\frac{W_j^2}{\sqrt{\sum_{j=1}^{m}\left[W_j\right]^2}}\right) \tag{26}$$

10. Mark $\overline{W_j}$ as a new set of factor index weight vector which is called gray relation projection weight vector.

$$\overline{W_j} = \frac{W_j^2}{\sqrt{\sum_{j=1}^{m} W_j^2}} \tag{27}$$

$$D_j = \sum_{j=1}^{m} F_{ij}\overline{W_j} \tag{28}$$

11. Evaluation.

    According to the projection value of each scheme, the scheme can be sorted and evaluated. The larger the projection value is, the closer the scheme is to the ideal scheme which indicates the better PV potential of urban buildings.

4 Case Study

As detailed in Sect. 3, this study uses a three-stage process to determine the comprehensive potential for rooftop PV development. In order to verify the effectiveness of the proposed evaluation model, this study used the data of Panzhihua as a sample to calculation. The test aimed to illustrate how the proposed comprehensive evaluation model can be applied to the rooftop PV system potential evaluation and the analysis of development in the future.

4.1 Research Case Area

Panzhihua is located at the junction of Sichuan and Yunnan in Southwest China where there are abundant solar energy resources. There are many sunny days and strong solar radiation. The average annual sunshine time is about 2300–2700 h and the annual radiation is directly in the high value area of Sichuan solar radiation. The location of the study area is shown in Fig. 3. According to *Panzhihua City Master Plan*, five types of land with high building density are selected as research objects in this study. These are residential land, administration and public services land, commercial and business facilities land, industrial land, and logistics and warehouse.

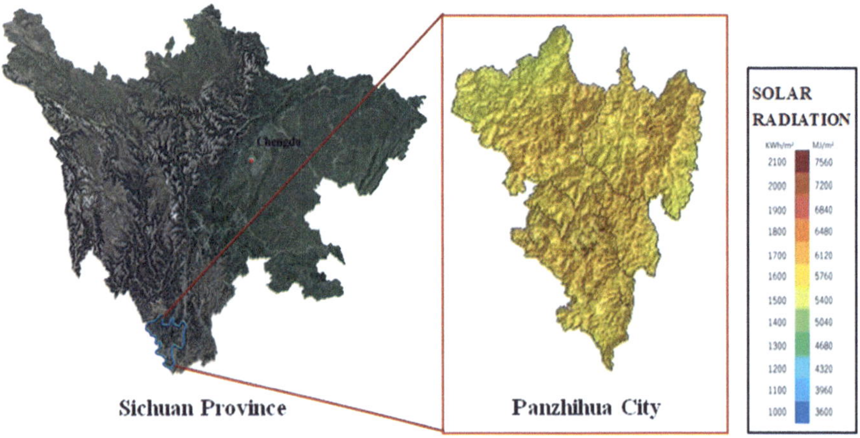

Fig. 3 Research area

Table 5 Planned land area (hm^2)

Residential land	Administration and public services	Commercial and business facilities	Industrial land	Logistics and warehouse
2446.44	911.70	701.90	3020.96	497.68

It is to evaluate and sequence to quantify the PV potential of urban buildings. And it proposes theoretical basis for the rapid development of urbanization in China. It further helps the government departments to formulate the PV development goals of buildings. The planned land area is shown in Table 5.

4.2 Calculation Result of PV Generation Potential

4.2.1 Technical Potential Value

Based on the classification standards for urban construction land, the assessment scope includes five major types of land in Panzhihua. The study excludes types of street and transportation, municipal utilities, and green space, which has less construction on the ground. Land area data are all from *Panzhihua City Master Plan (2011–2030)*. The selection of the PV module's inclination is also very important. According to the results calculated by PVsyst software, the range of the best dip angle in the whole year is 27–29°. This study selects the median value of 28° and the annual total radiation of the dip angle is 2256 KWh/m^2. According to the parameters of polysilicon cells commonly used at present and the selected PV module model, it is concluded that the distance between modules should be 4.40 m. And the effective area coefficient of PV module is 0.68 when the PV module is installed at the angle of 28°. According to the formula, the specific calculation results of each value are shown in Table 6.

According to the calculation results, the technical potential is larger for residential land and industrial land in Panzhihua. It is due to the relatively larger area of these two types of land. From the absolute value, it can be seen that there is a certain difference between the power generation calculated by the formula and by the software. Figure 4 shows a comparison diagram of the two types of power generation.

It can be seen that the power generation value simulated by the software is slightly higher than that calculated by the formula. The line chart visually shows the deviation rate of the power generation values obtained by the two types of methods. It can be seen from the figure that the power generation amount obtained by the software simulation is about 2% higher than that calculated by the formula. And the larger the land area, the smaller the effect of the deviation between the two types of calculation results. To facilitate the acquisition of data required for calculation, the subsequent calculation and analysis of this study are based on software-simulated power generation.

Table 6 List of rooftop PV power generation of buildings in Panzhihua

Land use	Land area (hm^2)	Gross roof area (hm^2)	The PV-suitable rooftop area (hm^2)	Annual power generation by formula (GWh/year)	Software-simulated power generation (GWh/year)
Residential	2446.44	2055.01	1130.26	2080.68	2122.78
Administration and public services	911.70	765.83	421.21	775.40	791.08
Commercial and business facilities	701.90	589.60	324.28	596.96	609.04
Industrial	3020.96	2537.61	1395.68	2569.31	2621.24
Logistics and warehouse	497.68	418.05	229.93	423.27	431.84

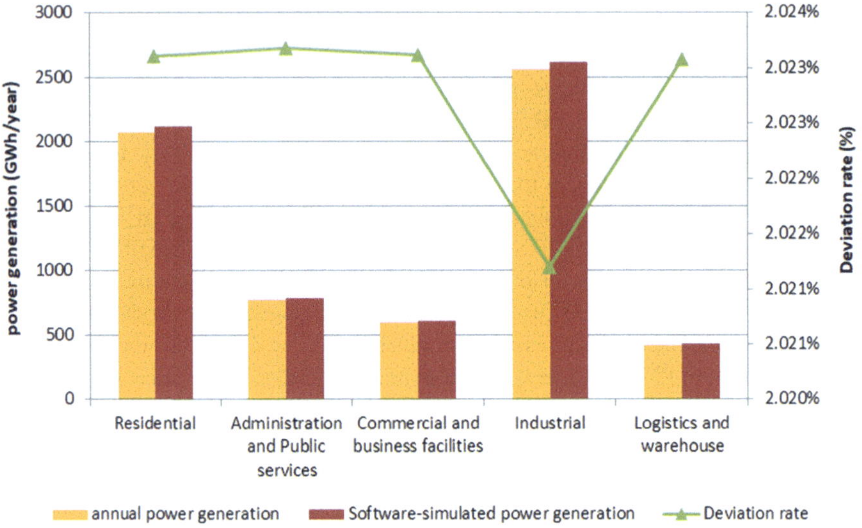

Fig. 4 Annual power generation of rooftop PV systems in Panzhihua

4.2.2 Environmental Potential Value

The environmental potential of solar power is mainly reflected by reducing the consumption of conventional energy and no direct discharge of any. Compared with thermal power, PV power generation can effectively reduce the emissions of smoke, carbon dioxide, sulfur dioxide, nitrogen oxides, and others. The annual emission of effective substances reduced in the life cycle of a PV system is calculated by multiplying the amount of power with the corresponding emission coefficient. The relative pollutant emission reduction of each kilowatt hour of roof PV is shown in Fig. 5.

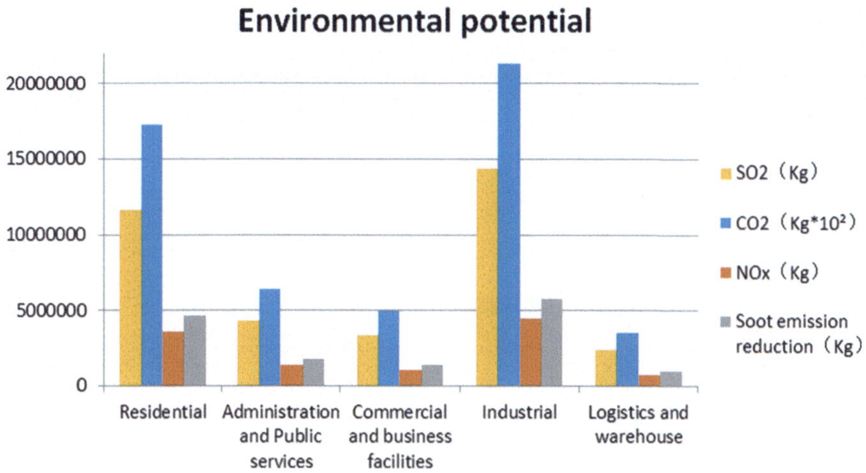

Fig. 5 The estimation of the emission reduction of air harmful substances in rooftop PV system

It can be seen from the histogram that CO_2 emission reduction effect of various harmful substances is the most obvious followed by SO_2. The emission reduction of each land use object is directly related to the amount of power generation. And the difference of power generation directly leads to the difference in the amount of emission reduction. Among them, industrial land and residential land have the best CO_2 and SO_2 emission reduction effect.

4.2.3 Economic Potential Value

The cost of PV power generation is affected by various factors, such as initial investment of the system, the on-grid electricity price, the amount of power generated by the system, subsidy policy, and discount rate. The above factors are included in the calculation formula of NPV. And the mathematical meaning of the calculation result is straightforward and easy to understand. IRR is used to indicate the anti-risk ability during the operation of the project. It is a supplement to the NPV calculation results to avoid a large NPV due to the large scale of the project. This is helpful for investors to identify development targets with positive NPV and acceptable financial risk level. To directly compare the economic benefits of rooftop PV, this study assumes that all the power generated by PV system is connected to the grid. According to formula (3), the calculation results of NPV and IRR with $E_{\mathrm{PVconsume}} = 0$ are as shown in Fig. 6.

The line chart visually shows the NPV calculation results of various types of objects. As can be seen from the figure, the NPV value advantage of industrial land is obvious. It is mainly due to the large proportion of industrial land area and directly leads to large NPV data. Although the proportion of other land occupation is different, the difference of NPV calculation results is not obvious. It can be clearly

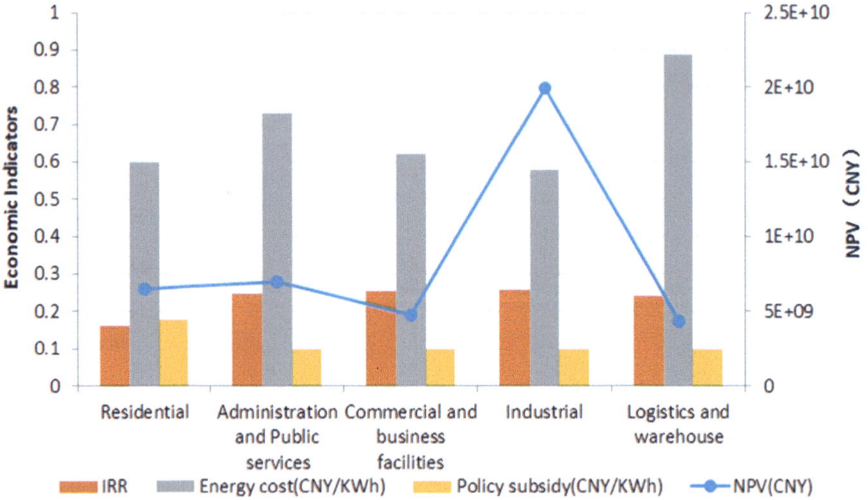

Fig. 6 The histogram of economic indicator potential

seen from the histogram that the IRR of residential land is significantly lower than that of the other four types of land. However, the IRR values of the remaining four types of land are not significantly different and the ability to resist risks is comparable. At present, the average civil electricity price in Panzhihua is around 0.52 yuan/kWh. And the industrial electricity price is about 0.71 yuan/kWh. Compared with the energy cost of various objects calculated by PVsyst software, rooftop PV system has certain economic advantages for industrial and commercial areas. At the same time, it can be seen through the cost analysis that solar power generation has no advantages for the other three types of land. At this time, the government's incentive subsidy policy has become the key to promote the further development of solar energy. According to the histogram of policy subsidy, the policy subsidies for other land objects are the same except for the slightly higher policy subsidies for residential land. However, through the analysis of the above results, it can be seen that the subsidized preferential policies for residential land have also not exerted certain advantages. Even though the area of residential land is relatively large, the performance of various economic indicators is still weak.

4.3 Evaluation Results of Comprehensive Potential

4.3.1 Calculation of Index Weight

The combination of CRITIC and MSD method can fully consider the discreteness, correlation, and contrast strength of data [37]. And, it enhances the reliability of objective weights. According to formula (14), the weights of the subsystems and the weight of the integrated system are calculated. Among them, the technical potential and the environmental potential subsystem indicators are completely linear related. So the weight value is only calculated by MSD. The calculation results are shown in Table 7.

Make full use of the actual statistical data of the case area to calculate the objective weight of each indicator. According to the calculation results, it can be seen that the economic potential plays a decisive role in the evaluation of the rooftop PV development potential. In terms of comprehensive weight, IRR and policy subsidy are the most important factors to determine the potential. Secondly, two economic indicators, energy cost and NPV, also have great influence. NPV has a lower weight value in the economic potential part because its calculation result is easy to cause large numerical value due to large scale. The available area on the roof determines the amount of power generation. And the power generation is directly related to the emission reduction of harmful substances in the air. Therefore, the complete linear correlation of these indicators makes the indicators have the same weight. And there is no significant difference in impact strength.

4.3.2 Comprehensive Potential Evaluation Analysis

Due to limited space and complicated calculation process, it is only selected the evaluation process of economic potential as an example to illustrate. The specific details of economic potential are shown in Table 8.

The scheme set is $U = $ {Residential, Administration and public services, Commercial and business facilities, Industrial, Logistics and warehouse} and index set is $V = $ {NPV, IRR, Energy cost, Policy subsidy}. Among them, the energy cost indicator belongs to the cost indicator, and the rest belong to the benefit indicator.

According to the data given in Table 8, can be obtained as the factor indicator X_0 of the relatively optimal design scheme.

$$X_0 = (19.92\text{bn}, 0.26, 0.58, 0.18).$$

Therefore, the attribute matrix of scheme set U to index set V as

$$\begin{bmatrix} x_0 \\ x_1 \\ x_2 \\ x_3 \\ x_4 \\ x_5 \end{bmatrix} = \begin{bmatrix} 19.92\text{bn} & 0.26 & 0.58 & 0.18 \\ 6.49\text{bn} & 0.16 & 0.60 & 0.18 \\ 6.98\text{bn} & 0.25 & 0.73 & 0.10 \\ 4.77\text{bn} & 0.26 & 0.62 & 0.10 \\ 19.92\text{bn} & 0.26 & 0.58 & 0.10 \\ 4.41\text{bn} & 0.24 & 0.89 & 0.10 \end{bmatrix}$$

After initial value treatment, it can be obtained that $\Delta\text{min} = 0.00$, $\Delta\text{max} = 0.78$. Then by formulating (20), (21), and (22), $\Phi = 0.31$, smaller than 1/3, so ρ is 1.25

Table 7 The results of the index weights

	Economic potential				Technical potential			Environmental potential			
	NPV	IRR	Energy cost	Policy subsidy	Gross roof area	The PV-suitable rooftop area	Power generation	SO_2	CO_2	NO_x	Soot emission reduction
Subsystem weight	0.188	0.311	0.183	0.318	0.333	0.333	0.334	0.250	0.250	0.250	0.250
Comprehensive weight	0.080	0.283	0.090	0.169	0.054	0.054	0.054	0.054	0.054	0.054	0.054

Table 8 Values of each economic indicator

Variables	NPV	IRR	Energy cost	Policy subsidy
Residential	6.49bn	0.16	0.60	0.18
Administration and public services	6.98bn	0.25	0.73	0.1
Commercial and business facilities	4.77bn	0.26	0.62	0.1
Industrial	19.92bn	0.26	0.58	0.1
Logistics and warehouse	4.41bn	0.24	0.89	0.1

times Φ, $\rho = 0.39$. By formulating (23), the gray relation discriminate matrix R is obtained as

$$R = \begin{bmatrix} 1.00 & 1.00 & 1.00 & 1.00 \\ 0.32 & 0.46 & 0.90 & 1.00 \\ 0.32 & 0.90 & 0.60 & 0.41 \\ 0.29 & 0.98 & 0.83 & 0.41 \\ 1.00 & 1.00 & 1.00 & 0.41 \\ 0.29 & 0.84 & 0.47 & 0.41 \end{bmatrix}$$

According to the MSD and CRITIC method, the objective weight coefficient is $\omega = (0.188, 0.311, 0.183, 0.318)$. By formulating (27), it can get a new set of weight vectors, that is, the weight vector of gray relation projection ω'_j

$$\omega'_j = (0.13, 0.36, 0.13, 0.38)$$

Finally, the projection of each program is obtained as

$$(\text{D1}, \text{D2}, \text{D3}, \text{D4}, \text{D5}) = (0.70, 0.60, 0.65, 0.78, 0.56)$$

Thus, the economic potential of the five types of land is ranked as follows: Industrial > Residential > Commercial and business facilities > Administration and public services > Logistics and warehouse.

Based on the above principles, the remaining technical potential, environmental potential, and comprehensive potential were evaluated. The evaluation results are summarized in following Table 9.

Therefore, in the case area of Panzhihua, the comprehensive development potential of rooftop PV for five types of construction land is as follows: Industrial > Commercial and business facilities > Administration and public services > Logistics and warehouse > Residential.

Table 9 Evaluation results

Variables	Economic potential	Technical potential	Environmental potential	Comprehensive potential
Residential	0.70	0.75	0.80	0.72
Administration and public services	0.60	0.46	0.52	0.77
Commercial and business facilities	0.65	0.43	0.49	0.802
Industrial	0.78	1.00	1.00	0.91
Logistics and warehouse	0.56	0.41	0.47	0.73

4.4 Result Analysis and Discussion

4.4.1 Subsystem Potential Value

To comprehensively consider the development potential of rooftop PV, this study analyzes the potential of the five types of land from three aspects of economy, technology, and environment. The five types of land show different advantages in various aspects because of their different land use properties and area proportion. Based on the case calculation results in Sect. 4.3, the potential value radar maps of the three subsystems are plotted as shown in Fig. 7.

1. Technical potential: In the technical potential subsystem, the amount of power generation is directly related to the total roof area and the effective area of PV modules. And the indicators are completely linear related. Therefore, the MSD method is directly used for calculating index weight. From Fig. 7a and Table 9, it can be clearly seen that the ranking of technical potential is: Industrial (1) > Residential (0.75) > Administration and public services (0.46) > Commercial and business facilities (0.43) > Logistics and warehouse (0.41). Among them, the industrial land and residential land have obvious technological potential advantages. And their advantages are directly derived from the absolute advantages of their land area ratio. It can be seen from Table 5 that the area of industrial and residential land accounts for 39.86% and 32.28% of the total area of five types respectively. The calculation of rooftop PV power generation depends on the actual effective area of the roof obtained by the coefficient method. So the proportion of the original area of various types of land is particularly important.
2. Environmental potential: From Fig. 7b and Table 9, it can be clearly seen that the ranking of environmental potential is: Industrial (1) >Residential (0.80) > Administration and public services (0.52) > Commercial and business facilities (0.49) > Logistics and warehouse (0.47). Among them, the environmental benefit advantage of industrial land is the most obvious. The main reason is the large proportion of industrial land and the large amount of rooftop PV power generated under the same conditions. It directly contributes to a significant reduction in the emissions of environmentally harmful substances. Industrial land and residential land make great contribution to CO_2 and SO_2 emission reduction.

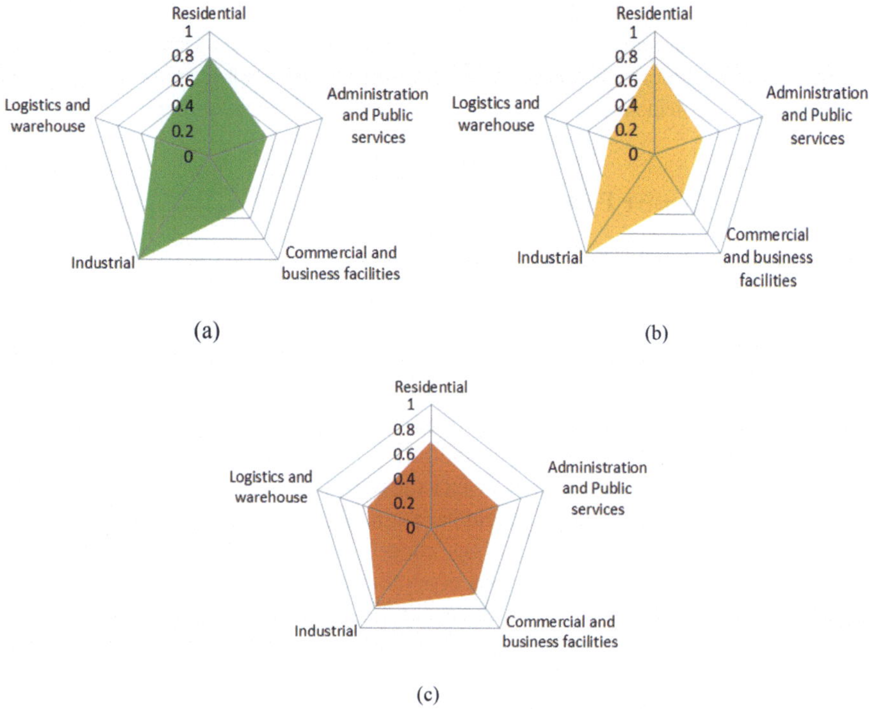

Fig. 7 The radar chart of subsystem potential evaluation. (**a**) Radar map of economic potential. (**b**) Radar map of technical potential. (**c**) Radar map of environmental potential

3. Economic potential: From Fig. 7c and Table 9, it can be clearly seen that the ranking of economic potential is:Industrial (0.78) > Residential (0.70) > Commercial and business facilities (0.65) > Administration and public services (0.60) > Logistics and warehouse (0.56). There is no obvious advantage of the five types of land in the evaluation of economic potential. One of the main reasons is that the economic indicators are no more significant correlations. Economic potential assessment needs to measure the combined effects of many indicators, such as investment [34], power generation, policy subsidies [20], and financial risks. Through the weight value of indicators in Table 7, it can be seen that IRR (0.311) and policy subsidy (0.318) have a non-negligible role in the evaluation of economic potential. For example, commercial and business facilities, which has a smaller area share and performs poorly in both technology potential and environmental potential subsystems. But it performs well in the economic potential subsystem due to the good performance of its IRR value (0.26). On the contrary, residential land that performs well in both technical potential and environmental potential subsystems loses a clear advantage in the economic potential subsystem because its IRR performance is at a disadvantage. It can be seen through the case study not only in the Panzhihua area but also in the entire range of rooftop PV technology promotion. The level of financial risk

represented by IRR and the local subsidy policy are important factors. It determines the economic viability of rooftop PV in a region. Therefore, making appropriate supporting policies and controlling the long-term return rate of rooftop PV projects are the top priority of rooftop PV development.

4.4.2 Comprehensive Potential Value

In the previous section, the development potential of the rooftop PV economy, technology, and environment was analyzed separately. But the five types of land showed different potential results after integrating the three perspectives. The results are shown in Fig. 8. Among the five types of land, the comprehensive potential of industrial land is the highest, while that of residential land is the lowest. Commercial and business facilities land is the second in the evaluation of comprehensive potential. But it is not outstanding in the three subsystems. The evaluation results seem to be a little unexpected, but in fact they are not. From the analysis in Sect. 4.2.3, it can be seen that residential land has some advantages in the evaluation of the subsystem by virtue of its relatively large proportion of area. But a closer look will reveal that the performance of various economic indicators is still weak. It can be clearly seen from Table 8 that the rankings of the four economic indicator values of residential land in the five types of land are: NPV is 3/5; IRR is 5/5; energy cost is 4/5, and policy subsidy is 1/5. Obviously, the IRR of residential land is in a clear disadvantage among the five types of land, though the policy subsidy has the greatest

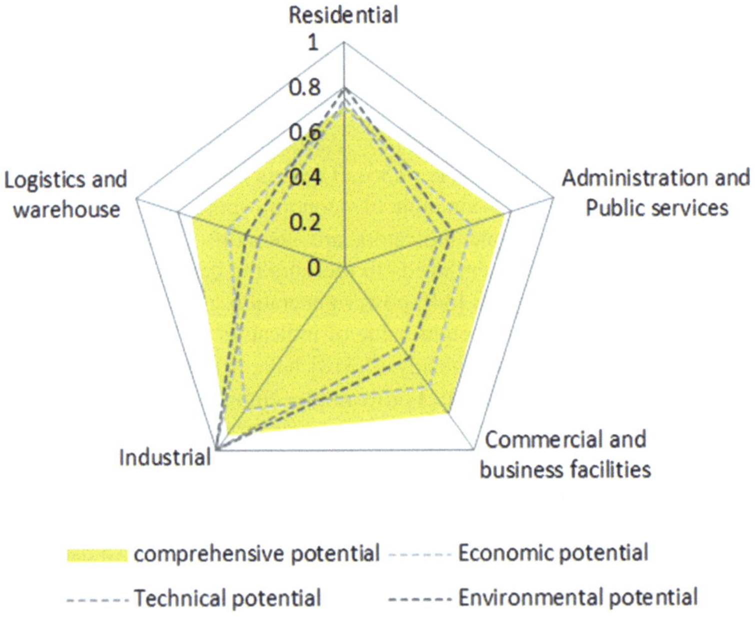

Fig. 8 The radar chart of comprehensive potential evaluation

support. But it has not played a certain advantage. At the same time, the roof property rights of residential buildings are complex and there are certain difficulties in implementation. Even if the area proportion is large, it is still not the main target of roof PV implementation. Based on the above reasons, residential land is at the bottom of the comprehensive potential evaluation of rooftop PV. And industrial land is still in the best position in the comprehensive potential evaluation of roof PV due to its excellent performance in all indicators and no obvious short board. At the same time, it can be seen from the case study that industrial land accounts for a large proportion of the city area, power consumption, and emissions of harmful substances. And the industrial electricity price is also relatively higher. These advantages and disadvantages can be exploited and improved through the improvement of rooftop PV technology. So it has a great advantage to use rooftop PV technology in the industrial land. Commercial and business facilities land as the largest dark horse, its poor performance in the three subsystems is mainly due to its smaller area, just 701.9 hm^2. Although the advantage is not obvious in the absolute number, its potential is still strong. Through the observation of the comprehensive weight, it can be found that the outstanding evaluation result of the comprehensive potential of commercial land mainly comes from its excellent IRR value. The weight after the GRPM vector modified, that is to say the gray relation projection weight vector, is as high as 0.5574. It directly contributes to the improvement of the potential value of commercial land.

Through the above case analysis, it can be found that the available roof area and power generation among the technical potential are the basis of evaluating the utilization potential of rooftop PV. But they are not the key influencing factors that determine the comprehensive potential level. The abundance of local solar energy resources directly determines whether a region is suitable for the promotion of rooftop PV technology. The difference of suitable area of building roofs in different regions will lead to huge difference of PV power generation. This is also the significance of many scholars who initially studied the PV utilization potential of building roofs. But no matter how great the utilization potential is, it cannot develop smoothly without the support of economic feasibility. Therefore, through this case study, it clearly shows the importance of economic potential in the comprehensive potential assessment. In particular, the indicators of IRR and policy subsidy in economic potential play an absolutely guiding role in the evaluation of comprehensive potential. Better economic performance can stand out even with slightly worse technical potential. Through the real data research of Panzhihua case can help to more effectively refine and summarize the practical problems in the development of rooftop PV. It can be seen not only in Panzhihua area but also in the entire scope of the promotion of rooftop PV technology. The level of financial risk represented by IRR and the local subsidy policy are important factors that determine whether rooftop PV in a region can be successfully promoted. Therefore, making appropriate supporting policies and controlling the long-term return rate of rooftop PV project are the most important issues in the development of rooftop PV.

4.5 Strategy Suggestion

The advantages of rooftop PV technology are obvious, but its promotion process in China has been faced with various obstacles.

4.5.1 Management Suggestion

Supporting policies and measures are the cornerstone of the development of emerging technologies. Combined with the research results of this chapter, the following suggestions are put forward on the deficiencies of the current roof PV development.

1. Without flexible and feasible supporting policies and regulations, even the best solar PV technology cannot be built on the roofs of cities, let alone give full play to its advantages in all aspects. Therefore, it is particularly necessary for relevant departments to make full use of regional resource advantages and formulate specific policies for the promotion of solar energy utilization, at the same time, through the establishment of appropriate incentive policies to mobilize the enthusiasm of the whole people to participate. And it promotes the large-scale use of rooftop PV technology in the region.
2. According to the analysis done, the policy subsidy has an important impact on the development potential of rooftop PV. In the case of no obvious price advantage of solar power generation, the government's incentive subsidy policy has become the key to promote the further development of solar energy. Scholars should conduct further in-depth research on different development objects and different roof properties, so that local government departments can set up appropriate subsidy policies based on project characteristics. At the same time, rooftop PV technology in different development periods has various differences. And relevant departments should also make timely adjustments to the subsidy policy according to the development cycle. The state should strive to promote the industrialization of rooftop power generation and support the R&D, production, sales, and use of rooftop power generation equipment, so as to make them more economical.
3. While actively promoting rooftop PV technology, the government should focus on reducing its short-term costs, increasing financing channels, and reducing investment risk. The government should try to guarantee the long-term return on investment of rooftop PV, so as to attract more people willing to install rooftop PVs. In particular, due to the scattered residential PV market and the lack of suitable financing tools, the development of PV industry is greatly limited. At present, it should continue to explore suitable business models for rooftop PV, such as attracting more funds and technical management through the market-oriented operation mode of state-owned enterprises, private enterprises, cooperation, foreign enterprises, joint ventures, joint-stock system, and other modes, so as to ensure the healthy and standardized development of PV rooftop plan.

4.5.2 Proposition

1. Promotion of residential buildings rooftop PV.
   In Western countries, especially in Europe, the development of PV in the later stage has focused on small-scale household distributed PV power plants. It not only meets the electricity demand of each family but also brings benefits to users through the residual electricity network while alleviating the environmental pressure. Through the case study of this chapter, it can be found that residential land occupies a large proportion of building area and has a large number of developable spaces. But the evaluation result is poor in development potential. One of the reasons is that the current development strategy is not suitable for residential buildings. However, in order to promote the rooftop PV technology, it is a key step for the government to support small PV power plants other than large-scale industrial and commercial power plants. Expansion of a rooftop PV promotion road for residential buildings will vigorously promote the development of rooftop PV technology in China and promote the diversified development of PV projects.
2. Strengthen the use of IPO.
   IPO has been applied to more and more research fields. Strengthening the application of IPO in the field of renewable energy technology promotion can further help researchers understand the public's concerns and attitudes. It will also help people truly understand the needs of the market and the current disadvantages. IPO can also play an important role in exploring the rooftop PV business model, which is suitable for residential buildings. In addition, it is indeed necessary to conduct more research to include public opinions in the development of rooftop PV. It will help resolve the contradictions caused by one-way advancement model and promote the future use of renewable energy and rooftop PV technology. Policy makers can use public opinion to adjust policies in time to get a positive response from the public.

5 Conclusions and Future Research

This chapter presented an evaluation method of the development potential of rooftop PV based on IPO. Firstly, the study using keyword mining and IPO data extraction combined with literature research established the comprehensive potential evaluation index system of rooftop PV. Then, the index values of each evaluation object are calculated according to the development potential model. Finally, the GRPM is used to evaluate the comprehensive rooftop PV potential of different objects. This chapter analyzes the key factors that affect the development potential level of rooftop PV. And it discusses the shortcomings of the current development mode of rooftop PV in China. That provides developmental suggestions for policy makers, investors, users, and other stakeholders of rooftop PV technology.

With the increasingly serious energy crisis and the rapid development of urbanization process, PV and building integrated design especially rooftop PV will become an important trend of urban development and energy utilization. At the same time, as the technical support for the rapid development of the current society, the Internet has injected new thinking and new impetus into the research of traditional issues. Therefore, the concept of IOT is introduced into the promotion and development of new energy. This chapter introduces the IPO data into the comprehensive evaluation innovatively. It made up for the lack of social impact in the previous study of rooftop PV potential evaluation. With the gradual improvement of PV efficiency and the decrease of PV product price, the popularity of building rooftop PV utilization is improved under the guidance of public opinion constantly. And the comprehensive potential of building rooftop PV is bound to be greatly improved.

This research is novel, but there is still much room for further research in the future. The current research is mostly on the macro level and more in-depth research on the micro level is needed for the comprehensive promotion of rooftop PV technology as follows. (1) The type and nature of building roof has a significant impact on the installation of rooftop PV. Therefore, it is necessary to conduct in-depth research on the differences of various links of different objects and explore the characteristics of their development. It will facilitate the formulation of policies. (2) Residential buildings will be the main object of the development of rooftop PV in the future. And it is of great significance to explore the ways to widely promote rooftop PV in China's residential buildings.

References

1. Romero Rodríguez, L., Duminil, E., Sánchez Ramos, J., & Eicker, U. (2017). Assessment of the photovoltaic potential at urban level based on 3D city models: A case study and new methodological approach. *Solar Energy, 146*, 264–275.
2. Peng, J., & Lu, L. (2013). Investigation on the development potential of rooftop PV system in Hong Kong and its environmental benefits. *Renewable and Sustainable Energy Reviews, 27*, 149–162.
3. Byrne, J., Taminiau, J., Kurdgelashvili, L., & Kim, K. N. (2015). A review of the solar city concept and methods to assess rooftop solar electric potential, with an illustrative application to the city of Seoul. *Renewable and Sustainable Energy Reviews, 41*, 830–844.
4. Bergamasco, L., & Pietro, A. (2011). Scalable methodology for the photovoltaic solar energy potential assessment based on available roof surface area: Application to Piedmont Region (Italy). *Solar Energy, 85*, 1041–1055.
5. Suomalainen, K., Wang, V., & Sharp, B. (2017). Rooftop solar potential based on LiDAR data: Bottom-up assessment at neighborhood level. *Renewable Energy, 111*, 463–475.
6. Zhang, H., Wang, L. X., & Li, Z. (2017). Method and application of rooftop photovoltaic utilization potential evaluation in urban buildings. *Urban Problems, 2*, 33–39. (in Chinese).
7. Kelly, C., Sen, B., & Tatari, O. (2020). A system dynamics analysis of the alternative roofing market and its potential impacts on urban environmental problems: A case study in Orlando, Florida. *Resources Conservation and Recycling, 153*, 104556.

8. Schallenberg-Rodrıguez, J. (2013). Photovoltaic techno-economical potential on roofs in regions and islands: The case of the Canary Islands. Methodological review and methodology proposal. *Renewable and Sustainable Energy Reviews, 20*, 219–239.
9. Zhao, H. Y., Yang, R., Wang, C. H., Wijeratne, W. M., Liu, C. Y., Xue, X. L., & Abdeen, N. (2019). Effects of design parameters on rooftop photovoltaic economics in the urban environment: A case study in Melbourne, Australia. *Frontiers of Engineering Management, 6*, 315–367.
10. Sobkowicz, P., Kaschesky, M., & Bouchard, G. (2012). Opinion mining in social media: Modeling, simulating, and forecasting political opinions in the web. *Government Information Quarterly, 29*, 470–479.
11. Guan, W., Gao, H., Yang, M., Li, Y., Ma, H., Qian, W., & Yang, X. (2014). Analyzing user behavior of the micro-blogging website Sina Weibo during hot social events. *Physica A: Statistical Mechanics and its Applications, 395*, 340–351.
12. Qazi, A., Hussain, F., Abd Rahim, N., Hardaker, G., Alghazzawi, D., Shaban, K., & Haruna, K. (2019). Towards sustainable energy: A systematic review of renewable energy sources, technologies, and public opinions. *IEEE Access, 7*, 63837–63851.
13. Gan, L., Jiang, P., Lev, B., & Zhou, X. (2020). Balancing of supply and demand of renewable energy power system: A review and bibliometric analysis. *Sustainable Futures, 2*, 100013.
14. Sovacool, B. K. (2014). What are we doing here? Analyzing fifteen years of energy scholarship and proposing a social science research agenda. *Energy Research and Social Science, 1*, 1–29.
15. Ragini, J. R., Anand, P. M. R., & Bhaskar, V. (2018). Big data analytics for disaster response and recovery through sentiment analysis. *International Journal of Information Management, 42*, 13–24.
16. Wang, Y., Li, H., Zuo, J., & Wang, Z. (2019). Evolution of online public opinions on social impact induced by NIMBY facility. *Environmental Impact Assessment, 78*, 106290.
17. Dubois, E., Gruzd, A., & Jacobson, J. (2020). Journalists' use of social media to infer public opinion: The citizens' perspective. *Social Science Computer Review, 38*, 57–74.
18. Li, C. (2017). *Research on comprehensive benefit evaluation of photovoltaic power generation project based on life cycle*. Master's Thesis. Qingdao University of Science and Technology. (in Chinese).
19. Qazi, A., Raj, R. G., Tahir, M., Khan, S. U. R., Abraham, A., & Waheed, M. (2014). A preliminary investigation of user perception and behavioral intention for different review types: Customers and designers perspective. *The Scientific World Journal, 2014*, 1–8.
20. Qazi, A., Tamjidyamcholo, A., Raj, R. G., Hardaker, G., & Standing, C. (2017). Assessing consumers' satisfaction and expectations through online opinions: Expectation and disconfirmation approach. *Computers in Human Behavior, 75*, 450–460.
21. Tang, M., & Liao, H. (2019). From conventional group decision making to large-scale group decision making: What are the challenges and how to meet them in big data era? A state-of-the-art survey. *Omega, 2019*, 102141.
22. Sumper, A., Robledo-García, M., Villafáfila-Robles, R., Bergas-Jané, J., & Andrés-Peiró, J. (2011). Life-cycle assessment of a photovoltaic system in Catalonia (Spain). *Renewable and Sustainable Energy Reviews, 15*, 3888–3896.
23. Bayod-Rujula, A. A., Ortego-Bielsa, A., & Martínez-Gracia, A. (2011). Photovoltaics on flat roofs: Energy considerations. *Energy, 36*, 1996–2010.
24. Hong, T., Lee, M., Koo, C., Jeong, K., & Kim, J. (2017). Development of a method for estimating the rooftop solar photovoltaic (PV) potential by analyzing the available rooftop area using Hillshade analysis. *Applied Energy, 194*, 320–332.
25. Korsavi, S. S., Zomorodian, Z. S., & Tahsildoost, M. (2018). Energy and economic performance of rooftop PV panels in the hot and dry climate of Iran. *Journal of Cleaner Production, 174*, 1204–1214.
26. Sun, Y., Hof, A., Wang, R., Liu, J., Lin, Y., & Yang, D. (2013). GIS-based approach for potential analysis of solar PV generation at the regional scale: A case study of Fujian Province. *Energy Policy, 58*, 248–259.

27. Koo, C., Hong, T., Park, H. S., & Yun, G. (2013). Framework for the analysis of the potential of the rooftop photovoltaic system to achieve the net-zero energy solar buildings. *Progress in Photovoltaics, 22*, 462–478.
28. Mukherji, R., Mathur, V., Bhati, A., & Das Mukherji, M. (2019). Assessment of 50 kWp rooftop solar photovoltaic plant at The ICFAI University, Jaipur: A case study. *Environmental Progress and Sustainable Energy, 39*(3), 13448.
29. Asakereh, A., Soleymani, M., & Sheikhdavoodi, M. J. (2017). A GIS-based fuzzy-AHP method for the evaluation of solar farms locations: Case study in Khuzestan province, Iran. *Solar Energy, 155*, 342–353.
30. Sánchez-Lozano, J. M., García-Cascales, M. S., & Lamata, M. T. (2016). Comparative TOPSIS-ELECTRE TRI methods for optimal sites for photovoltaic solar farms. Case study in Spain. *Journal of Cleaner Production, 127*, 387–398.
31. Tang, L., Guo, D., Wu, J., & Tan, Q. (2014). Program evaluation and its application to equipment based on super-efficiency DEA and gray relation projection method. *Journal of Systems Engineering and Electronics, 25*, 1037–1042.
32. Zheng, G., Jing, Y., Huang, H., & Gao, Y. (2010). Application of improved grey relational projection method to evaluate sustainable building envelope performance. *Applied Energy, 87*, 710–720.
33. Wu, Y., Xu, C., Ke, Y., Chen, K., & Sun, X. (2018). An intuitionistic fuzzy multi-criteria framework for large-scale rooftop PV project portfolio selection: Case study in Zhejiang, China. *Energy, 143*, 295–309.
34. Wu, Y., & Zhou, J. (2019). Risk assessment of urban rooftop distributed PV in energy performance contracting (EPC) projects: An extended HFLTS-DEMATEL fuzzy synthetic evaluation analysis. *Sustainable Cities and Society, 47*, 101524.
35. Ma, L., Chen, H., Yan, H., Li, W., Zhang, J., & Zhang, W. (2018). Post evaluation of distributed energy generation combining the attribute hierarchical model and matter-element extension theory. *Journal of Cleaner Production, 184*, 503–510.
36. Feng, L., & Xiao-hui, C. U. I. (2002). Multi-criteria decision grey relation projection method and its application. *Systems Engineering-Theory and Practice, 1*, 017.
37. Song, D., Liu, C., Shen, C., Shi, X., Zang, L., & Feng, W. (2015). Multiple objective and attribute decision making based on the subjective and objective weighting. *Journal of Shandong University (Engineering Science), 45*, 1–9. (in Chinese).
38. Meadows, C. Z., Tang, L., & Liu, W. (2019). Twitter message types, health beliefs, and vaccine attitudes during the 2015 measles outbreak in California. *American Journal of Infection Control, 47*, 1314–1318.
39. Liu, D., Wang, W., & Li, H. (2013). Evolutionary mechanism and information supervision of public opinions in internet emergency. *Procedia Computer Science, 17*, 973–980.
40. Alrashoud, K., & Tokimatsu, K. (2020). An exploratory study of the public's views on residential solar photovoltaic systems in oil-rich Saudi Arabia. *Environmental Development, 2020*, 100526.
41. Klick, H., & Smith, E. R. A. N. (2010). Public understanding of and support for wind power in the United States. *Renewable Energy, 35*, 1585–1591.
42. Li, Y., Zhou, H., Lin, Z., Wang, Y., Chen, S., Liu, C., Wang, Z., Gifu, D., & Xia, J. (2020). Investigation in the influences of public opinion indicators on vegetable prices by corpora construction and WeChat article analysis. *Future Generation Computer Systems, 102*, 876–888.
43. Jin, J. (2020). Research on data retrieval and analysis system based on Baidu reptile technology in big data era. *Journal of Intelligent and Fuzzy Systems, 38*, 1203–1213.
44. Du, Y., Yi, Y., Li, X., Chen, X., Fan, Y., & Su, F. (2020). Extracting and tracking hot topics of micro-blogs based on improved Latent Dirichlet Allocation. *Engineering Applications of Artificial Intelligence, 87*, 103279.
45. Spertino, F., Di Leo, P., & Cocina, V. (2013). Economic analysis of investment in the rooftop photovoltaic systems: A long-term research in the two main markets. *Renewable and Sustainable Energy Reviews, 28*, 531–540.

46. Mangiante, M. J., Whung, P. Y., Zhou, L., Porter, R., Cepada, A., Campirano, E., Licon, D., Lawrence, R., & Torres, M. (2020). Economic and technical assessment of rooftop solar photovoltaic potential in Brownsville, Texas, USA. *Computers Environment and Urban Systems, 80*, 101450.
47. Baljit, S. S. S., Chan, H. Y., & Sopian, K. (2016). Review of building integrated applications of photovoltaic and solar thermal systems. *Journal of Cleaner Production, 137*, 677–689.
48. Cucchiella, F., D'Adamo, I., & Koh, S. C. L. (2015). Environmental and economic analysis of building integrated photovoltaic systems in Italian regions. *Journal of Cleaner Production, 98*, 241–252.
49. Le, T. D., Dobele, A. R., & Robinson, L. J. (2018). Information sought by prospective students from social media electronic word-of-mouth during the university choice process. *Journal of Higher Education Policy and Management, 41*, 1–17.
50. Sun, Y., Wang, R., Xiao, L., Liu, J., Yu, Y., & Zhuang, X. (2011). Economical and environmental analysis of grid-connected photovoltaic systems in China. *China Population, Resources and Environment, 21*, 88–94. (in Chinese).
51. Romano, S., Cozzi, M., Di Napoli, F., & Viccaro, M. (2013). Building agro-energy supply chains in the Basilicata region: Technical and economic evaluation of interchangeability between fossil and renewable energy sources. *Energies, 6*, 5259–5282.
52. Defaix, P., Van Stark, W., Worrell, E., & De Visser, E. (2012). Technical potential for photovoltaics on buildings in the EU-27. *Solar Energy, 86*, 2644–2653.
53. California Energy Commission. (2019) *Electricity consumption by County. ECDMS: energy consumption data management system.* Retrieved from http://www.ecdms.energy.ca.gov/elecbycounty.aspx
54. Denholm, P., & Margolis, R. (2008). *Supply curves for rooftop solar PV-generated electricity for the United States.* National Renewable Energy Laboratory [NREL].
55. Lopez, A., Roberts, B., Heimiller, D., Blair, N., & Porro, G. (2012). *U.S. renewable energy technical potentials: A GIS-based analysis.* National Renewable Energy Laboratory (NREL).
56. Gutschner, M., Nowak, S., Ruoss, D., Togweiler, P., & Schoen, T. (2002). *Potential for building integrated photovoltaics.* International Energy Agency [IEA] PVPS Task, 7.
57. Liu, L. (2014). Environmental impact and benefit analysis of solar photovoltaic power generation. *Energy Conservation & Environmental Protection, 6*, 54–56. (in Chinese).
58. Gan, L., Wang, Y., Lin, Z., & Lev, B. (2019). A loss-recovery evaluation tool for debris flow. *International Journal of Disaster Risk Reduction, 37*, 101165.
59. Dakoulakid, M., & Rapayannakis, L. (1995). Determining objective weights in multi le criteria problems: The CRITIC method. *Computers and Operations Research, 22*(7), 763–770.
60. Märkle-Huß, J., Feuerriegel, S., & Neumann, D. (2020). Cost minimization of large-scale infrastructure for electricity generation and transmission. *Omega, 96*, 102071.
61. Huang, W., Zhou, W., Chen, J., & Chen, H. (2019). The government's optimal subsidy scheme under manufacturers' competition of price and product energy efficiency. *Omega, 84*, 70–101.

Index

F. P. García Márquez, B. Lev (eds.), *Introduction to Internet of Things in Management Science and Operations Research*, International Series in Operations Research & Management Science 311,
https://doi.org/10.1007/978-3-030-74644-5

B

T

U

V

The manufacturer's authorised representative in the EU is Springer Nature Customer Service Centre GmbH, Europaplatz 3, 69115 Heidelberg, Germany. If you have any concerns regarding our products, please contact ProductSafety@springernature.com

Printed and bound by CPI Group (UK) Ltd, Croydon, CR0 4YY
30/09/2026
02225452-0013